# 2G Bomb

## RTIs Shook North Block

# *Attention Authors*

Manas Publications is fighting a war to tell the world that India can win the battle not only by the bullet but also by pen. There is no dearth of intellectuals in our country, but their knowledge is confined to them only. No sincere effort has been made by any other publisher to channelise their knowledge in national interest, which is why the talent of large number of intellectuals remain latent. An author always gives the raw material in the shàpe of a manuscript and it is the job of the publisher to convert it into a beautiful book. Manas always motivates the intellectuals by publishing their manuscripts since more than four decades and would like to publish your manuscript too. If you or your colleagues have any manuscript ready for publication or are working on it, kindly contact us with a detailed synopsis and list of contents for its best publication. If you wish, we can also suggest you a suitable title for writing related to your area of expertise. Manas is known for its publishing quality and commitments. We take utmost care in production and give wide publicity to the book as well as its author through our national and international distribution network.

# 2G Bomb

## RTIs Shook North Block

**Vivek Garg**
Advocate & RTI Activist

**Manas Publications**
**(We convert Fighters into Writers)**
**New Delhi-110002 (INDIA)**

**MANAS PUBLICATIONS**
(Publishers for IAS, IPS, IFS, IRS, Defence, Press, Judges etc.)

4402/5-A, Ansari Road (Opp. HDFC Bank)
Darya Ganj, New Delhi-110 002 (India)
**Off. ✆ 23260783, 23265523; Fax: 011-23272766**
**E-mail: manaspublications@vsnl.com**
**manaspublications@yahoo.com**
**manaspublications@gmail.com**

We have tried our level best to print the best possible quality of the documents, received from the PMO/ Ministries in photostat mode



**ISBN** 978-81-7049-421-8
₹ 995/-



*Designed at*
**Manas Publications**

*Printed in India at*
HS Offset Press, Delhi
and published by **Mrs Suman Lata** for
Manas Publications, 4402/5-A, Ansari Road
(Opp. HDFC Bank),
Darya Ganj, New Delhi-110 002 (INDIA)

# PREFACE

Corruption starts from the top. The best example to prove this logic is the 2G spectrum scam. This scam cost the country approximately Rs 1,76, 645 crores, according to the CAG report. The amount involved in 2G spectrum scam is so huge that one cannot imagine that this scam could have materialised without the involvement of the top political masters. How come the then Telecom Ministers A Raja and Dayanidhi Maran could indulge in this huge swindling on their own, with the Prime Minister's Office and the Ministry of Finance unable to sniff the 'dirty spectrum air'?

This question also teased my mind, and then 2G spectrum scam became yet another cause for me to expose corruption at high places. For quite some time now, I have been seeking information from different government departments to get to the bottom of many a scam involving gross misuse of precious public funds in various government projects and schemes. Now, the 2G spectrum scam, the Commonwealth Games 2010 scam and the rotten grain scam figure prominently in my fight against corruption list.

Regarding the 2G spectrum and Commonwealth Games scams, I have filed a series of applications under the RTI Act in the PMO, Ministry of Telecommunication and Information Technology, Ministry of Finance and Ministry of Home Affairs. From these offices, I have not yet got all the documents sought under the RTI Act. They are providing us documents on the pick-and-choose basis. Still many documents connected with the 2G scam have not been supplied by the PMO and other departments. Maybe, the involvement of some big fish in the 2G scam is the main reason of these documents not reaching me.

When I got a bunch of documents from the PMO, I found the controversial 'Office Memorandum' of March 25, 2011 prepared by the Ministry of Finance, which they had sent to the PMO. This note is quite an eye-opener, as it prima facie indicates the role of the then Finance Minister Shri P Chidambaram in the 2G spectrum mess. After studying the note with the help of my friends, I gave it to the media to bring it in the public domain. Because of the hue and cry raised by this note in political circles and among people, I thought it proper to bring this note and other documents in the book form to make public the 2G spectrum scam.

The best way to curb scams is to keep a check on the financial powers of the ministers or officers. In this task, the Right to Information (RTI) Act, 2005 has the great potential of proving a highly effective tool. In fact, the RTI Act has transformed the whole of India into people's real parliament by empowering the masses to elicit information from the government on any issue. Now, a common man, like an elected Member of Parliament (MP), is empowered to make government accountable by inquiring about the implementation (wrong or right) of government policies and its budgetary expenditures.

Since Independence, India has made rapid strides in all walks of development and human endeavour, yet all is not that rosy on many fronts. Today, infrastructure development should be the utmost priority of the government. Many ambitious schemes for development have been launched by the government, but their full benefits could not be realized because of poor infrastructure, corruption and technological inadequacies, thus wasting public resources.

Needless to say, our country is today in the clutches of many self-centred leaders, lacking a pragmatic vision. Poor political will has led to a stunted growth environment. India is often dubbed as a soft state, not having the will to tackle national issues with a firm hand. Cobbling together of various political parties to usurp power has further damaged the prospect of expressing a strong national will to address serious concerns on priority. Hard bargaining, inherent in coalition politics, and an attempt to settle scores at the cost of the nation just do not allow the focus on issues that matter. Moreover, the crafty and corrupt among politicians are always engaged in queering the pitch against their political opponents. They are the major roadblocks on the way to building a national consensus on resolving important issues that have been lingering for decades. Our leaders of diverse political hues inflame the fragile emotions and passions of the masses, provoking them into flagrant violation of law.

Rampant corruption in our body-politic poses a serious challenge to the growth prospects of India. Looking back, we see a long trail of scams such as Jain Hawala case, Harshad Mehta's shares scam and Telgi stamp scam. But no lessons have been learnt from these scams. People at the helm are still busy bestowing benefits and bounties on their henchmen and cronies without any regard for the rule of law, justice and equality. In 2010, Transparency International (TI) ranked India 87th on its corruption index of 178 countries. Here an interesting fact is that China is at the 78th position in this index. It implies that we are nine places ahead of China in corruption as per the TI index.

Computerization of government services, e-banking, economic reforms and the RTI Act have helped little in tackling the corruption and making the system more transparent. The economic reforms of 1991 have reduced the red tape, bureaucratic hurdles and the Licence-Permit Raj to a great extent. But, corruption can be removed only if it is rooted out first at the top. Then as a cascading effect everything else down the line will become corruption-free. The big fish must be caught first and penalized properly.

Vivek Garg
Advocate & RTI Activist

*Dedicated to*

My Grand Parents
and all
Patriots of India

**Speed Post A.D.**
**Right to Information**

**PRIME MINISTER'S OFFICE**

South Block
New Delhi - 110 101

No. RTI/2388/2011-PMR

Dated: 29th July, 2011

To:

Shri Vivek Garg
18/1, Ground Floor
Shakti Nagar
Delhi - 110 007

Subject: Application under Right to Information Act, 2005.

Sir,

In continuation of this office's memorandum of even number dated 24.6.2011, transferring your application dated 23.6.2011, received on 23.6.2011, to the Department of Telecommunications for action as appropriate; the matter was also referred to office for providing inputs on points 1 to 13. Information provided by the office, is enclosed (2 pages). A copy of documents referred to therein are enclosed (537 pages).

2. Insofar as the request in point 5 of the application is concerned, the office has provided a third party reference marked 'Top Secret' and has informed that there is no other letter etc. exchanged between PM / PMO and Minister / Ministry of External Affairs on 2G Spectrum / Licence matter. Further, for the purpose of section 11 of the Right to Information Act, 2005, a decision on disclosure has been considered in terms of the said document in the record. The said letter attracts the provisions of section 11 of the Right to Information Act, which envisages that where a Central Public Information Officer (CPIO) intends to disclose any information or record or request received under the Act, which has been supplied by a third party, the CPIO shall invite the third party to make submissions in writing or orally, regarding whether the information should be disclosed, and such submissions of the third party shall be kept in view while taking decision on request seeking disclosure. The matter has been processed under section 11(4) as per statutory requirements and further response will be provided after due process is completed.

3. For the purpose of section 19 of the Right to Information Act, 2005, Shri Amit Agrawal, Director, is the appellate authority in respect of this office.

Yours faithfully,

Encl: As above

(Sanjukta Ray)
Deputy Secretary and
Central Public Information Officer
☏ : 2307 4072

## CHRONOLOGY OF THE SPECTRUM SCAM (LIST OF DATES)

1. 13-April-07: DoT sends a reference to TRAI seeking review of existing procedure to grant licenses in each circle in view of spectrum shortage and whether there should be limit placed. Also seeks review of M&A conditions and rollout obligations, in addition to few other issues.

2. May 2007 : A Raja takes over as Telecom Minister

3. Aug 2007: TRAI recommends no cap, no M&A till roll out obligations are met and no changes in roll out obligations i.e. continue to be linked to effective date of license. Also recommends and market based pricing for determining entry fee

4. 25-Sep-2007: A Raja sends press release to announce sudden cut of date of 25-Sep-2007.

5. 1-Oct-2007: 575 applications at an average of 26 applications for each of the 22 circles received.

6. 15-Oct-2007: TRAI protests against issuing fresh licenses. DoT ignores. Letter not in public domain

7. 19-Oct-2007: DoT sends out press release announcing 'no cap' is accepted but change in rollout obligations and M&A norms. TRAI protests again. Ignored again.

8. 25-Oct-2007: Secretary DoT D S Mathur and Manju Madhavan write detailed note seeking auctions for allocation licenses a/ spectrum as the only legally defendable option.

9. 26-Oct-2007: DoT sends request for Law Ministry opinion.

10. 1-Nov-2007 Law Ministry declines. Says to send matter to GOM. Raja declines.

11. 2-Nov-2007: PM cautions A Raja. Informs about NTP 99 and spectrum shortage. Direction to consider auction and benchmark pricing at 2007 rates. Raja refuses. Says he will proceed with first-come-first-served.

12. 26-Dec-2007: Raja writes to Prime Minister informing him that he will execute the decision in line with existing policy and that he has consulted External Affairs Minister and has received advice of Solicitor General of India.

13. Dec 2007: D S Mathur refuses to sign files. Manju Madhavan (Member Finance) proceeds on leave in protest. Takes premature retirement in February 2008. D S Mathur retires 31-Dec-2007.

14. 1-Jan-2008: Siddharth Behura joins as Secretary DoT.

15. 3-Jan-2008: Prime Minister acknowledges A Raja letter dated 26-12-07.

16. 10-Jan-2008: LOIs issued, pricing licenses /2G spectrum at 2001 prices of Rs. 1,658 crores for pan India licenses. Arbitrary cutoff date advanced from 1-10-07 to 25-9-07. Only 122 applications qualify. FCFS definition changed. Fist fights in Sanchar Bhawan over who would pay first. Outrage in the media.

17. 14-Jan-2008: TRAI writes 3rd protest letter. Raja ignores.

18. Feb-Mar-2008: Licenses granted.

19. 22-Apr-2008: New M&A guidelines issued; TRAI recommendations circumvented. Acquisition allowed. Merger linked to 3 years and not rollout.

20. 23-Sep- 08: Swan closes deal with Etisalat

21. 29-Oct-08 Unitech closes deal with Telenor

22. 30-Oct-2008: DoT puts out press release defending its actions.

23. 4 Nov-2008 : Swan and Unitech inform DoT of 45% and 60% stake sale to Etisalat and Telenor for Rs.9,800 crores and Rs. 11,620 crores respectively - 7 times higher price - without a single customer or any income/cash flow.

24. 5-Nov-08: A Raja directs Telecom Commission to ban sale of promoters' equity after Swan/Unitech deals are done.

25. 7-Nov-2008: DoT puts out second press release defending its own actions as well as Swan and Unitech. Memo to Telecom Committee to ban sale of promoter's equity

26. May-2009: Raja reappointed as Telecom Minister in UPA-2.

27. 21-Oct-2009: CBI registers FIR against DoT and private companies citing criminal conspiracy, and loss to the exchequer, under Prevention of Corruption Act.

28. Jan 2010: CAG begins performance audit.

29. 11-May 2010: TRAI issues recommendations equating 3G price as current price for 26. Confirming 6.2 MHz as contracted spectrum.

30. Mid-2010: 3G auctions / BWA auctions yield over Rs.1 Lakh crores. All money is deposited within 10 days. CAG launches investigation.PIL filed in Supreme Court.

31. Sept 2010: PIL hearing begins in Supreme Court.

32. Oct 2010: DoT provides Para-by-Para reply to CAG.

| | | |
|---|---|---|
| 33. | Nov-2010: | CAG report finalized. Rs.1.76 crore loss to exchequer. Indicts Raja. Indicates collusion between DoT officials and industry. Media and opposition parties cry for Raja's removal. Parliament stalled. |
| 34. | Nov 2010: | DoT, CBI, Raja file affidavits in Supreme Court claiming DoT has followed TRAI's recommendations and raising questions about CAG's loss calculation and defending STel and Unitech's calculations as indicative of loss. |
| 35. | 14-Nov-2010: | A Raja resigns. |
| 36. | 16-Dec-2010: | Supreme Court judgment expanding probe to include CAG report including losses |
| 37. | 7-Jan- 2011: | Kapil Sibal holds press conference claiming CAG loss as 'zero' |

SECRET

F.No. 3/11/2011 – Inf (Part)
Ministry of Finance
Department of Economic Affairs

New Delhi, March 25, 2011,

**Office Memorandum**

**Sub: Allocation and pricing of 2G spectrum**

A copy of basic facts prepared on allocation and pricing of 2G spectrum is enclosed.

2. This has been seen by the Finance Minister.

28/3/11
(Dr. P.G.S. Rao)
Dy. Director,
Infrastructure and Investment Division

Ms. Vini Mahajan,
Joint Secretary,
Prime Minister's Office
South Block, New Delhi – 110001

## Chronology of basic facts related to pricing and allocation of 2G spectrum

**Facts of the case**

1. Based on the decision of the Union Cabinet dated October 31, 2003, guidelines for the Unified Access Service (UAS) were issued on November 11, 2003 which allowed for UAS licences to provide basic and / or cellular licences using any technology in the defined service area.

2. The Union Cabinet had authorized DoT to finalise, with the approval of the Minister-in-charge, the details of implementation of the UASL regime, including the calculation of the entry fee[1] depending upon the date of payment based on the principles given by TRAI in its recommendations. In the context of the release of adequate spectrum needed for the growth of the telecom sector, the Union Cabinet in October 2003 had decided that the Department of Telecommunication and Ministry of Finance would discuss and finalise spectrum pricing formulae which would include incentive for efficient use of spectrum as well as disincentive for sub-optimal usage.

3. The licence fee for UAS licences was reduced by 2%, across the board, with a further reduction by 2% of AGR for the first two cellular licensees (for a period of 4 years with effect from April 01, 2004) in order to spur investment and growth, and, ultimately yield more revenue to Government. The financial implication of the proposal was estimated at ₹ 968 crore for the first four years, and, ₹ 885 crore per annum thereafter. The proposal to the above effect, initiated by the then Minister of Communications and Information Technology (Shri Arun

[1] TRAI, in its recommendations dated October 27, 2003 had recommended the fee paid by the 4th cellular operator to be benchmark for migration of basic player to the new access regime.

Shourie) was approved by the then Minister of Finance (Sri Jaswant Singh) on December 12, 2003, without any examination as regards financial implications.

4. TRAI, in its recommendations dated May 13, 2005, has indicated that in the existing licensing framework, entry fee includes onetime spectrum charge. TRAI recommended that as in the existing framework the spectrum charges should have two components: **onetime spectrum charges and annual spectrum charge**. It was recommended that there should be no one time spectrum charges for allocation of IMT-2000 spectrum to the existing service providers. As regards the new entrants, the onetime spectrum charges would be equal to UASL entry fee in that services area minus the component of registration charge based on the entry fee paid by new BSO (entered in/after 2001), specified by TRAI in its recommendations on Unified licensing regime dated January 13, 2005. TRAI also recommended that the existing method of annual spectrum charge in terms of percentage of revenue share should continue.

5. In response to the TRAI recommendation dated May 13, 2005, DEA as per relevant notings and in letter December 21, 2005 to DoT indicated that, for allocation of additional spectrum, while price discovery through auction may not be appropriate, the hybrid option of a base fee, combined with revenue share, appears to be the most appropriate. It was also recommended by DEA that the issues should be put up for consideration and appropriate decision by the Committee of Secretaries (CoS) and thereafter, by a Group of Ministers (GoM). DEA did not question the methodology suggested by TRAI on issues of one time and annual spectrum charges.

6. The thrust of the Union Cabinet decision of October 31, 2003, in regard to spectrum pricing was for MoF and DoT to "...discuss and finalize spectrum pricing formula, which will include incentive for efficient use of spectrum as well as dis-incentive for sub-optimal usages...". Though there was no basic disagreement between the two Departments on the basic thrust of the TRAI recommendations on pricing in 2005, DEA had advised DoT to take up the matter in CoS and thereafter, by a GoM. This was presumably not done by DoT. The matter was also not followed up further by DEA.

7. A Group of Ministers (GoM) was constituted by Cabinet Secretariat on February 23, 2006, on the issues of vacation of Defence spectrum and raising of resources for the purpose. DEA, vide D.O. letter dated March 28, 2007 asked DoT to include issues relating to 'spectrum pricing' within the ambit of the GoM. It was, however, not specifically communicated whether 'spectrum pricing' meant only spectrum usage charges or entry fee and spectrum usage charges. The view of DoT was that the spectrum pricing is within the normal work carried out by that Ministry as indicated in their letter dated April 02, 2007. In a D.O letter, dated April 19, 2007, to the Cabinet Secretary, Finance Secretary had indicated that since these issues would have economic and financial ramifications, they need to be discussed in the GoM. The contention of the DoT that these issues are within the normal work was not entirely correct. It was explained that a sound policy on spectrum allocation and pricing will not only result in optimal utilization of spectrum, but would also have revenue implications. Vide OM dated May 17, 2007, Cabinet Secretariat advised DEA that Finance Secretary and Secretary(DoT) may discuss for resolving the issue of inclusion of spectrum pricing in the ToR of GoM and advise the Cabinet secretariat about the decision taken

in the matter. DEA sent an OM to DoT on 18.05.2007 indicating that technology neutrality and spectrum price must be included in the ToR of the GoM. In its letter dated June 06, 2007 Finance Secretary requested Secretary, DoT to include spectrum pricing in the ToRs for the GoM. It was also said that the methodology to be followed for 'spectrum pricing' would logically follow the vacation of spectrum which is the main task of GoM. A view was taken in DEA then that the matter may be resolved through correspondence, failing which meeting with DoT could be held. In its letter dated June 15, 2007 on the subject, DoT indicated that since spectrum pricing and charges for the use of spectrum is a dynamic issue, it is to be reviewed and considered from time to time in the context of the changing technology and international best practices in consultation with TRAI. Thus DoT precluded the role of MoF, if any, in finalizing spectrum pricing. This letter however does not appear to have been received and processed on the file of DEA. Thereafter, DEA did not take up the issue further, either with the DoT or with the Cabinet Secretariat. A chronology of events is enclosed at Annex- I.

8. DEA explicitly took up the issue of fixation of entry fee on November 22, 2007. In the context of the three crossover licenses for CDMA operators issued by DoT, DEA had argued that it is not clear how the rate of ₹ 1600 crore determined as far back as in 2001, has been applied for a license given in 2007 without any indexation, let alone current valuation. It was also said that all further action to implement the said licenses may be stayed. While the intent of DEA was to settle this issue in a generic sense for all licenses, the letter itself referred only to the crossover licenses. In response, DoT vide their letter dated November 29, 2007 indicated that the decision to allot the dual technology licences at the 2001 entry fee was justified on account of the

decisions taken in the Cabinet meeting held on October 31, 2003 and TRAI recommendations dated August 28, 2007. (The TRAI recommendation of August, 2007 was not placed before the Full Telecom Commission). This was also not further responded to by DEA. No follow up appears to have been done from DEA/DoT as per the available records.

9. As a response to the DoT letter dated November 29, 2007, the then Director (Infra) initiated a note highlighting the need to revise the entry fee. This note, dated December 17, 2008, while it was marked to Joint Secretary (On tour)/Additional Secretary (Economic Affairs [AS (EA)] does not seem to have been put up to the next level of consideration. Records also indicate that the then AS (EA) put up on 09.01.2008, in a separate file, a comprehensive concept paper on the extant telecom sector policy. The subject header of the note mentioned the references of the DEA letter of November 22, 2007 and the DoT reply of November 29, 2007. The note recommended both revision of the entry fee fixed in 2003 as well as adoption of an auction methodology for determination of the spectrum usage charges. The position paper was prefaced with a note of the then AS(EA) dated January 09, 2008, which *inter alia* mentioned that she had been directed to attend the meeting of the full Telecom Commission, which had been scheduled to be held on January 09, 2008 and had now been postponed to January 15, 2008. This position paper was used by the then FM as a basis of his 'secret note' to the Prime Minister on January 15, 2008 wherein, an auction based mechanism was recommended for future allocation of spectrum (**beyond** the "start up" spectrum), with the spectrum allocations having been made in the past to be treated as a-

closed chapter. The recommendation was in the context of spectrum usage charges and not with regard to the entry fee.

10. A Full Telecom Commission meeting took place on January 15, 2008. One of the agenda item was pricing of spectrum. However, it only included annual spectrum charge (revenue share) and not the entry fee. MoF representative who attended the meeting did not raise the issue of revision of entry fee.

11. The conclusions arising from the paras 9 and 10 *ante* can be summarized as follows: the DoT response of November 29, 2007 was brought to the notice of the then Finance Minister on 09.01.08, along with suggestions to argue for revision of the entry fee and adoption for auction with spectrum usage charges as the bid parameter; the fact that a Telecom Commission meeting on the issue was scheduled on January 15, 2008 was also mentioned; no response, however, was sent by DEA to DoT either on the issues raised by DoT in the communication dated November 29, 2007, or with reference to the impending meeting of the Telecom Commission; no intervention on entry fee were suggested in this meeting by DEA representatives; and, finally, a note was sent by the then Finance Minister to the Prime Minister on January 15, 2008 wherein auction of spectrum was argued, but only with reference to spectrum beyond the 'start up' spectrum. The licenses allotted in 2007 and 2008 only carried the 'start up' spectrum embedded with them. The note of the Finance Minister did not deal with the need, if any, to revise entry fee or the rate of revenue share. The issue of revision of entry fee was taken up by the MoF subsequently in November 11, 2008.

12. Subsequently, in a meeting held on January 30, 2008 between the then Ministers of Finance and Telecommunications, it was noted by the

then Finance Minister that he was for now not seeking to revisit the current regimes for entry fee or revenue share.

13. Secretary DoT formally wrote to DEA on February 8, 2008 enclosing an approach paper[2], wherein, DoT proposed to price allocation of spectrum beyond 4.4 MHz and, enhancement of spectrum usage charges. It is indicated in the approach note that Secretary(Finance) was of opinion that auctioning is legally possible for initial allotment of spectrum of 4.4 MHz. DoT indicated that as 4.4 MHz is a part of the licence agreement, no spectrum acquisition charge is supposed to be levied. The approach paper states that even if it is priced, it will also disturb the level playing field and the present LoI holders who have already paid entry fee are likely to go for litigation. Initial entry fee for licence may be construed as the de-facto price of initial spectrum i.e. ₹ 1650 crore for pan-India licence. Based on the DoT letter, an internal note on the subject was prepared in DEA on February 11, 2008, wherein the entire range of spectrum was proposed to be charged for both new and old operators, using the entry fee as the price of embedded spectrum and indexing it with the increase in the AGR of the telecom sector between 2003-04 and 2007-08. The note also ruled out the option of auctioning spectrum for various reasons explained therein. A note for discussion was put up by the Finance Secretary on April 07, 2008, outlining the proposals in respect of both 2G and 3G spectrum bands. After subsequent discussions with DoT, and, in response to a draft note for Cabinet of DoT, for financial approval for creation of the Air Force Network (AFNET), DoT were informed with the approval of FM on April 08, 2008 that all allotments of spectrum, **beyond** 4.4 MHz, may be specifically priced and charged for and the spectrum

[2] It was suggested by DoT that it would be placed in the meeting of the Telecom Commission for appropriate decision

usage charges may be calibrated with regard to circle specific "scarcity value" of spectrum instead of basing it on bandwidth as has been the practice. The then Finance Minister sent a "non paper" to the then Minister of Telecommunications on April 21, 2008 conveying that an 'in principle' decision may be taken to price the spectrum beyond 4.4 MHz, as had been suggested by DoT.

14. In a meeting between the then Finance Secretary and Secretary, DoT on April 24, 2008 DEA adopted the following position: spectrum usage charge may be linked to circle specific "scarcity value"; spectrum upto 6.2 MHz may not be priced; and, spectrum beyond 6.2 MHz may be priced using the base price of ₹ 375 crore per MHz indexed to growth in Adjusted Gross Revenue (AGR) with reference to the year 2003-04. In subsequent meetings DEA presented its stand that spectrum usage charge may be revised as a percentage of AGR; spectrum upto 6.2 MHz may not be priced; and, spectrum beyond 6.2 MHz may be priced using the base price of Rs 266 crore per MHz indexed to growth in Gross Domestic Product (GDP) with reference to the year 2003-04. This position was thereafter communicated to DoT vide DO letter dated June 27, 2008 of the then AS(EA). Further meetings were held between the then Finance Minister and the Minister of Telecom on May 29, 2008 and June 12, 2008. Subsequently, in a meeting held under the Chair of the Prime Minister, on July 4, 2008 (as recorded in the note of the then Finance Secretary dated July 6, 2008), the then Finance Minister and Minister of Telecommunications agreed to the proposals on enhancement of spectrum usage charges and pricing of spectrum based on indexing the base price (₹ 266 crore per MHz) and compounding using SBI PLR from existing allottees of spectrum beyond 6.2 MHz.

However, the issue of revision of entry fee was not discussed in the meeting.

15. A meeting of the Telecom Commission was convened on November 11, 2008 to discuss issues relating to one time spectrum charge and spectrum usage charges. Approval of the then FM was taken on the same lines as had been agreed to in the PMO meeting on July 4, 2008. The enhancement of spectrum usage charges was expected to yield revenue of ₹ 4,149 crore annually, an increase of ₹ 1,270 crore over the annual revenue yield ( ~ ₹ 3,000 crore) on the current rate structure. However, in addition, DoT were also asked vide OM dated November 11, 2008 to suggest a mechanism for updating the entry fee of ₹ 1,658 crore (fixed in 2003-04), for all allotments of licences after January 01, 2009. Thus MoF raised the issue of updating the entry fee albeit only for the licences allotted after January 01, 2009. Thus MoF implicitly agreed to imposition of same entry fee as that prevailing in 2001 for licences allotted upto December 31, 2008.

16. It is, therefore, clear that there were consultations between MoF and DoT in the first half of 2008, on the formula for charging 2G spectrum based on indexation to the PLR of the SBI, which related only to the allocations beyond 6.2 MHz. In the matter presently under consideration (i.e., allotment of 2G licenses in 2007-08) spectrum allocations were not made beyond 6.2 MHz, on the pricing of which, DoT and MoF were in agreement. On the other hand, the new licensees have only got 4.4 MHz of spectrum each.

17. Secretary (Finance) had suggested to go for auction for initial spectrum of 4.4 MHz in early February, 2008. DoT was not keen to do the same since it had said that it will disturb the level playing field and the present LoI holders who had already paid entry fee were likely to go

for litigation. DoT opined that 4.4 MHz is, a part of the licence agreement and initial entry fee for licence may be construed as the de-facto price of initial spectrum. There was a way out by invoking clause 5.1 of the UAS license, which *inter alia*, provide for modification at any time the terms and conditions of the Licence, if in the opinion of the Licensor it is necessary or expedient to do so in public interest or in the interest of the security of state or for the proper conduct of the telegraphs. DoT could have invoked this clause for cancelling licences in case MoF had stuck to the stand of auctioning the 4.4 MHz spectrum. Perhaps some litigations would have arisen as a consequence. It may be mentioned that while the UAS licenses were signed between February 27 and March 07, 2008, spectrum allocations were done starting only in April, 2008, almost 4 months after the LoIs were issued. However, these were not charged (beyond the normal spectrum usage charges) since there was consensus, at the levels of the Ministers concerned, that spectrum beyond the 'start up' levels only should be charged.

18. Detailed replies on the issues raised by the Members of the PAC during the oral evidence of the Finance Secretary were sent to the Lok Sabha Secretariat on July 21, 2010. Comments of the Department of Economic Affairs on the draft performance audit report on the issue of licences and allocation of 2G spectrum were sent to the Director General of Audit on August 11, 2010. These were put up for the first time to the FM for information when copies of these were forwarded to the Cabinet Secretary under intimation to the Prime Minister's Office (PMO) on January 05, 2011.

सत्यमेव जयते

**DAYANIDHI MARAN**

MINISTER OF COMMUNICATIONS & INFORMATION TECHNOLOGY

***Confidential***

Respected Prime Minister,

D.O. No. L-14047/09/2005-NTG (Pt.)

03 JUN 2005

Vide your office letter dated 10th February, 2005, you were kind enough to approve the thrust areas for the Ministry, one of which was the spectrum allocation policy. My Ministry also made detailed presentation to you on all the 4 thrust areas, including the one involving spectrum. Recently, the Telecom Regulatory Authority of India (TRAI) has made certain recommendations on spectrum related issues released by them on 13th May, 2005. Around that time, certain newspaper reports appeared regarding this issue. Your office has desired our comments, which my Ministry has separately submitted to your office.

2. However, I wish to apprise you on some important and crucial issues relating to the working of the Chairman, TRAI in general and the recommendation TRAI has made out of context in connection with the management of the RF spectrum which is the responsibility of the Wireless Planning and Coordination (WPC) Wing in my Ministry.

3. I have been observing the working of TRAI and particularly the style of working of the Chairman Mr. Pradeep Baijal. Being responsible for its working, I have answered many questions in the Parliament as well as references from Hon'ble Members of Parliament and issues raised in the Department's Consultative Committee. In the case of Reliance Infocomm, just to give one example, instead of taking timely and stern action at their end, TRAI simply passed it on to the Department of Telecommunications on the ground that TRAI is not equipped to take action. Furthermore, the Chairman's penchant of constantly voicing his opinion to the Press and Media has been a source of constant embarrassment to the Department. Person holding such a high office as that of Chairman TRAI should exercise restraint of high office and not give press interviews on matters of policy, which are completely within the domain of the Government. On many

ELECTRONICS NIKETAN, 6, C.G.O. COMPLEX, NEW DELHI-110003
PHONE : 24329191, 24369191 FAX : 24362333

occasions (and I may refer to the issue of unbundling of the local loop, co-location, niche operators, Rural Access Providers, Broadband etc) his remarks are at variance with the adopted Government Policy. I strongly suspect that in matters where his recommendations were not accepted by my Ministry, instead of accepting the position, he has been giving unwarranted inputs to interested parties perhaps with the ulterior agenda of having his recommendations find acceptance in Government by putting undue pressure on the Department. Such attitude needlessly compromises the position of the Ministry. I would imagine that once TRAI has given its recommendation, the Chairman has no business to air his views in the Press and Media defending his recommendations as their acceptance or otherwise is the sole prerogative of the Government which it would in any case exercise in public interest.

4. Coming to the specific issue of RF Spectrum, in November, 2003, my Ministry had sought views of Telecom Regulatory of India (TRAI) on the following three issues in the context of their recommendations dated 27.10.2003 on Unified Licensing Regime:

- Efficient utilization of spectrum
- Spectrum allocation procedure
- Spectrum pricing.

5. Unfortunately, TRAI inordinately delayed giving their recommendation on the specific issues. It finally gave its recommendation only in May, 2005, after a period of 18 months. Also, TRAI has included their views on some other issues, most notably that of 3G Spectrum and its pricing. The Government had not asked for recommendations on 3G at all. This is a sensitive issue having external policy ramifications. TRAI should have quickly given its recommendations on the specific issues raised by us. It unnecessary delayed its recommendations. At one place TRAI has now suggested that there will be no one time spectrum charges for allocation of IMT-2000 (3G) spectrum to the existing service providers. At another place

they have recommended bidding process. It has also suggested for examining this issue by Group of Ministers.

6. Not only that, within a week of giving the recommendation, the Chairman aired his views on the press saying that the revenue model will be preferable in spectrum allocation for 3G.

7. I feel that on both these grounds TRAI has transgressed the mandate given to it. On the pricing issue, it is our considered view that it is the prerogative of the Ministry to decide in the matter after considering various aspects connected thereto in consultation with other major stakeholders.

8. As regards the examination of the issue by the Group of Ministers, it is the PM's prerogative to set up a GOM on any particular issue. It is not for the TRAI to suggest such a mechanism.

9. I am separately examining the modalities of spectrum allocation for 3G Services. Regarding the need for making more spectrum available which is a prerequisite for the growth of Cellular Mobile Services (including 3G Services) in the country, we have as indicated above, already made a detailed presentation before you when you were kind enough to spare time to review the thrust areas. I am concerned about spectrum requirements and I have requested the Hon'ble Defence Minister for his help in getting adequate spectrum vacated from Defence Services. We would separately submit our proposals in this regard for your kind consideration and to evolve an appropriate mechanism to pursue the same. I am confident that we shall be able to evolve a comprehensive Spectrum Allocation Policy under your guidance. This will be a policy fair to all the cellular operators without giving anyone undue advantage, either in terms of early entry or bandwidth, and conducive to the rapid growth of this vital sector.

10. It is necessary for Chairman, TRAI to be advised to behave himself with dignity and restraint. However, his conduct and irrepressible desire to go before the media have been constant sources of embarrassment to the Government. So far I have not made any public comment on his utterances. However, if he continues in this manner, I may be left with no option but defend the Department's stand publicly to correct the negative impression he likes to give of the Government.

With Kind Regards,

Yours sincerely,

(DAYANIDHI MARAN)

Dr. Manmohan Singh,

Hon'ble Prime Minister of India,

South Block,

New Delhi - 110 011.

Dy No:- 2 /MOC-IT /R /2006

सत्यमेव जयते

**DAYANIDHI MARAN**
MINISTER OF COMMUNICATIONS &
INFORMATION TECHNOLOGY

11th January, 2006

Respected Prime Minister,

It has been brought to my notice that the PMO had in a letter dated 23rd November 2005, addressed to the Deputy Chairman, Planning Commission (a copy of which was received in our office on 6th January 2006) indicated that you have approved the Group of Ministers for looking into the entire gamut of issues relating to spectrum availability and its allocation. This is in pursuance of the recommendations made in the Mid Term Appraisal (MTA) of the Tenth Plan.

2. I am happy to inform you that Telecommunications in India are registering an unprecedented growth in the last one year. The growth rate is accelerating as can be witnessed from the fact that as against a monthly increase of 1.25 million lines when the UPA Government took over, 3.24 million lines have been added in the month of October 2005, 3.79 million in the month of November 2005 and the month of December 2005 saw a record increase of 4.88 million lines. This clearly would not have been possible but for the policies of this Department including in respect of spectrum allocation and management.

3. The fact however remains that this growth needs to be sustained and further enhanced if we are to meet the target of 250 million lines by the year 2007 set by this Department. The one major bottleneck is the availability, not allocation of spectrum for telecommunication services, and particularly through vacation of spectrum occupied by the Defence Services, as recognised by the MTA. It is therefore necessary that the proposed GoM should focus its attention on this aspect of vacation of Spectrum by the Defence and also early migration to digital terrestrial

contd. 2

ELECTRONICS NIKETAN, 6, C.G.O. COMPLEX, NEW DELHI-110003
PHONE : 24329191, 24369191 FAX : 24362333

:: 2::

broadcasting by Prasar Bharti and not allow itself to be diverted by any other issues such as spectrum allocation, 3G, etc. which are solely within the purview of this Department and which can be well handled by it .

4. I therefore request that the Terms of Reference (ToR) of the GoM be formulated as separately communicated by this Department (copy of the proposed ToR is enclosed) and the GoM requested to give its report within a period of 6 months and not by March 2007 as proposed by the Planning Commission.

With Kind Regards

Yours sincerely,

(DAYANIDHI MARAN)

End: As above

Dr. Manmohan Singh,
Hon'ble Prime Minister of India,
South Block,
New Delhi.

**GOM 2006 – Draft Terms of Reference**

The Mid Term Appraisal (MTA) of the $10^{th}$ Five Year Plan has identified spectrum as a scarce national resource and the consequential need for its optimum use by all. Adequate availability of spectrum for telecom services has been recognised as a significant area and the need for a formalized institutional arrangement for vacation of appropriate spectrum from existing users like Defence.

The Prime Minister has approved, in principle, the constitution of a Group of Ministers (GOM) for address these issues.

The Terms of Reference of the GOM are as follows:

- To recommend measures to make available adequate additional spectrum for growth of telecom sector to achieve high teledensity.
- To make necessary funds available to the Ministry of Defence in particular for replacement of analogue/old equipment with alternate systems or more spectrally efficient equipment;
- To recommend measures for vacation of the spectrum in a time bound manner.
- To suggest measures for early introduction of efficient digital terrestrial broadcasting for vacation of spectrum for other services in line with international practices;

The Group of Ministers will be serviced by the Office of WPC Wing, Department of Telecommunications, Ministry of Communications & IT.

The GOM will give its report within a period of six months.

-------

सत्यमेव जयते

प्रधान मंत्री

**Prime Minister**

New Delhi
January 13, 2006

Dear Shri Maran ji,

I have received your letter of January 11, 2006 regarding formulation of the Terms of Reference of the Group of Ministers constituted to look into issues relating to spectrum availability for telecommunication services.

With warm regards,

Yours sincerely,

Manmohan Singh
(Manmohan Singh)

Shri Dayanidhi Maran
Minister of Communications &
Information Technology
New Delhi

D.O. No. L-14047/01/06-NTG
SECRET

सत्यमेव जयते

**DAYANIDHI MARAN**
MINISTER OF COMMUNICATIONS &
INFORMATION TECHNOLOGY

Respected Prime Minister, 28 FEB 2006

You may kindly recall my meeting with you on 1st February, 2006 when we had, inter-alia, discussed the issue of the Group of Ministers relating to the vacation of spectrum by the Defence. You had kindly assured me that the Terms of Reference of the GOM would be drawn up exactly the way we wanted, which was to focus only on the issue of vacation of spectrum. I am, however, surprised to note that the GOM as constituted has much wider Terms of Reference, some of which I feel impinge upon the work normally to be carried out by the Ministry itself.

2. I shall be grateful if you could kindly instruct the concerned to modify the Terms of Reference as suggested by us, which are enclosed.

With Kind Regards,

Yours sincerely,

(DAYANIDHI MARAN)

Dr. Manmohan Singh
Hon'ble Prime Minister of India,
South Block,
New Delhi.

## GOM 2006 – Draft Terms of Reference

The Mid Term Appraisal (MTA) of the 10th Five Year Plan has identified spectrum as a scarce national resource and the consequential need for its optimum use by all. Adequate availability of spectrum for telecom services has been recognised as a significant area and the need for a formalized institutional arrangement for vacation of appropriate spectrum from existing users like Defence.

The Prime Minister has approved, in principle, the constitution of a Group of Ministers (GOM) to address these issues.

The Terms of Reference of the GOM are as follows:

- To recommend measures to make available adequate additional spectrum for growth of telecom sector to achieve high teledensity.
- To make necessary funds available to the Ministry of Defence in particular for replacement of analogue/old equipment with alternate systems or more spectrally efficient equipment;
- To recommend measures for vacation of the spectrum in a time bound manner.
- To suggest measures for early introduction of efficient digital terrestrial broadcasting for vacation of spectrum for other services in line with international practices;

The Group of Ministers will be serviced by the Office of WPC Wing, Department of Telecommunications, Ministry of Communications & IT.

The GOM will give its report within a period of six months.

-------

D. O. No. ... 2006-Conf.

सत्यमेव जयते

**DAYANIDHI MARAN**
MINISTER OF COMMUNICATIONS &
INFORMATION TECHNOLOGY

16th November, 2006

Respected Prime Minister,

Vide Cabinet Secretariat's Memorandum of even number dated 10th November, 2006, the composition of Group of Ministers (GOM) on vacation of spectrum has been revised. You were kind enough to give me time to discuss the terms of reference for the Group of Ministers on vacation of spectrum. In consonance of the discussions, the terms of reference of the GOM has been prepared by us and enclosed. I solicit your kind approval to the same so as to enable us to vacate the required spectrum from the major users for the growth of the Telecom sector. At the cost of repetition, I may mention that we are on course towards achieving the target of 250 million subscribers by December, 2007 which I had put before you in the last UPA meeting held after completion of two years of the UPA Government. Early vacation of the spectrum by Defence, Space, etc. will go a long way in helping us to reach our milestones at the earliest.

With Kind Regards.

Yours sincerely,

Dayanidhi Maran.

**( DAYANIDHI MARAN )**

Ack. being put up separately.

**Dr. Manmohan Singh,**
Hon'ble Prime Minister,
South Block,
New Delhi.

ELECTRONICS NIKETAN, 6, C.G.O. COMPLEX, NEW DELHI-110003
PHONE : 24329191, 24369191 FAX : 24362333

Draft Terms of Reference of the GOM are as follows:

- To recommend measures for vacation of adequate additional spectrum by the existing large users such as Defence, Space, Para-military, etc., in a time bound manner for the growth of mobile telephony and broadband sectors in the country, in the overall national interest;

- To recommend alternate frequency bands / media for migration of such existing usages, keeping in mind the nature of technology upgradation;

- To estimate and identify the resources required by the concerned Ministries and their phasing, for putting in place necessary alternate systems by such users to enable migration;

- To suggest measures for early introduction of spectrum efficient digital terrestrial broadcasting for vacation of spectrum for other services in line with international practices.

The Group of Ministers will be serviced by the WPC Wing, Department of Telecommunications, Ministry of Communications and Information Technology

D.O. No. 3/11/2003-Inf

भारत सरकार Government of India
वित्त मंत्रालय Ministry of Finance
आर्थिक कार्य विभाग Department of Economic Affairs

सत्यमेव जयते

Preeti Madan
Director (Infra.)
Tel. No. 011-23092500

13th June 2005
नई दिल्ली / New Delhi, ..........................

Dear Shri Agrawal,

Kindly refer to your letter of ID No. 180/31/C/26/05-ESI dated 26th May 2005, enclosing therewith copies of press clippings on the issues of allocation of additional spectrum to mobile operators and soliciting this Department's report/comments on it.

2. The issues involved has since been analysed in this Ministry and after detailed deliberations it is felt that taking a position on such a critical and sensitive issue without having recourse to all the relevant facts and the formal position of the administrative Ministry would neither be appropriate nor advisable.

3. It is, therefore, suggested that PMO may consider initiating the process of by calling a meeting of all the relevant parties and stakeholders. Alternatively, Department of Telecom may be asked to circulate a concept paper on which different Ministries, including Department of Economic Affairs could offer comments.

With regards,

Yours sincerely,

Preeti Madan
(Preeti Madan)

Shri Amit Agrawal
Deputy Secretary
Prime Minister's Office

**Prime Minister's Office**

New Delhi – 110 011

Subject: Allocation of additional spectrum to mobile operators.

In the context of the TRAI's recommendations dated 13.5.05 on spectrum related issues, a number of references have been received and media reports have been published. These have raised issues regarding the possible revenue that could be generated for the Government on selling additional spectrum space, issues concerning a level playing field between GSM and CDMA operators and the need to have a feasible policy for providing necessary capital expenditure to existing users (like MoD) to upgrade technology for enabling them to vacate spectrum for commercial use.

2. In the above context, a discussion note is enclosed. Principal Secretary to PM would be taking a meeting at 3:30 pm on 16.8.05 in South Block to discuss and arrive at a suitable course of further action in the matter.

3. Kindly make it convenient to attend the meeting.

(Amit Agrawal)
Deputy Secretary
Tel. 2301 2613

Member Secretary, Planning Commission
Defence Secretary
Secretary, Department of Economic Affairs
Secretary, Department of Telecommunications

---

PMO ID No. 180/31/c/26/05-ES.I Dated: 29.7.05

Encl: As above.

**DISCUSSION NOTE ON ALLOCATION OF ADDITIONAL SPECTRUM TO MOBILE OPERATORS**

A number of references received and media reports published have raised issues regarding the possible revenue that could be generated for the Government on selling additional spectrum space and also issues concerning a level playing field between GSM and CDMA operators in the context of the TRAI's recommendations dated 13.5.05 on spectrum related issues.

2. Four distinct issues have been raised in respect of the TRAI recommendations dated 13.5.05 on spectrum. These are:

(i) GSM operators are apparently unhappy with the recommendations of TRAI for a review of the existing norms of spectrum allocation *vis-à-vis* roll out obligations, which are distinct for CDMA and GSM operators. TRAI has recommended 'equal' treatment of both sets of operators, and a review for this purpose. This is perceived by GSM operators as resulting in higher availability of spectrum to CDMA operators in a spectrum scarce scenario, which, they argue, militates against a level playing field. DOT's view appears to be that the present system is based on equitable treatment rather than equal treatment.

(ii) CDMA operators are apparently unhappy with the TRAI recommendation for earmarking the '1900 MHz band' for 3G services. There is overlap in frequency bands in use (i) in USA by CDMA operators for 2G/2.5G/3G services, and (ii) in Europe by GSM operators for 3G services. CDMA operators contend that earmarking of this band for 3G services automatically rules out use of the overlapping USPCS '1900 MHz band' desired by them. The USPCS '1900 MHz band' can be readily used by them for expanding services from the telecom equipment and dual band mobile handsets already invested in for the existing operations in the '800 MHz band' currently assigned to them. Any other band would require fresh investments. Further, GSM operators would be able to begin 3G services earlier as dual band handsets for the frequency band envisaged are not immediately in the market.

(iii) GSM operators are apparently unhappy with the TRAI recommendation for allocating additional spectrum in the '800 MHz band' to CDMA operators. They contend that this would enable them to not only roll out 2G/2.5G services to a greater number of subscribers but would also enable them to roll out 3G services ahead of

GSM operators, who would have to wait till the recommended '1900 MHz band' is vacated by MOD.

(iv) Shri Ratan Tata has raised issue with the TRAI recommendation that spectrum for 3G services should be given on annual revenue basis without any entry charges to make services more affordable. Shri Tata had written to Minister of Telecommunications suggesting that license for 3G services be given only on a nationwide basis and an entry charge of Rs. 1,500 crore be charged. Copy of Shri Tata's letter is attached.

**Discussion**

(i) ***Review of spectrum assignment requirements for CDMA and GSM operators***

3. There are two competing alternative technologies for mobile communication services, *viz.*, GSM & CDMA. The US mobile telephony system is based on CDMA, while the European mobile telephony system is based on GSM. India, along with Japan and Korea, is one of the few countries where both GSM and CDMA technologies have been extensively deployed. 3G services are based either on the WCDMA standard (which has evolved from the GSM standard) or the CDMA 2000 1x / EV-DO / EV-DD (which have evolved from the CDMA standard).

4. Mobile service licences are technology neutral. However, after obtaining licence, the service provider has to opt for a particular technology standard while applying for assignment of spectrum frequencies to the WPC (DoT). Both technology standards operate in specified bands which are fixed as per the National Frequency Allocation Plan 2002. Both standards have different frequency bandwidth requirements and DoT have been assigning frequencies starting from a minimum and increasing the frequencies assigned as the service provider reaches certain subscriber number milestones. The bandwidths initially assigned are thus unequal and, further, the milestones for giving additional bandwidth are also unequal. This is evident from the following table:

| SN | Spectrum frequency assignment stages | GSM | CDMA |
|---|---|---|---|
| 1 | Initial assignment of spectrum frequencies | 4.4 + 4.4 MHz / 6.2 + 6.2 MHz | 2.5 + 2.5 MHz |
| 2 | Service area subscriber base required for enhanced assignment of frequencies | 5 lakh | Between 1.5 to 4 lakh for various categories of service areas |
| | Enhanced assignment | Between 6.2 + 6.2 to 8 + 8 MHz | 3.75 + 3.75 MHz |

| 3 | Service area subscriber base required for maximum assignment of frequencies | 10 lakh | Between 5 to 10 lakh for various categories of service areas |
|---|---|---|---|
| | Maximum assignment | Between 8 + 8 to 10 + 10 MHz | 5 + 5 MHz |

5. ***DoT appear to be of the view that this difference in the quantum and subscriber base conditions between the two standards is necessary given inherent variations in technolog and necessary for optimal spectrum use based on subscriber base growth. In this view, this 'unequal' frequency assignment is 'equitable' from the point of view of ensuring competition between competing technology standards. TRAI's view apparently is that the frequency assignment should be equal. Thus, there is an implicit difference of viewpoints regarding what the expression 'technology neutral' means.***

(ii) ***Overlap in frequency bands in use (a) in USA by CDMA operators for 2G/2.5G/3G services, and (b) in Europe by GSM operators for 3G services***

6. Generally, separate spectrum needs to be allocated for various technology standards due to technological reasons. In India, CDMA operators are currently allocated spectrum in the '800 MHz band' while GSM operators are allocated spectrum in the '900 MHz band' and '1800 MHz band'. In USA, only CDMA operators are there and they are allocated spectrum in the '1900 MHz band' in what is referred to as the USPCS band (1850-1910 MHz paired with 1930-1990 MHz). In Europe, only GSM operators are there and they are allocated spectrum in the '1900 MHz band' in what is referred to as the IMT-2000 core band (1920-1980 MHz paired with 2110-2170 MHz). ***Thus, there is a clear overlap between the band assigned to CDMA operators in USA and the band assigned for 3G services and used by GSM operators in Europe.*** The International Telecommunications Union (ITU) has recommended five spectrum bands for 3G, which are referred to as IMT-2000 bands and, one of these, is also in the '1900 MHz band' and is referred to as 'IMT-2000 core band' (1920-1980 MHz paired with 2110-2170 MHz). ***TRAI have recommended that the ITU recommendations of reserving the '1900 MHz band' for 3G services be followed. The National Frequency Allocation Plan (NFAP) formulated by the Wireless Planning Cell in DoTis understood to be in line with TRAI recommendations. CDMA operators are apparently of the persuasion that this favours GSM operators at their cost and distorts the level playing field.***

7. The IMT-2000 core band is not a unique requirement for 3G GSM services (unlike what the expression 'core' may suggest) and any of the five ITU recommended IMT-2000 bands may be used for 3G services. ***However, mobile handsets currently available in the***

***market are based on the IMT-2000 core band frequencies and using a different frequency band would, therefore, significantly alter the expenditure requirements and also result in initial delay till such time as handsets are available in the new frequency band.***

8. A somewhat recent development has been the development and deployment of ***new equipment in Japan and Korea permits both CDMA and GSM operators to simultaneously operate in the '1900 MHz band'.*** There are unconfirmed reports that China too may be opting for this. DoT have intimated that ***Telecom Equipment Manufacturers' Association (TEMA) are understood to be of the view that such equipment is likely to be available in 12 months. In any case, the '1900 MHz band' is currently in use by Defence Services and its vacation may be expected to take time, which might turn out to be of a similar duration.***

(iii) ***<u>Use of additional spectrum to be assigned to CDMA operators in bands already licensed to them on the basis of subscriber base conditions for 3G services</u>***

9. CDMA operators have requested for additional spectrum to cater to the growing volume and requirements of the existing 2G / 2.5G operators as the spectrum currently allocated is insufficient. ***The current infrastructure for CDMA services is largely capable of providing 3G services as well, provided additional spectrum is made available.*** In case of CDMA (and unlike in case of GSM), technology permits that spectrum can be used for simultaneously providing 2G / 2.5G as well as 3G type of services.

10. ***The apprehension of GSM operators appears to be that if CDMA operators are made additional spectrum available in the existing 800 MHz band, they will be able to roll out 3G services right away, whereas the proposed earmarking of the '1900 MHz band' for 3G services would be available only after some time as it would require vacation of the spectrum by MOD and, therefore, the CDMA operators would get an early mover advantage vis-à-vis GSM operators.***

11. However, 3G being a broadband service, the quantum of spectrum required for any significant roll out is substantial. A total of only 14 frequency channels only are available whereas the maximum entitlement of each of 4 licensed CDMA operators is for 4 frequency channels. Thus, against a maximum entitlement of 16 frequency channels, only 14 are available. In several of the commercially more attractive circles, these are already allocated and, only in some circles a very small number of frequency channels are available today for assignment. ***These channels are to be provided as per subscriber base conditions already committed to*** and mentioned above for meeting the existing 2G/2.5G service roll out needs.

4

which should lead to ***limited possibility of any significant roll out of 3G services with this limited spectrum.***

(iv) ***<u>One time entry spectrum charges for 3G services</u>***

12. TRAI has recommended that spectrum for 3G services should be given on annual revenue basis without any entry charges to make services more affordable. DOT is understood to be considering initial charges as well, to ensure economic utilisation of scarce resource and to guard against the likelihood hoarding of this valuable asset to boost the asset position of companies. Shri Tata had written to Minister of Telecommunications suggesting that license for 3G services be given only on a nationwide basis and an entry charge of Rs. 1,500 crore be charged. On the basis of 60 MHz bandwidth in the IMT-2000 core band being parcelled in spectrum licenses of 5 MHz each (both CDMA and GSM operators are expected to require a minimum of this quantity of the spectrum for roll out), the one-time receipts may be estimated as up to Rs. 18,000 crore. ***Shri Tata has made coupled this offer with the condition of nationwide spectrum allocation as against the current practice of circle-wise (and, since December 2004 in respect of CDMA operators, SDCA-wise) spectrum allocation and his concern might be getting a nationwide footprint and limiting the field for competition, given the heavy investments that 3G services would require and the likely escalation in a bidding scenario for interested investors seeking to secure spectrum in all circles.***

**Comments:**

13. Thus, both sets of operators have joined issues on various recommendations. In addition, Shri Tata has raised the issue of entry charge for 3G services. ***The recommendations of TRAI were requested by DoT in 2003 in the context of a unified service licence. The recommendations are not binding on the Government, nor are they a necessary part of the process by which the Government has to arrive at a decision.***

14. There is no immediacy regarding the issue at paragraph 2(i) above.

15. Regarding the issue at paragraph 2(ii) above, the assignment of the '1900 MHz band' for 3G services is in line with ITU recommendations. The dual technology equipment is also likely to be available within a reasonable timeframe of 12 months according to the Telecom Equipment Manufacturers' Association and time is also required for vacating this band from MoD uses and making them available to operators. Thus, CDMA operators may have a realistic opportunity for preparing themselves in time for the actual roll out. CDMA is a proprietary closed source standard owned by the US-based MNC Qualcomm, while GSM is

an open standard. It is possible that pressure in the matter is being raised by the US based franchisee manufacturers of CDMA equipment (rather than by the domestic CDMA service providers), who may lose out to the East Asian based franchisee manufacturers who would get the market in the proposed scenario.

16. Regarding the issue at paragraph 2(iii) above, CDMA operators are understood to be entitled for allotment of additional spectrum in their existing bands as per their licence conditions and this is also required for catering to the subscriber needs. The TRAI recommendations are apparently merely reiterate what is already committed to.

17. The basic dispute arises from the unavailability of spectrum. Both sets of operators require additional spectrum bands to be allocated: GSM operators require separate spectrum for 3G services and for 2G/2.5G services, while CDMA operators require it for 2G/2.5G services (which can automatically be used for 3G services as well). The solution lies in making adequate spectrum available. This is only possible by vacating existing spectrum. In view of affordability, entry charges on spectrum for 2G/2.5G services have not been kept and nor do they appear desirable. On the other hand, 3G services have a realistic potential for raising such entry charge revenues. A key bottleneck in vacating spectrum has been the migration difficulties, including costs on capital expenditure, that existing users like MOD would have to bear. 3G spectrum entry revenues, if charged, could be used to meet spectrum vacation costs, meeting not only 3G spectrum requirements but also 2G/2.5G spectrum requirements.

18. The preparation of a clear spectrum allocation policy along with a roadmap for meeting future requirements was last considered at length in the report of the Spectrum Management Committee constituted by PMO in December 1998. However, the recommendations were only used as an input by the GoT for preparing the National Telecom Policy of 1999 which only incorporates the broad unexceptionable statements regarding spectrum allocation and did not deal with the extensive and specific recommendations made by the Committee. As a result, the spectrum scenario has continued to be increasingly constrained with the emergence and growth of new technology standards (CDMA), increase in number of licensees (from 2 GSM operators to 4 GSM + 4 CDMA operators), and lack of desired progress in vacation of spectrum by MoD and other users (MoD uses both 'NATO bands' and 'non-NATO bands', unlike most other countries which operate on one or the other).

6

19. On this key issue of unavailability of adequate spectrum, there is need to have a feasible policy for providing necessary capital expenditure to existing users to upgrade technology for enabling them to vacate spectrum for commercial use. While the Spectrum Management Committee constituted by PMO in December 1998 had made specific recommendations which have not yet been operationalised, there may now be need for review on account of any changes that have taken place in technology and the developments in the regulatory frame that have taken place since.

Most Immediate

PRIME MINISTER'S OFFICE

**New Delhi 110 011**

Subject: Allocation of additional spectrum to mobile operators.

Kindly refer to this Office ID of even number dated 29.7.05 on the above subject.

2. The meeting scheduled to be held at 3:30 p.m. on 16.8.05 will now be held at 3:30 p.m. on 5.9.05 in South Block.

3. Kindly make it convenient to attend the meeting.

(Amit Agrawal)
Deputy Secretary
Phone: 23012613

Member Secretary, Planning Commission
Defence Secretary
Secretary, Department of Economic Affairs
Secretary, Department of Telecommunications

PMO ID No. 180/31/c/26/05-ES I Dated: 16.8.05

**Secret**

**Prime Minister's Office**

South Block, New Delhi – 110 011

Subject: Spectrum policy related issues.

Principal Secretary to PM will be taking a meeting to discuss the constitution of a Group of Ministers for resolving spectrum policy related issues on 17.1.06 at 6:00 p.m. in PMO to discuss the matter. Drafts prepared by the DoT and the Planning Commission for the proposed Terms of Reference for the Group of Ministers are enclosed.

2. The addresses of this note are requested to kindly make it convenient to attend the meeting.

(Amit Agrawal)
Deputy Secretary
Tel.: 2301 2613

Member Secretary, Planning Commission

Defence Secretary

Secretary, Department of Telecommunications

Secretary, Department of Economic Affairs

---

PMO ID no. 180/31/C/26/2005-ES.I Dated: 14.1.06

Encls.: as above

राजीव रत्न शाह
**RAJEEVA RATNA SHAH**

सदस्य-सचिव
भारत सरकार
योजना आयोग
योजना भवन, संसद मार्ग
नई दिल्ली - 110001

***Member-Secretary***
Government of India
Planning Commission
Yojana Bhavan, Parliament Street
New Delhi-110 001
Tele : 23096574 Fax : 23096575
Email : rrshah@nic.in

**D. O. NO. 13040/65/2005-C&I**

**10th January, 2006**

Dear Sri Nair,

With reference to PMO I.D. No. 180/31/C/26/05-ES.I dated 23rd November, 2005 addressed to Deputy Chairman, Planning Commission relating to Constitution of a Group of Ministers (GOM) to look into allocation of spectrum to mobile operators and related issues. Draft order with Terms of Reference (TOR) is attached for perusal.

2. I am sending a copy of the draft TOR to Department of Telecommunications, requesting them to provide their inputs to PMO directly. Since Deputy Chairman, Planning Commission is out of station, the final version of TOR would be sent to you on his arrival and approval.

Regards,

Yours sincerely,

10/1/2006

**(Rajeeva Ratna Shah)**

**Shri T.K.A. Nair,**
Principal Secretary to the Prime Minister,
Prime Minister's Office
South Block,
New Delhi

Draft

**F.NO.M-**
**Government of India**

ORDER

**Subject: Constitution of a Group of Ministers for Looking into Spectrum Related Issues**

The task of preparation of a clear spectrum allocation policy along with a roadmap for meeting the future requirements (earlier assigned to Spectrum Management Committee by PMO in December, 1998) has acquired urgency in light of the rapid roll out of mobile services and the consequent demand for allocation of additional spectrum currently occupied by Defence & Paramilitary Forces. Furthermore, the spectrum needs of broadband based rural services and the dispersed nature of communication requirements in rural areas makes it necessary that we identify some unlicensed bands (esp ISM) for outdoor, public usage to enable wireless ISPs, public interactive services & other service providers. Finally, it is important to take note of technological innovations which are opening up new options, which have the potential of converting spectrum scarcity into spectrum abundance. Accordingly, the Mid Term Appraisal of the Tenth Five Year Plan has suggested the need for a formalized institutional arrangement in the form of a Group of Ministers to discuss issues relating to spectrum allocation, including all the issues related to vacation of certain spectrum bands by Defence and Paramilitary Forces.

2. Recognizing that envisioning a progressive spectrum allocation policy which optimizes spectrum usage, balancing the interests of stakeholders, fairly, transparently and adequately, will require high level priority intervention and resolution of issues cutting across various sectors, Prime Minister has approved the Constitution of a Group of Ministers for looking into the entire gamut of issues relating to Spectrum. The composition of the Group of Ministers will be as follows:-

| | |
|---|---|
| **Shri Pranab Mukherjee, Minister of Defence** | **Chairman** |
| **Shri Shivraj V Patil, Minister of Home** | **Member** |
| **Shri P Chidambaram, Minister of Finance** | **Member** |
| **Shri Dayanidhi Maran, Minister of Communications & IT** | **Member** |
| **Shri M S Ahluwalia, Dy. Chairman, Planning Commission** | **Member** |
| **Shri Priyaranjan Dasmunsi, Minister of I & B** | **Member** |
| **Shri Prithviraj Chavan, Minister of State for Space** | **Member** |

Department of Telecommunications will provide the background, technical papers and inputs for the Group. The Group will be serviced by Planning Commission.

C:\Documents and Settings\Administrator\Desktop\Spectrum GOM TOR 100106.doc

Page 1 of 3

3 **Terms of Reference**

A Vacation & Reallocation of Spectrum

(a) Determine the quantum of additional spectrum requirement and identify frequency bands 3G+NG (next generation) services for major users viz.

(i) Cellular-mobile services,
(ii) Defence & Paramilitary Forces,

for both (i) short term (i.e. less than one year) & (ii) Medium term (i.e. less than five years)

(b) Based on current occupation of spectrum, clearly delineate a **transition path** for enabling users like **Defence & Paramilitary Forces** to migrate to the more appropriate spectrum slots identified at (a) above, keeping in mind technology upgradation, nature of usage and procurement procedures. The transition path should clearly lay down phasing and sequencing of steps and a feasible time-frame to enable step by step monitoring.

(c) Correspondingly suggest a **transition path for cellular & mobile services** to step into the spectrum bands vacated by security forces and allocated to them. Finalize transparent guidelines and criteria for additional allocation of spectrum to operators.

(d) Estimate, quantum of **funds** required to enable security forces to procure state-of-the-art equipment, technologically appropriate for the assigned spectrum. Estimate, year wise fund-flow requirements, to bring about a smooth transition.

(e) Suggest a **Spectrum Pricing Policy** and examine the possibility of creation of a **Spectrum Relocation Fund.** Indicate likely source and quantum of resources so generated and guidelines for the operation of the fund. The Pricing Policy would need to look at both the spectral efficiency and sectoral business viability / profitability models, which would vastly vary in case of voice, data/ text and images (i.e. television / broadband internet). Spectrum Pricing Policy may, as far as possible, aim at Revenues fully offsetting the cost of vacation of spectrum.

(f) Suggest guidelines to encourage and incentivise introduction of **spectrum efficient technologies.**

(g) To modify existing **procurement procedures** of Defence & Internal Security agencies, authorizing them to accelerate equipment procurement to enable them to observe spectrum-vacation-timelines.

B. Dispute Resolution

(h) Suggest a **dispute resolution mechanism** for amicably resolving disputes among stakeholders, relating to spectrum usage. The disputes are bound to

C:\Documents and Settings\Administrator\Desktop\Spectrum GOM TOR 100106.doc

Page 2 of 3

arise since we have opted for a multi-technology (i.e. both GSM & CDMA) and multi-user (seven or more service providers) environment.

C. <u>Technology Neutrality</u>

(i) Suggest ways to bring about resilience in Spectrum Management Policy & Procedures to ensure technology neutrality and service neutrality.

D. <u>Rural Networks & Delicensed Bands</u>

(j) For faster rural coverage, identify licence exempt spectrum bands, like sub GHz and 5 GHz for proliferating inexpensive TV broadcasting and rural wireless broadband networks. For ultimately achieving ubiquitous rural broadband, the following options may be examined:-

i allow use of unlicensed bands (esp ISM) for outdoor, public usage to enable wireless ISPs, public interactive services and other service providers.

ii since rural wireless services are best served by long ranges, consider reallocation of UHF band (470 – 520 - 585 MHz) or (620 - 720 MHz) for fixed and mobile services in urban areas and/or WiFi / WiMAX technologies in rural areas.

iii examine the option of moving away from fixed spectrum allocations to innovative options such as software defined radios or cognitive radios.

iv allow higher power levels for unlicensed WiFi bands, through antennae gain.

(k) To match country's Spectrum Allocation Policy with best international practices in line with the requirements of ITU and our own national priorities.

The underlying principle for this exercise is that smart regulation will not only improve usage of spectrum, but will also subserve public interest best. Given the urgency associated with the case, the Group of Ministers may submit its recommendations by March 2007.

(Name)
Jt. Secretary

To

All Members

Copy to:

1. Prime Minister's Office
2. Cabinet Secretary
3. Secretaries of all concerned Ministries

Tel. : +91-11-2371 9898
Fax : +91-11-2371 1514
e-mail: jssarma@nic.in

Dr. J. S. SARMA
सचिव Secretary

**Secret**

भारत सरकार
संचार एवं सूचना प्रौद्योगिकी मंत्रालय
दूरसंचार विभाग
संचार भवन, नई दिल्ली-110 001
Government of India
Ministry of Communications & Information Technology
Department of Telecommunications
Sanchar Bhawan, New Delhi-110 001

D.O. No.L-14047/01/2006-NTG
January 10, 2006

Dear Shri Usmani,

Please refer to your letter No.180/31/C/26/05-ESI dated November 23, 2005, addressed to the Deputy Chairman, Planning Commission where it has been indicated that Hon'ble Prime Minister has approved, in principle, the constitution of a Group of Ministers(GoM) for looking into various issues relating to vacation of spectrum, etc. In this regard, please find enclosed the proposed Terms of Reference as approved by the Minister of Communications & IT.

With kind regards,

Yours sincerely,

(*J.S. Sarma*)

*Encl: As above*

Shri Jawed Usmani,
JS to Prime Minister,
PMO, South Block,
New Delhi.

SURENDRA PRAKASH GOYAL
MEMBER OF PARLIAMENT
(LOK SABHA)

सत्यमेव जयते

92, South Avenue
New Delhi - 110 011

April 07, 2006

Dear Mr. Prime Minister,

I welcome your recent observation that Government is working towards releasing additional spectrum for use of commercial telecom operators so that the growth of this dynamic sector is not constrained by the shortage of this vital and scarce resource, which is rightly called the oxygen for the telecom business. I also welcome Government's reported decision to set up a GoM to tackle issues like the allocation and utilization of spectrum etc. This step is all the more appreciable in view of the fact that additional spectrum which will be vacated by the Defence will need to be allocated amongst GSM and CDMA operators and also in view of the fact that GSM appears to be unjustifiably being favoured and preferred over CDMA in the matter of Spectrum allocation.

2. The Government had already hiked FDI sectoral cap to 74%. Added to this is a private initiative of an entry of new operators. As a result, the demand for Spectrum is bound to considerably increase. In such a competition scenario, it is necessary to ensure that there is transparency as well as level playing field for both the operators.

3. Radio Frequency Spectrum is a national resource, which is limited. How much teledensity is reached through the wireless route in India will depend on how the spectrum policy is formulated and allocation is done. At present the Spectrum is allocated to GSM and CDMA at the ratio of 2:1 i.e. 10 MHz per licence area to GSM and 5 MHz per licence area to CDMA. This needs to be revised in the light of facts namely, the ability to provide services in far flung or rural areas or 10% coverage to achieve the target of 250 million subscribers by the end of next year. This is possible only if there is a level playing approach as well as appreciation of technologies.

4. While GSM system is prevalent in Europe, the CDMA technology is operational in USA. Both have pluses and minuses, but we have to weigh this in the light of our requirements of reaching rural population rather than concentrating on metros. From this point of view the CDMA has several advantages, which cannot be ignored while allocating Spectrums.

5. In any case in our country, it is more important at this stage of development to move beyond mere technology factor. Government should be technology neutral, while formulating spectrum policy. It is therefore necessary that this policy does not lean towards one side or another and as and when

-1-

SURENDRA PRAKASH GOYAL
MEMBER OF PARLIAMENT
(LOK SABHA)

92, South Avenue
New Delhi - 110 011

-2-

the quota is raised, it should be equally divided between the two operators without discrimination on technological, geographical or financial or number of subscribers.

6. **It is therefore essential that the GoM should review the Spectrum policy *de novo* and lay down clear-cut guidelines about spectrum allocations to be followed by the DoT or Spectrum Management Committee/WPC. In other worlds, the GoM should provide detailed blue print for the purpose and its implementation or management only should be left to these agencies. This will ensure that both the operators will be treated on par and decisive role is vested in the GoM and not these agencies, which may tend to be partisan and selective as our experience shows.**

7. According to recent newspaper reports Wireless Planning Commission (WPC) of DoT considering **allocating spectrum for fifth and sixth CDMA carriers on the basis of their meeting the subscriber criteria.** If the newspaper reports are believed to be true, these criteria will not bring improvement and efficiency of spectrum usage but it will lead to utter confusion and will not be fair and transparent in allocation of spectrum as subscriber base of particular operator can vary from time to time. This will also lead to uncertainty in policy application. **It would be more appropriate if this aspect is also examined and consider by GoM.**

8. Even the Standing Committee on Information Technology in its report of December 2005 had deprecated the injudious allocation of spectrum and stressed the need to have a clear-cut road map for the country in order to cater to the short-term spectrum requirements beyond 2007. The Committee had, therefore, desired that the Government should come out with a comprehensive and transparent Spectrum policy, dispensing with all earlier loopholes. **I, therefore, feel that GoM is the most appropriate forum to address this issue.**

9. The Committee had also recommended that Spectrum may be released keeping in view the need for "eventual harbonization of the Spectrum allocation policy in accordance with the international norms" At the same time, the Committee desired that "while releasing the Spectrum, adequate opportunity should be given to both the technologies to expand in a balanced manner" and "Government should take into consideration the legitimate spectrum needs of the existing operators". Even in regard to 3G and emerging services in the existing bands, the Committee had desired that Government should provide simultaneous opportunities to both GSM and CDMA operators. **These recommendations and observations of the Parliamentary Standing Committee deserve to the given serious thought and full weight while formulating the Spectrum Policy.**

SURENDRA PRAKASH GOYAL
MEMBER OF PARLIAMENT
(LOK SABHA)

92, South Avenue
New Delhi - 110 011

-3-

10. However, I am surprised that even before the GoM meets to address the issue, according to press reports, the DoT has already pre-empted the core issue by announcing norms for additional spectrum allocation to both GSM and CDMA operators in the ratio of 2:1 ignoring the TRAI's recommendations. Even in regard to this additional allocation, the GSM service providers have been given a favourable treatment. This announcement appears to have been made in indecent haste inasmuch as additional spectrum from the Defence is yet to be released. The DoTs announcement is therefore nothing but presenting a *fate accompli* and rendering the GoM ineffective. This is yet another instance of the bureaucracy having an upper hand over political leadership, which is accountable to Parliament. Hence I request you to look into this aspect immediately and direct the DoT retract or keep on hold the announcement until the GoM formulates a comprehensive spectrum policy for the approval of the Union Cabinet and additional spectrum is made available from the Defence.

11. I, therefore feel that all these issues can best be addressed by GoM in a better, comprehensive and futuristic way than be left to be determined by DoT or any other wing of Government. I total disagree with the reported official views that the GoM should focus only on how to get spectrum for Defence or spectrum bands and the like. In fact these are technical maters, which may be left to be sorted out at an official level and a High Level body like GoM should concentrate on laying down detailed guidelines for spectrum allocation. I do hope that you will kindly apprise the GoM of my concern and reasoning while formulating the National Spectrum Policy. It is my firm belief that a policy blue print for Spectrum arrangement that focuses on efficient and equitable allocation across different services providers can alone lead to faster growth and expansion of telecom sector.

With regards,

Yours sincerely,

(Surendra Prakash Goyal)

Dr. Manmohan Singh,
Prime Minister,
Government of India,
**New Delhi.**

**P. S. GADHAVI**
MEMBER OF PARLIAMENT
(LOK SABHA)

सत्यमेव जयते

☎ : 02832 - 251177 (R)
256177 (O)
MF-8, ODHAVDHAM APPARTMENT,
OPP. RADIO STATION,
BHUJ-KUTCH. PIN-370 001.

June 9, 2006.
Date :

To

Dr. Manmohan Singhji,
Hon'ble Prime Minister,
Government of India,
South Block, New Delhi.

Respected Sir,

I would like to draw your kind attention to recent news report appearing in a local daily of repute from Haryana and also a national daily (copy enclosed for your immediate reference).

This is very disturbing news especially when various issues related to Telecom is at forefront of all controversies. On May 24, 2006 in a press conference shown on leading television channels, I heard Telecom Minister of UPA Government defending the subscriber figures announced by various telecom operators and said "we are following the best of international practices, which is very stringent in subscriber counting and definitely we believe the operators." But looking at the news article appearing in "Dainik Bhaskar", this does not seems to be ground reality. I rather feel that it will not few thousand but few million customers on all India basis. We have a very recent example of more or less similar fraud in the IPO scam.

I also feel that this is not only an issue of an overstating of subscriber base but this is also an issue of internal security. Not verifying customers before issuing SIM cards or having multiple connections in name of few fictitious individuals is nothing but playing with national security. By doing this, companies like Reliance and Hutch, Essar (as indicated in newspaper report) are doing harm to national security.

In recent past, issue of spectrum and its allotment on subscriber base was in news. Now, it is evident that telecom companies reported in the article are involved in racket of forging subscriber base. It is all the more important that all further allotment of spectrum should be stopped till the time all the subscriber figures are verified by a third party independent auditor. Issue like this raised many important questions like :

(i) Why are the telecom operators overstating subscriber figures? Is this for spectrum hoarding?

RESI. : 10/B, HIMATNAGAR COLONY, BHUJ (KUTCH) 370 001 (GUJARAT)
77, SOUTH AVENUE, NR. TIN MURTI, NEW DELHI-110 011. TEL. : (011) 23794965

**P. S. GADHAVI**
MEMBER OF PARLIAMENT
(LOK SABHA)

सत्यमेव जयते

☎ : 02832 - 251177 (R)
256177 (O)
MF-8, ODHAVDHAM APPARTMENT,
OPP. RADIO STATION,
BHUJ-KUTCH. PIN-370 001.

Date :

- 2 -

(ii) How is Government planning to tackle the issue of internal security? (Not to forget that in all the terrorist attacks including that on Parliament & Ayodhya, it was mobile, which played a vital role in communication).

(iii) Why is Government not willing to look at integrated telecom & spectrum policy? (If a comprehensive spectrum policy is set up, then no company will resort to these cheap ways of inflating subscriber numbers and compromising with internal security).

(iv) Why is Telecom Minister shying away from addressing these serious issues of national concern and seem to be on the side of defaulting telecom operators?

I would like you to order a probe in this regard and make a statement clarifying the fact by which people of this country and all of us can know about the real fact.

With regards,

Yours sincerely,

( P.S. GADHAVI )

RESI. : 10/B, HIMATNAGAR COLONY, BHUJ (KUTCH) 370 001 (GUJARAT)
77, SOUTH AVENUE, NR. TIN MURTI, NEW DELHI-110 011. TEL. : (011) 23794965.

RAJEEV CHANDRASEKHAR
MEMBER OF PARLIAMENT
RAJYA SABHA

12th May,2007

Respected Prime Minister,

I write to you in connection with the recent Announcement of a Global Auction of spectrum for 3G services by the Department of Telecommunications and a subsequent article in Economic Times dated 10th May, 2007 in that connection. (A copy of the Article is attached).

Firstly, I must congratulate you and the Government in taking the decision for a global auction of spectrum. I believe that is in the best National interests.

The article attached quoting one of the corporate currently in the Telecom sector is trying to make out a tenuous case of restricting bidders for 3G on some frivolous grounds. As someone who has personal experience of various forms of arguments and logic that have been used in the past to distort what is the correct thing to do, I would like to make some points so that such lobbying does not derail the government from the right path.

That 3G is a separate service is a principle accepted all over the world. The regulator and the government here have also agreed to this principle. Therefore there seems to be no dispute that these should be separate licenses. The key issue seems to be the commercial terms of allocating Spectrum.

It is true that in the early 90s when the Government was actively trying to encourage investors and helping build out the telecom sector, the terms of spectrum were far kinder and gentler. Even there in the mid 90s and subsequently spectrum allocation or license allocation was through a global auction without any restrictions on new players.

...2/-

Jupiter Innovision Centre, No. 54 Richmond Road, Bangalore 560 025 India.
Tel : 91-80-25585908 Fax : 91-80-25587843
E-mail : rajeev.c@nic.in

-2-

Spectrum is clearly a valuable natural resource of the Government and people of India. When spectrum is being allocated in present day, when the telecom sector is well developed and valuable (Note the current valuations of Hutch sale to Vodafone), there is clearly no justification in allotting spectrum in any way but a transparent auction. An auction process has been used in the Telecom sector before for the $4^{th}$ round of cellular licenses and as well more recently very successfully by the I&B Ministry for FM licenses.

Given that there cant be any argument against auction, a case is now sought to be made by this corporate, that the bidders must be restricted through some arbitrary criterion – in this case Indian companies or existing operators or both. This is quite ridiculous and goes against the objectives of an auction. There were no such restrictions on the $4^{th}$ round of cellular licenses nor were there any restrictions like this in the recent FM licenses. Which would lead one to believe, that the only objective of the restricting bidders would be to depress the real price of spectrum being allotted.

This argument being made must be rejected with the contempt it deserves notwithstanding the fact that it comes from a so-called reputed Indian corporate. It is against national interest and against every precedence and practice of exacting maximum value for spectrum. This suggestion is even more ironical given the almost opposite view taken by the same company when it was trying to get into Cellular through the WLL route in the whole WLL scam not many years ago.

In short, I wish to reiterate that the decision of the Government to actively seek out through the process of a Global transparent Auction with no restrictions on participants, the best price for 3G spectrum/licenses - is the correct one for the country and its people. This is consistent with practices in the past and in other sectors like FM. Resources raised through such a process can be invaluable in addressing rural tele-density and other investment requirements of the government in rural and urban infrastructure. The government must not allow lobbying of the kind in this reported letter to compromise this approach and to perpetuate oligopolies of the kind that you recently referred to in a speech.

...3/-

-3-

I am sure given my history of association of Telecom, there will be some accusations of me having some agenda or the other. I have none, except to make sure the wrongs that so characterized the conduct of Telecom policy in the past years are not repeated today or ever again in the future.

Thanking you

Very Truly Yours

RAJEEV CHANDRASEKHAR

Dr. Manmohan Singh
Hon`ble Prime Minister
Government of India
New Delhi

*Copy to:*

1) *Thiru Dayanidhi Maran*
*Honble Minister of Telecommunications and IT*

2) *Thiru P Chidambaram*
*Honble Minister of Finance*

**TOP SECRET**
**COPY 1 of 1**

**Government** of India
**Ministry** of External Affairs
***

Sub: **Telecom Licences and Spectrum issues.**

The Hon'ble **Prime** Minister had asked for my views on the subject **mentioned** above. On the basis of the information provided **by** the Ministry of Communication & Information **Technology** (MOCIT), I have the following observations to make:

(i) The licences **and** spectrum allocation, presently, is being done under **the "Guidelines for Unified Access Services Licence"** notified on **14 December** 2005. Therefore, it is **assumed** that the **"POLICY"** which is being referred to in a **number** of cases before the **"Telecom Dispute Settlement Appellate Tribunal"** is what is stated in these guidelines of **14** December 2005.

**Para 11** of these **guidelines** clearly say that "*the licences shall be issued **without** any restriction on the number of entrants for provision of Unified Access Services in a service area*".

PM wants it examined pl.
-sd-
Private Secretary to PM
28.12.2007
-sd-
Principal Secretary to PM
28.12.2007
Jt.Secretary to PM

***Department of Telecommunications (DOT) may continue to follow this policy till any further changes are made in this regard.***

(ii) **Para 38** of **these** guidelines, *inter alia*, states that "*additional spectrum **may** be considered for allocation after ensuring optimal **and** efficient utilization of the already allocated spectrum, **taking** into account all types of traffic and **guidelines/criteria prescribed from time to time***".

Norms notified in **March 2006** by DOT specified for the first time that allocation **of** additional spectrum beyond start-up spectrum would **be made** on reaching certain minimum number of subscribers.

***Therefore, any allocation of spectrum post-March 2006 will have to be according to these norms.***

(iii) **In August 2007,** Telecom Regulatory Authority of India (**TRAI**) suggested **revised** norms which were stringent than the earlier ones. **In October 2007,** Telecommunication Engineering Centre **(TEC)** of DOT has recommended even more stringent **norms. A third Committee** set up under Additional Secretary **(DOT)** is taking another look at the norms. *No notification post-March 2006 has been issued so far.*

***It is clear that the notified norms so far are only those issued in March 2006.***

1

TOP SECRET
COPY 1 of 1

(iv) While it is the **prerogative of the Government to frame, revise and change the policy**, it is also the responsibility of the **government** to do so in a transparent manner and then **follow the** stated policy both in letter and spirit. **Thus, it is essential for DOT to issue the new norms immediately so that the spectrum allocation is done in a transparent manner.** Enforcement of stringent norms may lead to **change** in the entitlements of existing licence holders and **may** increase the availability of the spectrum for new licen**se holders**/crossover LOI holders.

(v) It is also impor**tant** to take this step in view of the large number of court **cases**. Even though no stay has been granted to the litigants **so** far on the assurance given by the Government that the **"POLICY"** would be followed in the spectrum allocation, ***it can lead to problems if we do not have a clearly stated policy and norms in this regard.***

(vi) As stated by **the** *Solicitor General in his note, an affidavit has been* ***filed by*** *the Government saying that spectrum would be first* ***allocated*** *to existing operators,then to persons to whom* ***licences were*** *issued in December 2006, and thereafter to the* ***persons to whom*** *LOIs have been issued for cross-over technology.* **If** such an affidavit has already been filed, it closes our **options** as the matter is *subjudice*.

*Otherwise, in all fairness,* ***the*** *allocation from the available spectrum may be made* ***on the*** *following basis:*

(a) Existing operators
(b) To those who **were** issued licences in December 2006 and who **were** issued LOIs for crossover technology on **"first-come-first-served"** basis.

(vii) According to DOT, **the grant of licences is "technology neutral"** and no further licence fee will be payable by existing licence holders if they ask for more spectrum for crossover. **Yet, CDMA operators who want to crossover to GSM technology** have been asked to pay another tranche of licen**ce fee** which is equivalent to fee paid by new licence holders. **This** may be termed as **"Crossover fee"** to distinguish it **from** licence fee.

(viii) While under the **existing** policy, the Government may keep on issuing new **licences**, the criteria for the grant of licences may be **strengthened** and put in public domain at the earliest.

(Pranab Mukherjee)
External Affairs Minister
26 December 2007

**Hon'ble Prime Minister**

**CONFIDENTIAL**

**NOTE BY THE SOLICITOR GENERAL FOR THE HON'BLE MINISTER OF EXTERNAL AFFAIRS, MR PRANAB MUKHERJEE.**

There are four issues which are dealt with separately:

I. **Challenge to criteria for additional GSM Spectrum**

The COAI and the three members (who are petitioners) contend that the existing criteria for allocation of additional GSM Spectrum (March 2006) are adequate and should not be reviewed or made tighter. There is no substance in this contention for the following reasons:

(A) The existing criteria are outdated and unrealistic. This can be demonstrated by a simple example. Bharti Airtel in Delhi is providing service to 36 lakh subscribers. Presently it has Spectrum of 10 MHz. Under the existing criteria, requirement is 10 Lakh subscribers for 10 MHz, 16 Lakh subscribers for 12.4 MHz and 21 Lakh subscribers for 15 MHz. Clearly Bharti's own figures show how outdated the existing criteria are. Indeed, if Bharti Airtel is servicing 36 Lakh customers on 10 MHz Spectrum, how can the existing criteria be said to be "rational" or "adequate"?

(B) As against this, TRAI recommended revised criteria for Delhi and Mumbai. For 10 MHz Spectrum, the minimum subscriber base is 20 lakhs. For 12.4 MHz, it is 30 Lakhs. Bharti would be entitled to 15 MHz when it reaches a subscriber base of 50 Lakhs.

(C) TEC's recommendations are more scientific. For instance, TEC does not group Delhi and Mumbai together. Mumbai norms are stricter and these are obviously justified having regard to the topography of Mumbai.

(D) At the instance of the cellular operators, the Committee headed by the Additional Secretary has been considering the entire issue. COAI has its nominee on this Committee. Instead of cooperating with the Committee with substantial contentions, some of the cellular operators are resorting to the use of intemperate language to criticize the reports of the technical experts which are no substitute for argument.

(E) NTP99 made it absolutely clear that Government retains full right to review Spectrum utilization from time to time, keeping in view the emerging scenario of Spectrum availability, optimal use of Spectrum, requirements of market and other interests of public. This is reflected in the licence contents also.

(F) It can be demonstrated that additional Spectrum has been given to some of these operators without any rational basis.

II. **Crossover technology**

(i) COAI contends that there is a contractual right which limits the entry of new players. There is no substance in this plea. As a matter of fact, this plea was raised in 2001-2003 in relation to the WLL controversy and the TDSAT, by a majority, rejected this contention. The Chairman was in a minority. The COAI filed an SLP in the Supreme Court against the order of the TDSAT which was withdrawn, a fact which is suppressed in the pending petition. On the contrary, Justice Wadhwa's judgment is quoted as if it was a binding opinion of the Tribunal.

(ii) It can hardly be disputed that the UASL is technology neutral. The requirement for indicating technology arose only when an application was made to the WPC for grant of Spectrum because GSM Spectrum and CDMA Spectrum operate on different bands.

(iii) This matter has been duly considered by the Regulator. The Regulator has recommended crossover and this recommendation has been accepted by Government. It is a matter of policy taken in larger public interest with a view to increasing competition and benefiting the consumer at large.

(iv) Hence, the pleas taken by COAI, are not tenable.

III. **Manner in which Spectrum will be allocated.**

The contention that applicants for crossover technology will be given preference is not correct. Though the present licence holders (December 2006 category) awaiting initial Spectrum are having contractual rights over existing operators and the new applicants, the affidavit filed by the Government says that Spectrum will be first allocated to existing operators, then to persons to whom licences were issued in December

2006, and thereafter to the persons to whom LOIs have been issued for crossover technology. The COAI can have no real grievance in this behalf since their apprehensions have been shown to be ill founded.

**IV. The issue of new telecom licences**

COAI has no legal right or authority to contend that new licences cannot be issued. The NTP (99) broadly categorises service providers as Access Service Providers. The whole basis of this changed on 31 October 2003 when the UASL system was brought about. Paragraph 11 of the amended guidelines issued on 14 December 2005 expressly provides that licences shall be issued without any restriction on the number of entrants for provision of Unified Access Services. As a matter of fact, a specific reference was made to TRAI as to whether there should be a cap for the number of licences in any area. TRAI recommended that there should be no cap on the number of service providers for a service area. This has been accepted by the Government. Thus Government is obliged to scrutinize the pending applications and if the applicants are found eligible, to issue licences on a first-come-first-served basis. Once an applicant becomes licencee after complying with the LOI conditions, the applicant then becomes eligible for spectrum as per the WPC guidelines.

Government of India
Ministry of Communications and Information Technology
Department of Telecommunications
Sanchar Bhawan, 20 Ashoka Road, New Delhi-110 001.

No.10-21/2005-BS.I(Vol.II)/49 dated, the 14th December, 2005.

**SUB: GUIDELINES FOR UNIFIED ACCESS SERVICES LICENCE.**

Consequent to opening of Internet Telephony and merger of Chennai & Tamilnadu Service Area, following are the broad Guidelines for grant of Unified Access Services Licence in a Service Area.

1. The applicant must be an Indian company, registered under the Indian Companies Act'1956.
2. The applicant company shall submit the application in duplicate in the prescribed Application form enclosed as (Annexure-III), for each Service Area separately.
3. The applicant company can apply for Licence in more than one service area subject to fulfillment of all the conditions of entry.
4. The applicant company shall pay a processing fee along with the application ( Two copies) of Rs. 15,000/- in the form of Demand Draft/Pay Order from a Schedule Bank payable at New Delhi issued in the name of Pay & Accounts Officer (Headquarter) DOT and the same shall not be refunded for any reason whatsoever.

5.0

5.A The total composite foreign holding including but not limited to investments by Foreign Institutional Investors (FIIs), Non-resident Indians (NRIs), Foreign Currency Convertible Bonds (FCCBs), American Depository Receipts (ADRs), Global Depository Receipts (GDRs), convertible preference shares, proportionate foreign investment in Indian promoters/investment companies including their holding companies, etc., herein after referred as FDI, will not exceed 74 per cent.

The 74 per cent foreign investment can be made directly or indirectly in the operating company or through a holding company and the remaining 26 per cent will be owned by resident Indian citizens or an Indian Company (i.e. foreign direct investment does not exceed 49 percent and the management is with the Indian owners). It is clarified that proportionate foreign component of such an Indian Company will also be counted towards the ceiling of 74%. However, foreign component in the total holding of Indian public sector banks and Indian public sector financial institutions will be treated as 'Indian' holding. The licensee will be required to disclose the status of such foreign holding and certify that the foreign investment is within the ceiling of 74% on a half yearly basis.

5.B The majority Directors on the Board including Chairman, Managing Director and Chief Executive Officer (CEO) shall be resident Indian citizens. The appointment to these positions from among resident Indian citizens shall be made in consultation with serious Indian investors. Serious investor has been defined below in para 5.G(ii).

5.C The Share Holder Agreements (SHA) shall specifically incorporate the condition that majority directors on the Board including Chairman, Managing Director and Chief Executive Officer (CEO) shall be resident Indian citizens and shall also envisage the conditions of adherence to Licence Agreement.

5.D FDI upto 49 per cent will continue to be on automatic route. Foreign Investment Promotion Board (FIPB) approval shall be required for FDI in the licensee company/Indian promoters/investment companies including their holding companies if it has a bearing on the overall ceiling of 74 per cent. While approving the investment proposals, FIPB shall take note that investment is not coming from unfriendly countries.

5.E The investment approval by FIPB shall envisage the conditionality that Company would adhere to licence Agreement.

5.F FDI shall be subject to laws of India and not the laws of the foreign country/countries.

5.G (i) There shall be a non-obstante clause in the licence which confers powers upon the licensor to cancel the licence under certain defined circumstances.

(ii) In order to ensure that at least one serious resident Indian promoter subscribes reasonable amount of the resident Indian shareholding, such resident Indian promoter shall hold at least 10 per cent equity of the licensee company.

(iii) The Company shall acknowledge compliance with the licence agreement as a part of Memorandum of Association of the Company. Any violation of the licence agreement shall automatically lead to the company being unable to carry on its business in this regard. The duty to comply with the licence agreement shall also be made a part of Articles of Association.

(iv) Chief Technical Officer (CTO)/Chief Finance Officer (CFO) shall be resident Indian citizens. The Licensor can also further notify key positions to be held by resident Indian citizens.

(v) The Company shall not transfer the following to any person/ place outside India:-

(a) any accounting information relating to subscriber (except for roaming/billing) (Note: it does not restrict a statutorily required disclosure of financial nature) ;

(b) user information (except pertaining to foreign subscribers using Indian Operator's network while roaming); and

(c) details of their infrastructure/network diagram except to telecom equipment suppliers/manufacturers who undertake the installation, commissioning etc. of the infrastructure of the licensee Company on signing of non-disclosure agreement.

(vi) The Company when entering into roaming agreements with service providers outside India must provide, on demand, the list of such users (telephone numbers, in case of foreign subscribers using Indian Operator's network while roaming).

3

(vii) The Company must provide traceable identity of their subscribers. However, in case of providing service to roaming subscriber of foreign Companies, the Indian Company shall endeavor to obtain traceable identity of roaming subscribers from the foreign company as a part of its roaming agreement.

(viii) No traffic (mobile and landline) from subscribers within India to subscribers within India shall be hauled to any place outside India. For this purpose, the location of satellites serving for domestic traffic shall not be treated as outside India.

(ix) No Remote Access (RA) shall be provided to any equipment manufacturer or any other agency out side the country for any maintenance/repairs by the licensee. However, RA may be allowed for catastrophic software failure (such as failure to boot up etc.) which would lead to major part of the network becoming non-functional for a prolonged period, subject to meeting the following conditions:-

(a) An identified Government agency (Intelligence Bureau) will be notified, when RA is to be provided.

(b) Remote Access password is to be enabled for a definite period only and only for access from pre-approved locations of the Original Equipment Manufacturer (OEM) Vendors and only for the equipments specifically under repair/maintenance.

(c) The control of Remote Access i.e. activation, transfer of data, termination etc. shall be within the country and not at a Remote location, abroad.

(d) The Government agency will be given all support to record the transactions for on-line monitoring.

(e) Any equipment or software that forms part of the overall monitoring shall not be permitted to have remote access under any circumstances.

(f) The terms catastrophic software failure, major part of the network, and prolonged period used under this clause shall be defined by Licensor from time to time.

(x) It shall be open to the Licensor to restrict the Licensee Company from operating in any sensitive area from the National Security angle.

(xi) In order to maintain the privacy of voice and data, monitoring shall only be upon authorisation by the Union Home Secretary or Home Secretaries of the States/Union Territories.

(xii) For monitoring traffic, the licensee company shall provide blind access of their network and other facilities as well as to books of accounts to the security agencies.

(xiii) In case of not adhering to Licence conditions envisaged in para 5.G, the licence(s) granted to the company shall be deemed as cancelled and the licensor shall have the right to encash the performance/financial bank guarantee(s) and the licensor shall not be liable for loss of any kind.

5.1 The conditions at paras 5.A to 5.G above shall also be applicable to the existing companies operating telecom service(s), which had the FDI cap of 49%.

6 The detail of non-refundable Entry fee, Category of service area, Financial bank guarantee , performance bank guarantee, Networth and Paid up equity capital required under the Unified Access Services Licence for each service area is as per Annexure-I. The prescribed paid-up equity capital shall be maintained during currency of the licence.

7 The licence for Unified Access Services shall be issued on non-exclusive basis, for a period of 20 years, extendable by 10 years at one time within the territorial jurisdiction of a licensed Service Area.

8 No single company/ legal person, either directly or through its associates, shall have substantial equity holding in more than one LICENSEE Company in the same service area for the Access Services namely; Basic, Cellular and Unified Access Service. 'Substantial equity' herein will mean 'an equity of 10% or more'. A promoter company/ Legal person cannot have stakes in more than one LICENSEE Company for

the same service area. A certificate to this effect shall be provided by the applicant's company Secretary alongwith application.

9 The applicant company shall have a minimum paid up equity capital of the amount indicated in Annex-I for the respective Service Area on the date of the application and shall submit a certificate to this effect shall be provided by the applicant's company Secretary alongwith application.

10 The applicant and promoters of applicant company should have a combined net-worth of amount as detailed in the Table below:

| Net-worth | Total Minimum Net-worth required. |
|---|---|
| Rs.30 Crores for each Category C Service Area<br>Rs.50 Crores for each Category B Service Area<br>Rs.100 Crores for each Category A Service Area | 100 X+50 Y+30 Z where X,Y & Z is respectively the Number of A, B & C Service Areas for which either LOI/ Licence have been issued or applied for in the name of applicant. |

The net-worth of only those promoters shall be counted who have at least 10% equity stake or more in the total equity of the company. Here networth shall mean as the sum total, in Indian Rupees, of paid up equity capital and free reserves. While counting Net-worth the foreign currency shall be converted into Indian Rupees at the prevalent rate indicated by the Reserve Bank of India as on the date of Application received.The minimum networth & paid-up capital shall be maintained during currency of the Licence

11 Licences shall be issued without any restriction on the number of entrants for provision of Unified Access Services in a Service Area.

12 SCOPE OF THE LICENCE:

(a)(i) The Unified Access Services cover collection, carriage, transmission and delivery of voice and/or non-voice MESSAGES over LICENSEE's network in the designated SERVICE AREA and includes provision of all types of access services.

Access service provider can also provide Internet Telephony , Internet Services and Broadband Services. If required , access service provider can use the network of NLD/ILD service licensee. In addition to this, except those services listed in para 12(b)(i) licensee cannot provide any service / services which require a separate licence. The access service includes but not limited to wireline and / or wireless service including full mobility, limited mobility as defined in clause 12 (c) (i) and fixed wireless access. However, the licensee shall be free to enter an agreement with other service provider(s) in India or abroad for providing roaming facility to its subscriber under full mobility service unless advised / directed by Licensor otherwise. The LICENSEE may offer " Home Zone Tariff Scheme (s)" as a subset of full mobile service in well defined geographical Areas through a tariff of its choice within the scope of orders of TRAI on the subject. Numbering and interconnection for this service shall be same as that of Full mobile subscribers.

(a) (ii) Leased circuit is defined as virtual private network (VPN) using circuit or packet switched (IP Protocol) technology apart from point to point non-switched physical connections/ transmission bandwidth . Public network is not to be connected with leased circuits/ CUGs.

(a) (iii) The access service providers can provide broadband services including triple play i.e. voice, video & data.

(b) (i) Further, the LICENSEE can also provide Voice Mail, Audiotex services, Video Conferencing, Videotex, E-Mail , Closed User Group (CUG) facilities over its network to the subscribers falling within its SERVICE AREA on non-discriminatory basis. The Licensee cannot provide any service except as mentioned above, which require a separate licence. However, an intimation before providing any other VALUE ADDED SERVICE has to be sent to the LICENSOR and TRAI.

(ii) No separate Entry Fee shall be charged for Voice Mail / Audiotex, Video Conferencing, Videotex, E-Mail service provided by the LICENSEE. However, all the revenue earned by the LICENSEE through these service shall be counted towards

7

the revenue for the purpose of paying LICENCE Fee under the LICENCE AGREEMENT.

(c) (i) In respect of subscriber availing limited mobility facility, the mobility shall be restricted to the local area i.e. Short Distance Charging Area (SDCA) in which the subscriber is registered. While deploying such systems, the LICENSEE has to follow the SDCA based linked numbering plan in accordance with the National Numbering Plan of the respective SDCA within which the service is provided and it should not be possible to authenticate and work with the subscriber terminal equipment in SDCAs other than the one in which it is registered. Terminal of such subscriber in wireless access system can be registered in only one SDCA. Multiple registration or Temporary subscriber/ Subscription facilities in more than one SDCA using the same Subscriber terminal in wireless access systems is not permitted and the same Subscriber Terminal can not be used to avail Limited Mobile facility in more than one SDCA. The system shall also be so engineered to ensure that hand over of subscriber does not take place from one SDCA to another SDCA under any circumstances, including handover of the calls through call forwarding beyond SDCA. The Licensee must ensure that the mobility in case of such limited mobile service/ facility remains restricted to SDCA.

(d). In case of Fixed Wireless in Local Loop service, the terminal used for fixed wireless services should be strictly confined to the premises of the subscriber where the telephone connection is registered.

13 The applicant will be required to pay one time non-refundable Entry Fee based on the Letter of Indent (LOI) before signing the Licence Agreement, as per annexure-I.

14 In addition to the non refundable Entry fee described above, the Licensee shall also pay Licence fee annually @ 10/8/6% of **Adjusted Gross Revenue (AGR) for category A/B/C service areas respectively** excluding spectrum charges.

8

15 Licence Fee shall be payable in four quarterly installments during each financial year (FY). Quarterly installment of licence fee for the first three quarters of a financial year shall be paid within 15 days of the completion of the relevant quarter. This Fee shall be paid by the LICENSEE on the basis of actual revenue (on accrual basis) for the quarter, duly certified with an affidavit by a representative of the LICENSEE, authorized by the Board Resolution coupled with General Power of Attorney. However, for the last quarter of the financial year, the LICENSEE shall pay the Licence Fee by 25th March on the basis of expected revenue for the quarter, subject to a minimum payment equal to the actual revenue share paid of the previous quarter.

16 Any delay in payment of Licence Fee, or any other dues payable under the LICENCE beyond the stipulated period will attract interest at a rate which will be 2% above the Prime Lending Rate (PLR) of State Bank of India existing as on the beginning of the financial year (1st April ) in respect of the licence fees pertaining to the said financial year. The interest shall be compounded monthly and a part of the month shall be reckoned as a full month for the purpose of calculation of interest.

17 In case, the total amount paid on the self-assessment of the LICENSEE as quarterly LICENCE Fee for the 4 (four) quarters of the financial year, falls short by more than 10% of the payable LICENCE Fee, it shall attract a penalty of 50% of the entire amount of short payment. This amount of short payment along with the penalty shall be payable within 15 days of the date of signing the audit report on the annual accounts, failing which interest shall be further charged as per terms of Condition in above para-16. However, if such short payment is made good within 60 days from the last day of the financial year, no penalty shall be imposed.

18 The Fee/royalty payable towards (Wireless Planning and Coordination Wing(WPC)) WPC Charges shall be payable at such time(s) and in such manner as the WPC Wing of the DoT may prescribe from time to time.

9

19 The LICENSEE shall pay spectrum charges in addition to the Licence Fees on revenue share basis as notified separately from time to time by the WPC Wing. However, while calculating 'AGR' for limited purpose of levying spectrum charges based on revenue share, revenue from wireline subscribers shall not be taken into account.

20 Further royalty for the use of spectrum for point to point links and other access links shall be separately payable as per the details and prescription of Wireless Planning & Coordination Wing. The fee/ royalty for the use of spectrum /possession of wireless telegraphy equipment depends upon various factors such as frequency, hop and link length, area of operation and other related aspects etc. Authorization of frequencies for setting up Microwave links by Licensed Operators and issue of Licenses shall be separately dealt with WPC Wing as per existing rules.

21 The Fees, charges and royalties for the use of spectrum and also for possession of Wireless Telegraphy equipment shall be separately securitised by furnishing FBG of an amount equivalent to the estimated sum payable annually in the proforma annexed, to WPC, valid for a period of one year, renewable from time to time till final clearance of all such dues.

22 The applicant company shall submit Financial Bank Guarantee (FBG) of amount equal to Rs. 50, 25 and 5 Crores for category 'A' 'B' & 'C' service areas respectively before the date of signing the licence agreement in the prescribed Proforma given in the Licence Agreement. Initially, FBG shall be valid for a period of one year and shall be renewed from time to time for such amount as may be directed by the Licensor. The applicant shall also submit Performance Bank Guarantees (PBG) of amount equal to Rs. 20, 10 and 2 Crores for category 'A' 'B' & 'C' service areas respectively in the prescribed Proforma given in the Licence Agreement before signing the licence. PBG shall be valid for a period of three year and shall be renewed from time to time. FBG and PBG must be from any Scheduled Bank or Public Financial Institution duly authorized to issue such Bank Guarantee.

23 The application shall be decided, so far as practicable, within 30 days of the submission of the application and the applicant company shall be informed

accordingly. In case the applicant is found to be eligible for grant of licence for UNIFIED ACCESS Service an Letter of Intent (LOI) will be issued. The applicant shall be required to deposit Entry Fee and submit Bank Guarantees / other documents and sign the licence agreement within a period as mentioned in the letter(LOI) from the date of issue of the letter (LOI) failing which the offer of grant of licence shall stand withdrawn at the expiry of permitted period.

24 In case the applicant is found to be not eligible for the grant of licence for UNIFIED ACCESS service the applicant shall be informed accordingly. Thereafter the applicant is permitted to file a fresh application if so desired.

25 LICENSEE shall ensure "Roll-out obligations" that

(i) Atleast 10% of the District Headquarters (DHQs) will be covered in the first year and 50% of the District Headquarters will be covered within three years of effective date of Licence.

(ii) The choice of District Headquarters/towns to be covered and further expansion beyond 50% District Headquarters/towns shall lie with the Licensee depending on their business decision.

(iii) There is no requirement of mandatory coverage of rural areas.

26 On completion of one year from the effective date of Licence and meeting the coverage criteria stipulated for first year,the PBG shall be reduced to Rs.10/5/1 crores for category 'A'/'B'/'C' service areas on self-certification provided by the Licensee. Further on fulfilling the roll out obligations as stipulated in clause 34 of Licence agreement, the balance PBG shall be released on receipt of test certificate / test certificates issued by TEC in respect of coverage.

27 The LICENSEE shall be responsible for, and is authorized to own, install, test and commission all the Applicable system for providing the Unified Access Services under this Licence agreement.

28 The LICENSEE shall commission the Applicable Systems within one year from the effective date of the Licence. The date of Test Certificate issued by Telecom Engineering Centre of DOT will be reckoned as the date of commissioning the service

11

for the purpose of calculating liquidated damage charges in terms of Condition 35 Part V. However, the LICENSEE may start providing service to customers at any time without the need of specific approval of the Licensor.

29 **Liquidated damages:**In case the LICENSEE fails to bring the Service or any part thereof into commission (i.e., fails to deliver the service or to meet the required coverage criteria/ network roll out obligations) within the period prescribed for the commissioning, the Licensor shall be entitled to recover LD charges @ Rs. 5 Lakh (Rupees: Five Lakhs) per week for first 13 weeks; @ Rs 10 lakhs for the next 13 weeks and thereafter @ Rs. 20 lakhs for 26 weeks subject to a maximum of Rs. 7.00 crores. Part of the week is to be considered as a full week for the purpose of calculating the LD charges. For delay of more than 52 weeks the Licence may be terminated under the terms and conditions of the Licence agreement. The week shall means 7 Calendar days from (from midnight) Monday to Sunday; both days inclusive and any extra day shall be counted as full week for the purposes of recovery of liquidated damages.

30 The Licensor may also impose a financial penalty not exceeding Rs. 50 crores for violation of terms and conditions of licence agreement This penalty is exclusive of Liquidated Damages as prescribed above.

31 Change in the name of the Licensee company shall be permitted in accordance with the provisions under the Indian Companies Act, 1956.

32 The Licence shall be governed by the provision of Indian Telegraph Act, 1885, Indian Wireless Telegraphy Act, 1933 and Telecom Regulatory Authority of India Act, 1997 as modified or replaced from time to time.

33 Licensee shall make its own arrangements for all infrastructures involved in providing the service and shall be solely responsible for installation, networking, operation and commissioning of necessary equipment and systems, treatment of subscriber complaints, issue of bills to its subscribers, collection of its component of revenue, attending to claims and damages arising out of his operations.

34 The applicant company shall make its own arrangements for Right of Way (ROW). However, the Central Government has issued necessary notification conferring the requisite powers upon the licensee for the purposes of placing telegraph lines under Part III of the Indian Telegraph Act'1885. Provided that non-availability of the ROW

12

or delay in getting permission / clearance from any agency including WPC delay shall not be construed or taken as a reason for non-fulfillment of the Rollout obligations.

35 The Licensee shall provide the details of the technology proposed to be deployed for operation of the service. The technology should be based on standards issued by ITU/TEC or any other International Standards Organization/ bodies/Industry. Any digital technology having been used for a customer base of one lakh or more for a continuous period of one year anywhere in the world, shall be permissible for use regardless of its changed versions. A certificate from the manufacturers about satisfactory working for a customer base of one lakh or more over the period of one year, shall be treated as established technology.

36 The subscriber terminals employed in the network shall be of a type/ model certified by an internationally accredited agency with respect to ITU/ETSI/TEC/ International standardization bodies such as 3GPP/3GPP-2/ETSI/IETF/ANSI/EIA/TIA/IS or any other international standard as may be approved by the Government. . Only such category of subscriber unit as has been granted such a certificate shall be brought into and operated within India under this Agreement. The mode of ownership of subscribers' terminal equipment will be at the option of the subscriber.

37 For wireless operations in SUBSCRIBER access network, the frequencies shall be assigned by WPC wing of the Department of Telecom from the frequency bands earmarked in the applicable National Frequency Allocation Plan and in coordination with various users. Initially a cumulative maximum of upto 4.4 MHz + 4.4 MHz shall be allocated in the case of TDMA based systems @ 200 KHz per carrier or 30 KHz per carrier or a maximum of 2.5 MHz + 2.5 MHz shall be allocated in the case of CDMA based systems @ 1.25 MHz per carrier, on case by case basis subject to availability. While efforts would be made to make available larger chunks to the extent feasible, the frequencies assigned may not be contiguous and may not be the same in all cases or within the whole Service Area. For making available appropriate frequency spectrum for roll out of services under the licence, the type(s) of Systems to be deployed are to be indicated.

13

38 Additional spectrum beyond the above stipulation may also be considered for allocation after ensuring optimal and efficient utilization of the already allocated spectrum taking into account all types of traffic and guidelines / criteria prescribed from time to time. However, spectrum not more than 5 + 5 MHz in respect of CDMA system or 6.2 + 6.2 MHz in respect of TDMA based system shall be allocated to any new Unified Access Services Licensee. The spectrum shall be allocated in 824-844 MHz paired with 869 - 889 MHz, 890 - 915 MHz paired with 935 - 960 MHz, 1710 – 1785 MHz paired with 1805 – 1880 MHz.

39 In the event, a dedicated carrier for micro-cellular architecture based system is assigned in 1880 - 1900 MHz band, the spectrum not more than 3.75 + 3.75 MHz in respect of CDMA system or 4.4 + 4.4 MHz in respect of TDMA system shall be assigned to any new Unified Access Services Licensee.

40 In case of provision of bandwidth by the Licensee through the satellite media, the Licensee shall abide by the prevalent Government orders, directions or regulations on the subject like satellite communication policy, V-SAT policy etc.

41 For use of space segment and setting up of the Earth Station etc., the Licensee shall directly coordinate with and obtain clearance from Network Operations and Control Centre (NOCC), apart from obtaining SACFA clearance. The clearance from other authorities shall also be obtained by the Licensee.

42 The LICENSEE shall register demand/request for telephone connection without any discrimination from any applicant, at any place in the licensed service area and provide the SERVICE, unless otherwise directed by the LICENSOR. The LICENSEE shall not in any manner discriminate between subscribers and provide service on the same commercial principle and shall be required to maintain a transparent, open to inspection, waiting list. The LICENSEE shall clearly define the scope of Service to the Subscriber(s) at the time of entering into contract with such Subscriber(s). LICENSOR shall have right to impose suitable penalty, not limited to a financial penalty, apart from any other actions for breach of this condition. The LICENSEE shall launch the SERVICE on commercial basis only after commencement of registration in the manner prescribed. Before commencement of SERVICE in an area, the LICENSEE shall notify and publicize the address where any subscriber can register demand /request for

telephone connection. Any change of this address shall be duly notified by the LICENSEE.

43 The licensee shall provide independently or through mutually agreed commercial arrangements with other Service Providers all public utility services including TOLL FREE services such as police, fire, ambulance, railways/road/air accident enquiry, police control, disaster management etc. While providing emergency services such as police, fire, ambulance etc. it shall be ensured that such calls originated shall be delivered to the control room of the concerned authority for the area from where call is originated.

44 LICENSEE shall be free to carry intra-Service Area long distance traffic without seeking additional licence. However, subject to technical feasibility, the subscriber of the intra-Service Area long distance calls, shall be given the choice to use the network of another Service Provider in the same service area, wherever possible. The LICENSEE can also make mutual agreements with National Long Distance Operators for carrying intra Circle Long Distance traffic.

45 The LICENSEE shall ensure adherence to the National FUNDAMENTAL PLAN ( Which includes National Numbering, routing and Transmission plan issued by Department of Telecommunications and technical standards as prescribed by LICENSOR or TRAI, from time to time. In case of providing choice of Long Distance Operator, the equipment shall support the selection facilities such as dynamic call-by-call selection and pre-selection as per prevailing regulation, direction, order or determination issued by LICENSOR or TRAI on the subject.

46 It shall be mandatory for the LICENSEE to provide interconnection to all eligible Telecom Service Providers as well as NLD Operators whereby the subscribers could have a free choice to make inter-circle/ international long distance calls through NLD/ ILD Operator. For international long distance call, the LICENSEE shall normally access International Long Distance Operator's network through National Long Distance Operator's network subject to fulfillment of any Guidelines/ Orders/ Directions/ Regulation issued from time to time by Licensor/ TRAI. The LICENSEE shall not refuse to interconnect with the International Long Distance Licensee directly in

situations where ILD Gateway Switches/ Point of Presence (POP), and that of Access Provider's (GMSC/ Transit Switch) are located at the same station of Level -I TAX .

47 Direct interconnectivity among all Telecom Service Providers in the licensed SERVICE AREA is permitted. LICENSEE shall interconnect with other Service Providers, subject to compliance of prevailing regulations, directions or determinations issued by TRAI. The interconnection shall have to be withdrawn in case of termination of the respective licensed networks of another Telecom service provicers within one hour or within such time as directed by the LICENSOR in writing, after receiving intimation from the LICENSOR in this regard.

48 Interconnection between the networks of different SERVICE PROVIDERs shall be as per National Standards of CCS No.7 issued from time to time by Telecom Engineering Centre (TEC) and also subject to technical feasibility and technical integrity of the Networks and shall be within the overall framework of interconnection regulations issued by the TRAI from time to time. However, if situation so arises, INTERCONNECTION with R2MF signaling may be permitted by LICENSOR.

49 The LICENSEE may enter into suitable arrangements with other service providers to negotiate Interconnection Agreements whereby the interconnected networks will provide the following:

(a) To meet all reasonable demand for the transmission and reception of messages between the interconnected systems.

(b) To establish and maintain such one or more Points of Interconnect as are reasonably required and are of sufficient capacity and in sufficient numbers to enable transmission and reception of the messages by means of the Applicable Systems,

(c) To connect, and keep connected, to their Applicable Systems.

50 The terms and conditions of interconnection including standard interfaces, points of interconnection and technical aspects will be as mutually agreed between the service providers, subject to compliance of prevailing regulations, directions and determinations issued by TRAI from time to time.

51 The Interconnection Tests with network of other Service Provider may be carried out by mutual arrangement.

52 For the purpose of providing the SERVICE, the LICENSEE shall install his own equipment so as to be compatible with other service providers' equipment to which the LICENSEE's Applicable Systems are intended for interconnection.

53 The Licensee shall comply with any order, direction, determination or regulation as may be issued from time to time by the Licensor or TRAI as the case may be.

54 The charges for accessing other networks for inter-network calls shall be based on mutual agreements between the service providers conforming to the Orders/Regulations/Guidelines issued by the TRAI from time to time.

55 The LICENSEE shall operate and maintain the licensed Network conforming to Quality of Service standards to be mutually agreed in respect of Network- Network Interface subject to such other directions as LICENSOR or TRAI may give from time to time. Failure on part of LICENSEE or his franchisee to adhere to the QUALITY OF SERVICE stipulations by TRAI and network to network interface standards of TEC may be treated as breach of Licence terms.

56 In the interests of security, suitable monitoring equipment as may be prescribed for each type of system used will be provided by the LICENSEE for monitoring as and when required by LICENSOR. The specific orders or directions from the Government, issued under such conditions, shall be applicable.

57 The LICENSEE shall provide necessary facilities depending upon the specific situation at the relevant time to the Government to counteract espionage, subversive act, sabotage or any other unlawful activity.

58 The LICENSEE shall make available on demand to the person authorized by the LICENSOR, full access to the switching centers, transmission centers, routes etc. for technical scrutiny and for inspection, which can be visual inspection or an operational inspection.

59 All foreign personnel likely to be deployed by the LICENSEE for installation, operation and maintenance of the LICENSEE's network shall be security cleared by the Government of India prior to their deployment. The security clearance will be

obtained from the Ministry of Home Affairs, Government of India, who will follow standard drill in the matter.

60 The LICENSEE shall ensure protection of privacy of communication and ensure that unauthorized interception of messages does not take place.

61 The network resources including the cost of upgrading/ modifying interconnecting networks to meet the service requirements of the LICENSEE will be mutually negotiated keeping in view the orders and regulations issued by the TRAI from time to time.

62 LICENSEE can appoint any franchisee not limited to Cable Service Provider for provision of last mile linkages including suitable rural exchanges to provide service. However, all responsibilities for ensuring compliance of terms & conditions of the LICENCE shall vest with the LICENSEE. The terms of franchise agreement between LICENSEE and his franchisee shall be settled mutually by negotiation between the two parties involved.

63 The LICENSEE shall not, without the prior written consent of the LICENSOR, either directly or indirectly, assign or transfer this LICENCE in any manner whatsoever to a third party or enter into any agreement for sub-Licence and/or partnership relating to any subject matter of the LICENCE to any third party either in whole or in part i.e. no sub-leasing/partnership/third party interest shall be created. Provided that the LICENSEE can always employ or appoint agents and employees for provision of the service.

64 The LICENSEE shall not employ bulk encryption equipment in its network. Any encryption equipment connected to the LICENSEE's network for specific requirements has to have prior evaluation and approval of the LICENSOR or officer specially designated for the purpose. However, Any encryption equipment connected to the LICENSEE's network for specific requirements has to have prior evaluation and approval of the LICENSOR or officer specially designated for the purpose. However, the LICENSEE shall have the responsibility to ensure protection of privacy of communication and to ensure that unauthorised interception of MESSAGE does not take place.

65 LICENSOR shall have the right to take over the SERVICE, equipment and networks of the LICENSEE or revoke/terminate/suspend the LICENCE either in part or in whole of the Service area in the interest of national security or in case of emergency or war or low intensity conflict or any other eventuality in public interest as declared by the Government of India. Any specific orders or direction from the Government issued under such conditions shall be immediately applicable to the LICENSEE without loss of time and shall be strictly complied with. Further, the LICENSOR reserves the right to keep any area out of the operation zone of the service if implications of security so require. Provided any taking over or suspension of licence, issuance of an order and exclusion of an area, as described above shall neither be a ground of extension of licence period or expansion of area in different corner or reduction of duly payable fee.

66 The LICENSOR reserves the right to modify at any time the these guidelines and terms and conditions of the LICENCE, if in the opinion of the LICENSOR it is necessary or expedient to do so in public interest or in the interest of the security of the State or for the proper conduct of the telegraphs. The decision of the LICENSOR shall be final and binding in this regard.

67 LICENSEE will ensure that the Telecommunication installation carried out by it should not become a safety hazard and is not in contravention of any statute, rule or regulation and public policy.

68 The LICENSEE shall take necessary measures to prevent objectionable, obscene, unauthorized or any other content, messages or communications infringing copyright, intellectual property etc., in any form, from being carried on his network, consistent with the established laws of the country. Once specific instances of such infringement are reported to the LICENSEE by the enforcement agencies, the LICENSEE shall ensure that the carriage of such material on his network is prevented immediately.

69 The LICENSEE is obliged to provide, without any delay, all the tracing facilities to trace nuisance, obnoxious or malicious calls, messages or communications transported through his equipment and network, to authorized officers of Government of India including Police, Customs, Excise, Intelligence Department officers etc. when such information is required for investigations or detection of crimes and in the interest of

19

national security. Any damages arising on account of LICENSEE's failure in this regard shall be payable by the LICENSEE.

70 In case any confidential information is divulged to the LICENSEE for proper implementation of the Agreement, it shall be binding on the LICENSEE and its employees and servants to maintain its secrecy and confidentiality.

71 The LICENSOR or its authorized representative shall have right to inspect the sites used for extending the Service and in particular but not limited to, have the right to have access to leased lines, junctions, terminating interfaces, hardware/software, memories of semiconductor, magnetic and optical varieties, wired or wireless options, distribution frames, and conduct the performance test including to enter into dialogue with the system through Input/output devices or terminals. The LICENSEE will provide the necessary facilities for continuous monitoring of the system, as required by the LICENSOR or its authorized representative(s). The Inspection will ordinarily be carried out after reasonable notice except in circumstances where giving such a notice will defeat the very purpose of the inspection.

72 In case any confidential information is divulged to the LICENSEE for proper implementation of the Agreement, it shall be binding on the Licensee and its employees and servants to maintain its secrecy and confidentiality.

73 The terms and conditions applicable to the licence for Unified Access Service shall be given in detail in the Licence Agreement.

74 Applications are to be submitted to the Assistant Director General (BS-III), Department of Telecommunications, Room No.713, Sanchar Bhavan, 20 Ashok Road, New Delhi-110 001.

(R.K.GUPTA)
Assistant Director General(BS-III)
on behalf of President of India
ph. +91-11-23036574

ANNEXURE-I

(Amount in Rs. Crores)

| S.No | Service Area | Category | Entry fee | FBG Required | PBG required | Networth | Paid up equity capital of Applicant Company |
|---|---|---|---|---|---|---|---|
| 1 | West Bengal | B | 1.0000 | 25.00 | 10.00 | 50 | 5 |
| 2 | Andhra Pradesh | A | 103.0100 | 50.00 | 20.00 | 100 | 10 |
| 3 | Assam | C | 5.0000 | 5.00 | 2.00 | 30 | 3 |
| 4 | Bihar | C | 10.0000 | 5.00 | 2.00 | 30 | 3 |
| 5 | Gujarat | A | 109.0100 | 50.00 | 20.00 | 100 | 10 |
| 6 | Haryana | B | 21.4600 | 25.00 | 10.00 | 50 | 5 |
| 7 | Himachal Pradesh | C | 1.1000 | 5.00 | 2.00 | 30 | 3 |
| 8 | Jammu & Kashmir | C | 2.0000 | 5.00 | 2.00 | 30 | 3 |
| 9 | Karnataka | A | 206.8300 | 50.00 | 20.00 | 100 | 10 |
| 10 | Kerala | B | 40.5400 | 25.00 | 10.00 | 50 | 5 |
| 11 | Madhya Pradesh | B | 17.4501 | 25.00 | 10.00 | 50 | 5 |
| 12 | Maharastra | A | 189.0000 | 50.00 | 20.00 | 100 | 10 |
| 13 | North East | C | 2.0000 | 5.00 | 2.00 | 30 | 3 |
| 14 | Orissa | C | 5.0000 | 5.00 | 2.00 | 30 | 3 |
| 15 | Punjab | B | 151.7500 | 25.00 | 10.00 | 50 | 5 |
| 16 | Rajasthan | B | 32.2500 | 25.00 | 10.00 | 50 | 5 |
| 17 | Tamilnadu | A | 233.0000 | 50.00 | 20.00 | 100 | 10 |
| 18 | Uttar Pradesh (West) | B | 30.5500 | 25.00 | 10.00 | 50 | 5 |
| 19 | Uttar Pradesh (East) | B | 45.2500 | 25.00 | 10.00 | 50 | 5 |
| 20 | Delhi | A | 170.7000 | 50.00 | 20.00 | 100 | 10 |
| 21 | Kolkata | A | 78.0100 | 50.00 | 20.00 | 100 | 10 |
| 22 | Mumbai | A | 203.6600 | 50.00 | 20.00 | 100 | 10 |

21

**ANNEXURE-II**

**SERVICE AREA (TELECOM CIRCLES/ METROS) AND THE AREAS COVERED BY THEM FOR THE PURPOSE OF THIS LICENCE**

| Sl. No. | Name of Telecom Circle/ Metro Service Area | Areas covered | Category |
|---|---|---|---|
| 01. | West Bengal | Entire area falling within the Union Territory of Andaman & Nicobar Islands and area falling within the State of West Bengal and the State of Sikkim excluding the areas covered by Kolkata Metro Service Area. | B |
| 02. | Andhra Pradesh | Entire area falling within the State of Andhra Pradesh. | A |
| 03. | Assam | Entire area falling within the State of Assam. | C |
| 04. | Bihar | Entire area falling within the re-organised State of Bihar and newly created State of Jharkhand pursuant to the Bihar Reorganisation Act, 2000 (No.30 of 2000) dated 25th August, 2000. | C |
| 05. | Gujarat | Entire area falling within the State of Gujarat and Union Territory of Daman and Diu, Silvassa (Dadra & Nagar Haveli). | A |
| 06. | Haryana | Entire area falling within the State of Haryana except Pachkula town and the local areas served by Faridabad and Gurgaon Telephone exchanges. | B |
| 07. | Himachal Pradesh | Entire area falling within the State of Himachal Pradesh | C |
| 08. | Jammu & Kashmir | Entire area falling within the State of Jammu & Kashmir including the autonomous council of Ladakh. | C |
| 09. | Karnataka | Entire area falling within the State of Karnataka | A |
| 10. | Kerala | Entire area falling within the State of Kerala and Union Territory of Lakshadeep and Minicoy. | B |
| 11. | Madhya Pradesh | Entire area falling within the re-organised State of Madhya Pradesh as well as the newly created State of Chattisgarh pursuant to the Madhya Pradesh Reorganisation Act, 2000 (No:28 of 2000) dated 25th August, 2000. | B |
| 12. | Maharashtra | Entire area falling within the State of Maharashtra and Union Territory of Goa, excluding areas covered by Mumbai Metro Service Area. | A |
| 13. | North East | Entire area falling within the States of Arunachal Pradesh, Meghalaya, Mizoram, Nagaland, Manipur and Tripura. | C |
| 14. | Orissa | Entire area falling within the State of Orissa. | C |

| 15. | Punjab | Entire area falling within the State of Punjab and Union territory of Chandigarh and and Punchkula Town of Haryana. | B |
|---|---|---|---|
| 16. | Rajasthan | Entire area falling within the State of Rajasthan. | B |
| 17. | Tamilnadu | Entire area falling within the State of Tamilnadu and Union Territory of Pondichery including Local Areas served by Chennai Telephones, Maraimalai Nagar Export Promotion Zone (MPEZ), Minzur and Mahabalipuram Exchanges | A |
| 18. | Uttar Pradesh-West | Entire area covered by Western Uttar Pradesh with the following as its boundary districts towards Eastern Uttar Pradesh : Pilibhit, Bareilly, Badaun, Etah, Mainpuri and Etawah. It will exclude the local telephone area of Ghaziabad and Noida. However, it will also include the newly created State of Uttaranchal pursuant to the Uttar Pradesh Re-organisation Act, 2000 (No.29 of 2000) dated 25th August, 2000. | B |
| 19. | Uttar Pradesh – East | Entire area covered by Eastern Uttar Pradesh with the following as its boundary districts towards Western Uttar Pradesh : Shahjahanpur, Farrukhabad, Kanpur and Jalaun. | B |
| 20. | Delhi | Local Areas served by Delhi, Ghaziabad, Faridabad, Noida, and Gurgaon Telephone Exchanges | Metro |
| 21. | Kolkata | Local Areas served by Calcutta Telephones. | Metro |
| 22. | Mumbai | Local Areas served by Mumbai, New Mumbai and Kalyan Telephone Exchanges | Metro |

**NOTE:**

1. Yenum, an area of Union Territory of Pondicherry is served under Andhra Pradesh Telecom Circle in East Godavari LDCA.

2. The definition of Local areas of exchanges will be as applicable to the existing cellular operators, i.e. at the time of grant of cellular Licences in Metro cities.

3. The definition of local areas with regard to the above service area as applicable to this Licence is as per definition applicable to Cellular Mobile Service Licences as in the year 1994 & 1995, when those Licences were granted to them. This is in accordance with respective Gazette Notification for such local areas wherever issued and as per the statutory definition under Rule 2 (w) Indian Telephones Rules, 1951, as it stood during the year 1994/1995 where no specific Gazette Notification has been issued.

## MINISTRY OF FINANCE

### Note on Spectrum Charges

The first licenses for cellular mobile telephone services were awarded in 1994 for 8 cellular operators in four metro cities. The operators were bound by a ceiling tarrif and call charge, and were required to pay a license fee spread over ten years. The annual payment ranged from a minimum of Rs.1 crore in the first year to Rs.24 crore per year in the seventh year for various metros. More licenses were awarded in 1995 based on a bidding process. The bids were based on license fees spread over a ten year license period but did not include spectrum charges. Charges for spectrum were payable separately and these licensees were charged for spectrum at Rs.4,800 per voice channel and Rs.1200 for each additional station.

2. In the year 1999, NTP-99 was announced. The existing operators (including basic services operators) were permitted to migrate to provide cellular mobile services with effect from 1st August 1999 on payment of "license fee" and "spectrum charges". At this point of time, the following three charges were levied:-

(i) entry fee - based on a bidding process;
(ii) charges for spectrum (at the present rate);
(iii) revenue sharing (collected as a license fee).

3. In 2002, licenses were issued to a fourth cellular operator based on bidding for the entry fee.

4. On 27th October 2003, TRAI recommended that the existing entry fee charged from the fourth cellular operator would be the entry fee for the new Universal Access Services License (UASL) regime.

contd...

: 2 :

5. Cabinet approved the recommendations of the TRAI with regard to implementation of the Universal Access Services License regime (for basic and cellular services) and authorised DoT to finalise the details of implementation including the calculation of the entry fee depending on the date of payment based on the, principles given by TRAI in its recommendations.

6. A GoM constituted for the purpose made certain recommendations. Cabinet approved the recommendations on release of adequate spectrum, namely,

- (i) DoT and MoF would discuss and finalise the pricing formula for spectrum which will include incentive for efficient use of spectrum;
- (ii) the allotment of additional spectrum would be transparent, fair and equitable; and
- (iii) the long-term (5-10 years) spectrum requirements would be worked out by DoT.

7. It is therefore clear that there are three separate concepts:

- (i) entry fee;
- (ii) charges for spectrum;
- (iii) revenue share.

8. (i) **Entry Fee:** The present entry fee is based on the highest bid received in 2001, namely, Rs.1,651 crore if operating over the entire country. DoT has taken the stand that entry fee is **not** in the nature of spectrum charges or license fees.

(ii) **Charges for spectrum**: Currently, spectrum charges are fixed at 2 per cent, 3 per cent or 4 per cent of Adjusted Gross Revenue (AGR) depending upon the spectrum bandwidth. The rate goes up from 2 per cent to 4 per cent as the bandwidth increases from 4.4 + 4.4 MHz to 10 + 10 MHz. There are two more rates of 5 per cent and 6 per cent for higher bandwidth, but spectrum in this range has not yet been allotted.

contd...

: 3 :

Start up spectrum is allocated as part of the license. Initial allotment is up to 4.4 + 4.4 MHz for TDMA based systems and up to 2.5 + 2.5 MHz for CDMA based systems. It is also provided that additional spectrum may be considered after ensuring optimal and efficient utilisation of the spectrum allocated.

(iii) **Revenue share** (also described as **license fee**): Currently, revenue share is a percentage of AGR. With effect from 1.4.2004, the share is 10 per cent for category 'A', 8 per cent for category 'B' and 6 per cent for category 'C'.

9. This note does not deal with the need, if any, to revise entry fee or the rate of revenue share. This note deals with spectrum charges for 2G spectrum.

10. **Spectrum is a scarce resource.The price for spectrum should be based on its scarcity value and efficiency of usage. The most transparent method of allocating spectrum would be through auction. The method of auction will face the least legal challenge. If Government is able to provide sufficient information on availability of spectrum, that would minimize the risks and, consequently, fetch better prices at the auction. The design of the auction should include a reserve price.**

11. The auction could be for a "one-time payment" for the additional spectrum or "an annual rent" for the additional spectrum Once the price is discovered, additional spectrum should be allocated to all bidders at that price.

12. In addition, if a licensee sells his license (including the spectrum) to another person, it could be stipulated that the licensee should share with the Government a part of the premium/profit gained by him through the sale.

contd...

: 4 :

13. This leaves the question about licensees who already hold spectrum over and above the start up spectrum. In such cases, the past may be treated as a closed chapter and the payments made in the past for additional spectrum (over and above the start up spectrum) may be treated as the charges for spectrum for that period. However, prospectively, such licensee should pay for the additional spectrum that he holds, over and above the start up spectrum, at the price discovered in the auction. This will place old licensees, existing licensee seeking additional spectrum and new licensees on par so far as spectrum charges are concerned.

**(P. Chidambaram)**
**Finance Minister**
**15.1.2008**

**PRIME MINISTER**

**Ministry of Finance**
**Department of Economic Affairs**

---

**July 04, 2008**

## Spectrum Issues – Update

**(Update on Papers dated February 11, April 17 & 29, and June 11, 20, 27 & 30, 2008)**

1. Meetings took place between Finance Minister and Minister of Telecommunications on May 29, 2008 and June 12, 2008 to resolve outstanding issues relating to allocation and pricing of 2G and 3G spectrum bands. The DEA paper, in following paragraphs, attempts to consolidate the position on the outstanding issues.

2. The issues that are taken up for discussion in this paper are summarized as under:

i. Raising spectrum usage charges for 2G spectrum
ii. Pricing of spectrum for 2G allocations
iii. Method of allocation of 3G spectrum

**I. Spectrum Usage Charge for 2G Spectrum**

3. Spectrum usage charge is pegged to the bandwidth[1] and is calibrated as a percentage of the Adjusted Gross Revenue (AGR). In view of historical legacy reasons and the administrative issues involved in changing an established practice, **it was decided to continue with the current practice of levying spectrum usage charges on the basis of varying percentages of AGR for different bandwidths of spectrum.**

4. **It has been agreed to raise the rates as indicated in Table 1 below. This will yield revenue of Rs 4,149 crore in 2008-09, an increase of Rs 1,270 crore over the revenue yield on the current rate structure.**

---

[1] Frequency Spectrum is divided into Bands. Bandwidth refers to the difference between the lower and higher limits of each Band.

**Table 1: Spectrum usage charges and Revenue Implications thereof for 2008-09**

| Bandwidth Range (MHz) | Spectrum Usage Charges as a % of AGR | |
|---|---|---|
| | Existing Rates | Proposed Rates |
| Upto 4.4 | 2% | 3% |
| 4.4 - 6.2 | 3% | 4% |
| 6.2 – 8.0 | 4% | 5% |
| 8.0 – 10.0 | 4% | 6% |
| 10.0 – 12.5 | 5% | 7% |
| 12.5 – 15.0 | 6% | 8% |
| **Revenue Implication for 2008-09 (in Rs Cr)** | **2,879** | **4,149** |

**Source: DoT Finance**

## II. Pricing of Spectrum for 2G Allocations

5. It is legally and administratively tenable to impose a two part tariff for spectrum: a fixed, one-time "upfront" spectrum price for allowing the allottees to use a public resource for private profit; and, a recurring spectrum usage charge, whereby Government shares the profits accruing to the operator. However, due to historical legacy reasons, spectrum allocations upto 6.2 mhz for GSM (5 mhz for CDMA) shall not be charged both from new and existing operators.

6. **It has been agreed that the "base price" shall be determined by taking the entry fee of Rs.1,650 crore (determined in 2003-04) for pan-India operation of UASL licensees as the price of spectrum for 6.2 mhz of bandwidth for GSM operators** (a similar exercise is possible for CDMA operators also). This translates to an embedded price of Rs.266 crore/mhz (for pan India operation).

7. Since the unit price determined as above relates to 2003-04, it needs to be indexed to reflect the increase in the price level. Two options have been worked out.

8. **In the first option, the embedded price of spectrum is updated using SBI PLR, compounded on a monthly basis, from the date of allotment of additional spectrum beyond 6.2 mhz, upto March 31, 2008, for the purpose of determining the amount payable by existing operators as on March 31, 2008.** The indexing factor works out to 1.52 and represents the time value of the price of spectrum for the

duration over which it remained unrecovered from the operators. For new operators, who are allotted spectrum beyond 6.2 mhz after March 31, 2008, the putative spectrum price as on March 31, 2008 would be updated to the date of allotment using the same methodology of compounding the SBI PLR on a monthly basis.

9. **In the second option, the indexation is made using the number of times by which GDP (at current market prices) has gone up between 2003-04 and 2007-08, in order to determine the amount payable by existing operators, for spectrum beyond 6.2 mhz, as on March 31, 2008.** This is premised on the assumption that the growth in GDP reflects, in a rough and simple manner, the "scarcity" value of spectrum, i.e., the GDP growth rate can be used as a proxy parameter for updating the embedded price of spectrum, as derived from the 2003-04 Entry Fee. This indexation works out to 1.7. For operators who will be allotted spectrum beyond 6.2 mhz after March 31, 2008, the updating factor will be indexed to the GDP (at current market prices) for the year in which the spectrum allocation beyond 6.2 mhz takes place, with the base year remaining the same, i.e., 2003-04.

10. **Broad Estimates indicate that while the methodology using PLR would yield Rs 3,028 crore the revenue yields in the option using GDP would be Rs 3,400 crore, by way of upfront charge for spectrum beyond 6.2 mhz allotted upto March 31, 2008.**

11. The lacuna in the first option is that over the last five years, SBI PLR rates have had an inverse relationship with nominal GDP as well as GDP at factor cost. This implies that in a growing economy, when the demand for spectrum will rise, the first option will, in fact, undervalue its price. (Annex may be seen)

12. These rates shall be applicable for the entire duration of the initial license period of 20 years for all operators. Extension in license period and the conditions for extension shall be as per the extant policy at the time of expiry of the license.

**III. Method of Allocation of 3G spectrum**

13. DEA and DoT have agreed that allotment of 3G spectrum will be made on the basis of the International Competitive Bidding (ICB), with reiteration of the existing mandatory "roll out" clause. The present criteria for pre-qualification will be followed for 3G auction, viz., all interested parties eligible for the UASL license will participate. A non-licensee who succeeds in obtaining 3G spectrum in the ICB process, for a particular circle, would be granted a license to operate 3G services in that circle.

---

CONFIDENTIAL.

SANDEEP DIKSHIT
Member of Parliament
(Lok Sabha)

सत्यमेव जयते

C-I/16, Pandara Park,
New Delhi - 110003
Ph. : 23782963, 23782965

Dr Manmohan Singh,
Honourable Prime Minister of India,
New Delhi

Honourable Prime Minister

December 14, 2010

The last three months have been tumultuous for the Government and the Congress Party. The various reports, especially the CAG report on the 2G Spectrum allocation has somehow turned against us, and the general mood is one of looking at the UPA Government and the Congress Party with suspicion.

If I may summarise the issue :

- The CAG report, clearly a motivated and unprofessional document has made the country believe that there has been a "loot" to the extent of Rs. 1,76,000 crores.
- It is Mr A Raja and the DMK that may take the blame in Tamil Nadu, but elsewhere, thanks largely to yellow journalism by the media, the belief spreading is that the Congress party has indulged in this "massive scam".
- While we have initiated steps that will ultimately and speedily bring justice, the Opposition demand for a Joint Parliamentary Committee has become the corner stone of this national mood. The Opposition, assisted by the ill informed media has been able to make people believe that the Government is running away from any probe and hence has much to hide.
- As a Government and as a Party we have been both late and lazy in putting the real picture has not been put across to the nation.
- It is now a challenge for all of us to ensure that in the few months before the Budget Session and the elections in four states, we are able to show decisive action to the people, and change this mood.

Sir, in all humility, I have a suggestion to make. I know that you are a leader of impeccable integrity and a leader whose vision, whose fearlessness in action for the greater national good and whose abilities make us proud. Today, there is a sustained campaign by both the Opposition and rogue elements in the media and our bureacracy and private sector to malign this image, thereby denting both the UPA and our party. At the centre of this is the issue of denying the JPC and hence the suspicion that we are reluctant to open ourselves up to independent scrutiny. While many of our leaders may say things contradicting this view, it is only Smt. Gandhi and you who have a credibility in people that can turn public opinion.

My suggestion is that you take the "bull by the horns" as they say, and write to the Public Accounts Committee and offer to appear before it to clear whetever they want to know from you. This will electrify the entire situation and will be a game changing move. Public opinion will receive a confidence building shock. I know Sir, that in many different ways you have done this – come out and defended our actions, be it the Nuclear Deal, the opening of our economy or any other. Whether, the PAC speaks to you or not, this unprecedented move would, once and for all establish yours, and your Governments credibility in the eyes of the people, and put all speculations to rest. Sir, politically we need to convince a doubting and unbelieving nation of our Governments integrity.

I have written to you and made this suggestion, with humility, and with great concern at what is being spoken and believed in the streets of our country. We cannot and should not be the "fall guys" in this episode. You have been a beacon of hope for all of us and a trend setter in many areas. This step of yours will set a completely new benchmark of probity and integrity in public life. Only you can do it.

With my deepest regards and respects,

Yours sincerely,

(Sandeep Dikshit)

AMAR SINGH
MEMBER OF PARLIAMENT
(RAJYA SABHA)
NATIONAL GENERAL SECRETARY & SPOKESMAN
(SAMAJWADI PARTY)

27, LODHI ESTATE,
NEW DELHI-110003
TEL. : 32565397 / 32542188 / 24616827
FAX : 91-11-24636299
Email : amarsingh@bol.net.in

सत्यमेव जयते

**July 2, 2008**

Respected Manmohan Singhji,

**Sub: Government can raise more than Rs. 15000 Crores for the use of spectrum by Indian Telecom Industry.**

In these challenging times when Government is finding it hard to meet subsidy obligations on account of fertilizer, food, etc., there is an area where revenue can easily be generated and substantial sum will be raised in a very short time.

I would like to draw your kind attention to the issue of charging of spectrum allotted to the Indian cellular operators. I have been following the numerous media reports on the subject for quite some time. It is a common knowledge that spectrum is a scarce resource and has to be utilized most efficiently and at the same time Government has to be compensated adequately from the huge profits the cellular industry is making out of the use of this scarce resource.

2. I am aware that this issue had caught your attention quite some time back while addressing the India Telecom – 2007 on 12th December, 2007. Some extracts of your speech are given below for reference;

Quote

> **"We must realize that we need to make use of this precious and limited resource in an optimal manner. All technological options must be explored to maximize its utilization. The policy regime for making spectrum available should be fair, transparent, equitable and forwarding looking. It should not create entry barriers to newcomers or barriers to the continued growth of the important sector. At the same time, the revenue potential to the government must not be lost sight of".**

Unquote

3. Without encroaching much on your valuable time, I will briefly draw your kind attention on the following important issues with respect to the allotment and charging of spectrum to the cellular operators:

(a) The cellular operators are entitled to get a start up spectrum of 4.4 MHz of GSM spectrum and 2.5 MHz of CDMA spectrum as per the existing license conditions immediately after the payment of an entry fee of Rs. 1650 Crores for pan India operations. Spectrum up to 6.2 MHz in respect of GSM and 5 MHz in respect of CDMA can, however, be allotted to the cellular operators based on justification.

(b) The license does not provide for allotment of spectrum beyond 6.2 MHz in GSM and 5 MHz in CDMA.

(c) Some of the GSM operators have been allocated spectrum beyond the contracted value of 6.2 MHz without payment of any additional spectrum fees.

Permanent Address : E-593, GREATER KAILASH - II, NEW DELHI - 110048 Phone : 29226507 / 29225377
OFFICE : 8, SOUTH AVENUE, NEW DELHI - 110011 PHONE : 23792324 / 23794913 FAX : 23794913 Email : asingh@sansad.nic.in

AMAR SINGH
MEMBER OF PARLIAMENT
(RAJYA SABHA)
NATIONAL GENERAL SECRETARY & SPOKESMAN
(SAMAJWADI PARTY)

सत्यमेव जयते

27, LODHI ESTATE,
NEW DELHI-110003
TEL. : 32565397 / 32542188 / 24616827
FAX : 91-11-24636299
Email : amarsingh@bol.net.in

4. I understand from various media reports that the Government is considering the following for charging the excess spectrum over and above 6.2 MHz allocated to the cellular operators.

(i) **Levying of one time fixed charges.** This involves two steps i.e. determining the per MHz charge and then indexing it

(a) Determination of the per MHz price of the spectrum. This could be done with the following options:

| S.N | Options | Impact | Observations |
|---|---|---|---|
| (i) | Start-up spectrum of 4.4 MHz in GSM and 2.5 MHz in CDMA | Rs.375 crores / MHz | • The entry fee of Rs.1650 crores entitles the operator for initial start-up spectrum of 4.4 MHz. Allocation of additional spectrum beyond start-up spectrum has been based on meeting the subscriber criteria. |
| (ii) | Contracted Spectrum of 6.2 MHz in GSM and 5 MHz in CDMA | Rs.266 crores / MHz | • The new operators, who have been issued the licenses this year have been allocated spectrum of 4.4 MHz in GSM and 2.5 MHz in CDMA |

**I suggest that per MHz price can be derived only on the basis of start up spectrum which comes along with the entry fee. Thus, the per MHz price should be derived by dividing Rs. 1650 Crores by 4.4 MHz i.e. Rs. 375 Crores per MHz.**

(b) Indexing the per MHz charge to the current value

The per MHz charge is based on the entry fee of 2001. Since the revenues of the cellular industry have grown up by more than 3.5 times, the per MHz charge could be derived by multiplying the per MHz price of 375 Crores by 3.5 i.e. Rs. 1312 Crores per MHz. I am aware that there could be several other methods of indexation like growth in GDP and PLR but these parameters reflect the overall national economics and not for the cellular industry alone which has grown much faster.

(c) The one time fixed charge as suggested above will promote spectral efficiency, ensure a level playing field, will be in line with the TRAI's recommendations of charging a one time fees and will ensure a higher share to the Government of the super normal profits accruing to the cellular operators because of the spectrum allotment beyond the contracted value.

(ii) **Levying of additional spectrum usage charge.**

There could be following options with the Government for levying the spectrum usage charges:

(a) **Keep existing spectrum charges:**

This will generate about Rs. 2800 Crores. However, keeping the existing charges intact will not promote spectral efficiency and does not recognize that every 2 MHz incremental allocation beyond the contracted value saves the operator approximately Rs. 7500 Crores in network expenditure over five years.

(b) **Accept TRAI recommendations of August 2007:**

TRAI had recommended no change in the spectrum usage charges up to 8 MHz and recommended an increase of only 1% beyond 8 MHz. In this scenario, the Government will get about Rs. 3500 Crores. However, this recommendation of TRAI

Permanent Address : E-593, GREATER KAILASH - II, NEW DELHI - 110048 Phone : 29226507 / 29225377
OFFICE : 8, SOUTH AVENUE, NEW DELHI - 110011 PHONE : 23792324 / 23794913 FAX : 23794913 Email : asingh@sansad.nic.in

AMAR SINGH
MEMBER OF PARLIAMENT
(RAJYA SABHA)
NATIONAL GENERAL SECRETARY & SPOKESMAN
(SAMAJWADI PARTY)

27, LODHI ESTATE,
NEW DELHI-110003
TEL. : 32565397 / 32542188 / 2461682
FAX : 91-11-24636299
Email : amarsingh@bol.net.in

also does not fully recognize the value of the spectrum allocated up to 8 MHz which is beyond the contracted value of 6.2 MHz. The recommended increase of only 1% beyond 8 MHz is much smaller than the value accruing to the operators.

(c) **Adopt stricter spectrum usage charge** over and above TRAI recommendations of August 2007.
Since the TRAI recommendations are too lenient, the Government can tighten the criteria of these recommendations, without changing the basic principles, on the following lines.

Apply increased charges to beyond 6.2 MHz instead of beyond 8 MHz and increase by 2% instead of 1%. This will give an estimated revenue of nearly Rs.5000 crores – incremental revenue of Rs.2000 crores in 2008-09.

5. **Suggestions**

I understand that the Department of Telecom is trying to take a very lenient view on levying the one time fixed charge and increasing the spectrum usage charges at the behest of some of the incumbent GSM cellular operators like Airtel and Vodafone at the cost of the exchequer. I will, thus, request you to give your personal attention to the matter as it deals with the efficient utilization of spectrum and at the same time raising the revenues to the Government of India. **Therefore, the spectrum beyond the contracted value of 6.2 MHz should be charged as follows:**

(i) **Levy a one time fixed spectrum charge at the rate of Rs. 375 Crores per MHz and index it with the AGR growth between 2003 & 2008. This will facilitate raising Rs. 10000 Crores to the Government.**

(ii) **Increase the spectrum charges as suggested in Para 4 c above. This will fetch Rs. 5000 Crores to the Government and at the same time will ensure spectral efficiency.** I would like to meet you regarding this before any decision is taken so that I may personally tell you about it.

**Thanking you**

**With** regards,

**Yours** affectionately,
Amar Singh

**(Amar Singh)**

**Dr. Manmohan Singh**
**Hon'ble Prime Minister of India**
**Government of India**
**New Delhi**

Permanent Address : E-593, GREATER KAILASH - II, NEW DELHI - 110048 Phone : 29226507 / 29225377
OFFICE : 8, SOUTH AVENUE, NEW DELHI - 110011 PHONE : 23792324 / 23794913 FAX : 23794913 Email : asingh@sansad.nic.in

सत्यमेव जयते

RAJEEV CHANDRASEKHAR
MEMBER OF PARLIAMENT
RAJYA SABHA

Member of Standing Committee on Information Technology
Member of Consultative Committee on Urban Development
Member of Parliamentary Forum on Youth

25 September, 2008

Respected Prime Minister

**Sub: Transparent approach to monetization of public assets like Spectrum**

I have written to you earlier on the issue of the need to have an open, market based method to establish value of Spectrum that the Government, from time to time, gives to the private sector for operating various services.

Since spectrum is an asset of the Government and people of India, it follows logically that when this asset is being transferred to any non-government entity or company, that the government is commercially compensated at the market value for that asset i.e. spectrum.

Recent news reports confirm that the arbitrage between the value that Government is receiving for spectrum and actual market value is to the tune of almost Rs 8-9000 Crores. On a base price of nationwide spectrum at Rs 1540 Crores appx (for all 23 circles), this is an appreciation in the hands of private sector of almost 600% in a few months.

I am basing this conclusion on recently published reports of a private company (Swan Telecom) which holds 13 licenses in 13 circles (states) in India (and paid less than Rs 1500 Crores) and has been valued at $2Billion (Rs 9400 Crores). Given that company has no operations, no infrastructure yet and no customers or revenues – it is safe to conclude that this value of Rs 9400 Crores is for the spectrum that the company owns/will own.

This transaction clearly establishes a market based and irrefutable evidence that the Governments pricing for spectrum of 4.4 MHz is far lower than actual market values for the asset and is causing a situation where considerable moneys is being lost to the exchequer and people of India.

211 North Avenue, New Delhi-110001 India
Tel: + 91-11-23094044 Fax : + 91-11-23094042
E-mail : rajeev.c@nic.in
www.rajeev.in

सत्यमेव जयते

As you know, I have raised this issue with you on more than one occasion and believe there is a need for a comprehensive public policy when it comes to commercial terms of monetization of public assets like spectrum, minerals, natural resources etc – i.e. a public policy that should be based on a simple objective and test of ensuring maximum benefit to the exchequer and public.

I hope given the latest piece of information, you will have your Government initiate a new public policy for pricing National assets like spectrum, minerals, etc.

Thanking you,

Very truly yours,

RAJEEV CHANDRASEKHAR

**Dr. Manmohan Singh**
Hon'ble Prime Minister
Government of India
New Delhi

**No.3/15/2008-Infra**
**Ministry of Finance**
**Department of Economic Affairs**
**(Infrastructure Division)**

**New Delhi, October 13, 2008.**

**Office Memorandum**

**Subject: Issues related to allocation and pricing of 2G Spectrum.**

Prime Minister's Office may refer to ID dated September 3, 2008 on the subject mentioned above. The issues raised in the memorandum submitted by Samajwadi Party to the Prime Minister are similar to those that have been raised by the Association of Unified Telecom Service Providers of India (AUSPI) in representations dated June, 30, July 2 and July 3, 2008 to the Minister of Finance. These issues have been referred to Department of Telecommunications (DoT) for examination and consideration in a meeting of the Telecom Commission.

2. So far no meeting of Telecom Commission has taken place on these issues. As soon as the meeting is held and a view is taken on the proposals of AUSPI by DoT, PMO will be informed of the position.

3. This issues with the approval of Secretary, Department of Economic Affairs.

**(Govind Mohan)**
**Director (Infra)**
**Telefax 23093881**

**Prime Minister's Office**
**(Ms. Vini Mahajan, Joint Secretary)**
**South Block,**
**New Delhi.**

Tel. : +91-11-2371 9898
Fax : +91-11-2371 1514
e-mail: sidbehura@yahoo.co.in

सत्यमेव जयते

**SIDDHARTHA BEHURA**
सचिव Secretary

भारत सरकार
संचार एवं सूचना प्रौद्योगिकी मंत्रालय
दूरसंचार विभाग
संचार भवन, नई दिल्ली-110 001
**Government of India**
**Ministry of Communications & Information Technology**
**Department of Telecommunications**
**Sanchar Bhawan, New Delhi-110 001**

Secy(EA)

D.O. No. P-11015/08/2008-PP
Dated: 6th October. 2008

JS(Infra)

Dear Ashok,

I am enclosing herewith a copy of the self-contained note, which I had sent to Principal Secretary to Prime Minister, on issues raised by Shri Amar Singh, MP in his letters to Hon'ble Prime Minister relating to pricing and spectrum allocation.

With regards,

Yours sincerely,

( Siddhartha Behura )

Encl: as above.

**Shri Ashok Chawla**
Secretary
Department of Economic Affairs
North Block
New Delhi – 110 001.

8/10

No. P-11015/08/2008-PP

**Subject: Pricing and Spectrum Allocation Policy and Loss in Revenue to the Government due to Alleged Hoarding and Policy Issues.**

Reference letters from Hon'ble Shri Amar Singh, Member Parliament, PMO ID No. 180/31/C/26/08-ES-I (Vol.IV) dated 22nd August 2008 and PMO ID No. 670/71/C/8/2008-ES-I dated 3rd September 2008 regarding Pricing and Spectrum Allocation policy and loss in revenue to the Government due to alleged spectrum hoarding and policy issues.

2. Comments on the issues raised in the letters of Hon'ble MP and referred to in J. S. PMO's letter No.670/71/c/8/2008-ES-I dated 03.09.2008 are as under:

2.1 It is submitted that allotments of spectrum were made in accordance with the norms prevailing at the stage of allotment. Initial GSM spectrum (2x 4.4 MHz) has been allotted to mobile telecom operators as per relevant provision of their Service Licence Agreements, taking into account the request of the service providers, the guidelines/ orders and, subject to the availability of spectrum.

2.2 With the growth of service, the next installment of spectrum (2 x 1.8 MHz). to make the total spectrum upto 2 X 6.2 MHz has also been allotted taking into account their request, the guidelines/ orders/ criteria and subject to the availability of spectrum. Also, to achieve the objectives of continued growth of telecom services, further spectrum beyond 2 x 6.2 MHz has also been allotted to various operators, as per guidelines/ orders/ criteria in force at the time of such allotment. These criteria have been formulated and appropriately reviewed periodically, taking into account TRAI recommendations and development of technological features, etc.

2.3 In the beginning when the telecom sector was in a nascent stage, additional spectrum upto 6.2 MHz., beyond the initial 4.4 + 4.4 MHz spectrum, was allotted to GSM operators, based on their request, justification and subject to availability of spectrum. In this regard, it is pertinent to mention that the Para 13 (ii) and (iv) of the earlier licenses of 1994 and 1995 (reproduced below) are similar to the current condition 43.5 (iv) of the UASL licence, as far as Government's (licensor) powers to modify the licence conditions.

*13 (ii) The Authority reserves the right to modify at any time the terms and conditions of the licence, if in the opinion of the Authority it is necessary or expedient to do so in the interests of the general public or for the proper conduct of telegraphs or for security considerations and reasons.*

*13 (iv) "Notwithstanding anything contained anywhere else in the license, the Authority's decision shall be final"*

Cont. 2

**UASL License Agreement:**

*Clause 43.5.(i) Initially a **cumulative** maximum of up to 4.4 MHz + 4.4 MHz shall be allocated in the case of GSM **based** systems and maximum of 2.5 MHz per carrier in case of CDMA based systems, on **case** by case basis subject to availability.*

*Clause 43.5.(ii) Additional spectrum beyond the above stipulation may also be considered for allocation **after** ensuring optimal and efficient utilization of the already allocated spectrum taking into account all types of traffic and guidelines / criteria prescribed from time to time. However, spectrum not more than 5 + 5 MHz in respect of CDMA system or 6.2 + 6.2 MHz in respect of GSM based system shall be allocated to any new Unified Access **Service** Licensee.*

*Clause 43.5 (iv) The licensor has right to modify and / or amend the procedure of allocation of spectrum including quantum of spectrum at any point of time without assigning any reason.*

**Migrated UASL License Agreement (from CMTS):**

*Clause 43.5.(i)Initially a **cumulative** maximum of up to 4.4 MHz + 4.4 MHz shall be allocated in the case of GSM **based** systems and maximum of 2.5 MHz per carrier in case of CDMA based systems, on **case** by case basis subject to availability.*

*Clause 43.5.(ii)The licensee operating wireless services will continue to provide such services in already allocated/ contracted spectrum.*

*Clause 43.5 (iv)The licensor **has** right to modify and / or amend the procedure of allocation of spectrum **including** quantum of spectrum at any point of time without assigning any reason.*

It is thus apparent that none of the conditions of the license agreement have been violated. There is a power to "modify and / or amend the procedure of allocation of spectrum including quantum of spectrum at any point of time without assigning any reason"

Extract of the relevant provisions of the licensing agreements are enclosed at Annexure I-III.

2.4 During 2005-06, the Telecom Engineering Centre had analyzed the practical traffic capacity (and consequentially the subscriber base) which can be derived/served by a particular amount of spectrum, taking into account the demographic features of the respective service areas as well as the technological features for spectrum efficiency, as available at that time. For the purpose of allotment of additional spectrum, the criteria took into account the active subscribers & the peak traffic. Based on this the orders for allocation of additional spectrum was issued in March 2006 (Annexure-IV). It may also be mentioned that the technological innovations are continuously taking place and various spectrum efficient technologies are evolving. Therefore, the criteria for efficient uses of spectrum are being continuously reviewed/updated.

Cont.3

2.5 Orders regarding the new subscriber base criteria for allotment of spectrum for GSM and CDMA, based on the TRAI Recommendations of August 2007, TEC study results of October 2007 and the recommendations of the Committee, which included academia and representatives from industry besides from DOT has been issued on 17th January 2008 (Annexure-V). Additional spectrum based on their request and taking into account the subscriber based eligibility criteria has also been allotted subject to availability of spectrum in a telecom service area. Usage charges are levied for all allotted spectrum and the service providers have to pay increased spectrum charges (as additional percentage of revenue share) for such additional spectrum.

2.6 The Government has announced policy guidelines in March 2006 and January 2008 and allocated spectrum above 6.2 MHz strictly in accordance with the license stipulation and guidelines.

3. Hon'ble M.P. has raised issues concerning availability of spectrum. In this regard it may be mentioned that spectrum in 1800 MHz is presently used by defence services. As and when it is made available/coordinated by them, same is being allotted to the telecom service providers.

4. On the issue of one time spectrum pricing for allotment beyond 6.2 MHz and increase in spectrum charges, it is submitted that several meetings were held with Ministry of Finance at the highest level wherein these issues were discussed at length as given under.

(i) It would not be possible to auction 2G spectrum in view of the past and current policies of the Government, which inter-alia, involves allotment of spectrum based on subscriber base and future uncertain availability of spectrum. This unit price for 1 MHz of 2g spectrum would have to be calculated by dividing Rs.1650 cr by 6.2 MHz, and not 4.4 MHz as suggested by Hon'ble MP Shri Amar Singh in his letter to the Prime Minister. This is because, as provided in the license. the BSNL , MTNL have been given 6.2 MHz initially followed by others since the license conditions provide for allocation of 6.2 MHz. Any attempt to do otherwise is likely to result in litigation.

(ii) Spectrum has a scarcity value. It can be argued that it is scarce for all, whether the operator is new or old. In January 2008, Government have issued 120 licenses as well as dual technology licenses to Reliance Communications and TATA at the rate of Rs. 1650 crore for PAN India license, which is taken as the price of initial spectrum of 4.4/6.2 MHz. Therefore, any deviation from the rate at which the other operators are charged, would appear discriminatory and 'non-level playing field'.

(iii) In a meeting between Ministry of Finance and Department of telecommunications at the level of Hon'ble Finance Minister, it was therefore, decided that, given the circumstances and legacy of policy of allocation of

Cont. 4

spectrum, the only possible way the spectrum can be priced beyond 6.2 MHz, which would be sustainable and acceptable to the Industry, would be to price the spectrum at the unit price as Rs. 1650 divided by 6.2, along with PLR to take care of time value of money.

(iv) Spectrum usage charges.
The current and proposed spectrum usage charges along with the TRAI recommendation is as under.

| Spectrum(in MHz) | Charges as %age of AGR | | | Hon'ble M.P's proposal |
|---|---|---|---|---|
| | Existing | TRAI | Proposed | |
| Upto 4.4/2.5 | 2 | 2 | 3 | 2 |
| 6.2/5 | 3 | 3 | 4 | 3 |
| 8.0 | 4 | 4 | *5 | 5 |
| 10.0 | 4 | 5 | +6 | 7 |
| 12.5 | 5 | 6 | 7 | 9 |

*upto 8.2, +upto10.2

4.1 On the proposal of Hon'ble MP, the following points are made.

(i) The spectrum usage charge has not been revised since 2000-2001.

(ii) Hon'ble MP has suggested that no changes be made in spectrum charges upto 6.2 MHz but increase it beyond 6.2 MHz at 2% instead of 1%. TRAI had also recommended no change in the spectrum charges upto 6.2 MHz.

(iii)DOT has suggested an across the board increase of 1% with addition of a new slab at 8.0 MHz. effectively it will mean a 1% increase upto 8.0 MHz and 2% beyond that, compared to the existing rates. There is no rational justification to increase the rate only beyond 6.2 MHz.

(iv)The TRAI has agreed with the current proposal of DOT on spectrum usage charges.

(v) An estimation of the impact of 1% increase in 4.4 MHz spectrum indicate an average increase of Rs.1 cr on average revenues of over Rs.100 cr, which is not very significant especially in comparison to the pan India entry fee of Rs.1650 cr paid by the operator and the increasing future revenue streams.

4.2 The finally agreed proposals under consideration of the Government are as under.

(a) To levy one time spectrum charge beyond 6.2 MHz, which would be calculated by dividing the entry fee by 6.2 MHz. The same would be updated by using the PLR of SBI for time value of money. The spectrum charge per MHz for new allotments after 1/4/2008 shall also be according to same formula.

(b) To increase microwave access + backbone spectrum charges.

Cont. 5

An across the board increase of 1% on spectrum charges.

5. Hon'ble M.P. has also desired that the spectrum allotted on earlier guidelines should be taken back from the operators after the promulgation of the stricter guidelines issued in January 2008. Any such move to retrospectively modify extant guidelines would have legal and other ramifications. TATA and Reliance have gone to TDSAT against allotment of spectrum beyond 6.2 MHz and the Government in consultation with Solicitor General has finalized the reply which in turn states that all spectrum allocated beyond 6.2 MHz have been made strictly in accordance with the licence agreement and guidelines issued in the subject.

6. A Committee for allocation of spectrum has been constituted to recommend the methodology to be followed for allocation of spectrum. Department of Telecom is also reviewing spectrum pricing in consultation with Ministry of Finance. This Ministry shall take into account valuable observation/ views of Hon'ble M.P. Shri Amar Singh and shall consider the same while allocating and pricing of spectrum beyond 6.2 MHz.

No. J-14025/200(17)/2004-NT(GSM)
Government of India
Ministry of Communications & I.T.
Department of Telecommunication
(WPC Wing)
Sanchar Bhavan, 20, Ashoka Road, New Delhi-1

Date: the 29th March, 2006

ORDER

In suppression of all existing orders relating to subscriber base criteria for allotment of GSM spectrum, the following subscriber based criteria shall be followed :-

| Service Area | Minimum subscriber base (In Lakh) required for allotment of different amounts of GSM spectrum | | | | | |
|---|---|---|---|---|---|---|
| | 4.4 MHz | 6.2 MHz | 8 MHz | 10 MHz | 12.4 MHz | 15 MHz |
| Metro Service Area | | | | | | |
| Delhi & Mumbai | No criteria* | 3 | 6 | 10 | 16 | 21 |
| Chennai & Kolkata | No criteria* | 2 | 4 | 6 | 10 | 13 |
| Telecom Circles as Service Area | | | | | | |
| Category 'A' circle | No criteria* | 4 | 8 | 14 | 20 | 26 |
| Category 'B' circle | No criteria* | 3 | 6 | 10 | 16 | 21 |
| Category 'C' circle | No criteria* | 2 | 4 | 6 | 9 | 12 |

*Initial allotment for roll-out of the network

2. The spectrum allotment is subject to availability of spectrum.

3. The active subscribers and peak traffic averaged over a month (for a minimum of 40mErlangs per subscriber) in the Visitor Locator Register (VLR) would be taken into account for this purpose.

4. The enhanced revenue share for spectrum charges, as per orders in this regard would apply for the AGR for subscribers in complete service area.

5. This comes into force with immediate effect.

S/d
(Sukhpal Singh)
Assistant Wireless adviser
to the Government of India.
T.No. 23359562 Fax: 23716111

To,

1) All concerned.
2) Cellular Service providers
3) COAI

Government of India
Ministry of Communications & I.T.
Department of Telecommunication
WPC Wing, Sanchar Bhavan, New Delhi-11001

No. J-14025/200(17)/2004-NT Dated the 17th January, 2008

ORDER

In continuation of the orders dated 09-01-2008 relating to subscriber base criteria for allotment of CDMA spectrum, the following subscriber based criteria, in line with TRAI recommendations shall be followed, as an interim measure.

| Service Area | Subscriber base * (In Lakh) supported by CDMA spectrum in MHz. (eligibility for allotment of next step) | | | | |
|---|---|---|---|---|---|
| | 2X2.5 MHz * (2 carriers) | 2X3.75 MHz (3 Carriers) | 2X5 MHz (4 carriers) | 2X6.25 MHz (5 Carriers) | 2X7.5 MHz (6 carriers) @ |
| **Metro Service Areas.** | 5 | 20 | 30 | 50 | |
| **Telecom Circles as Service Area** | | | | | |
| Category 'A' and 'B' circles. | 8 | 50 | 80 | 100 | |
| Category 'C' circles. | 6 | 40 | 60 | 80 | |

@ Present upper limit for spectrum allotment.

* These are the figures of active subscribers (VLR) averaged over a month. In addition, peak traffic, averaged over a month should be 40 milli-Erlangs per active subscriber in the criteria.

2. The spectrum allotment is subject to availability of spectrum

3. The active subscribers and peak traffic averaged over a month (for a minimum of 40mErlangs per subscriber) in the Visitor Locator Register (VLR) would be taken into account, for this purpose.

4. The revenue share for spectrum charges, as per orders in this regard, would apply on the AGR for the complete service area.

5. This comes into force with immediate effect.

(D. JHA)
Assistant Wireless Adviser
Ph: 2303 6681

To:
1) All concerned.
2) Unified Access Service Providers/ Basic Service providers.
3) AUSPI.

## PRIME MINISTER'S OFFICE

South Block, New Delhi - 110 101

Reference is invited to this office's endorsement of even number dated 12.8.08 endorsing the letter dated 1.8.08 from Shri Ajay Chakraborty, MP on spectrum related issues for action as appropriate, under intimation to this office.

2. Intimation regarding the matter is awaited and may kindly be expedited.

(Amit Agrawal)
Director
☎ : 23012613

Secretary, Department of Telecommunications
Secretary, Department of Economic Affairs

PMO ID no. 180/31/C/26/2005 ES.I — Dated : 25.11.08

AMAR SINGH
MEMBER OF PARLIAMENT
(RAJYA SABHA)
NATIONAL GENERAL SECRETARY & SPOKESMAN
(SAMAJWADI PARTY)

27, LODHI ESTATE,
NEW DELHI-110003
TEL. : 32565397 / 32542188 / 24616827
FAX : 91-11-24636299
Email : amarsingh@bol.net.in

**November 17, 2008**

Respected Manmohan Singhji,

**Subject: Measures to Raise Additional revenue of over Rs 60000 crores from the Telecom Sector on the basis of market discovered price for the Excess Spectrum over 6.2 MHz held by Operators free of Cost**

This is further to my letter dated 22nd August'08 and my earlier letters dated 2nd July'08, 11th July'08 and 25th July'08, regarding the charging for the extra spectrum over 6.2 MHz allotted to the private cellular operators completely free of cost over and above their license conditions.

I understand that the imposition of One-time Spectrum Enhancement Charge for 2G Spectrum has now been deferred by the Department of Telecommunications.

I now see from media reports that the new telecom licenses with national presence based on Deals of Swan Telecom with UAE Government firm Etisalat and Unitech Wireless with Norway Government managed Telenor and are having market valuation upwards of $ 2 billion without assets, customers, infrastructure i.e.9500 to 10,000 crores. **Thus the per MHz price derived at these prices is Rs.2200 to Rs 2300 crores per MHz based on the start-up spectrum of 4.4 MHz allocated to these operators.**

The other telecom deals which have concluded in 2008 can also be the basis for determining per MHz price. The June'08 deal of Sh. Kumar Mangalam Birla led Idea Cellular with Telecom Malaysia (TMI) in June 2008 of Rs.7300 crores for 15% stake indicates that the market valuation of the company is Rs.48000 crores and thus amounting to **Rs.7800 crores per MHz** for the average spectrum held by this company. Also, In the recent deal in November 2008 of Sh Ratan Tata led TTSL with NTT DoCoMo, being reported in the media, of Rs.13000 crores for 26% stake indicates a market valuation of Rs.50000 crores and thereby **Rs.4400 crores per MHz** for the average spectrum held by this company.

I had brought to your attention the media reports in my earlier letter that the DoT is intending to adopt a lenient pricing of spectrum for the excess spectrum over 6.2 MHz to benefit certain dominant private operators – Bharti Airtel, Vodafone and Idea. The reports are stating that the per MHz price is being based on the entry fee of Rs.1650 crores divided by 6.2 MHz spectrum i.e. Rs 266 crore per MHz as the license provides for spectrum up to 6.2 MHz. Also, the appropriate indexation being stated to be adopted

1

Permanent Address : E-593, GREATER KAILASH - II, NEW DELHI - 110048 Phone : 29226507 / 29225377
OFFICE : 8, SOUTH AVENUE, NEW DELHI - 110011 PHONE : 23792324 / 23794913 FAX : 23794913 Email : asingh@sansad.nic.in

AMAR SINGH
MEMBER OF PARLIAMENT
(RAJYA SABHA)
NATIONAL GENERAL SECRETARY & SPOKESMAN
(SAMAJWADI PARTY)

27, LODHI ESTATE,
NEW DELHI-110003
TEL. : 32565397 / 32542188 / 24616827
FAX : 91-11-24636299
Email : amarsingh@bol.net.in

by the DoT is the prime lending rate and thereby, the per MHz charge at today's price being considered is Rs.400 crores per MHz.

The per MHz price based on the market discovery with the deals in 2008 is approximately Rs.8000 crores per MHz based on the Sh. Kumar Mangalam Birla led Idea Cellular deal with Telecom Malaysia in June and the Government should be able to raise over Rs.60,000 crores as Fixed One-time Spectrum Charge from the operators who have been allotted extra spectrum over 6.2 MHz. This would include Sh. Sunil B Mittal led Bharti Airtel – Rs.15000 crores, Vodafone- Essar– Rs.14000 crores and Sh. Kumar Mangalam Birla led Idea Cellular - Rs.6500 crores.

The lenient approach, as reported by the media, being suggesting by DoT would result in the revenue of just Rs.3500 crores including Bharti Airtel – Rs.800 crores, Vodafone Essar – Rs.700 crores and Idea Cellular – Rs.350 crores.

With the lenient approach of PLR basis, vis-à-vis the Market valuation of Rs.8000 crores per MHz, the savings to the operators are Bharti Airtel – Rs.14000 crores, Vodafone Essar – Rs.13000 crores, Idea Cellular – Rs.6000 crores and at the great loss to the Government exchequer. Clearly, this seems to be a part of a grand design to benefit the dominant private operators.

The table below provides the comparison of the approaches:

| Indexation Basis | Value Estimation method | Value MHz for all circles Rs Crore | Index | Value MHz with Indexation for all circles (Rs Crore) | Govt Exchequer revenue Rs crore | Operator Excess Spectrum Value (Rs Crore) Airtel | Vodafone | Idea |
|---|---|---|---|---|---|---|---|---|
| PLR based Lenient approach | Entry fee of Rs 1650 for 6.2 MHz spectrum | 266 | 1.6 | 426 | 3500 | 820 | 750 | 350 |
| Market Price Discovery Options based on deals | | | | | | | | |
| Market Price Discovery Basis | Details | | | Value - MHz for all | Govt Exchequer | Operator Excess Spectrum Airtel | Vodafone | Idea |
| Swan with UAE Government firm Etisilat deal in Aug 08 | Value of 900 Mn$ for 45% stake i.e EV 2 Bn$ or Rs 9400 crore Spectrum 4.4 Mhz | | | 2200 | 18000 | 4300 | 4000 | 1800 |
| Unitech with Norway Government firm Telenor deal in Oct 08 | Value of Rs 6120 crore for 60% stake i.e EV Value Rs 10,200 crore Spectrum 4.4 Mhz | | | 2300 | 19000 | 4440 | 4050 | 1900 |
| Sh Kumar Mangalam Birla led Idea Cellular with Telecom Malayisa deal in June 08 | Rs 7294 crore for 15% EV Rs 48626 crore Spectrum Avg Spectrum per circle 6.2 MHz | | | 7800 | 65000 | 15000 | .14000 | 6500 |
| Sh Ratan Tata led TTSL with NTT-DOCOMO deal in November 08 | Rs 13070 crore for 26% EV Rs 50250 crore Spectrum Avg CDMA per circle - 3.5 MHz i.e equivalent GSM 7 MHz GSM startup - 4.4 MHz ie Total of 11.4 Mhz avg/circle | | | [illegible] | 36000 | 8500 | 7800 | 3600 |



Permanent Address : E-593, GREATER KAILASH - II, NEW DELHI - 110048 Phone : 29226507 / 29225377
OFFICE : 8, SOUTH AVENUE, NEW DELHI - 110011 PHONE : 23792324 / 23794913 FAX : 23794913 Email : asingh@sansad.nic.in

AMAR SINGH
MEMBER OF PARLIAMENT
(RAJYA SABHA)
NATIONAL GENERAL SECRETARY & SPOKESMAN
(SAMAJWADI PARTY)

सत्यमेव जयते

27, LODHI ESTATE,
NEW DELHI-110003
TEL : 32565397 / 32542188 / 246168
FAX : 91-11-24636299
Email : amarsingh@bol.net.in

The pricing of spectrum beyond 6.2 MHz has only one logical option - pricing based in terms of current market value. The costing of spectrum should be done with complete economic prudence, maximizing the revenue interest of the Government Exchequer and accordingly this objective will be best met by adopting the market value pricing of Rs.8000 crores per MHz

**I urge the government to:**

- **Not succumb to the pressure of the dominant private GSM operators by adopting lenient and inappropriate spectrum pricing.**
- **Price spectrum beyond 6.2 MHz based of minimum 2200 crores per MHz and up to Rs.8000 Crores per MHz on the market valuation basis the deals in June08 to November08.**

**Thanking you**

**With** regards,

**Yours** affectionately,

Amar Singh

**(Amar Singh)**

**Dr. Manmohan Singh**
**Hon'ble Prime Minister**
**Government of India**
**152 South Block**
**New Delhi-110011**

3

Permanent Address : E-593, GREATER KAILASH - II, NEW DELHI - 110048 Phone : 29226507 / 29225377
OFFICE : 8, SOUTH AVENUE, NEW DELHI - 110011 PHONE : 23792324 / 23794913 FAX : 23794913 Email : asingh@sansad.nic.in

सत्यमेव जयते

प्रधान मंत्री

Prime Minister

New Delhi
24 November, 2008

Dear Shri Amar Singh ji,

I have received your letter of 17 November, 2008 regarding spectrum charges.

With regards,

Yours sincerely,

(Manmohan Singh)

Shri Amar Singh, MP
27, Lodhi Estate
New Delhi-110003

**No.180/31/C/26/2005-ES.1** **December 1, 2008**

**Copy, with a copy of the letter under reply forwarded to.**

**i. Secretary, Department of Telecommunications**
**ii. Secretary, Department of Economic Affairs**

**2. It is requested that comments in the matter may kindly be sent to this office.**

(Amit Agrawal)
Director
☎: 23012613

RAJEEV CHANDRASEKHAR
MEMBER OF PARLIAMENT
RAJYA SABHA

12th May,2007

Respected Prime Minister,

I write to you in connection with the recent Announcement of a Global Auction of spectrum for 3G services by the Department of Telecommunications and a subsequent article in Economic Times dated 10th May, 2007 in that connection. (A copy of the Article is attached).

Firstly, I must congratulate you and the Government in taking the decision for a global auction of spectrum. I believe that is in the best National interests.

The article attached quoting one of the corporate currently in the Telecom sector is trying to make out a tenuous case of restricting bidders for 3G on some frivolous grounds. As someone who has personal experience of various forms of arguments and logic that have been used in the past to distort what is the correct thing to do, I would like to make some points so that such lobbying does not derail the government from the right path.

That 3G is a separate service is a principle accepted all over the world. The regulator and the government here have also agreed to this principle. Therefore there seems to be no dispute that these should be separate licenses. The key issue seems to be the commercial terms of allocating Spectrum.

It is true that in the early 90s when the Government was actively trying to encourage investors and helping build out the telecom sector, the terms of spectrum were far kinder and gentler. Even there in the mid 90s and subsequently spectrum allocation or license allocation was through a global auction without any restrictions on new players.

...2/-

Jupiter Innovision Centre, No. 54 Richmond Road, Bangalore 560 025 India.
Tel : 91-80-25585908 Fax : 91-80-25587843
E-mail : rajeev.c@nic.in

सत्यमेव जयते

-2-

Spectrum is clearly a valuable natural resource of the Government and people of India. When spectrum is being allocated in present day, when the telecom sector is well developed and valuable (Note the current valuations of Hutch sale to Vodafone), there is clearly no justification in allotting spectrum in any way but a transparent auction. An auction process has been used in the Telecom sector before for the 4th round of cellular licenses and as well more recently very successfully by the I&B Ministry for FM licenses.

Given that there cant be any argument against auction, a case is now sought to be made by this corporate, that the bidders must be restricted through some arbitrary criterion – in this case Indian companies or existing operators or both. This is quite ridiculous and goes against the objectives of an auction. There were no such restrictions on the 4th round of cellular licenses nor were there any restrictions like this in the recent FM licenses. Which would lead one to believe, that the only objective of the restricting bidders would be to depress the real price of spectrum being allotted.

This argument being made must be rejected with the contempt it deserves notwithstanding the fact that it comes from a so-called reputed Indian corporate. It is against national interest and against every precedence and practice of exacting maximum value for spectrum. This suggestion is even more ironical given the almost opposite view taken by the same company when it was trying to get into Cellular through the WLL route in the whole WLL scam not many years ago.

In short, I wish to reiterate that the decision of the Government to actively seek out through the process of a Global transparent Auction with no restrictions on participants, the best price for 3G spectrum/licenses - is the correct one for the country and its people. This is consistent with practices in the past and in other sectors like FM. Resources raised through such a process can be invaluable in addressing rural tele-density and other investment requirements of the government in rural and urban infrastructure. The government must not allow lobbying of the kind in this reported letter to compromise this approach and to perpetuate oligopolies of the kind that you recently referred to in a speech.

...3/-

-3-

I am sure given my history of association of Telecom, there will be some accusations of me having some agenda or the other. I have none, except to make sure the wrongs that so characterized the conduct of Telecom policy in the past years are not repeated today or ever again in the future.

Thanking you

Very Truly Yours

RAJEEV CHANDRASEKHAR

Dr. Manmohan Singh
Hon`ble Prime Minister
Government of India
New Delhi

*Copy to:*

1) *Thiru Dayanidhi Maran*
*Honble Minister of Telecommunications and IT*

2) *Thiru P Chidambaram*
*Honble Minister of Finance*

*Abani Roy*
MEMBER OF PARLIAMENT
RAJYA SABHA
MEMBER STANDING COMMITTEE
ON RAILWAYS

NEW DELHI
17, FEROZ SHAH ROAD, NEW DELHI-110001
TEL.: 23782342, 23782167, FAX : 011-23782342
E-mail :-abani@sansad.nic.in

KOLKATA
R.S.P. OFFICE
124-C, LENIN SARANI, KOLKATA-700 013
TEL.: 22468049, 22461810

Date.........................

Dr. Manmohan Singh
Hon'ble Prime Minister
South Block,
New Delhi.

Dear Dr. Manmohan Singh,

It is heartening to note that in keeping with the phenomenal growth of Indian Telecom Industry your Government had introduced far reaching reforms in the Telecom Sector.

However, a lobby of major telecom operators, i.e. Cellular Operators Association of India (COAI) is working on the sole aim of furthering their interests at the cost of country's development and in other words blocking the entry of new entrants in the sector as they do not want competition.

It is needless to add that, these few operators, under the umbrella of COAI, have amassed 10 MHZ of spectrum each even though they are entitled to get only 6.2 MHZ of spectrum. This raises a question as to how and in what manner they have obtained the additional spectrum which needs to be investigated by the CBI.

The COAI had been instrumental in attacking the Government for allotting spectrum to Public Sector Companies, BSNL & MTNL, without realizing the fact that they have to take care of social obligations.

In view of the above, I would request you to ensure that the Government strongly defends its action in the TDSAT so that the monopolistic anti-developmental campaign launched by the COAI is rejected.

Thanking you,

With warm regards,

( Abani Roy ) 10.11.2007

**AMAR SINGH**
MEMBER OF PARLIAMENT
(RAJYA SABHA)
NATIONAL GENERAL SECRETARY & SPOKESMAN
(SAMAJWADI PARTY)

सत्यमेव जयते

27, LODHI ESTATE,
NEW DELHI-110003
TEL. : 32565397 / 32542188 / 2461682
FAX : 91-11-24636299
Email : amarsingh@bol.net.in

**November 12, 2007**

Respected Manmohan Singh ji,

I would like to draw your kind attention to some nefarious activities of the Cellular Operators Association of India (COAI) whose main aim is anti-consumer.

The COAI is holding the Department of Telecom, and in other words, the country to ransom by being a stumbling block for entry of new entrants in the sector.

Over the past 6 months some of the prominent members of the COAI have cartelized and increased the charges on consumers in a concerted manner. The increases have been as high as 30%, hurting the consumers.

Every time the Government brings about measures to improve spectrum efficiency to conserve the precious natural resource, the COAI has been opposing as they do not want to bring in efficiencies as it would entail them to invest more capital. In other words, COAI wants to thrive on Country's resources without any payment.

As per the licence agreements signed with the Government, these companies are entitled to get only 6.2 MHZ of spectrum. Curiously the companies in the forefront of litigation before the TDSAT on spectrum issues have amassed 10 MHZ spectrum each raising the question as to how and in what manner they obtained additional spectrum. This begs a CBI enquiry without any delay.

COAI and their principal sponsor have recently attacked the Government for allotting spectrum to the National Telecom companies, BSNL and MTNL forgetting that the National units have heavy social obligations to cater to.

The Department of Telecom should strongly defend their action in the TDSAT and expose the cartel, that is, COAI.

**Thanking you**

**With** regards,

**Yours** Sincerely,
Amar Singh

**(Amar Singh)**

**Dr. Manmohan Singh**
**Hon'ble Prime Minister**
**Government of India**
**152 South Block**
**New Delhi-110001**

Permanent Address : E-593, GREATER KAILASH - II, NEW DELHI - 110048 Phone : 29226507 / 29225377

सत्यमेव जयते

RAJEEV CHANDRASEKHAR
MEMBER OF PARLIAMENT
RAJYA SABHA

Member of Standing Committee on Information Technology
Member of Consultative Committee on Urban Development
Member of Parliamentary Forum on Youth

November 14, 2007

Dear Respected Prime Minister

This has regards to the release of Spectrum by Defence Ministry to DOT, and the planned sale of the Spectrum by DOT to Private Telecom Companies.

Although I have written to you earlier on this issue, I am reiterating through this letter again that all decisions relating to Spectrum allocation must pass the twin tests of public interest and transparency to the fullest.

Though there has been considerable rhetoric, noise and letter writing on this subject, I believe the issue can be narrowed down to two simple questions and I wish to bring them to your attention as the issues that your government and the Minister of Communications will have to explain and defend-

a. What is the commercial value of this spectrum TODAY as estimated by the Government (that is being recovered from the Defence Ministry) and why is it that the Government and Ministry is levying charges for spectrum that were discovered through a tender process. 6 years ago in 2001? Is it not commonsense that these prices are not relevant today when almost all asset classes have appreciated significantly in value and cost over the last 6 years?

b. Why are license or Spectrum award process not following a tender route - a route adopted for all previous licenses and as well for FM license under this very government?

Unless the Government, Ministry of Communications and/or DOT have clear and defendable answers to these two questions, it would be easy for anyone to conclude that the process and terms being followed by the Government for the sale of spectrum are against the best interests of the country.

I have further researched this subject in detail in anticipation of a debate in Parliament and have detected many serious deviations in the working of the DOT vis a vis the Law and Policy. I will separately seek out answers for these as well.

I would urge you to seek answers for the two questions raised above urgently and I look forward to your response.

Yours truly,

RAJEEV CHANDRASEKHAR

**Dr. Manmohan Singh**
Hon'ble Prime Minister
Government of India

211 North Avenue, New Delhi-110001 India
Tel: + 91-11-23094044 Fax : + 91-11-23094042
E-mail: rajeev.c@nic.in

# SHIV SENA PARLIAMENTARY PARTY

126 (II), PARLIAMENT HOUSE, NEW DELHI - 110 001
TEL. : 011-23014453; TELEFAX : 011-23034913

Ref. No. : SS-1/GoI/2007 Date : 23.11.2007

Respected Prime Minister.

As you may be aware that the question of allocation of electromagnetic spectrum to specific mobile phone companies has been engaging Government's attention and new rules are being framed for the purpose. The existing and new licensees are apprehensive of new rules detrimental to their interest owing to scarcity of available spectrum.

The Cellular Operators Association of India (COAI), a GSM industry lobby said the excessive hike in subscriber numbers was being done with a single point agenda to choke and deprive the existing GSM operators of spectrum and to facilitate a priority entry of select players into GSM. An increase in the subscriber linkage by as much as 800 percent in the revised criteria that was reviewed only last year, indicates that the objective is not to ensure spectrum efficiency but rather to ensure spectrum deficiency for the existing GSM operators.

Also, the defence ministry is insisting on getting an alternate optic fiber network with built-in encryption ready for its forces before any spectrum can be vacated. The entire process of vacation of around 60 Mhz of spectrum (covering both 2G and 3 G) could take up to two years, according to estimates.

It has to be recalled that throughout the world incumbent operators were given the license first whereas in our case it was delayed because of them. As a result by the time MTNL lunched its cellular service competitors where already around six years ahead of MTNL. This resulted in loss of vast business opportunity to MTNL in terms of subscriber base and revenue.

**In order to put an end to the controversies raised by vested interest TRAI has taken a prudent view and recommended that allocation of spectrum be made by the process of auction. Also we understand that M/s STel Telecom and some others for allocation of spectrum at Rs. 6000 crore as entry fee. Similarly there may be other offers too.**

By the method of auction the public exchequer may earn Rupees Forty Thousand Crore or even more. This amount will go a long way to implement schemes for poverty alleviation and public services including infrastructure.

In view of the foregoing the Shiv Sena Parliamentary Party strongly recommend that allocation of spectrum be made by auction only. This will be a clean and fair method. We solicit the intervention Hon'ble Prime Minister in this important case in the public interest.

With kind regards,

Yours sincerely,

Manohar Joshi
**Leader: Rajya Sabha**

Anant G Geete
**Leader: Lok Sabha**

**The Hon'ble Prime Minister**
**Government of India**
**New Delhi.**

RAJEEV CHANDRASEKHAR
MEMBER OF PARLIAMENT
RAJYA SABHA

Member of Standing Committee on Information Technology
Member of Consultative Committee on Urban Development
Member of Parliamentary Forum on Youth

November 26, 2007

Dear Thiru Raja

Thank you very much for the letter No. 219/M (C&IT) VIP/2007 dated November 21, 2007 and your efforts at clarifying the position of the DoT and your Ministry.

Firstly let me thank you for reaffirming your commitment to transparency and an equitable approach to the issue of allocating spectrum. I believe this is an important meeting of minds.

Firstly, I unreservedly endorse your efforts at increasing competition – which is clearly a desirable public policy objective because it delivers significant consumer benefit and I further, support your Ministry's views on the need for an open and unfettered approach to auctions for 3G licenses and spectrum, despite the TRAIs obviously flawed approach of restricted auctions.

As you are aware, I have been advocating the need for such an auction even for the 2G spectrum that the Defence Ministry is releasing. It is now clear to me, however that - given the December 2005 guidelines for UASL and its clause 11 and more specifically the critical fact that the DoT has entered into contracts with a large number of licensees by accepting fees from them – that it may be impractical to introduce auctions for these licensees and applicants, therefore I will agree with your view that introducing auctions at this stage may lead to a breach of contract by DoT and consequential litigations – both of which are not desirable outcomes.

I therefore would be willing to dilute my demand for auctions and be supportive of the Ministry's efforts at using the December 2005 guidelines at allotting spectrum to licensees/applicants with the following conditions:

a. That the DoT will immediately amend the existing Policy and the 2005 guidelines to ensure that all future licenses/spectrum (after this round of licensing) shall only be through an open, transparent multi round bidding process.

211 North Avenue, New Delhi-110001 India
Tel: + 91-11-23094044 Fax : + 91-11-23094042
E-mail : rajeev.c@nic.in

सत्यमेव जयते

b. That additional licenses are issued for new licensees are issued without delay so that the competitive landscape is increased and consumers start benefiting from this with minimum delay.

Let me also through this letter urge you also to commence a comprehensive review of the TRAI Act. As you are aware, I have urged in Parliament that such a review is long overdue, because of the number of areas of weakness in the current act, both in terms of accountability of the TRAI to Parliament and its independence from the DoT. I hope you will agree to the request and initiate the same

Very truly yours,

RAJEEV CHANDRASEKHAR

**Thiru. A Raja**
Minister of Communications and Information Te
Government of India
New Delhi

**Copy to:** Hon'ble Prime Minister of India
This refers to my letter dated 14th November 2007 on the subject.

**DR MURLI MANOHAR JOSHI**
Member of Parliament (Rajya Sabha)
CHAIRMAN
Parliamentary Standing Committee
on Commerce

123, Parliament House Annexe
New Delhi- 110 001
Tel.: 23034123, 23011991

CONFIDENTIAL

December 2, 2007

Dear Dr Manmohan Singh Ji

Recently media has reported that leading MNCs operating in the telecom sector have launched a tirade against the allocation of spectrum to BSNL and MTNL by the Government. The telecom sector is very important from various dimensions.

First, the issue of ensuring teledensity in the rural sector and the hilly and other far flung areas as well, deserves utmost consideration. In order to make the communication facilities available to the villages it is of paramount importance that the Government takes speedy measures which unfortunately the MNCs generally neglect - they only concentrate in the urban and high profit areas. On the other hand the PSUs are mandated to fulfil the social obligations and have to make efforts in this direction which is not a high profit business.

The media have reported that some private operators have been given free of cost spectrum far in excess of their eligibility as per the licensing norms. Further, they do not have any social responsibility to fulfil. The media also report that after the announcement of the new policy by DOT, these private operators wish to prevent the growth of BSNL and MTNL by depriving them of spectrum, that they require. Some operators have suggested that spectrum should be auctioned which means that there could be a case of hording and cartelization to the detriment of MTNL and BSNL.

The issue was also raised in the Parliament where a number of MPs demanded enquiry into the whole matter of grabbing the spectrum by few monopolistic companies.

I have also come across reports in Indian Express which say that Dubai Ports World, Chinese companies, china's new forex reserve fund, Saudi Telecom and even Vodafone as "areas of potential threat to national security" in a confidential note prepared by the Government's Joint Intelligence Committee. I need not impress upon you that the advancements in ICT require a very careful and alert watch on the security problems both internal and external. The terrorist elements on the one hand and the investments of shady money in the highly sensitive and defence-related industries on the other can not and should not be overlooked in the name of the flow of investments. The expansion of such

6, Raisina Road, New Delhi-110001 Tel. : 23718444, 23711144. Fax : 23711772
"ANGIRAS" 9/10-A Tagore Nagar, Anukul Baaerji Road, Allahabad-211002

DR MURLI MANOHAR JOSHI
Member of Parliament (Rajya Sabha)
CHAIRMAN
Parliamentary Standing Committee
on Commerce

123, Parliament House Annexe
New Delhi-110 001
Tel.:23034123, 23011991

-2-

investments may jeopardize our national security interests. PSUs, therefore, can not be weakened and Government cannot ignore the security aspects.

I would, therefore, request you to protect the interests of our PSUs, and the interests of the genuine players. Perhaps this can be achieved by ensuring a level playing field through a licensing policy which earns revenue to the Government, unearths the excess spectrum being used without meeting social obligations and protects the interests of PSUs, allows new players and permits the allocation under a technology-neutral licence so long the operator is using the spectrum honestly and efficiently.

I do believe that this issue will receive your utmost and serious consideration.

With regards,

Yours sincerely,

(Murli Manohar Joshi)

Dr Manmohan Singh
Prime Minister of India
South Block
New Delhi-110 011

6, Raisina Road, New Delhi-110001 Tel.: 23718444, 23711144, Fax: 23711772
"ANGIRAS" 9/10-A Tagore Nagar, Anukul Banerji Road, Allahabad-211002

AMAR SINGH
MEMBER OF PARLIAMENT
(RAJYA SABHA)
NATIONAL GENERAL SECRETARY & SPOKESMAN
(SAMAJWADI PARTY)

सत्यमेव जयते

27, LODHI ESTATE,
NEW DELHI-110003
TEL. : 32565397 / 32542188 / 2461682
FAX : 91-11-24636299
Email : amarsingh@bol.net.in

December 03, 2007

Respected Manmohan Singhji -

To bring the nefarious activities of the dominant GSM operators like Airtel, Vodafone and Idea to the notice of Parliament and the Government, I had given notices for Calling Attention Motion and Short Duration Discussion. However, I am informed that due to paucity of time, these may not be taken up for discussion during the remaining Session. Hence this letter to you, Hon'ble Prime Minister.

As you are aware, these three companies are mostly foreign owned – Vodafone – 67%; Airtel – 35% by Singtel and another about 30% by FIIs; Idea – 40% by FIIs. Eventhough foreigners are holding substantial/majority equity in these companies, real foreign direct investment is minimal. These companies are holding the country to ransom to perpetuate their own monopolistic hold on the telecom economy.

I have had occasions to interact with many stakeholders, especially the state owned BSNL and MTNL who are doing a yeoman service to the populace across the country and also meet the responsibilities of social obligations.

I am very much concerned that these national companies – BSNL & MTNL – are being attacked by private interests in the GSM lobby, the Cellular Operators Association of India.

At the outset, it is to be noted that the dominant players in the GSM field have cornered to themselves 10 MHZ of spectrum across all circles. This is in clear violation of the licensing conditions which stipulate that each operator is entitled to get only 6.2 MHZ of spectrum.

These dominant operators have hoarded spectrum and it is estimated that they have about 58 MHZ with them illegally. In this process, country's exchequer has lost substantial revenue, estimated at more than Rs.10,000 Crores. The Government must order a CBI enquiry to fix responsibility and bring the culprits to book for obtaining this illegal allocation and consequent revenue loss to the exchequer.

Government must take steps to get this spectrum returned immediately and given to new licensees who have been waiting in queue for almost a year now after paying requisite fees.

2

India would not be the first country where existing operators are asked to return excess spectrum. Vodafone has been ordered by the UK regulator to return excess spectrum to be given to new licensees. Similar actions have taken place in US, Argentina, Chile, etc.

TRAI and TEC, who have technical capabilities second to none, have recommended that operators should demonstrate a certain number of subscribers within the allotted spectrum to seek additional spectrum. The dominant GSM operators are questioning the same for the sole purpose of retaining their hegemony.

For the sake of fair competition, consumer benefits in terms of lower tariff and better service, it is imperative that Government allows new players in the cellular mobile sector.

This will help Government to additional entry fee upto Rs.6500 Crores and in excess of Rs.20000 crores by way of indirect and direct taxes as the new operators roll out their networks.

I request you to kindly consider the above so that anti-competition, anti-consumer activities of these three companies are not allowed to continue.

**Thanking you**

**With** regards,

**Yours** Sincerely

**(AMAR SINGH)**

**Dr. Manmohan Singh**
**Hon'ble Prime Minister**
**Government of India**
**152, South Block**
**New Delhi**

**S.M.LALJAN BASHA**
MEMBER OF PARLIAMENT
(RAJYA SABHA)
CHAIRMAN
JOINT PARLIAMENTARY COMMITTEE
ON WAKF

सत्यमेव जयते

OFF. : 128, PARLIAMENT HOUSE ANNEXE,
NEW DELHI-110 001
TEL. : 23034898, 23015733

RES. : AB-15, MATHURA ROAD.
NEW DELHI-110 002
TEL. : 23782136
FAX : 23782116
E-MAIL : gbasha@sansad.nic.in

Sub: Hoarding of telecom spectrum by monopolies..

Dear Dr. Manmohan Singh ji Dec. 3, 207.

The entire country has learnt that telecom companies have hoarded spectrum, which is a national resource . Private Telecom Companies have cornered the entire Mobile sector . This is Crony Capitalism. Recently, you said that excess spectrum , held by telecom companies should be returned. I doubt whether TRAI or Telecom secretary can do it. Your office must take the initiative , as I doubt whether TRAI /Telecom Ministry can face the biggest /richest people in the world, who own the telecom sector.

In last 10 years, private telecom companies have earned huge amounts and the promoters are amongst world's richest people. Obviously, this means that they enjoy a monopoly & are fleecing the consumer.Only Mexico permits this situation and the world's richest man is a Mexican telecom operator. Mexico is not a good example for India.

I wonder whether the public controversy about spectrum hoarding is a mere "staged" fight . This controversy might be stage-managed. The controversy convinces everyone that there is rivalry. But in reality, we now hear of an "AMICABLE" settlement engineered by Ministry of Telecom. After a media fight, the Minister calls a meeting and everyone is happy.

The main effort of existing telecom companies is to ensure that no new entrants get into telecom. New entrants will reduce their super profits.

**Suggestions :**

a. Newcomers must be encouraged. Any newcomer should be able to start a telecom company and offer better rates .There should be no ban on entry . It should be an open sector .

Permanent Add. : "Bismillah Manzil", Mithila Nagar Colony, Road No. 12, Banjara Hills, Hyderabad-500034 (A.P.)

2

b. Presently, the entire telecom sector of India is being manipulated and controlled by 2 or at most 3 people. Government should ensure that telecom prices are not so high-priced. TRAI is doing nothing,

It is obvious that by hoarding Spectrum, the existing dominant players want to prevent future entries. They have plans for the next 25 years. If government wants to bring down service costs, then there should be free entry for new-comers.

Huge fortunes were made within 10 years. Such abnormal profits result only from monopoly situations. If government had ensured that there was competition, then such profits would not have been made.

The Indian consumer had paid more than is due. Please ensure that there is competition . The role of TRAI and its utility is now being publicly questioned.

With regards

Yours sincerely,

6.12.2007

**Laljan Basha S.M.**

**Dr. Manmohan Singh,**
Prime Minister ,
New Delhi.

# SHIV SENA PARLIAMENT PARTY

126 (II), PARLIAMENT HOUSE, NEW DELHI - 110 001
TEL. : 011-23014453; TELEFAX : 011-23034913

Ref. No. : SS-1/GI/2007 Date : 5.12.2007

**Hon'ble Prime Minister,**

**(Regarding; Spectrum allocation)**

Further to our letter dated 23rd November, certain new facts have come to our light and we would like to make some more suggestions for your consideration:

The DoT has appointed an expert committee consisting of Professors from IIT Chennai and Delhi to review the concerns of GSM as well as CDMA operators regarding spectrum allocation. The Government must ensure that independence of this committee is not compromised, nor the Committee pressurized by any lobby to adjust its findings / recommendations to suit any specific category of operators. Finally, the scientific and technically viable recommendations as made by Telecom Engineering Center (TEC) should be adopted by the Government for allocation of spectrum to all opretors.

It has also been brought to our notice that the TRAI has not recommended auction for 2G spectrum i.e. 800-900-1800 MHz and this view has also been accepted by DoT and GoI in order to create competition and a level playing field between all operators- new and old.

Accordingly, our view is the Government should go by existing policies, practices, and procedures and allocate spectrum and licenses on a non-discriminatory basis. The Government also must expeditiously issue instructions for the allocation of spectrum to all the applicants based on established guidelines to enhance number of players, increase competition and reduce tariffs in the interest of millions of consumers.

Further, in line with TRAI's recommendation, DoT must auction all available spectrums for both 3G and WIMAX, as and when available for allocation, through a transparent auction process which many well garner over Rs. 50,000 cr. in spectrum fees to the GoI.

We hope these suggesting will receive due consideration.

With regards, Yours Sincerely,

**(MANOHAR JOSHI)**
**Leader: Rajya Sabha**

**(ANANT G. GEETE)**
**Leader: Lok Sabha**

**Dr. Manmohan Singh**
**Hon'ble Prime Minister,**
**Government of India**
**New Delhi.**

[illegible]
MEMBER OF PARLIAMENT
(LOK SABHA)

[illegible]
Boat Club Road,
Chennai - 600 028.
Tel. : 24342545

Dec. 14th., 2007.

Dear Prime Minister,

I would like to congratulate you on your statement that the policy regime in the telecom sector for spectrum should be "fair, transparent and promote competition". I cannot agree with you more as the spectrum controversy is leading to undesirable politicisation.

To put your words into action, I request you to immediately direct the Group of Ministers that is looking into the spectrum issue to formulate ways and means in which the Government could auction Spectrum' even if it poses problems for existing GSM players and the new entrants. This would be in public interest and would fetch critical funds ( approx. Rs. 40,000 crores ) which could contribute to the Government's flagship programmes like NREGP and Bharath Nirman. It would also send the right signals to the whole world that the Indian Government is in favour of open competition and is opposed to crony capitalism. There are 49 new applicants who want to enter the telecom market and their entry is being stalled because of the scarce spectrum.

A view is being aired that the auction of 2G spectrum would cause legal hassles, so it would be better to auction 3G spectrum. To my mind, this is an attempt to save the status quo and prevent new players from entering the booming telecom market.

I fail to understand why the Government cannot arrange for the telecom companies to sit together and devise a transparent way by which the spectrum could be a) optimally utilized and b) and also allow new providers to come in, so as to ensure that the public get the best deal and service.

A firm and timely intervention by you would go a long way in reinforcing the view that the Government, under your leadership, is in favour of fair play, transparency and competition.

I request you to please take immediate action in the matter in greater national interest.

With Regards,

Sincerely yours,

( R. Prabhu )

Hon'ble Prime Minister of India,
South Block,
New Delhi.

CHANDRA SHEKHAR DUBEY
MEMBER OF PARLIAMENT
(LOK SABHA)

Member
Consultative Committee on Coal, Mines & Power
Standing Committee on Coal, Steel & Mines
Mineral Advisory Council, Govt. of India

सत्यमेव जयते

17, Canning Lane,
New Delhi - 110 001
Tel. : 011-23782090

December 26th, 2007

The Hon'ble Prime Minister of India,
South Block,
NEW DELHI

Respected Sir,

I have been patiently following the developments taking place in the area of Frequency/Spectrum allocation to various Cellular Operators. I have also read the news item which indicated that your good self have reservations about the whole matter and as a result the whole matter has now been referred to Group of Ministers.

It is interesting to note that the Panel, set up by the Government with representatives from Department of Telecom, Telecom Engineering Centre and representatives of various Cellular Operators, has also failed to come out with a viable solution to the ranging spectrum controversy. When every interested party, be it Bharti Mittal of Airtel, Ambani of Reliance Communication or Ratan Tata of Tatateleservices has their own interest in mind it is not surprising if the Panel failed to come up with a viable solution to the spectrum problem. Now, I understand, Bharti Airtel has committed to pay Rs.2650 crore for a Unified Access Services Licence, which is Rs.1000 crore more than the existing licence fee for a pan-India operation. I am sure, in due course of time, the other established players in the sector will come up with better offers. The best option available to the Government will be to auction the Spectrum.

In the midst of all these, my concern is about the Public Sector entities who are lagging behind in increasing their customer base and generating surpluses. Private Operators entered the field only two decades back whereas the Public Sector entities have been in fixed-line telecom business for a much longer period. Their entry into the Cellular services and subsequent performance are not very impressive. With their long standing experience in the telecom line, these PSUs should have been able to check the rise of private operators but this has not happened.

I have been apprised that Shri AK Srivastava, DDG(AS), DoT has been instrumental in causing loss to the Government exchequer to the tune of several thousand crores of rupees by supporting the flawed licensing policy of DoT of first come first serve and cross over technology UAS licenses to Reliance and Tata on the considerations of personal benefit which is adversely effecting the national interest and policy. It is also understood that the same has been done by the aforesaid Officer to please his big bosses for which he has been rewarded by the benefited telecom service providers.

There was another Official of TRAI who played a vital role in promoting the cross over technology licenses has been dubious and questionable. In particular there are officers like Mr Sudhir Gupta, Advisor, TRAI and some others who have worked to benefit cross over technology companies for garnering undue personal benefits. The coterie of officers is well entrenched in their functionalities and working on the same post for number of years now, should be transferred to their parent cadres without any second thought.

DHANBAD : Zila Parishad Campus, Bekar Bandh Dhanbad (Jharkhand) • Tel. : 0326-2223311 (R)
RESIDENCE : [illegible]

CHANDRA SHEKHAR DUBEY
MEMBER OF PARLIAMENT
(LOK SABHA)

17, Canning Lane,
New Delhi - 110 001
Tel. : 011-23782090

Member
Consultative Committee on Coal, Mines & Power
Standing Committee on Coal, Steel & Mines
Mineral Advisory Council, Govt. of India

*Now I understand there were nearly 600 new corporate applicants when it was announced recently that "pan-India" licences will be issued. If new entrants with practically no experience in telecom business are willing to invest their money and hope to recover it with profit, then why the Government entities cannot make enough profit? I am forced to think. Is it because of lack of vision in their top management, or is it due to rampant corruption? My feeling is that it could be only due to corruption in all echelons of the decision making ladder. If there is a healthy competition, whether in telecom sector or any other sector for that matter, the final beneficiary is the consumer. In the present case, the Public Sector entities are well placed to check the rise of private sector but till date these entities have failed to make any impact. It is time that the Government steps in and takes corrective measures to set things right in the telecom sector. To begin with an audit of the persons manning various key positions, whether in the Telecom Companies of the Government or the Government departments supervising and controlling the functions of these Companies, may be undertaken to identify those who have been in that position for a long time, say more than 5-6 years. They should be replaced with a fresh set of persons with enough qualifications and experience. No one should be allowed to stick to their key position for say more than 3 years. This, in my view, will help weeding out corruption to some extent.*

*Furthermore, I may appreciate if your good self may kindly intervene in the matter and take appropriate action on the following so as to curb all illegal malpractice which are prevailing under the Telecom Sector:*

1. *In the interest of National Security there must be surveillance to keep watch on the Private Cellular Operators for any mis-use of Frequency/Spectrum over & above from their existing allotment quota in the near future.*
2. *Action may be initiated to take back the excess Spectrum allotted to any Cellular Operator.*
3. *Without the connivance of the officials in Department of Telecom, Telecom Engineering Centre of TRAI, no Cellular Operator could have been allocated additional spectrum over the above the initial contracted 4.4. Mega Hertz. Officials responsible for throwing away the scarce national resource of Spectrum and deriving personal benefit out of it should be brought to books. Exemplary action be taken against them so that no Government Official, in future, should dare to put the National Exchequer to such huge losses.*
4. *Government must initiate steps to streamline and strengthen the functioning of BSNL and MTNL by infusing fresh blood at the top level. These Government Companies have all the necessary infrastructure to grow and meet the demands of customers. Corruption and laxity on the part of the present top management has brought about dismal performance of these Companies. They should be immediately replaced with honest, dedicated, qualified and experienced persons with right type of vision for the growth of these companies. I am sure once this step is taken, things will automatically improve.*

*With deepest regards,*

*Yours Sincerely,*

*(CHANDRA SHEKHAR DUBEY)*

DHANBAD : Zila Parishad Campus, Bekar Bandh Dhanbad (Jharkhand) • Tel. : 0326-2223311 (R)
RESIDENCE : [illegible] 377 & 378, [illegible]

S.M. LALJAN BASHA
MEMBER OF PARLIAMENT
(RAJYA SABHA)
CHAIRMAN
JOINT PARLIAMENTARY COMMITTEE
ON WAKF

सत्यमेव जयते

OFF. : 128, PARLIAMENT HOUSE ANNEXE,
NEW DELHI-110 001
TEL. : 23034898, 23015732

RES. : AB-15, MATHURA ROAD,
NEW DELHI-110 002
TEL. : 23782136
FAX : 23782116
E-MAIL : gbasha@sansad.nic.in

Sub: Telecom policies :

Dear Dr. Manmohan Singh ji

Feb. 17, 2008.

I had written earlier on the need to increase competition in the telecom sector. Now, what has emerged is that 3 or 4 telecom players control entire telecom sector. If you look 6 years down the line, it is obvious that there will be 3 major players in the country and no more.

An oligarchic situation or " **crony capitalism**" to quote you, has emerged because existing players have managed to fix rules, so that new entrants cannot enter. The threshold for new telecom entrants has been raised so high that no new company can come and offer cheaper services .Only **Take-Overs** can happen.

Kindly consider the following ;

a. To keep open telecom sector for new entrants and new technology?
b. How to reduce the threshold for new entrants ?

c. How to have an **"anytime policy"** for new entrants and not some vague and un-fixed time in the future ? Such an **anytime open policy** will keep the existing dominating telecom players alert and cautious .

d. To examine role of **TRAI** . There is a feeling in the country that TRAI is loyal to private telecom companies. Now and then , some symbolic noise is made. Nothing serious or spontaneous, but orchestrated to the tune of telecom companies. Even a simple demand to reduce nuisance calls / SMS messages by marketing companies was not done . The scheme for tackling marketing calls was designed to fail and it has failed . This purposeful sabotage was done so that telecom companies will not lose revenue.

e. **Spectrum policy :**
The country wants to know why no auction was done and why highest revenues were not obtained. There is no transparency in this matter. I request you to review the entire episode of spectrum allotment and sale.

2

f. **Excess spectrum :**

The country is aware that excessive spectrum has been hoarded by telecom companies. A natural resource has been cornered by a few companies. Actually, majority of shares of such companies are closely held . Hence , excessive spectrum has gone to some individuals.

The country wants to know whether this is what a free economy means. That some private companies make super-profits , in the name of competition, when no competition exists ..

g. **High price of phone calls :**

If you adjust price of Indian phone tariff with Purchasing Power Parity of Rupee, then our calls are very expensive. What telecom companies and TRAI are doing is to simply convert the present price of phone calls in India into dollar-terms and then say our calls are cheap.. When compared to incomes in India and Western countries, our calls are over-priced.

That is why telecom companies make profits of tens of thousands of crores every year.. They make super-profits at the expense of the public .It is estimated that our phone calls cost 7 times as much calls in the USA. **TRAI** has not done anything to bring down prices .TRAI is not regulating anything at all.

You frequently mention the virtues of competition and that a free economy is good for India . Then I request you to control and reduce the emerging monopolies which have already established themselves in the telecom sector, all in the name of free enterprise.

I hope you will initiate action before it is too late..
With regards

Yours sincerely,

16. 2. 2008

**Laljan Basha S.M.**

Dr. Manmohan Singh
Hon. Prime Minister,
Govt. of India
New Delhi.

CHANDRA SHEKHAR DUBEY
MEMBER OF PARLIAMENT
(LOK SABHA)
Member
Consultative Committee on Coal, Mines & Power
Standing Committee on Coal, Steel & Mines
Mineral Advisory Council, Govt. of India

सत्यमेव जयते

17, Canning Lane,
New Delhi - 110 001
Tel : 011-23782090

February 26th, 2008

The Hon'ble Prime Minister of India,
South Block,
NEW DELHI

Respected Sir,

This is in continuation to my earlier letter dated 26th, December, 2007 and once again I may like to bring to your kind attention towards the recommendations of TRAI permitted an existing licensee to obtain allocation of Spectrum for alternate technology on payment of entry fee Tanta mounting to grant of a New Licenses to the existing licensee jumping and bypassing the waiting list for New Licenses. This cross over technology license grant recommendation has been against the M&A Policy as well as the Government Norms wherein the same entity cannot have two licenses for the same services in a service area.

The recommendation of TRAI to grant new 2G licenses including the cross over technology license at the existing entry fee caused a tremendous loss to the Government exchequer to the tune of several thousand crores of rupees which Government would have earned had it been able and willing to auction the 2G spectrum to the aspirants for cross over technology licenses as well as new licenses. There are number of operators/new entrants on public record offering payment of higher entry fee for the 2G spectrum. However, TRAI under MR. Sudhir Gupta failed to take in to account the publicly demonstrated market price for entry into the mobile services sector of the country while issuing these recommendations. It is not TRAI was not aware of the mechanism of auction which it had recommended for the 3G Spectrum as well as Broadband Spectrum. The issue of level playing field between the existing licenses and the new licensees as an excuse will also not work as policy decisions of the Government do change the terms and conditions for a new licensee without causing any prejudice to it.

CHANDRA SHEKHAR DUBEY
MEMBER OF PARLIAMENT
(LOK SABHA)

Member
· Consultative Committee on Coal, Mines & Power
Standing Committee on Coal, Steel & Mines
Mineral Advisory Council, Govt. of India

17, Canning Lane,
New Delhi - 110 001
Tel. : 011-23782090

In my opinion, the inter se priority for Spectrum allocation was deliberately kept vague in the recommendation so that it can be manipulated further.

It is also pertinent to mention here that the recommendations of TRAI to regularise the allocation of Spectrum above the contracted amount of 4.4GHz without charging commensurate one time entry fee charges for the same is without any sound rationale and basis. The same has been purportedly done on the basis of not been legally feasible and in the name of penetration in rural areas which are not tenable arguments for the reason that there is no shortage of Spectrum in rural areas and no opinion from Ministry of Law was taken in respect of legal feasibility of the imposition of additional entry fee for the Spectrum beyond the contracted amount.

But nevertheless the dubious role of two Officials of TRAI i.e. Shri Sudhir Gupta, Advisor & Shri AK Srivastava DDG Access Services (AS) DoT are making some doubts in my mind about their wholly nexuses with private operators. Shri Sudhir Gupta, Advisor has been working in TRAI on deputation from DoT since last about four years and is IN-CHARGE of Mobile Network Division in TRAI. Prior to that he has been working MTNL Delhi for about more than 10 years. Thus his total stay in Delhi is more than 14 years working in a cadre (ITS) and managed his post at same station which is spread all over the country. It appears that he was the key person involved in framing of the flawed recommendations of the TRAI in respect of the vexed issue of Spectrum. He has been close to several Telecom Operators as I mentioned above including those who got benefited from the cross over Technology License recommendations. Shri Gupta for his pliable attitude has been awarded record number of foreign trips abroad during last two years. I have been apprised that Shri Gupta is the officer responsible for creating chaos in the telecom sector by framing the recommendations in respect of Spectrum allocation and cross over technology.

In the light of above, I shall be highly obliged if your good self may kindly intervene in the matter and advised the Ministry of Information & Technology to initiate in depth enquiry into the matte but in the first instance Shri Sudhir Gupta, Advisor and Shri AK Srivastava DDG Access Services (AS) DoT should be transferred immediately.

With deepest regards,

Yours Sincerely,

(CHANDRA SHEKHAR DUBEY)

DHANBAD : Zila Parishad Campus, Bekar Bandh Dhanbad (Jharkhand)

AMAR SINGH
MEMBER OF PARLIAMENT
(RAJYA SABHA)
NATIONAL GENERAL SECRETARY & SPOKESMAN
(SAMAJWADI PARTY)

सत्यमेव जयते

27, LODHI ESTATE,
NEW DELHI-110003
TEL. : 32565397 / 32542188 / 24616827
FAX : 91-11-24636299
Email : amarsingh@bol.net.in

**July 11, 2008**

Respected Manmohan Singhji,

**Subject: Pricing and Spectrum Allocation Policy – Measures to raise additional revenue of over Rs.18000 Crores from the Telecom Sector**

Further to my letter of 2nd July 2008 on the above subject, I would like to bring to your attention the following for discussions so that issues do not get buried and decision taken in a hurry thus losing thousands of crores potential revenue from the booming Telecom Sector.

It may be recalled that pursuant to the New Telecom Policy, private firms were allowed to offer Mobile services for which a basic 4.4 Mhz spectrum was allocated to every successful firm in each circle. At the relevant period, the objective of the Government was to introduce wireless telephone services as a superior hi-technology, value rich option to supplement wireline services. Naturally, the expectations were guarded while awaiting the results from the new and fledgling area.

The introduction of mobile services with its attendant simplicity in terms of rollout and superior technical characteristics took on an unexpected turn towards mass proliferation in the process leaving behind fixed line services. Currently, the country is witnessing an unprecedented growth in this area at internationally unsurpassed rate. Some time in the year 2003-04, the government notified the universal access service license, which was an omnibus license bundled with 4.4 Mhz spectrum, to be raised till 6.2. Mhz based on compliance of certain norms.

The spectrum availability in 2003-04 was still manageable and presumably a distinction between the available bandwidth in 900 Mhz and 1800 Mhz was [illegible] of resulting in [illegible]

AMAR SINGH
MEMBER OF PARLIAMENT
(RAJYA SABHA)
NATIONAL GENERAL SECRETARY & SPOKESMAN
(SAMAJWADI PARTY)

27, LODHI ESTATE,
NEW DELHI-110003
TEL. · 32565397 / 32542188 / 24616827
FAX : 91-11-24636299
Email : amarsingh@bol.net.in

spectrum in both these bands with same conditions in the licence agreement. As the users increased phenomenally along with more service providers, the availability of spectrum became the core issue. Now there was need to not only price the allocation of spectrum on market determined supply demand conditions but also make a distinction between 900 Mhz and 1800 Mhz since the former is capex and opex efficient.

However, without considering these crucial factors, further spectrum beyond 6.2 Mhz was allocated to several service providers. The need for levying a market defined price for additional spectrum allotted beyond 6.2 Mhz was neither taken up nor the constraint provided in the licence agreement of a maxium limit of 6.2 Mhz was adhered to.

In the above background, DOT on pursuation from MOF and other governmental regulating and monitoring agencies has belatedly woken up to the need for realizing the 'one time' charges for the extra spectrum allocation. It is well appreciated that spectrum is a 'scarce' item and government world over generally try to obtain the highest value for it commensurate with its earning potential. The Gross revenue in the telecom sector in 2007-08 was well over Rs. 70000 crores and is likely to only increase further with greater penetration in rural areas. It is well known that the rural teledensity is less than 10% and hence the potential in the sector is enormous. If the required expansion in rural services is reckoned with the appalling shortage of spectrum availability, the inference is plain. The spectrum is too valuable to be priced at historical cost. The pricing of spectrum based on the entry represents historical cost and application of such a method would permanently bind the Government for all times to come to the original cost which has no correlation to the current value of the spectrum.

It is in the above background that there is need for the government to tread spectrum pricing cautiously while avoiding all pitfalls on account of inadequate pricing. The preferred method is 'Auction' but the additional spectrum allocation having become 'fait accompli',

AMAR SINGH
MEMBER OF PARLIAMENT
(RAJYA SABHA)
NATIONAL GENERAL SECRETARY & SPOKESMAN
(SAMAJWADI PARTY)

27, LODHI ESTATE,
NEW DELHI-110003
TEL. · 32565397 / 32542188 / 24616827
FAX : 91-11-24636299
Email : amarsingh@bol.net.in

there is need to look at the next best alternative. The idea of correlating the spectrum price to its earning potential comes immediately to mind and has parallels in other areas of economy. The relationship is obvious to every one and is understood easily besides being simple to evaluate. Thus pricing the spectrum based on the ratio between the current AGR being the monetary equivalent of earning potential and the AGR at the relevant time would provide an elegant and accurate method of fixing the price for additional spectrum allocated.

There can be a number of other methods like updation of historical cost per MHz with PLR and its variants or use of other parameters like GDP to index the cost of spectrum. These methods do not provide the correct valuation of spectrum over time. The PLR method suffers from a serious drawback in that it only relies on historical cost as its basis and therefore fails to 'value' the spectrum for its scarcity and today's earning potential. The PLR is only an interest for not collecting the money at the appropriate time and is not a valuation procedure.

For similar reasons the GDP cannot be the index for valuation of spectrum since the growth in GDP does not proportionately reflect the growth in the telecom sector.

Ideally, the indexation method must factor in the supply-demand characteristics of the spectrum for its scarcity and the potential for increasing revenue generation on a continued basis for every megahertz of additional spectrum allocation. Thus there is need to recognize the synergies in revenue generation with increasing spectrum allocation. Both these factors are captured in the AGR being the revenue generated out of spectrum. The Gross revenue of service provider represents the culmination of direct revenues as a result of spectrum utilization and indirect revenues depending entirely on spectrum and its usage, through increased sale of mobile accessories and related items.

AMAR SINGH
MEMBER OF PARLIAMENT
(RAJYA SABHA)
NATIONAL GENERAL SECRETARY & SPOKESMAN
(SAMAJWADI PARTY)

27, LODHI ESTATE,
NEW DELHI-110003
TEL. : 32565397 / 32542188 / 2461682
FAX : 91-11-24636299
Email : amarsingh@bol.net.in

The phenomenal growth in telecom and IT usage has led to a worldwide scramble for the limited spectrum still available for allocation. This has spurred a universal effort in introducing spread-spectrum on efficient usage of spectrum technologies to improve the output from spectrum. While technologies can be invented, there is need to implement them by the users. Since any introduction of newer technologies has an associated cost, there would generally be reluctance on the part of operators to adopt them. Hence, the need for a regulatory framework, in the form of incentives and disincentives. As a corollary to the aforesaid discussion it would be argued that to make the service providers move towards more efficient usage of spectrum, disincentive in the form of a higher indexation than AGR should be thought of. While the AGR approach has merits, considering the environment in our country with its proliferating number of service providers with increasingly scarce spectrum availability, the need to factor in an incentive for lower spectrum usage or conversely a disincentive against higher spectrum usage in the form of a multiple equivalent of the AGR growth would adequately 'value' the spectrum and address the concerns on its optimal usage. **The price of spectrum of Rs. 375 Crores per MHz discovered on the basis of license fees and indexing it with the AGR growth during the relevant period comes to about Rs. 1300 Crores per MHz. This should make the basis of charging the excess spectrum held by the telecom service providers beyond the contracted value of 6.2 Mhz.**

It may be noted that there are a minimum of 10 service providers in each and every service area of the country. This provides the consumers sufficient choice as well as puts lot of competitive pressure on the telecom service providers to keep their tariffs low.

I also understand that the DoT is looking into the reduction in Mobile Termination charges. This initiative, when implemented will further bring down tariffs. I am certain that the telecom tariffs which are already one of the lowest in the world will continue to go down further, as has happened in past too.

AMAR SINGH
MEMBER OF PARLIAMENT
(RAJYA SABHA)
NATIONAL GENERAL SECRETARY & SPOKESMAN
(SAMAJWADI PARTY)

सत्यमेव जयते

27, LODHI ESTATE,
NEW DELHI-110003
TEL. : 32565397 / 32542188 / 2461682
FAX : 91-11-24636299
Email : amarsingh@bol.net.in

I will also like to highlight that both the Government operators i.e. BSNL and MTNL are having about 2 to 3 MHz of excess spectrum throughout the country, which is not being fully utilized. We are here to protect, preserve and promote both the PSUs. These PSUs may be asked to consider the option to return the excess spectrum so that no additional burden is passed on to them. The spectrum so returned by BSNL/MTNL can be allotted to the telecom service providers awaiting grant of additional spectrum or the initial spectrum. **This would fetch another Rs. 3000 Crores to the Government.**

**I am sure if the Government analyses and adopts the measures outlined above (i.e. to levy one time charge for spectrum allotted in excess of 6.2 MHz @ Rs. 1300 Crores per MHz), there will be additional revenue generation of over Rs.18000 Crores from the Telecom Service Providers.**

**Thanking you**

**With** regards

**Yours** affectionately
Amar Singh

**(Amar Singh)**

**Dr. Manmohan Singh**
**Hon'ble Prime Minister of India**
**Government of India**
**152 South Block**
**New Delhi**

AMAR SINGH
MEMBER OF PARLIAMENT
(RAJYA SABHA)
NATIONAL GENERAL SECRETARY & SPOKESMAN
(SAMAJWADI PARTY)

सत्यमेव जयते

27, LODHI ESTATE,
NEW DELHI-110003
TEL. : 32565397 / 32542188 / 2461682
FAX : 91-11-24636299
Email : amarsingh@bol.net.in

Dr. Manmohan Singh
Hon'ble Prime Minister of India
South Block
New Delhi.

**Sub: Maximizing government revenue by charging excess spectrum usage by telecom players**

Respected Manmohan Singhji,

This is further to my letters dated 2nd July, 2008 and 11th July 2008 regarding raising nearly Rs. 18,000 crores by levying charges on the various private telecom service providers for the excess spectrum being used by them over and above their licence conditions.

The table below is a brief reflection of the extra spectrum over 6.2MHz which has been hoarded by the private cellular operators completely free of cost.

| Service provider | Extra over 6.2 MHz. |
|---|---|
| Aircel | 6.0 |
| Airtel | 21.4 |
| Vodafone | 20.4 |
| Idea | 12.6 |

(a) It is completely evident that such huge hoarding of extra spectrum is tantamount to a criminal waste of extremely scarce and expensive resources by the private players like Airtel, Vodafone and others.

(b) Media reports speak of government plans to charge this extra spectrum. Separate reports also state that the DOT under due pressure from GSM players like Airtel and Vodafone is considering taking a very lenient approach in fixing the costs of additional spectrum.

(c ) I firmly reiterate that your intervention in this issue is critical for two reasons:

Upholding the fairness and transparency, no decision should be taken that would lead to a huge scam especially when it saves thousands of crores for private operators like

AMAR SINGH
MEMBER OF PARLIAMENT
(RAJYA SABHA)
NATIONAL GENERAL SECRETARY & SPOKESMAN
(SAMAJWADI PARTY)

27, LODHI ESTATE,
NEW DELHI-110003
TEL. : 32565397 / 32542188 / 2461682
FAX : 91-11-24636299
Email : amarsingh@bol.net.in

Airtel and Vodafone who have been wrongfully hoarding this spectrum bereft of any payment of fees.

The costing of spectrum should be done with complete economic prudence maximizing the revenue interests of the government exchequer instead of the interests of private operators who have been enjoying this free spectrum all these years.

Consequent to the above, I hereby propose the levy of a one time spectrum charge at the rate of Rs 375 crores per MHz and index it with AGR growth between 2003 and 2008 ( in multiples of 3.5). In addition spectrum charges should be increased by 2% beyond 6.2 Mhz instead of 8MHz .

**Thanking you**

**With** regards.

**Yours** affectionately,

Amar Singh

**(AMAR SINGH)**

AMAR SINGH
MEMBER OF PARLIAMENT
(RAJYA SABHA)
NATIONAL GENERAL SECRETARY & SPOKESMAN
(SAMAJWADI PARTY)

27, LODHI ESTATE,
NEW DELHI-110003
TEL. : 32565397 / 32542188 / 2461682
FAX : 91-11-24636299
Email : amarsingh@bol.net.in

सत्यमेव जयते

August 22, 2008

Respected Manmohan Singh ji,

**Subject: Pricing and Spectrum Allocation Policy – Measures to raise additional revenue of over Rs.18000 crores from the Telecom Sector**

This is further to my letters dated 2nd July'08, 11th July'08 and 25th July'08 regarding the charging for the extra spectrum over 6.2 MHz allotted to the private cellular operators completely free of cost over and above their license conditions.

I had also suggested adopting a stricter spectrum usage charge of 2% per MHz beyond the 6.2 MHz. These measures would raise additional revenue of Rs.15000 – Rs.18000 crores from the telecom sector which I had detailed in my earlier letters. I now read from the numerous media reports that the DoT is rejecting the suggested methodology of computing the one time spectrum charge payable by the GSM players and also quantum of additional levy on the recurring spectrum usage charges, on the premise that it could land the government in court and that it needs to be sustainable and acceptable to the industry players.

There is clearly more to it than meets the eye, as this seems to be a part of a grand design to price the spectrum in a lenient manner to benefit certain dominant private operators – Airtel, Vodafone and Idea Cellular.

I would like to draw your attention first to the fact that the spectrum which is a scarce national resource, has been allocated since 2002 in an arbitrary manner without policy framework till March'06. Post 2006, the allocation was based on the policy guidelines which was designed with extremely lenient criteria. This has been a part of a grand design allowing spectrum to be hoarded by Airtel, Vodafone and Idea Cellular; while at the same time citing unavailability of spectrum for many years, at the behest of these operators, for any new licenses which could have been introduced in the industry.

The TRAI and DoT corrected the anomaly by revising the spectrum allocation criteria in January 2008 incorporating substantial tightening of norms and has since allotted start-up spectrum of 4.4 MHz to over 70 new circle licenses.

AMAR SINGH
MEMBER OF PARLIAMENT
(RAJYA SABHA)
NATIONAL GENERAL SECRETARY & SPOKESMAN
(SAMAJWADI PARTY)

सत्यमेव जयते

27, LODHI ESTATE,
NEW DELHI-110003
TEL. : 32565397 / 32542188 / 2461682
FAX : 91-11-24636299
Email : amarsingh@bol.net.in

It now seems from the media reports that the DoT is intending to adopt lenient pricing of spectrum at the behest of these operators.

I had recommended a one time per MHz charge beyond 6.2 MHz being determined based on the entry free of Rs.1650 crores and start-up spectrum allocation of 4.4 MHz with this entry fee. Thus, the per MHz price derived is a division of Rs.1650 crores by 4.4 MHz, i.e., Rs.375 crores per MHz. The media reports states that the DoT is determining the unit price as Rs.1650 crores entry fee divided by 6.2 MHz and not 4.4 MHz. The reasons provided are that the license provides for spectrum upto 6.2 MHz and it is the only way of determining the per MHz price. Also, the appropriate indexation being the Prime lending rate which takes care of the time value of money.

I am surprised as the entry fee entitles the operator for initial start-up spectrum of 4.4 MHz and not 6.2 MHz and the allocation of additional spectrum beyond start-up spectrum is on meeting the subscriber criteria. Over 70 start-up spectrum allocations in the circles this year also has been 4.4 MHz in GSM and not 6.2 MHz.

The indexation method based on PLR has serious drawbacks and fails to value the scarcity of spectrum for its earning potential today. I am surprised that the AGR, which was even recommended by the Ministry of Finance, has been reported to not being adopted, whereas it captures the maximum revenue for the government and represents the culmination of direct revenue as a result of spectrum utilization.

I do not understand the political and economic compulsions for the government to adopt the appropriate spectrum charges and letting go the opportunity to maximize revenue. This kind of move is intended to benefit Airtel, and Vodafone between Rs.1800 to Rs.2000 crores and Idea Cellular of Rs.700 crores.

On the subject of levying additional spectrum usage charge, I had recommended stricter norms of **2% per MHz** which will result in estimated revenue of Rs.5000 crores – incremental revenue of Rs.2000 crores in 2008-09. As per the media reports I read that the DoT is suggesting a 1% increase across the board as a large part of the revenue is provided by spectrum upto 6.2 MHz. This again seems to be clearly a grand design which will hit the new entrants the hardest as they would need to pay an increased charge of 50% for the start-up spectrum allocated. Also, this method of increase is a clear weakness of not supporting spectral efficiency as the per MHz charges (a % of AGR) reduces as the MHz

AMAR SINGH
MEMBER OF PARLIAMENT
(RAJYA SABHA)
NATIONAL GENERAL SECRETARY & SPOKESMAN
(SAMAJWADI PARTY)

सत्यमेव जयते

27, LODHI ESTATE,
NEW DELHI-110003
TEL. : 32565397 / 32542188 / 2461685
FAX : 91-11-24636299
Email : amarsingh@bol.net.in

allocation increases. And the increase is higher at lower spectrum allocation and is lower at higher spectrum allocation of 7 – 8 MHz band, where these private operators hold most of the spectrum in the circles.

The table below is a brief reflection of the proposed charges which is totally lopsided.

**The increased charges proposed up to Contracted Spectrum**

| GSM | Rates current | trai | proposed | Per MHz | Increase |
|---|---|---|---|---|---|
| 4.4 | 2% | 2% | 3% | 0.68% | 50% |
| 6.2 | 3% | 3% | 4% | 0.65% | 33% |
| CDMA | | | | | |
| | 2% | 2% | 3% | 1.20% | 50% |
| 3.75 | 2% | 2% | 3% | 0.80% | 50% |
| 5 | 2% | 2% | 3% | 0.60% | 50% |

The increase up to Contracted spectrum has weaknesses, primarily:

- ☐ It skews the level playing field as the new entrants are hit the hardest as they would need to pay increased charges.
- ☐ The Increase for GSM operators is 33% almost all the existing GSM operators have 6.2 MHz and beyond (except new operators with start-up spectrum of 4.4 MHz) whereas the increase for CDMA operators is 50%.

**Spectrum Charges beyond contracted spectrum of 6.2 MHz in GSM**

| GSM | Rates current | trai | proposed | Per MHz | Increase |
|---|---|---|---|---|---|
| 4.4 | 2% | 2% | 3% | 0.68% | 50% |
| 6.2 | 3% | 3% | 4% | 0.65% | 33% |
| 7.2 | 4% | 4% | 5% | 0.69% | 25% |
| 8 | 4% | 4% | 5% | 0.63% | 25% |
| 8.2 | 4% | 5% | 5% | 0.61% | 25% |
| 9.2 | 4% | 5% | 6% | 0.65% | 50% |
| 10 | 4% | 5% | 6% | 0.60% | 50% |
| 10.2 | 5% | 6% | 6% | 0.59% | 20% |
| 11.2 | 5% | 6% | 7% | 0.63% | 40% |
| 12.2 | 5% | 6% | 7% | 0.57% | 40% |
| 13.2 | 6% | 7% | 8% | 0.61% | 33% |
| 14.2 | 6% | 7% | 8% | 0.56% | 33% |
| 15.2 | not defined | 8% | 9% | 0.59% | |

The above increase has weaknesses, primarily:

- ☐ Per MHz charges (As % of AGR) reduces as MHz allocation increases. This does not support spectral efficiency.
- ☐ The increase is higher at lower spectrum allocation and is lower at higher spectrum allocation of 7 to 8 MHz band where most private operators hold spectrum.
- ☐ This also does not support the objectives of promoting spectral efficiency.

AMAR SINGH
MEMBER OF PARLIAMENT
(RAJYA SABHA)
NATIONAL GENERAL SECRETARY & SPOKESMAN
(SAMAJWADI PARTY)

सत्यमेव जयते

27, LODHI ESTATE,
NEW DELHI-110003
TEL. : 32565397 / 32542188 / 2461682
FAX : 91-11-24636299
Email : amarsingh@bol.net.in

The media reports state that The DoT is under huge pressure from Airtel, Vodafone and Idea Celluar and thereby taking a lenient approach.

Your intervention in this issue is critical for fairness and transparency and ensuring no decision should be taken that would lead to a huge scam when it benefits thousands of crores for operators like Airtel, Vodafone and Idea Cellular who have been hoarding the spectrum bereft of any payment of fees. The costing for spectrum should be done with complete economic prudence maximizing the revenue interest of the government exchequer.

**I urge the government to adopt the measures to:**

- **Price spectrum beyond 6.2 MHz on the basis of Rs.375 crores per MHz on the basis of the entry license fee and index it with the AGR growth during relevant period which comes to about Rs.1300 crores per MHz.**
- **Also increase the additional spectrum usage charges of 2% per MHz beyond 6.2 MHz**

The Government should not succumb to the pressure of the private GSM operators by adopting lenient and inappropriate spectrum pricing.

**Thanking you**

**With** regards

**Yours** affectionately,
Amar Singh

**(Amar Singh)**

**Dr. Manmohan Singh**
**Hon'ble Prime Minister**
**Government of India**
**152, South Block**
**New Delhi**

**AMAR SINGH**
MEMBER OF PARLIAMENT
(RAJYA SABHA)
NATIONAL GENERAL SECRETARY & SPOKESMAN
(SAMAJWADI PARTY)

27, LODHI ESTATE,
NEW DELHI-110003
TEL. : 32565397 / 32542188 / 2461682
FAX : 91-11-24636299
Email : amarsingh@bol.net.in

August 22, 2008

Respected Manmohan Singhji,

**Subject: Loss of Over Rs. 40,000 crores Revenue to the Government due to Spectrum Hoarding & Policy Issues**

It has been brought to my notice that Spectrum, which is a scarce and national resource, has been allocated since 2002 in an arbitrary manner, first without a policy framework till March 2006 and post 2006, based on policy guidelines which was designed with extremely lenient criteria leading to hoarding of this resource by certain dominant private operators Airtel, Vodafone & Idea Cellular. This has been a part of a grand design to allow spectrum to be allocated in an arbitrary and inefficient manner to these private dominant operators, while at the same time citing non availability of spectrum for many years at the behest of these operators for any new licenses which could have been introduced in the industry.

This manner of allocation has lead to revenue loss to the Government of over Rs 40,000 crores and simultaneously resulted in abnormal super profits to the private GSM operators by avoiding a large capital Cost and Operating expenditure using spectrum as a proxy to deploying Capex. The private operators, Airtel, Vodafone and Idea Cellular in this period managed to get spectrum of over 50 MHz across circles allocated, which was beyond contracted Spectrum of 6.2 MHz under their license also. This allocation has been made without payment of any Spectrum fee except for a token increase in Spectrum usage charges and does not reflect in any way the economic cost of the additional spectrum.

This has promoted the narrow and vested interests of a section of the telecom industry and has been anti consumer, anti competitive by not allowing increased competition citing scarcity, non availability of spectrum. These actions prevented entry of new players, curtailing competition in the sector and lead to the dominance and oligopoly situation of these private operators acting in tandem.

**Allocation up to March 2006 has been allocated without a policy framework to then existing operators.**

1. The Start up Spectrum in GSM allows 4.4 MHz spectrum allotment. There is no policy for Spectrum allocation beyond 4.4 MHz and the order dated

AMAR SINGH
MEMBER OF PARLIAMENT
(RAJYA SABHA)
NATIONAL GENERAL SECRETARY & SPOKESMAN
(SAMAJWADI PARTY)

27, LODHI ESTATE,
NEW DELHI-110003
TEL. : 32565397 / 32542188 / 2461682
FAX : 91-11-24636299
Email : amarsingh@bol.net.in

too beyond 6.2 MHz i.e from 6.2 MHz to 8 MHz. However, there are eleven instances of allotment of 6.2 MHz without a policy framework prior to 1st Feb 2002. The fact is that the criteria for moving from 4.4 MHz to 6.2 MHz was specified only in March 06. The details of this allotment is given below :

**List of operators who were allotted 6.2 MHz spectrum before 1.2.2002, without policy framework**

| S.No. | Licensee name at the time of allocation | Licensee name as of now | Service area | Date w.e.f. |
|---|---|---|---|---|
| 1 | Aircel Digilink India Ltd | Vodafone | Haryana | Jan-01 |
| 2 | Aircell Digilink India Ltd | Vodafone | Rajasthan | Jan-01 |
| 3 | Aircel Digilink India Ltd | Vodafone | UP(East) | Jan-01 |
| 4 | Bharti Cellular Ltd | Bharti Cellular Ltd | AP | Apr-00 |
| 5 | Bharti Cellular Ltd | Bharti Cellular Ltd | Chennai | Aug-99 |
| 6 | Bharti Cellular Ltd | Bharti Cellular Ltd | Delhi | Aug-99 |
| 7 | Bharti Cellular Ltd | Bharti Cellular Ltd | Karnataka | Apr-00 |
| 8 | BPL Cellular Ltd | BPL | Mumbai | Aug-99 |
| 9 | RPG Cellular Ltd | Aircel Ltd | Chennai | Mar-00 |
| 10 | Spice Comm Ltd | Spice Comm Ltd | Karnataka | Apr-00 |
| 11 | Spice Comm Ltd | Spice Comm Ltd | Punjab | Apr-00 |

2. In this period, the Allocation of Spectrum of 10 MHz has also been done without any policy framework. Up to March 2006, there were absolutely no subscriber linkage criteria for allotment of spectrum up to 10 MHz, but there are nine instances where operators have been allocated 10 MHz spectrum in the period July 03 to January 06. The details of this allotment is given below:

**List of operators who were allotted 10 MHz spectrum prior to March 2006, without policy framework**

| S.No. | Licensee name at the time of allocation | Licensee name as of now | Service area | Date w.e.f. |
|---|---|---|---|---|
| 1 | Aircel Ltd | Aircel Ltd | Tamil Nadu | Dec-04 |
| 2 | Bharti Cellular Ltd | Bharti Cellular Ltd | Delhi | Jul-03 |
| 3 | BPL Cellular Ltd | BPL Cellular Ltd | Mumbai | Sept-04 |
| 4 | Hutchison Essar Telecom | Vodafone | Delhi | Oct-03 |
| 5 | Hutchison Essar Telecom | Vodafone | Mumbai | Oct-03 |
| 6 | Bharti Cellular Ltd | Bharti Cellular Ltd | Mumbai | Jan-06 |
| 7 | Bharti Cellular Ltd | Bharti Cellular Ltd | Karnataka | Jan-04 |
| 8 | Fascel Ltd | Vodafone | Gujarat | May-05 |
| 9 | Idea Cellular Ltd | Idea Cellular Ltd | Maharashtra | Apr-04 |

3. Operators have also been allocated Start up Spectrum of 6.2 MHz instead of the allowed 4.4 MHz without any Policy framework.

**The March 06 guidelines for spectrum allocation beyond the contracted spectrum of 6.2 MHz based on a subscriber criteria was by design kept lenient allowing inefficient allocation and hoarding. Additionally, New operator licenses were not considered, citing Spectrum non-availability when it was available in abundance**

1. The dominant private GSM operators were able to serve 3-5 times of number of subscribers than what the criteria prescribed. They also added 150 million new subscribers without allocation of substantial additional

AMAR SINGH
MEMBER OF PARLIAMENT
(RAJYA SABHA)
NATIONAL GENERAL SECRETARY & SPOKESMAN
(SAMAJWADI PARTY)

27, LODHI ESTATE,
NEW DELHI-110003
TEL. : 32565397 / 32542188 / 24616
FAX : 91-11-24636299
Email : amarsingh@bol.net.in

spectrum clearly proving Inefficiency of the Spectrum allocation guidelines

2. This was finally reviewed by TRAI, TEC then DOT issued revised spectrum allocation criteria in January 08 incorporating substantial tightening of the norms.

| | Subscriber Norms for allocation in Millions | | | | | |
|---|---|---|---|---|---|---|
| | 8 / 8.2 MHz | | 10 / 10.2 MHz | | 8/ 8.2 MHz Increase | 10 / 10.2 MHz Increase |
| | Mar 06 Norms | Jan 08 norms | Mar 06 Norms | Jan 08 norms | | |
| Metros Delhi/Mumbai | 0.6 | 1.8 | 1 | 2.6 | 3.0 | 2.6 |
| [illegible] | 0.8 | 4.1 | 1.4 | 6.8 | 5.1 | 4.9 |
| [illegible] | 0.6 | 4.1 | 1 | 6.8 | 6.8 | 6.8 |
| [illegible] | 0.4 | 3.1 | 0.6 | 5.2 | 7.8 | 8.7 |

The subscriber allocation norms were finally tightened 2.5 to over 8 times as shown above, clearly proving the earlier norms being very lenient and also inefficient guidelines of March 06.

With this, Government corrected the anomaly of spectrum hoarding and inefficient allocation.

3. TRAI and DOT post correcting the anomaly of spectrum hoarding and anticompetitive practice through revised guidelines, also declared that no cap is there in terms of number of players as well as permitting allocation of Cross Technology Spectrum under same license.

4. Since January 2008, DOT has now allocated Start up Spectrum to Vodafone (7 circles), Idea Cellular (5circles), Aircel (14 circles), Reliance Communications (14 circles), Unitech (5 circles), Datacom (5 circles), Tata's (5 circles), Swan (13 circles), Stel (1 circle) , Loop Telecom (5 Circles)

**The key question is where did the startup spectrum which was declared 'not available' come from?** Also, spectrum has been allocated to the existing operators using an inefficient policy framework.

All the above actions, I understand, is a part of a large conspiracy to safeguard the interest of the existing dominant GSM payers with the involvement of some

Permanent Address : E-593, GREATER KAILASH - II, NEW DELHI - 110048 Phone : 29226507 / 29225377
OFFICE : 8, SOUTH AVENUE, NEW DELHI - 110011 PHONE : 23792324 / 23794913 FAX : 23794913 Email : asingh@sansad.nic.in

AMAR SINGH
MEMBER OF PARLIAMENT
(RAJYA SABHA)
NATIONAL GENERAL SECRETARY & SPOKESMAN
(SAMAJWADI PARTY)

27, LODHI ESTATE,
NEW DELHI-110003
TEL. : 32565397 / 32542188 / 2461682
FAX : 91-11-24636299
Email : amarsingh@bol.net.in

senior officials in the DOT, its Wireless Wing including Sh. P.K. Garg, Wireless Advisor in this period.

I would urge the Government to

a) Direct for a CBI enquiry to investigate
   - How the Spectrum was allocated without any Policy Guidelines till March 2006?
   - How Lenient Guidelines of March 2006 were framed for allocation of Spectrum which finally led to the tightening of norms by 2.5 to over 8 times?
   - Where did the Spectrum allocated to new operators come from and how was it not available earlier for the new operators?

b) Assign the officials in CAG, CVC and DRI to assess the National exchequer loss and to take necessary steps including prevent such activities in future.

c) Levy appropriate fees for the Spectrum allocated beyond the Contracted amount of 6.2 MHz or be asked to return the excess spectrum immediately.

I also plan to also raise this in the upcoming session of parliament.

**Thanking you**

**With** regards,

**Yours** affectionately,

Amar Singh

**(Amar Singh)**

**Dr. Manmohan Singh**
**Hon'ble Prime Minister**
**Government of India**
**152, South Block**
**New Delhi**

AMAR SINGH
MEMBER OF PARLIAMENT
(RAJYA SABHA)
NATIONAL GENERAL SECRETARY & SPOKESMAN
(SAMAJWADI PARTY)

27, LODHI ESTATE,
NEW DELHI-110003
TEL. : 32565397 / 32542188 / 2461682
FAX : 91-11-24636299
Email : amarsingh@bol.net.in

सत्यमेव जयते

**September 27th, 2008**

Respected Manmohan Singh ji,

**Subject: Pricing Spectrum Based on the current market valuations. Measures to Raise Additional revenue of over Rs 24000 crore from the Telecom Sector**

This is further to my letter dated 22nd August'08 and my earlier letters dated 2nd July'08, 11th July'08 and 25th July'08, regarding the charging for the extra spectrum over 6.2 MHz allotted to the private cellular operators completely free of cost over and above their license conditions.

I now see from media reports that the new telecom licenses with national presence are having market valuation upwards of $ 2 billion without assets, customers, Infrastructure i.e., Rs.9500 crores. **Thus, per MHz price derived at these prices is Rs.2200 crores per MHz based on the start-up spectrum of 4.4 MHz allocated to these operators.**

I had brought to your attention the media reports in my earlier letter that the DoT is intending to adopt a lenient pricing of spectrum for the excess spectrum over 6.2 MHz to benefit certain dominant private operators – Bharti Airtel, Vodafone and Idea. The reports are stating that the per MHz is being based on the entry fee of Rs.1650 crores divided by 6.2 MHz spectrum i.e. Rs 266 crore per MHz as the license provides for spectrum up to 6.2 MHz. Also, the appropriate indexation being stated to be adopted by the DoT is the prime lending rate and thereby, the per MHz charge at today's price being considered is Rs.400 crores per MHz.

On the basis of the per MHz price of Rs.2200 crores per MHz, based on the current market valuation, the government should be able to raise over Rs.18,000 crores as Fixed One time Spectrum charge from the operators who have been allotted extra spectrum over 6.2 MHz. This would include Bharti Airtel – Rs.4200 crores, Vodafone – Rs.4000 crores and Idea Rs.1800 crores.

AMAR SINGH
MEMBER OF PARLIAMENT
(RAJYA SABHA)
NATIONAL GENERAL SECRETARY & SPOKESMAN
(SAMAJWADI PARTY)

27, LODHI ESTATE,
NEW DELHI-110003
TEL. : 32565397 / 32542188 / 2461682
FAX : 91-11-24636299
Email : amarsingh@bol.net.in

The lenient approach, as reported by the media, being suggesting by DoT would result in the revenue of just Rs.3500 crores including Bharti Airtel – Rs.800 crores, Vodafone – Rs.700 crores and Idea Cellular - Rs.325 crores.

With this lenient approach of PLR basis, vis-a-vis the Market valuation of Rs 2200 crore per MHz, **the savings to the operators are Bharti Airtel – 3400 crore, Vodafone – Rs 3300 crore, Idea Cellular – Rs 1500 crore and at the cost to the Government exchequer.** Clearly, this seems to be a part of a grand design to benefit the dominant private operators.

In my earlier letter(copy attached), I had suggested the methodology to price the spectrum beyond 6.2 MHz based on Rs.375 cores per MHz linked to the entry license fee alongwith start-up spectrum of 4.4 MHz and index it with AGR growth ( 3.5 times) during the relevant period, which comes to Rs.1300 crores per MHz. This has also been the recommendation of the Ministry of Finance. This measure, if adopted, would raise additional revenue of over Rs.12000 crores from the fixed charges of spectrum beyond 6.2 MHz.

The table below provides the comparison of the approaches:

**Excess Spectrum Fixed Charge - Comparison**

| Indexation Basis | Value estimation method | Value/MHz for all circles (Rs. Cr) | Index | Value Per MHz with indexation for all circles (Rs. Cr) | Government Exchequer Revenue (Rs. Cr) | Operator Excess Spectrum Value (Rs Cr) | | |
|---|---|---|---|---|---|---|---|---|
| | | | | | | Airtel | Vodafone | Idea |
| PLR | Entry fee of Rs. 1650 Cr for 6.2 MHz spectrum | 266 | 1.5 | 299 | 3,500 | 800 | 700 | 325 |
| AGR growth between 2003 & present | Entry fee of Rs. 1650 Cr for 4.4 MHz spectrum | 375 | 3.5 | 1313 | 12,000 | 2,500 | 2,300 | 1,000 |
| New Licensee valuation without assets | Value of Rs. 9500 Cr. For 4.4 MHz Spectrum | NA | NA | 2200 | 18,000 | 4,200 | 4,000 | 1,800 |

Additionally, the recurring charges of 2%, as mentioned in my earlier letter, would raise over Rs.5000 to 6000 crores in 2008-9.

AMAR SINGH
MEMBER OF PARLIAMENT
(RAJYA SABHA)
NATIONAL GENERAL SECRETARY & SPOKESMAN
(SAMAJWADI PARTY)

27, LODHI ESTATE,
NEW DELHI-110003
TEL. : 32565397 / 32542188 / 2461682
FAX : 91-11-24636299
Email : amarsingh@bol.net.in

The pricing of spectrum beyond 6.2 MHz has two logical options. One option is based on the historic value of the spectrum with indexation based on AGR growth i.e. Rs 1312 crore per MHz. The other option is based on the current market valuation i.e. Rs 2200 crore per MHz. The costing of Spectrum should be done with complete economic prudence maximizing the revenue interest of the Government Exchequer and accordingly this objective will be best met by adopting the second option i.e. of Rs 2200 crore per MHz.

**I urge the government to:**

- **Not succumb to the pressure of the private GSM operators by adopting lenient and inappropriate spectrum pricing.**
- **Price the fixed charges for spectrum beyond 6.2 MHz based on the Market valuation basis i.e. Rs 2200 crore per MHz.**
- **Also increase the Recurring spectrum usage charges of 2% per MHz beyond 6.2 MHz as detailed in my earlier letter which is attached.**

I also plan to also raise this in the upcoming session of the Parliament.

**Thanking you**

**With** regards,

**Yours** affectionately,

Amar Singh.

**(Amar Singh)**

**Dr. Manmohan Singh**
**Hon'ble Prime Minister**
**Government of India**
**152 South Block**
New Delhi-11001

Dharampal Sabharwal
MEMBER OF PARLIAMENT
(RAJYA SABHA)

Confidential

D.O. No. 3018/SPS(S)/ND-08

Tel.: 23315733
Mobile: 9868181137
C-201, Swarna Jayanti Sadan,
Dr. B.D. Marg,
New Delhi - 110 001.

November 06, 2008

Dear Dr. Manmohan Singh ji,

**Illegal & undue favour shown to Swan Telecom**

You may be aware that since last several months, the affairs of ADAG Group is in the news and in our Parliament. The main trust of all these are the "undue favours" being shown to this group. The recent case pertains to favours shown by the Department of Telecommunication to Swan Telecom Private Limited (Swan Telecom) which has been given license early this year is based on an invalid application.

Swan Telecom Private Limited was a company incorporated by Anil Ambani Group in July 2006 (Details in Annexure 1). This company filed application for UAS License on 2nd March 2007. Swan Telecom was further sold by Anil Ambani to Dynamix Balwan Group (A real estate company owned by Shahid Balwan) & its associates. It is understood that the sale was done for a hefty consideration as the company was ahead in the queue. Department of Telecom has publicly said that they want to strictly abide by the so called first come first serve basis which is reproduced below:

The application was invalid on the date of filing as per clause 8 of the Guidelines for Unified Access Services License issued by the Ministry of Communications and Information Technology, Development of Telecommunications, Government of India No. 10-21/2005-BS.I (Vol.II)/49 dated 14th December 2005 which is reproduced below:-

> "8. No. single company/legal person, either directly or through its associates, shall have substantial equity holding in more than one LICENSEE Company in the same service area for the Access Services namely; Basic, Cellular and Unified Access Service. 'Substantial equity' herein will mean 'an equity of 10% or more'. A Promoter company/Legal person cannot have stakes in more than once LICENSEE Company for the same service area. A certificate to this effect shall be provided by the applicant's company secretary alongwith application."

As per the above clause Anil Ambani group which also owns Reliance Communications has operation in the circles where application for Swan Telecom was filed. For the purpose only 9.99% holding was shown against Reliance Communications. Instead of rejecting the invalid application concerned officers of the Department processed this application and gave the license to Swan.

The favours shown to Swan did not stop here, some of the other favours shown to Swan Telecom are:

1. Two officers of DoT namely Mr.R.J.S.Kushwaha & Mr.D.Jha were transferred from WPC as they refused to unduly favour Swan Telecom. After transfer of these officers, spectrum was allotted to Swan Telecom for Delhi.

Dharampal Sabharwal
MEMBER OF PARLIAMENT
(RAJYA SABHA)

सत्यमेव जयते

Tel. : 23315733
Mobile : 9868181147
C-201, Swarna Jayanti Sadan,
Dr. B.D. Marg,
New Delhi - 110 001.

2. BSNL which has never done any roaming agreement with any operator was forced to do a roaming agreement with Swan Telecom. The same favour was not extended to any other operator. I am told that the policy was made by BSNL only to suit Swan Telecom.

I would therefore request you to **order a high level investigations to enquire into**:

1. The application of Swan Telecom Limited on illegal application and license issued to them. The role of concerned DoT officers acting in collusion with Swan Telecom.
2. The transfer of WPC official and role of senior Department official in these transfers.
3. Role of BSNL official in entering in roaming agreement with Swan Telecom.

In view of above, I would request you that issues raised above and in the enclosed notes be addressed thoroughly and thoughtfully. If this is not done with the promptitude it deserves, I am afraid, it may give rise to another scam-like situation in this country.

With regards

Yours sincerely,

D.P. Sabharwal

(DHARAM PAL SABHARWAL)

Dr. Manmohan Singh,
Hon'ble Prime Minister,
Government of India,
New Delhi.

website : http://parliamentofindia.nic.in

## Annexure -1: Swan Telecom Private Limited

A. Swan Telecom Private Limited (the "Company") was incorporated on 13th July 2006 as Swan Capital Private Limited with registered office at 7th Floor, Raheja Point- 1, Jawaharlal Nehru Marg, Vakola Market, Santa Cruz (E), Mumbai – 400 055. The subscribers to the Memorandum of Association were:

| Person | No. of equity shares of Rs. 10 each |
|---|---|
| Himanshu Agarwal (employee of ADA Group) | 1 |
| Powersurfer Interactive (India) P Ltd. (A ADA Group Company) | 4,999 |
| Reliance Energy Management Services P Ltd. (an ADA Group Company) | 5,000 |
| Total | 10,000 |

On 22nd January 2007, the Company allotted equity shares of Rs. 10 each as given below:

| Person | No. of equity shares of Rs. 10 each |
|---|---|
| Tiger Trustees Private Limited (formerly Tiger Traders Private Limited) | 27,03,000 |
| Reliance Telecom Limited (a wholly owned subsidiary of Reliance Communications Limited) | 2,97,000 |
| Total | 30,00,000 |

On 2nd March 2007, the Company further allotted equity shares of Rs. 10 each as given below:

| Person | No. of equity shares of Rs. 10 each |
|---|---|
| Tiger Trustees Private Limited (formerly Tiger Traders Private Limited) | 9,55,06,000 |
| Reliance Telecom Limited (a wholly owned subsidiary of Reliance Communications Limited) | 1,04,94,000 |
| Total | 10,60,00,000 |

The Company made an application for Unified Access Service Licence (UASL) on 2nd March 2007 and the shareholders of the Company on that date were:

| Shareholder | No. of shares | Percent |
|---|---|---|
| Tiger Trustees Private Limited (formerly Tiger Traders Private Limited) | 9,82,19,000 | 90.10% |
| Reliance Telecom Ltd. (a wholly owned subsidiary of Reliance Communications Limited) | 1,07,91,000 | 9.90% |
| Total | 10,90,10,000 | 100.00% |

B. Tiger Trustees Private Limited was incorporated on 20th March 2006 as Tiger Traders Private Limited with registered office at Reliance Energy Centre, 3rd Floor, Santacruz East, Mumbai 400055. The shareholders of Tiger Trustees Private Limited as on 2nd March 2007 were:

| Shareholder | No. of shares | Percent |
|---|---|---|
| Swan Infonet Services Private Limited (formerly Parrot Consultants Private Limited | 5,000 | 50.00% |
| Swan Advisory Services Private Limited(formerly Zebra consultants Private Limited) | 5,000 | 50.00% |
| Total | 10,000 | 100.00% |

The directors of Tiger Trustees Private Limited on incorporation were:

| Name of the Director | Address |
|---|---|
| Mr. Ashish Karyekar (employee of ADA Group) | 704, Reliance Energy Quarters, Chembur, Receiving Station, Deonar, Mumbai 400088 |
| Mr. Paresh Rathod (employee of ADA Group) | 204, Reliance Energy Quarters, Chembur, Receiving Station, Deonar, Mumbai 400088 |

C. Swan Infonet Services Private Limited was incorporated on 17th March 2006 as Parrot consultants Private Limited with registered office at Reliance Energy Centre, 3rd Floor, Santacruz East, Mumbai 400055. The shareholders of Swan Infonet Services Private Limited as on 2nd March 2007 were.

| Shareholder | No. of shares | Percent |
|---|---|---|
| Tiger Trustees Private Limited (formerly Tiger Traders Private Limited) | 5,000 | 50.00% |
| Swan Advisory Services Private Limited (formerly Zebra Consultants Private Limited) | 5,000 | 50.00% |
| Total | 10,000 | 100.00% |

The directors of Swan Infonet Services Private Limited on incorporation were:

| Name of the Director | Address |
|---|---|
| Mr. Ashish Karyekar (employee of ADA Group) | 704, Reliance Energy Quarters, Chembur, Receiving Station, Deonar, Mumbai 400088 |
| Mr. Paresh Rathod (employee of ADA Group) | 204, Reliance Energy Quarters, Chembur, Receiving Station, Deonar, Mumbai 400088 |

D. Swan Advisory Services Private Limited was incorporated on 21st March 2006 as Zebra Consultants Private Limited with registered office at Reliance Energy

Centre, 3rd Floor, Santacruz East, Mumbai 400055. The shareholders of Swan Infonet Services Private Limited as on 2nd March 2007 were:

| Shareholder | No. of shares | Percent |
|---|---|---|
| Tiger Trustees Private Limited (formerly Tiger Traders Private Limited) | 5,000 | 50.00% |
| Swan Infonet Services Private Limited (formerly Parrot Consultants Private Limited ) | 5,000 | 50.00% |
| Total | 10,000 | 100.00% |

The directors of Swan Infonet Services Private Limited on incorporation were:

| Name of the Director | Address |
|---|---|
| Mr. Ashish Karyekar (employee of ADA Group) | 704, Reliance Energy Quarters, Chembur, Receiving Station, Deonar, Mumbai 400088 |
| Mr. Paresh Rathod (employee of ADA Group) | 204, Reliance Energy Quarters, Chembur, Receiving Station, Deonar, Mumbai 400088 |

**From the above, it is apparent that on 2nd March 2007,when the Company made application for Unified Access Services Licence, it was owned 100% by Reliance Communications Limited and its associates viz. Reliance Telecom Limited, Tiger Trustees Limited, Swan Infonet Services Private Limited, and Swan Advisory Services Private Limited. As pictorically presented below:**

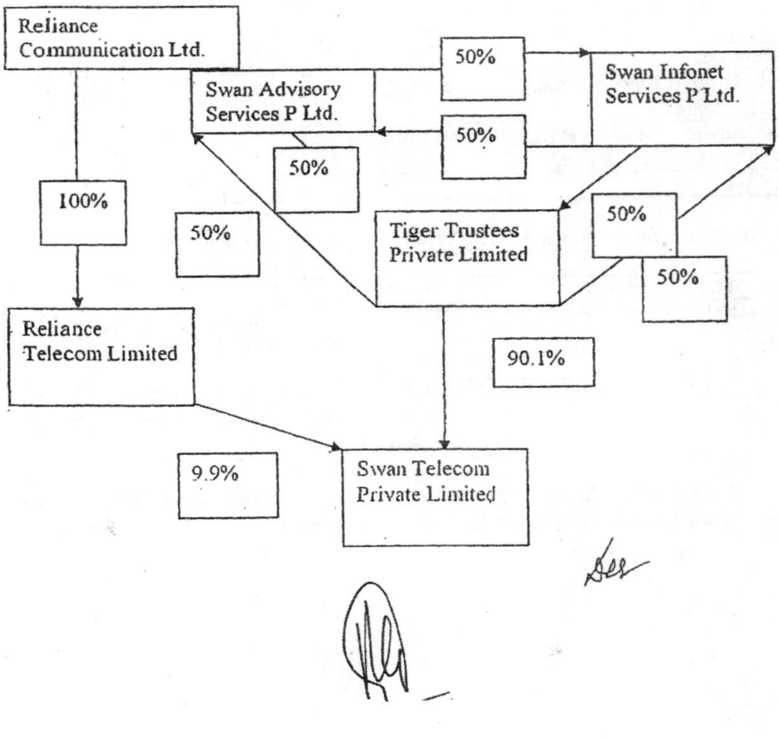

समाजवादी पार्टी

फोन : 011-23386842
फैक्स : 011-23382430

केन्द्रीय कार्यालय : 18, कॉपरनिक्स लेन, नई दिल्ली–110001

संदर्भ संख्या............. दिनांक............

मुलायम सिंह यादव
राष्ट्रीय अध्यक्ष

November 07, 2008

My dear Manmohan

**Subject:** **Pricing Spectrum Based on the current market valuations. – Measures to Raise Additional revenue of over Rs 18000 crores from already allotted excess spectrum**

One of the issues discussed during our Coordination Committee Meeting was raising over Rs.18000 Crores in the short term from the Mobile Telecom Sector by charging a one-time-fee against the excess spectrum obtained by them over and above the contracted 6.2 MHz under the licensing conditions and increase the spectrum usage charges by 2% above 6.2 MHz.

Dominant operators who are having excess spectrum to the tune of 54 MHz are Airtel, Vodafone and Idea.

Several letters were written highlighting the options available, copies enclosed. The steps suggested would in no way lead to increase in call charges paid by the common man.

- It was brought to the attention the media reports that DoT is intending to adopt a lenient pricing of spectrum for the excess spectrum over 6.2 MHz to benefit certain dominant private operators – Bharti Airtel, Vodafone and Idea.
- The reports are stating that the per MHz is being based on the entry fee of Rs.1650 crores divided by 6.2 MHz spectrum i.e. Rs 266 crore per MHz as the license provides for spectrum up to 6.2 MHz. The rationale being provided for dividing Rs.1650 crores by 6.2 Mhz is that some of the operators have been provided 6.2 MHz in the past and is thus likely to be acceptable to the operators. This per MHz price is being indexed as per PLR.
- The per MHz price of spectrum cannot be derived on the basis of 6.2 MHz as the entry fee of Rs.1650 crores entitles the operator for initial start-up spectrum of 4.4 MHz only and allocation of additional spectrum beyond start-up spectrum is based on meeting the subscriber criteria. There are only 13 instances of private operators being allocated 6.2 MHz start-up spectrum from the 201 instances of spectrum allotment. i.e. in over 90% cases, the start-up spectrum allotted has been 4.4 MHz. Accordingly, the per

समाजवादी पार्टी

फोन : 011-23386842
फैक्स : 011-23382430

केन्द्रीय कार्यालय : 18, कॉपरनिक्स लेन, नई दिल्ली–110001

संदर्भ संख्या............. दिनांक.............

मुलायम सिंह यादव
राष्ट्रीय अध्यक्ष

MHz price should be derived by diving Rs.1650 crores by 4.4 MHz i.e., Rs 375 Crores per MHz.

- It was suggested the methodology to price the spectrum beyond 6.2 MHz based on Rs.375 cores per MHz and index it with AGR growth ( 3.5 times) during the relevant period, which comes to Rs.1300 crores per MHz. This has also been the recommendation of the Ministry of Finance. This measure, if adopted, would raise additional revenue of over Rs.12000 crores from the fixed charges of spectrum beyond 6.2 MHz.
- The lenient approach, as reported in the media, would result in the revenue of just Rs.3500 crores including that from Bharti Airtel – Rs.800 crores, Vodafone – Rs.700 crores and Idea Cellular - Rs.325 crores.
- With this lenient approach of PLR basis, vis-a-vis the AGR Indexation methodology, the savings to Mr. Sunil Mittal (Airtel), Vodafone Essar and Mr. Kumar Mangalam Birla (Idea Cellular) will be Rs.1700 cores, Rs.1600 crores and Rs.700 crores respectively and at the cost to the Government exchequer. Clearly, this seems to be a part of a grand design to benefit the dominant private operators.
- I further recommend that the price of spectrum should also be assessed with the price discovery per MHz based on the 3G spectrum bid for 5 MHz. The Government could then finalize the price based on indexation with AGR or price discovered per MHz in 3G, whichever is higher.

The table below provides the comparison of the approaches:

| Indexation Basis | Value Estimation method | Value / MHz for all circles Rs Crore | Index | Value / MHz with Indexation for all circles (Rs Crore) | Govt Exchequer revenue Rs crore | Operator Excess Spectrum Value (Rs Crore) | | |
|---|---|---|---|---|---|---|---|---|
| | | | | | | Airtel | Vodafone | Idea |
| PLR | Entry fee of Rs 1650 for 6.2 MHz spectrum | 266 | 1.6 | 426 | 3500 | 820 | 750 | 350 |
| AGR growth between 2003 and 2007 | Entry fee of Rs 1650 for 4.4 MHz startup spectrum | 375 | 3.5 | 1313 | 12000 | 2500 | 2300 | 1000 |
| 3g price = 2 times reserve price estimated market price | Reserve price of Rs 2200 crore and 2 times of Rs 4400 crore for 5 Mhz | | | 880 | 7250 | 1700 | 1550 | 725 |
| PLR at current rate of 13.5% | Entry fee of Rs 1650 for 6.2 MHz spectrum | 266 | 1.88 | 500 | 4200 | 950 | 900 | 400 |
| PLR at current rate of 13.5% | Entry fee of Rs 1650 for 4.4 MHz spectrum | 375 | 1.88 | 705 | 6000 | 1350 | 1250 | 570 |

समाजवादी पार्टी

फोन : 011-23386842
फैक्स : 011-23382430

केन्द्रीय कार्यालय : 18, कॉपरनिक्स लेन, नई दिल्ली–110001

संदर्भ संख्या.............. दिनांक...........

मुलायम सिंह यादव
राष्ट्रीय अध्यक्ष

- Additionally, the recurring charges of 2%, as mentioned in my earlier letter, would raise over Rs.5000 to 6000 crores in 2008-9.
- The costing of Spectrum should be done with complete economic prudence maximizing the revenue interest of the Government Exchequer and accordingly this objective will be best met by the MHz spectrum price indexation with AGR or price discovered in 3G bidding, whichever is higher.

**I urge the government to:**

- **Not succumb to the pressure of the private GSM operators by adopting lenient and inappropriate spectrum pricing.**
- **Price the fixed charges for spectrum beyond 6.2 MHz** based on indexation with AGR or price discovered per MHz in 3G, whichever is higher.
- **Also increase the Recurring spectrum usage charges by 2% per MHz beyond 6.2 MHz.**

**Thanking you**

**With** Kind regards,

**Yours** Sincerely,

Mulayam Singh Yadav

**(Mulayam Singh Yadav)**

**Dr. Manmohan Singh**
**Hon'ble Prime Minister of India**
**Government of India**
**New Delhi**

GURUDAS DAS GUPTA

**MEMBER OF PARLIAMENT**
**(LOK SABHA)**
GENERAL SECRETARY,
ALL INDIA TRADE UNION CONGRESS

35-36, D.D.U. Marg,
Rouse Avenue
New Delhi-110002
Tel.:23217320 / 23220264
Mobile: 9868180640
Fax: 23222427

10.11.2008

My Dear Prime Minister,

From the on-goings in the telecom sector and the public outcry, it appears amply clear that 2G spectr.m allocation based on the First Comes First Served (FCFS) has robbed India off nearly Rs.50,000 crores.

After the sale of stakes in new telecom licenses Swan and Unitech, it is now crystal clear that a scarce national resource, i.e. 2G spectrum has been issued to private players on the basis of a twisted policy designed to encourage private profiteering, which is leading to unimaginable losses to the tune of 1% of India's GDP. In spite of this, no action seems to be forthcoming from the UPA Government.

Convoluted adoption of FCFS: To start with, let me clarify that FCFS that has been used to allocated 2G spectrum is nothing but a convoluted adoption of methodology mentioned in NTP 99 for allocation of additional spectrum to players who fulfil subscriber linked criteria first. It is common sense that when demand exceeds supply, auctions are the best way of determining fair market value of the scarce resource.

TRAI has misguided policy formulation: It defeats logic, why have UAS licenses not been auctioned as previously auctioned in 2001 for the allocation of the 4th cellular license? How has TRAI overruled recommendation 7.39 from 2003 TRAI recommendation titled 'Recommendation of TRAI on Unified Licensing', which recommends auctioning of licenses/spectrum. Was due consultation process and procedure followed by TRAI before recommending 'No auctions for 800, 900 and 1,800 MHz spectrum in its August 28, 2007 recommendations?

Private auctions Vs. Public auctions: The argument that low entry fee and license fee in perpetuity is a better option is most flawed. Where is the low entry fee? Telenor is paying the economic value of the license to UNITECH. The money has gone to a promoter and not the owner of the resource, i.e. the government. The input cost is the same. It is private auction vs. public auction. It is a promoter benefiting against the government.

...2/-

GURUDAS DAS GUPTA

MEMBER OF PARLIAMENT
(LOK SABHA)
GENERAL SECRETARY,
ALL INDIA TRADE UNION CONGRESS

35-36, D.D.U. Marg.
Rouse Avenue
New Delhi-110002
Tel.:23217320 / 23220264
Mobile: 9868180640
Fax: 23222427

-2-

of this country. That consumer would suffer if spectrum is auctioned appears to be a complete myth. It is private auctions versus public actions. In public auctions, the money goes to the government treasury, but in private auctions it goes towards private profiteering.

Revenue share argument is fallacious: It seems fallacious to argue that government cannot charge revenue share, if it auctions spectrum. In the case of 3G, where the government has proposed to auction spectrum, it is still planning to levy a 1% incremental revenue share of gross AGR. So why can't it be done for 2G? If it seems unfair to have the same revenue share being paid by existing operators, who got spectrum along with their licenses, have a reduced revenue share for new licensees who acquire spectrum via auctions.

It is being suggested that by not auctioning spectrum, DoT has created a goose that can lay golden eggs indefinitely. In an interview, the MOCIT states that from 2004 till the first quarter of 2008, the government has received Rs.55,000 crores in terms of license fee and revenue share. In the interview, for 2007-08 the revenue share plus license fee received by the government has been projected equal to Rs.24,381 crores. Even if any of these figures are to be believed, had the government auctioned 2G spectrum, current market valuations suggest that it would have raised about Rs.50,000 crores upfront as opposed to it having come over four years. Further, if the government were to invest it at a nominal 10%, it would recover Rs.5,000 crore per annum, besides the revenue share that would come from spectrum usage.

Merger guidelines: It may be noted that the merger guidelines that were put forth in April this year seemed to prevent mergers and acquisitions for a period of three years. However, the word 'acquisitions' were cleverly left out of the relevant text of the guidelines, suggesting that new licensees can sell out stake as per FDI policy. This laid out the clear path that the new licenses could follow, i.e. sell out stake and make huge profits.

From the sequence of events, it clearly appears that the policy has been twisted to allow private profiteering at the expense of the public exchequer. It appears that the entire game plan has been pre-planned. Thus, it appears that the policy that is depriving the exchequer of nearly Rs.50,000 crores seems to have been well thought through.

...3/-

GURUDAS DAS GUPTA

MEMBER OF PARLIAMENT
(LOK SABHA)
GENERAL SECRETARY,
ALL INDIA TRADE UNION CONGRESS

सत्यमेव जयते

35-36, D.D.U. Marg
Rouse Avenue
New Delhi-110002
Tel.:23217320 / 23220264
Mobile: 9868180640
Fax: 23222427

-3-

There are other deals to follow·Datacom, Loop and Aircel. Each of the concluded deals, have been done at 6 to 7 times what the companies paid for the licenses. They paid US $ 350 million each and have sold each license at valuations of around US $ 2 billion plus. Long and short government got only US $ 2.1 billion for these six licenses and speculators got about 12.6 billion. This is a loss of US $ 10 billion or only Rs.50,000 crores to be exchequer!

There is still time to save the country: It is not too late. The courts have ruled on more than one occasion that the government can change policy any time, especially under compelling corrupt circumstances such as this.

To begin with, the cleansing act has to start with the removal of those responsible for it. It is the responsibility of the MOCIT, Secretary, DoT, Chairman, TRAI, to ensure a policy framework that is in the interest of the nation. However, it appears that matters have been twisted in a manner such as to frame policy to benefit private pockets. It may be appropriate to hold those who are responsible for these misdeeds as stated above and discharge them of their responsibilities before the government manages to sully its image.

After their departure, the new UAS licenses should be cancelled and spectrum that has been allocated should be recalled as it has been allocated on a trial basis. In any case, none of the new licensees would have met the stringent roll out that is supposed to b. achieved within the first year, giving government sufficient reason to cancel their UAS licenses.

2G spectrum should then be auctioned such that its true value, which is being estimated at about Rs.50,000 crores based on the two private deals that have happened, accrues to the public exchequer.

I wish you take immediate action.

With kind regards,

Yours sincerely,

(GURUDAS DAS GUPTA)

The Prime Minister
South Block
New Delhi 110 001

AMAR SINGH
MEMBER OF PARLIAMENT
(RAJYA SABHA)
NATIONAL GENERAL SECRETARY & SPOKESMAN
(SAMAJWADI PARTY)

27, LODHI ESTATE,
NEW DELHI-110003
TEL. : 32565397 / 32542188 / 2461682
FAX : 91-11-24636299
Email : amarsingh@bol.net.in

November 17, 2008

Respected Manmohan Singh ji

**Subject:** **Measures to Raise Additional revenue of over Rs 60000 crores from the Telecom Sector on the basis of market discovered price for the Excess Spectrum over 6.2 MHz held by Operators free of Cost**

This is further to my letter dated 22nd August'08 and my earlier letters dated 2nd July'08, 11th July'08 and 25th July'08, regarding the charging for the extra spectrum over 6.2 MHz allotted to the private cellular operators completely free of cost over and above their license conditions.

I understand that the imposition of One-time Spectrum Enhancement Charge for 2G Spectrum has now been deferred by the Department of Telecommunications.

I now see from media reports that the new telecom licenses with national presence based on Deals of Swan Telecom with UAE Government firm Etisalat and Unitech Wireless with Norway Government managed Telenor and are having market valuation upwards of $ 2 billion without assets, customers, infrastructure i.e.9500 to 10,000 crores. **Thus the per MHz price derived at these prices is Rs.2200 to Rs 2300 crores per MHz based on the start-up spectrum of 4.4 MHz allocated to these operators.**

The other telecom deals which have concluded in 2008 can also be the basis for determining per MHz price. The June'08 deal of Sh. Kumar Mangalam Birla led Idea Cellular with Telecom Malaysia (TMI) in June 2008 of Rs.7300 crores for 15% stake indicates that the market valuation of the company is Rs.48000 crores and thus amounting to **Rs.7800 crores per MHz** for the average spectrum held by this company. Also, In the recent deal in November 2008 of Sh Ratan Tata led TTSL with NTT DoCoMo, being reported in the media, of Rs.13000 crores for 26% stake indicates a market valuation of Rs.50000 crores and thereby **Rs.4400 crores per MHz** for the average spectrum held by this company.

I had brought to your attention the media reports in my earlier letter that the DoT is intending to adopt a lenient pricing of spectrum for the excess spectrum over 6.2 MHz to benefit certain dominant private operators – Bharti Airtel, Vodafone and Idea. The reports are stating that the per MHz price is being based on the entry fee of Rs.1650 crores divided by 6.2 MHz spectrum i.e. Rs 266 crore per MHz as the license provides for spectrum up to 6.2 MHz. Also, the appropriate indexation being stated to be adopted

AMAR SINGH
MEMBER OF PARLIAMENT
(RAJYA SABHA)
NATIONAL GENERAL SECRETARY & SPOKESMAN
(SAMAJWADI PARTY)

27, LODHI ESTATE,
NEW DELHI-110003
TEL. : 32565397 / 32542188 / 2461682
FAX : 91-11-24636299
Email : amarsingh@bol.net.in

by the DoT is the prime lending rate and thereby, the per MHz charge at today's price being considered is Rs.400 crores per MHz.

The per MHz price based on the market discovery with the deals in 2008 is approximately Rs.8000 crores per MHz based on the Sh. Kumar Mangalam Birla led Idea Cellular deal with Telecom Malaysia in June and the Government should be able to raise over Rs.60,000 crores as Fixed One-time Spectrum Charge from the operators who have been allotted extra spectrum over 6.2 MHz. This would include Sh. Sunil B Mittal led Bharti Airtel – Rs.15000 crores, Vodafone- Essar– Rs.14000 crores and Sh. Kumar Mangalam Birla led Idea Cellular - Rs.6500 crores.

The lenient approach, as reported by the media, being suggesting by DoT would result in the revenue of just Rs.3500 crores including Bharti Airtel – Rs.800 crores, Vodafone Essar – Rs.700 crores and Idea Cellular – Rs.350 crores.

With the lenient approach of PLR basis, vis-à-vis the Market valuation of Rs.8000 crores per MHz, the savings to the operators are Bharti Airtel – Rs.14000 crores, Vodafone Essar – Rs.13000 crores, Idea Cellular – Rs.6000 crores and at the great loss to the Government exchequer. Clearly, this seems to be a part of a grand design to benefit the dominant private operators.

The table below provides the comparison of the approaches:

| Indexation Basis | Value Estimation method | Value/MHz for all circles Rs crore | Index | Value/MHz with indexation for all circles Rs crore | Govt Exchequer revenue Rs crore | Operator Excess Spectrum Value (Rs crore) Airtel | Vodafone | Idea |
|---|---|---|---|---|---|---|---|---|
| PLR based Lenient approach | Entry fee of Rs 1650 for 6.2 MHz spectrum | 266 | 1.6 | 426 | 3500 | 820 | 750 | 350 |

Market Price Discovery Options based on deals

| Market Price Discovery Basis | Details | | Value / MHz for all | Govt Exchequer | Operator Excess Spectrum Airtel | Vodafone | Idea |
|---|---|---|---|---|---|---|---|
| Swan with UAE Government firm Etisalat deal in Aug 08 | Value of 900 Mn$ for 45% stake i.e EV 2 Bn$ or Rs 9400 crore Spectrum 4.4 Mhz | | 2200 | 18000 | 4300 | 4000 | 1600 |
| Unitech with Norway Government firm Telenor deal in Oct 08 | Value of Rs 6120 crore for 60% stake i.e EV Value Rs 10,200 crore Spectrum 4.4 Mhz | | 2300 | 19000 | 4440 | 4050 | 1900 |
| Sh Kumar Mangalam Birla led Idea Cellular with Telecom Malaysia deal in June 08 | Rs 7294 crore for 15% EV Rs 48626 crore Spectrum Avg Spectrum per circle 6.2 MHz | | 7800 | 65000 | 15000 | 14000 | 6500 |
| Sh Ratan Tata led TTSL with NTT -DOCOMO deal in November 08 | Rs 13070 crore for 26% EV Rs 50250 crore Spectrum Avg CDMA per circle - 3.5 MHz i.e equivalent GSM 7 MHz GSM startup - 4.4 MHz ie Total of 11.4 Mhz avg/circle | | 4400 | 36000 | 8500 | 7800 | 3600 |

AMAR SINGH
MEMBER OF PARLIAMENT
(RAJYA SABHA)
NATIONAL GENERAL SECRETARY & SPOKESMAN
(SAMAJWADI PARTY)

27, LODHI ESTATE,
NEW DELHI-110003
TEL. : 32565397 / 32542188 / 2461682
FAX : 91-11-24636299
Email : amarsingh@bol.net.in

सत्यमेव जयते

The pricing of spectrum beyond 6.2 MHz has only one logical option - pricing based in terms of current market value. The costing of spectrum should be done with complete economic prudence, maximizing the revenue interest of the Government Exchequer and accordingly this objective will be best met by adopting the market value pricing of Rs.8000 crores per MHz

**I urge the government to:**

- **Not succumb to the pressure of the dominant private GSM operators by adopting lenient and inappropriate spectrum pricing.**
- **Price spectrum beyond 6.2 MHz based of minimum 2200 crores per MHz and up to Rs.8000 Crores per MHz on the market valuation basis the deals in June08 to November08.**

**Thanking you**

**With** regards,

**Yours** affectionately,

Amar Singh

**(Amar Singh)**

**Dr. Manmohan Singh**
**Hon'ble Prime Minister**
**Government of India**
**152 South Block**
**New Delhi-110011**

AMAR SINGH
MEMBER OF PARLIAMENT
(RAJYA SABHA)
NATIONAL GENERAL SECRETARY & SPOKESMAN
(SAMAJWADI PARTY)

27, LODHI ESTATE,
NEW DELHI-110003
TEL. : 32565397 / 32542188 / 2461682
FAX : 91-11-24636299
Email : amarsingh@bol.net.in

November 17, 2008

**Subject: Charging Annual Spectrum Charges for 2G spectrum, contrary to TRAI recommendation and at the behest of the private dominant operators which is also not pro level-playing field for new operators**

This is further to my letter dated 22nd August'08 regarding spectrum charges for the extra spectrum over 6.2 MHz allotted to the private cellular operators completely free of cost, as well as, the issue of annual spectrum charges for 2G spectrum.

I have now been given to understand that the Telecom Commission has reviewed the same and is increasing the spectrum usage charges by charging 1% across the board with a new slab at 8 MHz and beyond, where the increase is by 2%.

I would like to highlight that this decision is contrary to the TRAI recommendation in 2007, wherein it specifies that there should be no increase of spectrum usage charge up to 6.2 MHz in GSM and 5 MHz in CDMA. This was considering that the entry licensee fee of Rs.1650 crores for pan-India license includes the start-up spectrum as well as to ensure a level playing field for the new and existing operators. This also fulfilled the objectives of increasing the competition as well as acting as a pro-consumer measure.

**"Clause 2.83 – After examining various options for rationalizing the spectrum charges, the Authority, recommends adoption of revenue share spectrum charges as given in the table 8 below :**

| Spectrum | Current | Proposed |
|---|---|---|
| Upto 2x4.4 MHz | 2% | No change |
| Upto 2x6.2 MHz / 2x5 MHz | 3% | No change |
| Upto 2x8 MHz | 4% | No change |
| Upto 2x10 MHz | 4% | 5.00% |
| Upto 2x12.5 MHz | 5% | 6.00% |
| Upto2x15 MHz | 6% | 7.00% |
| Beyond 2x15 MHz | - | 8.00% |

A comparison of the current rates, TRAI's recommended rates and the Telecom Commission's proposed changes are given below:

AMAR SINGH
MEMBER OF PARLIAMENT
(RAJYA SABHA)
NATIONAL GENERAL SECRETARY & SPOKESMAN
(SAMAJWADI PARTY)

27, LODHI ESTATE,
NEW DELHI-110003
TEL. : 32565397 / 32542188 / 2461682
FAX : 91-11-24636299
Email : amarsingh@bol.net.in

| GSM | Rates current | Rates trai | Rates proposed | Per MHz | Increase |
|---|---|---|---|---|---|
| 4.4 | 2% | 2% | 3% | 0.68% | 50% |
| 6.2 | 3% | 3% | 4% | 0.65% | 33% |
| 7.2 | 4% | 4% | 5% | 0.69% | 25% |
| 8 | 4% | 4% | 5% | 0.63% | 25% |
| 8.2 | 4% | 5% | 5% | 0.61% | 25% |
| 9.2 | 4% | 5% | 6% | 0.65% | 50% |
| 10 | 4% | 5% | 6% | 0.60% | 50% |
| 10.2 | 5% | 6% | 6% | 0.59% | 20% |
| 11.2 | 5% | 6% | 7% | 0.63% | 40% |
| 12.2 | 5% | 6% | 7% | 0.57% | 40% |
| 13.2 | 6% | 7% | 8% | 0.61% | 33% |
| 14.2 | 6% | 7% | 8% | 0.56% | 33% |
| 15.2 | not defined | 8% | 9% | 0.59% | |

| Spectrum | TRAI Recommendations | Telecom Commission DOT proposal | Comments |
|---|---|---|---|
| upto Contracted spectrum including 4.4 MHz start up spectrum and 6.2 MHz spectrum in GSM | No Change | 1% increase | DOT proposal contrary to TRAI recommendation<br><br>No change recommended by TRAI as licence fee paid by new operator includes the strartup Spectrum<br><br>Also to ensure level playing field between new operators and existing opertors<br><br>New operators will be hit the hardest |
| Beyond 6.2 Mhz of spectrum in GSM | One time fee beyond 10Mhz of Rs 16 crore per MHz, 8 crore per MHz and 3 crore per MHz for based on category of circle<br><br>1% increase beyond 8 MHz | 1% Increase across board upto 8 Mhz and 2% beyond | Special category of 8MHz increase by 2% has little impact as most spectrum is held between 7 and 8 Mhz for the key operators and little Spectrum beyond 8 Mhz is held.<br><br>Charging One time fee recommended by TRAI has been derferred. |

It is clearly noticed from the above that:

a) It skews the level playing field, as the new entrants are hit the hardest, since they would need to pay increased charges. This is also contrary to the TRAI recommendation wherein it recommends no change in the spectrum charges up to 6.2 MHz for GSM and 5 MHz for CDMA.

b) The increase for new entrants with start-up spectrum is 50%, whereas, the increase for the existing operators with spectrum at 6.2 MHz is 33% and beyond 6.2 MHz to 8.2 MHz, the increase is 25%.

c) The per MHz charges (as % of AGR) reduces as MHz allocation increases. This does not support spectral efficiency.

d) The increase is higher at lower spectrum allocation and is lower at higher spectrum allocation of 7 - 8 MHz band where most private operators hold

AMAR SINGH
MEMBER OF PARLIAMENT
(RAJYA SABHA)
NATIONAL GENERAL SECRETARY & SPOKESMAN
(SAMAJWADI PARTY)

27, LODHI ESTATE,
NEW DELHI-110003
TEL. : 32565397 / 32542188 / 2461682
FAX : 91-11-24636299
Email : amarsingh@bol.net.in

spectrum. This also does not support the objective of promoting spectral efficiency.

e) Creating a special slab of 8 MHz and beyond where the charge increases by 2% instead of 1%, is clearly a grand design of increasing the charges where spectrum is not actually held by dominant private operators.

In my earlier letter, I had recommended an approach where there is no increase in spectrum charges up to contracted spectrum, which is also in line with the TRAI recommendation and meets the objective of a level playing field. I had also recommended the approach of charging for spectrum beyond 6.2 MHz by promoting the objective of spectral efficiency which has also been publicly stated by you. The letter dated 22nd April'08 is attached herewith for your ready reference.

**I would urge the Government to:**

- **Adopt the TRAI recommendation up to contracted spectrum and not charge 1% across the board, which is clearly at the behest of the existing dominant players and is against the interests of the new operators.**
- **Not to go ahead with the current proposal of 2G spectrum charge revision and refer the matter to the TRAI for review once again.**
- **Charge spectrum beyond contracted spectrum, which promotes spectral efficiency and do not allow creation of the new slab, which will not help the Government Exchequer and is clearly an attempt at lip-service increase on the behest of the dominant private operators.**

**Thanking you**

**With** regards,

**Yours** affectionately

Amar Singh

**(Amar Singh)**

**Dr. Manmohan Singh**
**Hon'ble Prime Minister**
**Government of India**
**152 South Block**
New Delhi-110011

**SITARAM YECHURY**
MEMBER OF PARLIAMENT
(RAJYA SABHA)
Leader
CPI(M) Group
CHAIRMAN
DEPARTMENT-RELATED PARLIAMENTARY
STANDING COMMITTEE ON TRANSPORT,
TOURISM AND CULTURE

सत्यमेव जयते

Off.: 124, Parliament House Annexe,
New Delhi-110 001
Tel. : 2303 4124, 2301 1973

A.K. Gopalan Bhavan, 27-29
Bhai Veer Singh Marg,
Gole Market, New Delhi-110001
Tel. : 23344918, 23747436

November 18, 2008

Dear Prime Minister,

I am constrained to draw your attention to the increasing evidence that the policy adopted for allocating the 4th license for 2 G by Government of India has caused a huge loss to the public exchequer – of more than Rs. 60,000 crore and has all the appearance of grave financial wrong-doing.

In my letter date 29th February, 2008 (enclosed), with regards to the telecom sector, I had drawn attention to the following:

- Spectrum is a scarce, national resource and needs to be allocated wisely and transparently
- Existing GSM operators should use the spectrum allocated to them efficiently before considering additional spectrum
- The CDMA operators being also given GSM spectrum and being allowed to jump the queue of new applicants is completely arbitrary
- The first come first served method of allocating license and spectrum is completely arbitrary and prone to manipulation
- Such a scheme will only encourage dummy companies and others to secure license and spectrum cheaply and then auctioning their shares/companies to earn windfall profits
  The cost put of Rs. 1,650 crore for the spectrum is nothing but a total give away of scarce national resources. This is a 2001 price and should never have been used as the price of license and spectrum in 2008.

All the above apprehensions have now been substantiated. The policy pursued by your Government under the stewardship of Mr. A. Raja as the Minister for Communications, not only has been totally arbitrary, but has produced a public loot of the exchequer of unprecedented amounts.

For the release of the fourth license and the spectrum needed for operationalising the corresponding Universal Access Service License in January 2008, The Communications Ministry adopted a completely inexplicable principle of 'first come first served' as well as a license fee based on 2001 price. These 2G licenses were priced at 2001 levels allegedly to ensure that the spectrum should not become expensive, presuming that the benefit would be passed on to the consumers. However, this was nowhere ensured through the license terms and conditions. As a result, the parties who had secured these licenses have sold or are selling their shares at huge profits.

The deal between UAE's telecom operator Etisalat and a Bombay-based builder's Swan Telecom has brought out the magnitude of largesse being doled out. Swan Telecom bought a license for 13 circles along with the necessary 2G spectrum for a paltry Rs. 1,537 crore. Subsequently, it has sold 45% of its stake to Etisalat for $900 million without putting up any infrastructure, let alone starting operations. This, therefore, is the market price for the spectrum is around $ 2 billion, as against the price of $300 milion SWAN paid. With the present exchange rate, this would mean that Swan had got a value 5.9 times of what it had paid just eight months earlier in January 2008 without having spent a single paisa in operationalising its license. The government has actually got only one-sixth of what it should have got, had it gone through a fresh auction route – a loss of Rs. 4,500 crore to the exchequer.

But this is not all. Even this loss proves to be an underestimate when one finds the details about the latest Unitech-Telenor (of Norway) deal. Here, Unitech like Swan had not spent a single paisa for executing its license. It has sold a 60 per cent stake of the telecom firm which had paid Rs. 1651 crore as license fee for all the 23 circles which it had applied for to Telenor. Obviously, Unitech got a better return on its sale because it has given away majority stake and had larger number of circles. Unitech has got 6,120 crores – and this is merely for spectrum. Since the debt component will be taken on by Telenor, Unitech has got a valuation which is seven times more than what it had paid. Based on this calculation, the loss to the government is about Rs. 5,500 crores.

There are also reports in the press of Turkcell, a leading Turkish telecom company and Europe's third largest operator being in talks to buy 51 per cent stake in Datacom solutions.

For a number of these corporations, who were awarded the so-called 'first come first served' licenses, the promoters are either unknown or shadow companies. This further reinforces the doubts regarding the *bona fides* of these companies as also the intent of the policy.

The argument of the government for using 'first come, first served' basis and offering prices discovered in 2001 to issue licenses -- an euphemism for scarce and costly spectrum, smacks of financial wrongdoing. The argument that the policy will ensure that the lower price that the new licensees had to pay will be passed on to the subscribers is clearly wrong. The deals which the new licensees and spectrum allottees have entered with the buyers makes clear that the benefit of low spectrum fees have accrued only to the licensees, who are fly by night operators securing spectrum only for speculative purposes. The total loss to the exchequer of giving away 2G spectrum in this way is over Rs. 60,000 crore and must rank as one of the biggest financial scams of all times in the country.

I would urge that you take immediate steps to scrap all licenses and subsequent spectrum allotments from the new licensees under this outrageous 'first come first served' basis at 2001 prices.It will also be keeping with your claim of valuing 'probity in public life' that an appropriate independent agency is assigned the task of fixing responsibility for this huge loss to the public exchequer.

With regards,

Yours sincerely

(Sitaram Yechury)

**Shri Manmohan Singh Ji**
**Hon'ble Prime Minister**
**Government of India**
**New Delhi**

FAX NO. :914023227942 Nov. 22 2008 05:09PM P1

.URAVARAM SUDHAKAR REDDY
Member of Parliament (Lok Sabha)
CHAIRMAN
STANDING COMMITTEE ON LABOUR
Dy. General Secretary
Communist Party of India

116, Parliament House Annexe,
New Delhi - 110001
Tel.: (011) 23034132
Telefax: (011) 23018010

D-1, M.S. Flats, Block A,
B.K.S. Marg, New Delhi-110001.
Tel.: 23315818, 23356568

Lr.No. 2682/ MPLS/NLG/08

Nov 22, 2008

**Dear Dr. Manmohan Singh jee,**

Namaskar. I am writing this letter to you, regarding the controversy about the spectrum allotment to some companies at much lower price and it is estimated that the Government has lost about 60,000 crores of rupees.

Unfortunately Telecom department frequently facing the allegations of scam. I remember that first controversy was the sale of "Videshi Nigam Ltd" to Tata's for a song by the then NDA Government. Even earlier Sri Sukhram was another controversial Minister for his convenience with Himalayaan Futuristic Company. Then came the allegation of preferring private cell phone companies by delaying the machinery of BSNL cell phones, thus forcing the public to go to private cell phone companies. Fortunately this trick did not work and people expressed their preference to public sector companies.

Now the latest decision of the Ministry on spectrum is being criticized by many experts and political parties. I care fully fallowed the statements and interviews of Hon'ble Minister Sri A. Raja. His defence is not at all convincing. Government collected 9000 crores awarding 120 licenses to nine companies. But Unitech Telecom sold 60% stake to Norwey based company "Telenor" for 6120 crores. Another company swan Telecom sold 45% stake to UAE Company "Etisalat" for R$ 40,000 crore. This resale of only part of two companies stake bringing huge profits to them will make every body to suspect that some thing gone wrong terribly in the Govt policy. The so-called lock in period etc will not help to whitewash the damage.

Prime Minister is the team leader of the cabinet. It is high time that you should step in to set right the things. You are answerable to the nation. Please answer by ordering a~ enquiry into the whole affair, at the earliest. I hope you will do the needful.

With regards,

Yours sincerely,

S Sudhakar Reddy

**(SURAVARAM SUDHAKAR REDDY)**

**Dr. Manmohan Singh**
**Hon'ble Prime Minister,**
**Government of India,**
**New Delhi.**

Abani Roy
MEMBER OF PARLIAMENT
(RAJYA SABHA)

17, Ferozshah Road
NEW DELHI – 110 001.
Tels. : 23782342, 9868181566(M)

सत्यमेव जयते

26.11.08

Dr. Manmohan Singh
Hon'ble Prime Minister
South Block
NEW DELHI.

Dear Sir,

This is further to my various letters on the above subject.

It is indeed, the Telecom Sector which has proved to be the success story of Indian reforms. India has become one of the most important country in the world which has seen tremendous growth in telecom services and the tele-density in the past 4 - 5 years.

However, in this euphoria we should not lose sight of certain aspects in the telecom service sector which needs careful consideration and proper investigation by the highest agency of the government due to large number of irregularities which have been committed in the management and allocation of the scarce resource of spectrum.

In the last 3-4 years the telecom sector regulator has been consistently maintaining that the new licenses should be issued after careful consideration of the availability of spectrum. However, few selected GSM operators (Airtel, Vodafone & Idea) under the umbrella of COAI and, in collusion with some senior officials in the DoT, namely Shri Siddhartha Behura – Secretary, J. S. Deepak – Jt. Secretary and Shri R. P. Agarwal – Wireless Advisor and Dr. Ashok Chandra – Jt. Wireless Advisor, have completely manipulated the government rules and regulations in a way that spectrum was issued to these operators indiscriminately without seeking any additional payment.

On the one hand DOT has been consistently maintaining that there is no spectrum available and on the other, spectrum was being selectively issued to these GSM operators without charging any fee. The allotment of spectrum beyond 6.2 MHz to these operators by the DoT had resulted in a colossal loss of more than Rs. 40,000/-crores to the national exchequer and gain to these select GSM operators.

Such indiscriminate and illegal allocation of spectrum to these select group of GSM Operators by the officials of DoT, after manipulating the Government guidelines, in the last 4-5 years needs investigation at the highest level.

Thanking you,

Yours sincerely,

( Abani Roy )

VIPLOVE THAKUR
MEMBER OF PARLIAMENT
(RAJYA SABHA)
PRESIDENT (H.P.C.C.)
SHIMLA

Member:
Standing Committee On Defence
Standing Committee On Health & Family Welfare

सत्यमेव जयते

10 Ferozshah Road,
New Delhi - 110 001
Ph.: 23355444

Vill. Birta
P.O. Ghurkari,
Kangra (H.P.)
Resi.: 01892-265500
Mob.: 09868-181003

D.O.No.MP(RS)/DEL/VIP/2009-634 URGENT February 14, 2009

**Dr. Manmohan Singh,**
Hon'ble Prime Minister of India,
7, Race Course Road,
New Delhi-110 011

**Sub. : Loss to Government due to separate spectrum charging on crossover technology**

Respected Dr. Sahib ji

I would like to bring your kind attention a decision wherein in the case of dual-technology licence (i.e. in a circle, a telecom operator is providing CDMA & GSM services under the same licence), in October 2007, Department of Telecommunications had decided to levy the spectrum charges on the individual spectrum / technology basis.

The above decision of DoT was contrary to Telecom Regulatory Authority of India's recommendations made in August 2007 wherein TRAI clearly recommended that in the case of dual technology licence, the concerned operator should pay spectrum charges / fee on the basis of combined spectrum held in that circle (i.e. applicable spectrum slab / charges on the combined spectrum of CDMA & GSM technology).

For instance, in its recommendations, TRAI stated that if a CDMA operator in a circle holds 5 MHz CDMA spectrum and 4.4 MHz of GSM spectrum, then for the purpose of spectrum charges, the slab rate for 9.4 MHz (5MHz+4.4MHz) of combined spectrum should be applicable. However, DoT made a policy that the applicable slab rate for 5MHz CDMA spectrum and 4.4MHz GSM spectrum will be applied separately.

It is surprising to note that in the case of applying the spectrum charges for 2G & 3G spectrums separately, DoT rejected the proposal on the grounds that it is operationally difficult to ascertain the separate revenue from 3G & 2G spectrum and extremely complicated to audit from DoT's point of view for the purpose of ascertaining the correct spectrum charges. However, in a case of levying the spectrum charges for CDMA & GSM technology, why these difficulties / concerns were clearly ignored by DoT.

.......2/-

VIPLOVE THAKUR
MEMBER OF PARLIAMENT
(RAJYA SABHA)
PRESIDENT (H.P.C.C.)
SHIMLA

Member:
Standing Committee On Defence
Standing Committee On Health & Family Welfare

10 Ferozshah Road.
New Delhi - 110 001
Ph.: 23355444

Vill. Birta
P.O. Ghurkari
Kangra (H.P.)
Resi.: 01892-265500
Mob.: 09868-181003

-2-

The said decision of DoT was clearly to benefit the CDMA players wherein the CDMA players would pay far lower rate of spectrum usage charges, despite having double the spectrum of the GSM operators. This decision of DoT is rendering huge financial largesse to the set of CDMA operators at the cost of huge loss to exchequer.

**How the loss will be incurred by the Government**

The stream-wise revenue of different technologies by DoT implies that % spectrum charges applicable would be based on spectrum slab of each technology i.e. 3% for CDMA - upto 5 MH (*as per DoT's proposed spectrum charges*) and 3% for GSM - upto 4.4 MH (*as per DoT's proposed spectrum charges*). Since no CDMA operator has more than 5 MHz of CDMA spectrum thereby it would attract minimum CDMA spectrum charges @ 3%.

Were the spectrum charges applied on total spectrum of operator (i.e. 9.4 MHz) as per GSM proposed slab rate on total Adjusted Gross Revenue (AGR) of operator, it would have earned much higher revenue to the Government than independent technology charging.

***E.g.*** (*based on DoT proposed Spectrum charges*) – In the above example individually, the operator would pay @ 3% for 5 MHz of CDMA spectrum and @ 3% for 4.4 MHz GSM spectrum. Assuming the AGR of Rs. 100 each for CDMA and GSM, the individual spectrum charges would be Rs. 6 (i.e. 3% of Rs. 100 of CDMA and 3% of Rs. 100 of GSM); ***whereas*** on total AGR of Rs. 200 the operator would pay Rs. 12 @ 6% (for 9.4 MHz spectrum the GSM spectrum charges are proposed @ 6%).

As per a fair assessment, in the first year itself, M/s. Reliance Communications Limited will save Rs.248 crores and Tata's Rs.187 crores and over a five year period, estimated advantage of Rs.1500 crores to Reliance and Rs.1200 crores to Tata. The total loss to the exchequer on account of these two companies will be over Rs.2700 crores in five years.

Please note that the above loss is an indicative loss to the Government and the same will continue to increase based on the increasing turnover of "Cross Over Technology operator", which includes Reliance & TATA.

.....3/-

VIPLOVE THAKUR
MEMBER OF PARLIAMENT
(RAJYA SABHA)
PRESIDENT (H.P.C.C.)
SHIMLA

Member :
Standing Committee On Defence
Standing Committee On Health & Family Welfare

10 Ferozshah Road,
New Delhi - 110 001
Ph. : 23355444

Vill. Birta
P.O. Ghurkari
Kangra (H.P.)
Resi. : 01892-265500
Mob. : 09868-181003

- 3 -

In this regard, I would therefore request you to order **a high level investigations** to inquire into:-

1. On what grounds, DoT decided to ignore TRAI's suggestion, which were in favour of exchaquer?

2. Whether DoT referred back their views on TRAI's suggestion / observations on the issue for TRAI reconsideration / response as the due process requires this procedure to be followed?

3. How DoT justified this loss to the Government especially when it is meant for selective CDMA operators, who were already benefited by getting the dual technology licence at much lower price of than that of the real market value.

In view of the above, I reqeust you that these issues are fully examined by the Government to avoid any scam / to give any undue benefits to a set of telecom operators and a huge loss to the exchequer.

**With high regards,**

Yours sincerely,

(VIPLOVE THAKUR)

***Spectrum Charges if Applied on Individual Stream-Wise AGR Basis:***

***@ DoT Proposed Rates***

| | Operator | AGR - CDMA *Individual* | AGR - GSM *Individual* | Spectrum Charges - on CDMA AGR *Individually* | Spectrum Charges - on GSM AGR *Individually* | *Total Individual* Spectrum Charges | *Annualized* Impact of Individual Spectrum Charges |
|---|---|---|---|---|---|---|---|
| | *RCOM* | One Quarter | One Quarter | One Quarter | One Quarter | One Quarter | Annualized |
| | Year 1 | 1,585.19 | 554.82 | 47.56 | 16.64 | 64.20 | 256.80 |
| | Year 2 | 1,585.19 | 792.60 | 47.56 | 23.78 | 71.33 | 285.33 |
| | Year 3 | 1,585.19 | 1,188.89 | 47.56 | 35.67 | 83.22 | 332.89 |
| | Year 4 | 1,585.19 | 1,585.19 | 47.56 | 47.56 | 95.11 | 380.45 |
| | Year 5 | 1,585.19 | 1,743.71 | 47.56 | 52.31 | 99.87 | 399.47 |
| (A) | RCOM Total | 7,925.95 | 5,865.20 | 237.78 | 175.96 | 413.73 | 1,654.94 |
| | *TATA* | One Quarter | One Quarter | One Quarter | One Quarter | One Quarter | Annualized |
| | Year 1 | 1,376.61 | 481.81 | 41.30 | 14.45 | 55.75 | 223.01 |
| | Year 2 | 1,376.61 | 688.31 | 41.30 | 20.65 | 61.95 | 247.79 |
| | Year 3 | 1,376.61 | 1,032.46 | 41.30 | 30.97 | 72.27 | 289.09 |
| | Year 4 | 1,376.61 | 1,376.61 | 41.30 | 41.30 | 82.60 | 330.39 |
| | Year 5 | 1,376.61 | 1,514.27 | 41.30 | 45.43 | 86.73 | 346.91 |
| | TATA Total | 5,883.05 | 5,093.46 | 206.49 | 152.80 | 359.30 | 1,437.18 |
| | Grand Total | 14,809.00 | 10,958.66 | 444.27 | 328.76 | 773.03 | 3,092.12 |

***Spectrum Charges if Applied on Combined AGR of CDMA+ GSM Basis:***

***@ DoT Proposed Rates***

| | Operator | Combined AGR (GSM + CDMA) | Spectrum Charges on Combined AGR | Annualied Spectrum Charges on Combined AGR | Difference in *Annualized* Total Individual Spectrum Charges vs. Combined Spectrum Charges |
|---|---|---|---|---|---|
| | I | II | III | IV | V |
| | *RCOM* | One Quarter | One Quarter | Annualized | Annualized |
| | Year 1 | 2,140.01 | 124.83 | 499.32 | 242.52 |
| | Year 2 | 2,377.79 | 138.70 | 554.80 | 269.47 |
| | Year 3 | 2,774.08 | 161.82 | 647.27 | 314.38 |
| (C) | Year 4 | 3,170.38 | 184.93 | 739.74 | 359.29 |
| | Year 5 | 3,328.90 | 194.18 | 776.72 | 377.26 |
| | RCOM Total | 13,791.15 | 804.46 | 3,217.86 | 1,562.92 |
| | *TATA* | One Quarter | One Quarter | Annualized | Annualized |
| | Year 1 | 1,858.42 | 102.56 | 410.24 | 187.23 |
| | Year 2 | 2,064.92 | 113.96 | 455.83 | 208.04 |
| | Year 3 | 2,409.07 | 132.95 | 531.80 | 242.71 |
| | Year 4 | 2,753.22 | 151.94 | 607.77 | 277.38 |
| | Year 5 | 2,890.88 | 159.54 | 638.16 | 291.25 |
| | TATA Total | 11,976.51 | 660.95 | 2,643.80 | 1,206.62 |
| | Grand Total | 25,767.66 | 1,465.41 | 5,861.65 | 2,769.53 |

| Annualied Loss to Govt @ Proposed DoT Rates | Rs. Cr. |
|---|---|
| *Year 1* | 429.76 |
| *Year 2* | 477.51 |
| *Year 3* | 557.09 |
| *Year 4* | 636.67 |
| *Year 5* | 668.51 |
| *Total Loss (Rs. Cr.)* | **2,769.53** |

RUDRA MADHAB RAY
MEMBER OF PARLIAMENT
(LOK SABHA)

1102 – Orissa Niwas
Chanakyapuri
New Delhi – 110 001
Mob. : 9013180235

3.11.09

**Dr. Manmohan Singh**
**Hon'ble Prime Minister of India**
**South Block,**
**New Delhi.**

**Respected Sir,**

We would like to bring to your kind attention the large scale fraud committed on the country in connivance of the previous government and officials of the ministry of Telecommunications.

Sh A Raja H' onble Minister of telecommunications in his statement to the media has pointed out that the fraud committed has resulted in the loss of more than Rs 1 Lac Crore to Government revenues. This is the biggest fraud in the history of the country. The loss has happened because of allotment of excess Spectrum free of cost to the operators violating the terms of the license regime.

The sector is a vital sector for the growth of the country and has see phenomenal growth but at a huge cost to the country. A scam of this proportion has enabled a few of the operators in cohorts with the previous government and senior officials of the ministry to make large sums of money.

The scarce spectrum resource was handed out to a chosen few operators in the period from 2003 to 2006. This was done with the connivance of the previous government and senior officials of the Ministry acting on their behalf.

The license granted by the government of India to telecom operators allows for only 4.4 Mhz of spectrum being allocated to the operator using GSM technology. This was granted to them on the basis of the entry fee paid by them for the license. There was no provision in the agreement for allotment of any additional spectrum. The officials of the ministry on the behest of the previous government issued spectrum to these companies without charging a single paise. The list of such companies and the amount of spectrum allocated is attached as Annexure 1. The scarce national resource was handed over these companies for use and earn crores out the same.

**Contd.....2/....**

RUDRA MADHAB RAY
MEMBER OF PARLIAMENT
(LOK SABHA)

1102 – Orissa Niwas
Chanakyapuri
New Delhi – 110 001
Mob. : 9013180235

सत्यमेव जयते

:: 2 ::

To cover up the issue some circulars were issued defining the basis of allotment of additional spectrum in March 2006 . The circular specified the allotment to be done based on the number of subscribers enrolled with the operator. Further the criteria of number of subscribers defined were again faulty. It is only in 2007 that TRAI and TEC relooked at the criteria. This faulty criterion allowed a set of operators to pocket huge amounts of money which otherwise they were required to spend on creating infrastructure while no charges were paid for the additional spectrum. This again enriched a set of operators and their supporters in the NDA government .

The circulars of the Department were flouted again wherein the department had decided in 2002, not to allow any additional spectrum in the 900 Mhz band and to allocate additional spectrum in 1800 Mhz only. The NDA government alongwith some senior officials of DOT ensured that the operators were provided additional spectrum in this band. Again no charges were taken from the operators. The list of such operators is annexed as Annexure 2 for ready reference. The allotment of spectrum in 900 Mhz again allowed these operator to pocket huge amounts which they would have had to spend on capital expenses.

We would request that an high level enquiry be setup to look into these issues and take appropriate action against the persons guilty of defrauding the nation of the legitimate resources which could have been utiised for the upliftment of the poor and downtrodden of the country.

Thanking You

With warm regrds

Encl: Annexure 1 & 2

Copy to:

1) Shri Pranab Mukherjee, Honourable Minister of Finance, GoI, New Delhi
2) Thiru A Raja, Honourable Minister of Communications & IT, GoI, New Delhi
3) CVC
4) Comptroller and Auditor General.

**Annexure 1**

**Telecom Operators allocated spectrum upto 10 MHz against the license conditions**

| S. No. | Telecom Operator | Telecom Circle | Date of allotment |
|---|---|---|---|
| 1 | Bharti | Delhi | 17.07.2003 |
| 2 | Vodafone | Delhi | 15.10.2003 |
| 3 | Bharti | Mumbai | 20.01.2006 |
| 4 | Vodafone (Hutch) | Mumbai | 15.10.2003 |
| 5 | BPL | Mumbai | 06.09.2004 |
| 6 | Vodafone (Hutch) | Kolkatta | 12.07.2006 |
| 7 | Bharti | Chennai | 15.11.2006 |
| 8 | Aircel | Chennai | 15.11.2006 |
| 9 | Vodafone (Fascel) | Gujarat | 13.5.2005 |
| 10 | Bharti | Karnataka | 03.12.2004 |
| 11 | Idea | Maharashtra | 01.04.2005 |
| 12 | Aircel | Tamil Nadu | 03.12.2004 |

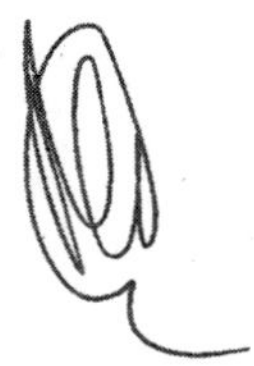

## Annexure 2

**Telecom Operators allocated spectrum in 900 Mhz against the circular of the Department of Telecommunications**

| S No | Telecom Operator | Telecom Circle | Date of Allotment | Spectrum allocated in 900 Mhz |
|---|---|---|---|---|
| 1 | Vodafone | Kolkatta | 30th June 2004 | 8 Mhz |
| 2 | Bharti | Punjab | 9th Feb 2004 | 7.8 Mhz |
| 3 | Bharti | AP | 9th Feb 2004 | 7.8 Mhz |
| 4 | Bharti | Karnataka | 9th Jan 2004 | 7.8 Mhz |
| 5 | Aircel | Tamil Nadu | 9th Jan 2004 | 7.8 Mhz |
| 6 | Spice | Punjab | 9th Jan 2004 | 7.4 Mhz |
| 7 | Idea | Maharashtra | 31st Dec 2003 | 7.8 Mhz |
| 8 | Vodafone | Gujarat | 14th Nov 2003 | 7.4 Mhz |
| 9 | BPL | Mumbai | 13th Jan 2003 | 8 Mhz |
| 10 | Bharti | Delhi | 17th July 2002 | 8 Mhz |
| 11 | Vodafone | Delhi | 17th July 2002 | 8 Mhz |
| 12 | Vodafone | Mumbai | 17th July 2002 | 8 Mhz |

जयप्रकाश नारायण सिंह
JAIPRAKASH NARAYAN SINGH
Member of Parliament
Rajya Sabha
Member-Standing Committee on Coal & Steel

सत्यमेव जयते

116, North Avenue
New Delhi-110001
Phone : 011-23093141
Mob. : 09868181381
Deoghar Ph. - 06432-225000
Mob.: 09431183181

**5th November, 2009**

Dr. Manmohan Singh
Hon'ble Prime Minister
South Block
<u>NEW DELHI.</u>

Dear Dr. Manmohan Singhji

The recent controversies in the telecom sector are real matter of concern to all citizens of the country, especially in view of the forthcoming 3G and BWA auction to be undertaken in the month of January 2010. Such controversies and alleged arbitrary practices will dampen the spirits of the operators, including the foreign operators who may be wishing to participate in the forthcoming auction and bring in the foreign direct investment.

The media reports are alarming that the spectrum allocation has been done in an inappropriate manner, causing lose to the national exchequer to the tune of about Rs. 1 Lakh Crore as stated by the Hon'ble Minister of Communication reported in the media today.

It is known that CBI is presently investigating the issue of license and spectrum allocation to some operators in January 2008 and the operators having made huge money by selling a part of their equity to the foreign operators.

However, it is painful that the actual lose to the exchequer to the tune of Rs. 1 Lakh Crore is being brushed aside and is not being investigated at all.

From the discussion with various quarters, I understand that the spectrum to the private operators has been issued from 1994-1995 onwards for the provision of cellular services. However, right from the beginning not even a single rupee has been charged. for the allocation of spectrum to the private operator which has been given as a state largesse. Not only the spectrum has been allocated beyond what has been contemplated in their licenses, this additional spectrum has also been allocated without any procedure or guidelines or systems being put in place. It is not surprising that the beneficiaries of this state largesse have acted in connivance with the powers within the DOT at all levels, be it official or political.

Contd......2/.....

जय जवान, जय किसान　　　　किसान सेवा, देश सेवा

जयप्रकाश नारायण सिंह
JAIPRAKASH NARAYAN SINGH
Member of Parliament
Rajya Sabha
Member-Standing Committee on Coal & Steel

सत्यमेव जयते

116, North Avenue
New Delhi-110001
Phone : 011-23093141
Mob. : 09868181381
Deoghar Ph. - 06432-225000
Mob.: 09431183181

:: 2 ::

The spectrum allocation has been done without even any study being made as to whether the spectrum allocation is being utilized efficiently or not. I also understand that the Hon'ble High Court of Delhi in one of the matters on the subject of spectrum allocation has adversely commented about the allocation of spectrum on the basis of some vague criteria and the operators serving much large number of subscribers within the given spectrum. This clearly shows that the operators earlier had much more spectrum than was required and they cornered the spectrum perhaps with a view to block the entry of new operators and gain at the cost of national exchequer.

It is surprising that today we are reading in the media about the value of spectrum being in thousands of crores whereas the same scarce spectrum has been given without any payment for additional spectrum. The only charge which the government made was for the usage of spectrum which varied from time to time based on the annual revenue. This usage charge cannot be equated with the initial cost of spectrum which has clearly led to loss to the national exchequer as has been reported in the media today.

The spectrum allocation issue needs to be investigated further and deeper right from the beginning as to how and when the spectrum was allocated and on what basis and why no charge was taken for the additional allocation of spectrum beyond what was mandated in the licence of the private operators.

With warm regards,

05.11.09

( Jaiprakash Narayan Singh )

CC :

a) Finance Minister
b) Minister for Communication & IT
c) CAG, New Delhi
d) Director, CBI
e) CVC, New Delhi.

सत्यमेव जयते

*Dr. M.V. Mysura Reddy*

**Member of Parliament (Rajya Sabha)**

Dated: 9th November, 2009.

***Respected Dr. Manmohan Singhji,***

There has been a lot of discussion in the media in the last few days on the issue of spectrum allocation and the irregularities alleged to have been committed by the Department of Telecom while allocating the scarce spectrum to the private operators at a throw away prices. The truth of allegations will be known finally when the CBI completes its investigation for any further appropriate action.

Due to the heat generated on the subject, I tried to examine the issue in a little more detail and found that there has been complete arbitrariness followed in the process of spectrum allocating right from the beginning. Spectrum allocation was being made without any proper guidelines or notifications ever issued by DoT (WPC) for spectrum management and allocation. The allegations being made and the astronomical figures being quoted for the alleged loss to the exchequer will pale into insignificance if the entire process of spectrum allocation is examined right from the beginning.

There have been large number violations in the allocation of spectrum to the private operators without payment of any additional fee for spectrum allocation. So far the public has been misled by the claims of the interested parties that a huge amount of money has been paid for the spectrum utilization in the form of spectrum usage charges paid annually based on the revenue percentage basis. To make the things clear I delved a little more into the subject and found the extra charges are being confused with the payment of spectrum usage charges and **in fact no amount has ever been paid for obtaining additional spectrum** (more than 6.2MHz which was originally mandated in the license). It is no wonder that the valuations of the cellular operators, who started their services in 1994-95, skyrocketed within a short time whenever they obtained additional spectrum.

20, Gurudwara, Rakab Ganj Road, New Delhi - 110 001. Ph : 011-23738231, Telefax : 011-23352002 Cell : 9868181119
E-mail : mv.mysurareddy@sansad.nic.in
Road No.12, Banjara Hills, Hyderabad. Ph : 040-23305759
Member - Standing Committee on Defence

*Dr. M.V. Mysura Reddy*

**Member of Parliament (Rajya Sabha)**

Specific cases have also come to my notice where the orders of the WPC itself were violated in allocating spectrum to the cellular operators especially during the period 2002-04. The DoT order dated 1.2.2002 specifically prescribed that spectrum beyond 6.2 to 8.0 MHz will be allocated to the operators only in 1800 MHz band but it is seen from the records that three/four cellular operators obtained spectrum beyond 6.2MHz also not in 1800 MHz band as was mandated in the DoT order dated 1st Feb 2002 (refer annexure I) but in more precious 900MHz band. (refer annexure II).

The significance of this violation can be understood on a simple principle that efficiency of 900MHz band is double than efficiency of the 1800MHz band for the cellular operations.

Spectrum to the operators was given upto 10 MHz without Subscriber Link Criteria policy norm which came out only in March 2006. Even the DoT order dated 1st Feb 2002, mentioned about the annual fees for spectrum utilization and no one-time charge for allotment of spectrum upto 10 MHz. Though the order mentioned the payment of revenue share, but no upfront charge was prescribed. Further, this order only mentioned that additional allocation of spectrum could be considered only after a suitable subscriber base as may be prescribed. However, this criteria prescribed was released in the year 2006 i.e. after a gap of almost 4 years. Thus the operators got spectrum upto 10MHz without any criteria or policy or guidelines and without any upfront charges. This free period allowed the incumbent operators to improve their financial strength and gave them opportunity to earn supernormal profits. Spectrum above contracted spectrum worth thousands of crores was distributed free of cost and at the cost of public exchequer without any upfront amount whereas the license conditions clearly indicated that contracted spectrum was upto 6.2 MHz only.

It is clear from the above that the spectrum scam hasn't started now. In fact it was in existence even i.e. from 2001 onwards without any policy or guidelines, spectrum was assigned to benefit the incumbent operators.

In view of the above what needs to be investigated is the spectrum allocation practices right from the beginning of the private cellular industry in the country since the scarcity of the spectrum and its valuation was equally the same at that time as is being made as today.

20, Gurudwara, Rakab Ganj Road, New Delhi - 110 001. Ph : 011-23738231, Telefax : 011-23352002 Cell : 9868181119
E-mail : mv.mysurareddy@sansad.nic.in
Road No.12, Banjara Hills, Hyderabad. Ph : 040-2330575

*Dr. M. V. Mysura Reddy*
**Member of Parliament (Rajya Sabha)**

Investigation in the entire spectrum allocation process would reveal much greater loss to the exchequer than what is being alleged today. Request you to order an in depth investigation through CBI and CVC so that bigger spectrum scam can also be unearthed.'

With warm regards,

Yours Truly,

**(M. V. MYSURA REDDY)**

Encld.: As-above.
***Dr. Manmohan Singh***
Hon'ble Prime Minister of India
**NEW DELHI.**

Copy to:-
1. The Hon'ble Minister for Finance
2. The Hon'ble Minister for Communication & IT
3. The Director – CBI
4. Central Vigilance Commissioner
5. Comptroller & Auditor General

## Annexure I

Government of India
Ministry of Communications
Department of Telecommunications
WPC Wing

No. L-14041/06/2000-NTG Dated: 01.02.2002

**ORDER**

Subject:-Allocation of additional Cellular Radio Frequency Spectrum to the Cellular Mobile, Telephone Service (CMTS) Providers.

In order to meet the requirements of growth of subscribers, it has been decided to assign additional spectrum upto 1.8 Mhz + 1.8 Mhz to the CMTS operators. Any operator may apply for allotment of additional spectrum after reaching a customer base of 4 Lakh or more under a license in a service area, after which the process of allotment would be initiated ; however, actual assignment of the spectrum would be made, subject to availability and coordination on case to case basis, after a customer base of 5 Lakh or more has been reached in the service area. This additional assignment will be beyond already allocated spectrum of 6.2 Mhz + 6.2 Mhz. The additional spectrum of 1.8 Mhz + 1.8 Mhz would be assigned in 1800 Mhz Band.

2. The cellular licensees are to pay spectrum charge with effect from 1.8.99 on revenue share basis at the rate of 2 % of Adjusted Gross Revenue (AGR) for spectrum upto 4.4 Mhz + 4.4 Mhz and 3% of AGR f. spectrum upto 6.2 Mhz + 6.2 Mhz.

3. Further, for this additional spectrum of 1.8 Mhz + 1.8 Mhz, if assigned for any one or more places in a Service Area, beyond 6.2 Mhz + 6.2 Mhz, an additional charge of 1% of AGR will be levied. Thus, the total spectrum charge to be paid by such operators would be 4% of AGR from the Service in the respective Service Area. This spectrum charge of 4% of AGR would also cover allocation of further spectrum , which may become possible to allocate in future subject to availability, to add up to a total spectrum allocation not exceeding 10 Mhz + 10 Mhz per operator in a Service Area. Such additional allocation could be considered only after a suitable subscriber base, as may be prescribed, is reached.

4. This order is issued in partial modification to the order of even number dated 22nd September, 2001; other terms and conditions of the said order shall remain unchanged.

1|2|1

(R. K. Srivastava)
Engineer

Copy to :

1. All concern
2. Cellular Operators Associations of India (COAI)
3. Cellular Service Providers

**List of operators given 900 MHz band in violation of DOT's own orders.**

WPC issued an order on 1.2.2002 vide No. L14041/06/2000-NTG prescribing that spectrum beyond 6.2 upto 8 MHz will be allocated to the operators **only in 1800 MHz band.**

**However, the following list shows allocation of 900 MHz band beyond 6.2 MHz also, even after having issued the order on 1.2.2002 against such allocation.**

| S. No. | Name of the Operator | Name of the Circle | Spectrum in 900 MHz | Date of allocation |
|---|---|---|---|---|
| 1 | Bharti | Delhi | 8 | 17.07.2002 |
| 2 | Vodafone | Delhi | 8 | 17.07.2002 |
| 3 | Vodafone | Mumbai | 8 | 17.07.2002 |
| 4 | BPL | Mumbai | 8 | 13.01.2003 |
| 5 | Vodafone | Kolkatta | 8 | 30.06.2004 |
| 6 | Idea | Maharashtra | 7.8 | 31.12.2003 |
| 7 | Vodafone | Gujarat | 7.4 | 14.11.2003 |
| 8 | Bharti | AP | 7.8 | 09.02.2004 |
| 9 | Bharti | Karnataka | 7.8 | 09.01.2004 |
| 10 | Aircel | Tamil Nadu | 7.8 | 09.01.2004 |
| 11 | Bharti | Punjab | 7.8 | 09.02.2004 |
| 12 | Spice | Punjab | 7.4 | 09.01.2004 |

**Allocation of additional spectrum from 4.4 to 6.2 MHz without any policy framework or guidelines and also without any additional payment for spectrum.**

## Bharti

| S. No. | Name of the Circle | Date of allotment |
|---|---|---|
| 1 | Delhi | 31.12.1996 |
| 2 | Kolkatta | 28.12.1999 |
| 3 | Chennai | 29.01.1998 |
| 4 | AP | 03.04.2000 |
| 5 | Himachal Pradesh | 19.9.2003 |
| 6 | Karnataka | 03.04.2000 |
| 7 | Punjab | 28.12.1999 |
| 8 | Rajasthan | 10.8.2000 |

## Vodafone

| S. No. | Name of the Circle | Date of allotment |
|---|---|---|
| 1 | Delhi (Hutch Essar) | 31.12.1996 |
| 2 | Mumbai (Hutchison Max) | 4.02.1997 |
| 3 | Kolkatta (Hutch Essar) | 28.01.1997 |
| 4 | Gujarat (Fascel) | 6.03.2000 |
| 5 | Kerala (Hutch Mobile) | 28.12.1999 |
| 6 | Maharashtra (Hutch Mobile) | 28.12.1999 |
| 7 | Tamil Nadu (Hutch Mobile) | 28.12.1999 |

## Idea

| S. No. | Name of the Circle | Date of allotment |
|---|---|---|
| 1 | AP | 27.12.2000 |
| 2 | Gujarat | 9.08.2000 |
| 3 | Haryana (Idea Mobile) | 28.12.1999 |
| 4 | Karnataka (Spice Com.) | 03.04.2000 |

| | | |
|---|---|---|
| 5 | Kerala (Idea Mobile) | 28.12.1999 |
| 6 | Maharashtra | 9.8.2000 |
| 7 | MP (BTA Cellcom) | 9.9.2002 |
| 8 | Punjab (Spice Com.) | 03.04.2000 |
| 9 | UP (W) | 28.12.1999 |

## Aircel

| S. No. | Name of the Circle | Date of allotment |
|---|---|---|
| 1 | Chennai | 01.03.2000 |
| 2 | Haryana | 02.01.2001 |
| 3 | Rajasthan | 02.01.2001 |
| 4 | Tamil Nadu | 06.10.1999 |
| 5 | UP (E) | 02.01.2001 |

## BPL

| S. No. | Name of the Circle | Date of allotment |
|---|---|---|
| 1 | Mumbai | 01.12.1996 |

## Reliance Telecom Limited

| S. No. | Name of the Circle | Date of allotment |
|---|---|---|
| 1 | Assam | 06.10.2003 |
| 2 | Bihar | 28.12.1999 |
| 3 | Himachal Pradesh | 26.08.2005 |
| 4 | MP | 08.01.2001 |
| 5 | North East | 20.01.2006 |
| 6 | Orissa | 05.09.2001 |
| 7 | West Bengal | 28.02.2004 |

Allocation of **spectrum upto 10 MHz** without any policy framework or any guidelines and without any additional payment for spectrum.

| S. No. | Name of the Company | Name of the Circle | Date of allotment |
|---|---|---|---|
| 1 | Bharti | Delhi | 17.07.2003 |
| 2 | Vodafone (Hutch) | Delhi | 15.10.2003 |
| 3 | Bharti | Mumbai | 20.01.2006 |
| 4 | Vodafone (Hutch) | Mumbai | 15.10.2003 |
| 5 | BPL | Mumbai | 06.09.2004 |
| 6 | Vodafone (Hutch) | Kolkatta | 12.07.2006 |
| 7 | Bharti | Chennai | 15.11.2006 |
| 8 | Aircel | Chennai | 15.11.2006 |
| 9 | Vodafone (Fascel) | Gujarat | 13.5.2005 |
| 10 | Bharti | Karnataka | 03.12.2004 |
| 11 | Idea | Maharashtra | 01.04.2005 |
| 12 | Aircel | Tamil Nadu | 03.12.2004 |

सत्यमेव जयते

**RAJEEV CHANDRASEKHAR**
MEMBER OF PARLIAMENT
RAJYA SABHA

Member of Standing Committee on Information Technology
Member of Consultative Committee on Finance
Member of Parliamentary Forum on Youth
Co-Chairman, Vigilance & Monitoring Committee, Bangalore Urban District

Respected Prime Minister,

26 November, 2010

**Sub. :** **Huge 2G Spectrum Losses – Need for Urgent Government Action**

This is in continuation to my various letters addressed to you on the subject and particularly, the letter written to you dated 11 May 2010 (copy enclosed herewith).

You will agree that Governments and Parliaments have a moral duty to act in Public Interest, and for any Government that lives by this belief - as I am sure your Government does - it must be its priority to identify the wrongdoers and recover the monies lost as a consequence of the cheap sale of spectrum.

There are many ways of recovering moneys from the different types of operators (new and old) relating to spectrum (new spectrum and additional spectrum). Some of the options available to the Government are :

a. Windfall taxes for those who have gained by resale of their cheap licenses.

b. Cancellation of licenses and re-auction of spectrum for illegal licenses. An alternate to cancellation and re-auction is to give the licensees the opportunity to pay up the balance license fees (calculated as the difference between the 3G license fees and what they have paid for 2G).

c. Existing operators to pay for extra spectrum at 3G benchmark rates or surrender them and buy them back through a re-auction of spectrum.

If the Government is serious about its obligations to public interest, then they would pursue the above instead of relying on arguments that are already being made expectedly to sweep this under the carpet.

The two arguments that are being used, i.e., investor interest and consumer interest, should not be allowed to come in the way of the action to achieve the twin objectives outlined above.

1

11th Floor, Major Tower, Sir M. Vishweshvaraiah Center, Dr. B. R. Ambedkar Veedhi, Bangalore-560001 India
Ph : 91-80-22863600, Tel/Fax : 91-80-22863680
E-mail : rajeev.c@nic.in
www.rajeev.in

I would like to make the following points for your consideration:

I. **Argument of Investor Interest**

The argument of investor interest should not be used and has no place in whatever action is decided by the Government.

(a) Telecom investors the world over and in India understand the need to currently pay market prices for spectrum – in a market like India which has little or no market or sectoral risk, and is poised to become one of the largest in the world. Those investors that do not understand the need to pay the market price for spectrum must be asked to learn that it is the case. The Government, and indeed the taxpayer, is not obliged to provide backstops for investors who take investment decisions based on illegal licenses and spectrum giveaways. Maybe there is an argument to improve the quality of investors we are attracting to our country and a change in the perception that robber baron investors are the ones that succeed in India.

(b) It is clear, according to the CAG report, that several of these companies have made false representations to acquire spectrum fraudulently. Clearly, those who made such false representations cannot be spared.

(c) The CAG has also pointed out that many existing Operators also have excess spectrum. As you are aware, these are all highly profitable companies with significant market capitalizations and value. Paying for this extra spectrum will be insignificant for their economics and true investors understand the need to pay market value for Spectrum.

(c) Moreover, any sector will do well to improve the quality of investors – especially from amongst those who have never been interested in investments. Majority of these new Telecom licensee companies had bought the license to sell it at a profitable value. Their interest is of no consequence since they would sell in any event. On the other hand, it is the buyer / operator whose interest is paramount, and under the circumstances, a cleaning up of the system and removal of such unwanted and undesirable elements would only add to the investor confidence – both Indian and global.

(c) Also, since vast majority of these companies have not made any significant rollouts, they have no case for arguing that their licenses are kept intact. Apart from TRAI recommendations based on lack of rollout, there is clear evidence that several companies have merely met the rollout obligations on paper – thus fooling the Government with a view to sell the licenses on the completion of three years, as per the current merger guidelines. Most companies will reach that stage by January / February 2011.

2

(d) Since the DoT has already circumvented TRAI's explicit recommendations that no M&As should take place till rollout obligations were met, by dropping the ban on acquisitions and modifying the merger guidelines to three years from date of license, rather than rollout – it is clear that these companies have, in collusion with officials in the Department, set out a dangerous plan which the Government must prevent with immediate effect.

II. <u>Argument of Consumer Interest</u>

The argument of consumer interest is, in any event, a non-issue for multiple reasons including :

(a) These companies hardly have any consumers in their circles. Their combined market share is in a lower single digit percentage.

(b) Each of these circles has multiple operators, and therefore, consumers can easily switch between operators and will have plenty of choice even if all the fraudulently acquired licenses / spectrum are withdrawn.

(c) With Mobile Number Portability on the anvil, every single subscriber with such dubious operators can simply change their operator with their current number intact, cost of such migration can be borne by the licensee.

So in conclusion, there is absolutely no case made out either for investor interest or consumer interest that will come in the way of the action that Government must take to recover the moneys and penalize the wrongdoers in this Spectrum Scam.

I hope that this communication will help forewarn the government of a second resultant scam, unless immediate steps are taken.

Yours Sincerely,

RAJEEV CHANDRASEKHAR

Dr. Manmohan Singh
Hon'ble Prime Minister
Government of India
New Delhi

3

D.O. No..1368./MP/LS/VIP/..

**Maheshwar Hazari**
Member of Parliament
(Lok Sabha)
**Member :**
• Standing Committee, Petroleum & Natural Gas
• Consultative Committee, Power
**Chairman :**
• District Vigilance & Monitoring Committee
For Rural Development Programmes, Samastipur (Bihar)

14-C, Ferozshah Road,
New Delhi-110001
Phone : 23327374
23327375

सत्यमेव जयते

Ref. No. ..............................

Dated 29 NOV 2010

Dr. Manmohan Singh ji,
Hon'ble Prime Minister of India
Govt. of India
South Block
New Delhi

**Subject:** **Conduct of CAG is questionable as to how the issue of 9 licenses issued to Vodafone did not figure in the recent CAG report. Enquiries should be conducted immediately by the Chief Vigilance Commissioner (CVC) and Central Bureau of Investigation (CBI) in connection with financial irregularities and huge benefits provided to Vodafone Essar Limited (Vodafone) owned by Mr. Shashi Ruia, which has caused over Rs.13600 Crores loss to public Exchequer in respect of allotment of spectrum for Mumbai Circle and issue of 9 new licenses in 2004 – 2007.**

Respected Dr. Manmohan Singh ji,

The CAG report 2010 on telecom issues has caused much uproar in both the houses of parliament. The CAG has come up with a figure pointing to potential loss of Rs.1,76,645 Crores on account of allotment of 2G spectrum to the new and dual technology licensees and the allotment of excess spectrum beyond the entitlement. I believe that this has been the biggest exposure in recent times.

2. I remember that the Government suffered a similar loss in 1999 wherein the licensees of Cellular Mobile services for Metros were rewarded by abrogating them with the tender conditions and relieving them with the license fee and royalty charges as committed by them while getting the licenses. Not only, the license fee was dropped in favour of revenue share, even the licensing period was increased from 10 years to 20 years without any additional fees. Since the licenses involved in this case were for Delhi, Mumbai, Kolkata and Chennai, which are the potential revenue earning areas, one could understand the potential loss to the Government on account of such undue favours to the operators of these Metro Cities viz. S/Shri Sunil Mittal, Kumar Manglam Birla, Shashi Ruia etc.

1

**Maheshwar Hazari**
Member of Parliament
(Lok Sabha)
**Member :**
• Standing Committee, Petroleum & Natural Gas
• Consultative Committee, Power
**Chairman :**
• District Vigilance & Monitoring Committee
For Rural Development Programmes, Samastipur (Bihar)

14-C, Ferozshah Road
New Delhi-110001
Phone : 23327374
23327375

Ref. No. ..............................

Dated ....................

**In such cases, the CAG in their report of 2000, gave definitive figures for losses incurred to the Government, but no action has been taken, while the losses as per CAG report of 2010 are on presumptive basis as per CAG's own admission in the report.**

3. Incidentally, these operators continued to get additional favours and no investigations were carried out at that time for the loss of revenue to the Government. Vodafone owned by Shri Shashi Ruia, paid a total of Rs.21 Crores licenses fee for 3 years for Mumbai License i.e. Rs.3 Crores for the first year, 6 Crores for the second year and Rs.12 Crores for the third year and after that stopped payment of license fee and the royalty charges.

4. Government did not take any action against Shri Shashi Ruia for non payment of License Fee and in fact rewarded him by relieving him of the license fees in favour of revenue share and also gifted him a 20 years License instead of the existing 10 years license without any charges.

5. Shri Shashi Ruia managed to get 10 MHz of spectrum against the entitlement of 6.2 MHz and most of it in the 900 MHz premium band. Shri Ruia got 8 MHz of spectrum out of 10MHz in 900 MHz band against the policy of the DoT that no operator would get spectrum more than 6.2 MHz in 900 MHz band. This helped Shri Shashi Ruia to save thousands of crores CAPEX and OPEX and on the other hand deprived other operators to get spectrum in the 900 MHz premium band, causing them to invest more in the other bands and also created a non level playing field for a new operator from day one.

6. The 3G auction has concluded recently and the Government has **auctioned 5 MHz of 3G** spectrum in Mumbai at a price of Rs.3247 Crores. As such 10 MHz of spectrum **will cost Rs.12000 Crores based on TRAI recommendations of treatment of allotment in 900 MHz at 1.5 times the 3G price and by applying multiplication factor of 1.3 in case allotted spectrum exceeds 8 MHz.** While Vodafone paid only Rs.21 Crores of License Fee during the last 15 years for 10 MHz of spectrum. This establishes a clear and continued nexus between Shri Shashi Ruia and the DoT and WPC officials right from day one.

2

[signature]

**Maheshwar Hazari**
Member of Parliament
(Lok Sabha)
**Member :**
• Standing Committee, Petroleum & Natural Gas
• Consultative Committee, Power
**Chairman :**
• District Vigilance & Monitoring Committee
For Rural Development Programmes, Samastipur (Bihar)

14-C, Ferozshah Road,
New Delhi-110001
Phone : 23327374
23327375

Ref. No. ..............................

Dated ..................

7. On going through the report, it is noticed that the report only takes into account the new licenses issues in 2008, and the excess spectrum and spectrum issued under dual technology. The report has completely ignored the licenses issued between 2004 and 2007 to Vodafone , at 2001 prices. It is beyond my understanding as to why CAG chose to ignore the losses incurred to the Government on account of the 9 licenses issued by DOT between 2004 and 2007 to Vodafone. The details of these licenses are as under :

| Sl. No. | Service Area | Effective Date of Licence |
|---|---|---|
| 1 | Assam | 05-12-06 |
| 2 | Bihar | 05-12-06 |
| 3 | Himachal Pradesh | 05-12-06 |
| 4 | Jammu & Kashmir | 05-12-06 |
| 5 | Madhya Pradesh | 20-03-07 |
| 6 | North East | 05-12-06 |
| 7 | Orissa | 05-12-06 |
| 8 | Uttar Pradesh (West) | 13-02-04 |
| 9 | West Bengal | 23-03-04 |

**8. In case of these 9 licenses, the potential loss to the exchequer, would be an additional amount of Rs 1600 Crores. Thus the total loss to the exchequer on account of benefits provided to Vodafone would be about Rs 13600 Crores**

**9. Request**

**The Government should immediately order investigations by the Chief Vigilance Commissioner (CVC) and Central Bureau of Investigation (CBI) in connection with irregularities and undue benefits granted to Sh Shashi Ruia owned Vodafone resulting into over Rs.13600 Crores to Exchequer in respect allotment of spectrum for Delhi Circle and specifically on the following:**

**Maheshwar Hazari**
Member of Parliament
(Lok Sabha)
Member :
• Standing Committee, Petroleum & Natural Gas
• Consultative Committee, Power
Chairman :
• District Vigilance & Monitoring Committee
For Rural Development Programmes, Samastipur (Bihar)

14-C, Ferozshah Road,
New Delhi-110001
Phone : 23327374
23327375

Dated ..................

Ref. No. ..............................

i) **Allotment of spectrum of 10 MHz spectrum at near zero price for Mumbai Circle to Vodafone resulting in loss of Rs 12000 Crores to the Government exchequer.**

ii) **Omission of 9 licenses issued to Vodafone between 2004 and 2007 at 2001 prices, by CAG in its report of 2010 resulting into a loss of Rs.1600 Crores.**

iii) **Criminal nexus between Shri Shashi Ruia and DoT officials for benefitting Vodafone, causing huge loss to the Government Exchequer and creation of monopoly against the tenets of competition and free market.**

With warm regards,

Yours Sincerely,

Maheshwar Hazari

( Maheshwar Hazari )

Copy for kind information:

1. Shri Pranab Mukherjee , Hon'ble Minister of Finance,
2. Shri Kapil Sibal, Hon'ble Minister of Communication & Information Technology,
3. Shri Vinod Rai, Comptroller and Auditor General of India,
4. Shri P.J. Thomas, Central Vigilance Commissioner,
5. Dr. Murli Manohar Joshi, Chairman, Committee – Public Accounts (PAC)
6. All Members of PAC.
7. Ms. Vini Mahajan, Joint Secretary PMO

4

Immediate

सत्यमेव जयते

ASHWANI KUMAR MP

Member, Public Accounts Committee of Parliament
Member, Standing Committee of Parliament on External Affairs

November 20, 2010

Respected Dr. Sahib,

I. The Opposition has repeatedly stalled the functioning of Parliament over their demand for constituting a JPC on the ground that the PAG cannot be a substitute for JPC because the latter has larger powers and a wider jurisdiction to investigate the 2G Spectrum issue.

The enclosed piece by Riccardo Pelizzo and Rick Stapenhurst extracted from Pelizzo, R; Stapenhurst, R; and Olson, D.2006 entitled "Parliamentary Oversight for Government Accountability" WBI Working Papers – World Bank PP. 23-35" would show that the jurisdiction of PAC is wide enough to summon and receive depositions from public officials on issues under investigation. There is no specific bar upon the PAC from seeking clarifications even from Ministers, if required. (See Chart in Annexure/B.) It has also being brought about in various studies including the one by PRS Legislative Intent that "about 75% recommendations of the PAC were accepted by the Government during the period of the 14th Lok Sabha".

From the enclosed Note 'A' which contains relevant extracts from information on Committee on Public Accounts on http://164.100.24.208/ls/committees/p17.htm?comm_code=26 it is clear that "the functions of the Committee extend beyond the formality of expenditure to its wisdom, faithfulness and economy". The PAC may thus examine cases involving losses and financial irregularities including negligence resulting in loss or extravagance. The Committee is entitled to express disapproval or pass strictures in the above situations. It is now well established that the PAC is competent and indeed called upon to discuss "points of financial discipline and principle". Although the PAC is not concerned with questions of policy in the broad sense which must remain in the domain of the Executive, the Committee is not absolutely precluded from pointing to the wisdom or otherwise of the policy where extravagance, waste or loss of public funds resulted from is implementation. In this view of the matter I believe that the Opposition's claim for a JPC can and should be forcefully and publicly rebutted.

II. HEARING IN THE SUPREME COURT

(A) Government Lawyers arguing in the Suprme Court on Tuesday (23rd Nov) should focus, on showing on an overall basis that this was not a case of inaction by the PMO and that, even assuming that the Sanctioning Authority was under a duty to take a decision either way, the discretion could not have been fairly exercised without the results of an independent official investigation being available to the PMO.

18, Ashok Road, New Delhi-110 001 Telefax: 23354222
C-9, Friends Colony (East), New Delhi - 110 065 Tel : 26832102, Telefax : 26842758
E-mail : contactaklawchambers@gmail.com

सत्यमेव जयते

ASHWANI KUMAR MP

Member, Public Accounts Committee of Parliament
Member, Standing Committee of Parliament on External Affairs

(B) In my considered view, the submissions should be limited to the allegation of delay without getting into the argument on whether the representation for sanction of prosecution was properly presented or not. This point even if available in law could have been agitated under normal circumstances in subordinate courts, but in the present circumstances and at this stage it may not be prudent to focus on a technicality, in which case there is a risk of keeping the issue alive. The end objective should be to convince the court that upon the results of the investigations being available (which may not be to far away) a suitable view would be taken.

(C) Submissions to be advanced in the Supreme Court should not be canvassed in the media as a matter of policy.

With deepest regards

Yours sincerely,

Ashwani Kumar

(ASHWANI KUMAR)

DR. MANMOHAN SINGH JI
HON'BLE PRIME MINISTER
7, RACE COURSE ROAD
NEW DELHI

18, Ashok Road, New Delhi-110 001 Telefax: 23354222
**C-9, Friends** Colony (East), New Delhi - 110 065 Tel : 26832102, Telefax : 26842758
**E-mail :** contactaklawchambers@gmail.com

*Sushil Kumar Singh*
Member of Parliament
(Lok Sabha)

Member .
(i) Estimate Committee
(ii) Standing (Committee & IT)
(iii) Consultative (Petroleum)

सत्यमेव जयते

16A, Ferozshah Road
New Delhi-110001

Singh Kothi
Aurangabad (Bihar)

Telephone :
New Delhi : 011-23354155
Fax : 011-23354156
Aurangabad : 06186-226300

29 November, 2010

Dr. Manmohan Singh ji,
Hon'ble Prime Minister of India
South Block
New Delhi

Subject: **The Government should immediately order investigations by the Chief Vigilance Commissioner (CVC) and Central Bureau of Investigation (CBI) in connection with irregularities and undue benefits granted to Mr. Sunil Bharti Mittal owned Bharti Airtel Limited (Bharti) resulting into over Rs.12000 crs to Exchequer in respect allotment of spectrum for Delhi Circle and specifically on the following:**

i) **Allotment of spectrum of 10 Mhz in 900 MHz band at near zero price for Delhi Circle to Bharti resulting in loss of Rs 12074 Crores to the Government exchequer.**

ii) **Criminal nexus between Shri Sunil Mittal and DoT officials for benefitting Bharti, causing huge loss to the Government Exchequer and creation of monopoly against the tenets of competition and free market.**

Respected Pradhan Mantriji,

Since the tabling of CAG report on the issue of licenses and allocation of 2G spectrum in both the houses of Parliament, the people of this country have been exposed to a scam involving a potential loss of Rs.1,76,645 Crores on account of allotment of 2G spectrum to the new and dual technology licensees and the allotment of excess spectrum beyond the entitlement. I believe that this has been the biggest exposure in recent times.

Sushil Kumar Singh
Member of Parliament
(Lok Sabha)

Member :
(i) Estimate Committee
(ii) Standing (Committee & IT)
(iii) Consultative (Petroleum)

सत्यमेव जयते

16A, Ferozshah Road
New Delhi-110001

Singh Kothi
Aurangabad (Bihar)

Telephone :
New Delhi : 011-23354155
Fax : 011-23354156
Aurangabad : 06186-226300

I understand that the Government suffered a similar loss in 1999 wherein the licensees of Cellular Mobile services for Metros were rewarded by abrogating them with the tender conditions and relieving them with the license fee and royalty charges as committed by them while getting the licenses. Not only, the license fee was dropped in favour of revenue share, even the licensing period was increased from 10 years to 20 years without any additional fees. Since the licenses involved in this were for Delhi, Mumbai, Kolkata and Chennai, which are the potential revenue earning areas, one could understand the potential loss to the Government on account of such undue favours to the operators of these Metro Cities viz. S/Shri Sunil Mittal, Kumar Manglam Birla, Sashi Ruia etc.

Incidentally, these operators continued to get patronage of CAG and CVC as no investigations were carried out at that time for the loss of revenue to the Government. Shri Sunil Mittal, who paid a total of Rs.14 Crores licenses fee for 3 years for Delhi License i.e. Rs.2 Crores for the first year, 4 Crores for the second year and Rs.8 Crores for the third year and after that stopped payment of license fee and the royalty charges.

Government did not take any action against Shri Sunil Mittal for none payment of License Fee and in fact rewarded him by reliving him of the license fees in favour of revenue share and also gifted him a 20 years License instead of the existing 10 years license without any charges.

Shri Sunil Mittal arranged to get 10 MHz of spectrum against the entitlement of 6.2 MHz and most of it in the 900 MHz premium band. Shri Mittal got 8 MHz of spectrum out of 10MHz in 900 MHz band against the policy of the DoT that no operator would get spectrum more than 6.2 MHz in 900 MHz band. This helped Shri Sunil Mittal to save thousands of crores CAPEX and OPEX on the other hand deprived other operators to get spectrum in the 900 MHz premium band, causing them to invest more in the other bands.

2

*Sushil Kumar Singh*
Member of Parliament
(Lok Sabha)

Member :
(i) Estimate Committee
(ii) Standing (Committee & IT)
(iii) Consultative (Petroleum)

सत्यमेव जयते

16A, Ferozshah Road
New Delhi-110001

Singh Kothi
Aurangabad (Bihar)

Telephone :
New Delhi : 011-23354155
Fax : 011-23354156
Aurangabad : 06186-226300

It may kindly be recalled that recently the Government has auctioned 5 MHz of 3G spectrum in Delhi at a price of Rs.3317 Crores. As such 10 MHz of spectrum **will cost Rs.12074 Crores based on TRAI recommendations of treatment of allotment in 900 MHz at 1.5 times the 3G price and by applying multiplication factor of 1.3 in case allotted spectrum is above 8 MHz.** While Bharti paid only Rs.14 Crores of License Fee during the last 15 years for 10 MHz of spectrum. This establishes a clear and continued nexus between Shri Sunil Mittal and the DoT and WPC officials right from day one.

**Request**

**The Government should immediately order investigations by the Chief Vigilance Commissioner (CVC) and Central Bureau of Investigation (CBI) in connection with irregularities and undue benefits granted to Mr. Sunil Bharti Mittal owned Bharti Airtel Limited (Bharti) resulting into over Rs.12000 crs to Exchequer in respect allotment of spectrum for Delhi Circle and specifically on the following:**

i) **Allotment of spectrum of 10 Mhz in 900 MHz band at near zero price for Delhi Circle to Bharti resulting in loss of Rs 12074 Crores to the Government exchequer.**

ii) **Criminal nexus between Bharti Airtel and DoT officials for benefitting Bharti, causing huge loss to the Government Exchequer and creation of monopoly against the tenets of competition and free market.**

With kind regards,

Yours,

(Sushil Kumar Singh)

3

*Sushil Kumar Singh*
Member of Parliament
(Lok Sabha)

Member :
(i) Estimate Committee
(ii) Standing (Committee & IT)
(iii) Consultative (Petroleum)

16A, Ferozshah Road
New Delhi-110001

Singh Kothi
Aurangabad (Bihar)

Telephone :
New Delhi : 011-23354155
Fax : 011-23354156
Aurangabad : 06186-226300

**Copy for kind information:**

1. Shri Pranab Mukherjee , Hon'ble Minister of Finance,
2. Shri Kapil Sibal, Hon'ble Minister of Communication & Information Technology,
3. Shri Vinod Rai, Comptroller and Auditor General of India,
4. Shri P.J. Thomas, Central Vigilance Commissioner,
5. Shri Ashwani Kumar, Director, CBI
6. Dr. Murli Manohar Joshi, Chairman, Committee – Public Accounts (PAC)
7. All Members of PAC.
8. Ms. Vini Mahajan, Joint Secretary PMO

4

**RUDRA MADHAB RAY**
Member of Parliament
(Lok Sabha)
Kandhamal, Orrisa

**Member:**
- Standing Committee on Railways
- Consultative Committee on Social Justice & Empowerment
- Committee on MPLADS

सत्यमेव जयते

200, North Avenue,
New Delhi-110011
Phone: 06842-255966
0674-2390332
Mobile: 9437006400, 9013180235
E-mail: rmray.Mpplb13@gmail.com

Ref. No. .......................... Date ..............................

**Shri Ashwini Kumar**
**Director, Central Bureau of Investigation (CBI)**
**Block No. 4, 6th Floor**
**CGO Complex**
**Lodhi Road**
**New Delhi-110003**

**Subject:** **Investigations in relation to criminal nexus and conspiracy of Mr. Sunil Bharti Mittal, owner of Bharti Airtel Limited (Bharti) and Bharti with the officials of DOT in connection with spectrum allocation**

**Dear Sir,**

Dec.-2010

**This is regarding the CAG Report on the issue of licenses and allocation of 2G spectrum, which was tabled in both the Houses of Parliament on 16.11.2010. It has been alleged by the CAG** that there was a potential loss of `1,76,645 Crores because of the allotment of 2G spectrum in 2008 at the prices arrived in 2001.

2. I would like to draw your attention to para 4.10 of the CAG Report wherein the CAG had estimated a potential loss of `36993 Crores on account of allotment of 150 MHz of spectrum beyond the contracted quantity **absolutely free to some of the companies like Bharti owned by Shri Sunil Mittal/ Idea owned by Shri**

**Kumar Mangalam Birla, Vodafone owned by Shri Sashi Ruia** and BSNL and MTNL owned by Government. The CAG has devoted less than a page for this potential loss whereas the complete report is covering about 80 pages. This appears to me a bigger scandal than the one quoted in the press.

3. It pains me to note that a lot of hue and cry has been made by the CAG and in the media that the new licenses were issued in 2008 at the price derived in 2001 and as such the government has suffered a potential loss of 1,76,000 crores. It may be brought to your notice that the scarce spectrum was not only allotted in 2008 to the new licensees but was also allotted to the existing operators and that too absolutely free, unlike the new licensees where they were charged. An analysis of the spectrum allotment in 2008-2009 has revealed that Bharti continued to get the additional spectrum even up to March, 2009, beyond its entitlement and without any payment at all.

4. The details of spectrum allotment to Bharti from January, 2008 till March, 2009 are given below:

| S. No. | Date of Allotment of excess spectrum (beyond 6.2 MHz.) | Amount of Spectrum Allotted in MHz). | Service Area |
|---|---|---|---|
| 1. | 10.01.2008 | 1.8 | West Bengal (Within the contracted limit) |
| 2. | 27.05.2008 | 1.4 | Andhra Pradesh |
| 3. | 30.07.2008 | 0.6 | Tamil Nadu |
| 4. | 24.09.2008 | 0.2 | Karnataka |
| 5. | 03.10.2008 | 0.2 | Bihar |

| | | | |
|---|---|---|---|
| 6. | 14.11.2008 | 1.0 | Maharashtra |
| 7. | 30.11.2008 | 1.0 | Bihar |
| 8. | 23.12.2008 | 1.8 | North East (Within the contracted limit) |
| 9. | 23.12.2008 | 2.0 | Rajasthan |
| 10. | 21.01.2009 | 1.0 | U.P (East) |
| 11. | 09.03.2009 | 1.0 | Maharashtra |
| 12. | 09.03.2009 | 0.8 | Andhra Pradesh |
| | **Total** | **12.8** | |

5. It would be seen from above that Bharti got 12.8 MHz of scarce spectrum, most of it beyond the contracted amount, absolutely free. This allotment of spectrum has helped Bharti in saving thousands of crores of rupees worth CAPEX and OPEX but the Government got nothing.

6. I am surprised that the spectrum continued to be allotted to Bharti without any charges even after having come across that Swan and Unitech have divested a portion of their stake at a much higher cost than at which the 4.4MHz was acquired by them. Surprisingly, the CAG has quietly ignored such serious issues for the reasons best known to them.

7. **To commence investigations and complete the same on an urgent basis in relation to criminal nexus and conspiracy of Mr. Sunil Bharti Mittal, owner of Bharti Airtel Limited (Bharti) and Bharti with the officials of DOT in connection with:**

(i) **How Bharti was allotted excess spectrum of 32.4 MHz, which is beyond the contracted quantum of spectrum, absolutely free,**

**across Pan India, causing a loss to the Government exchequer in excess of 40,000 Crores.**

**(ii) The intent of allotment of excess spectrum was to create a monopolistic status for Bharti, which helped Bharti to capture in excess of 32% of Telecom revenue market share, which violated provisions of The Competition Act, 2002.**

**(iii) The criminal conspiracy continued by allotting excess spectrum free of cost to Bharti right up to 31 March, 2009, while the new licensees were not allotted any spectrum.**

**(iv) New licensees have been highlighted in the 2010 Audit Report of CAG, whereas the issue of excess spectrum at no cost to Bharti right up to 31 March 2009 has almost escaped the attention of the CAG. Why?**

**I will also request and urge you to please summon and interrogate Shri Sunil Mittal in the same manner as the Chairmen/ Managing Directors/ CEOs of other companies in connection with the criminal case filed on various telecom matters.**

With regards,

Yours sincerely,

**(Rudra Madhab Ray)**

1/12/10.

Copy for kind information:

1. Dr. Manmohan Singh, Hon'ble Prime Minister of India
2. Shri Pranab Mukherjee , Hon'ble Minister of Finance,

3. Shri Kapil Sibal, Hon'ble Minister of Communication & Information Technology,
4. Shri Vinod Rai, Comptroller and Auditor General of India,
5. Shri P.J. Thomas, Central Vigilance Commissioner,
6. Dr. Murli Manohar Joshi, Chairman, Committee – Public Accounts (PAC)
7. All Members of PAC.
8. Ms. Vini Mahajan, Joint Secretary PMO
9. Shri Nitin Gadkari, President, BJP
10. Smt. Sushma Swaraj, The Leader of Opposition, Lok Sabha, New Delhi
11. Shri Arun Jaitley, The Leader of Opposition, Rajya Sabha, New Delhi

*Sushil Kumar Singh*
Member of Parliament
(Lok Sabha)

Member :
(i) Estimate Committee
(ii) Standing (Committee & IT)
(iii) Consultative (Petroleum)

16A. Ferozshah Road
New Delhi-110001

Singh Kothi
Aurangabad (Bihar)

Telephone :
New Delhi : 011-23354155
Fax : 011-23354156
Aurangabad : 06186-226300

3rd December, 2010

Dr. Manmohan Singh ji,
Hon'ble Prime Minister of India
Govt. of India
South Block
New Delhi

**Subject: Allotment of 21 new Telecom Licenses in 2004 & 2006 at 2001 prices issued to Aircel / Dishnet owned by Dr. Pratap Reddy and allotment of excess spectrum absolutely free in 2004 / 2006 needs investigation on urgent basis. The conduct of CAG also needs to be investigated as to how the issue of such licenses did not figure in his Audit Report.**

Respected Dr. Manmohan Singh ji,

I draw your kind attention to the Report on the Issue of Licenses and Allocation of 2G Spectrum prepared by the Comptroller and Auditor General of India (CAG) and tabled in both the houses of Parliament on 16th November, 2010. The CAG has alleged a potential loss of Rs.1,76,645 Crores because of the issue of Telecom Licenses in 2008 at a price discovered in 2001.

2. I notice from the report that the potential loss has been worked out on account of licenses issued in 2008 and the excess and dual technology spectrum allotted in 2008 and 2009. A number of questions crop up in my mind about this report i.e.:

i) Whether no new Telecom Licenses were issued between 2004 to 2007 and if issued, why these were not included in this Report of the CAG or were they included in any earlier CAG Report?

*Sushil Kumar Singh*
Member of Parliament
(Lok Sabha)
Member :
(i) Estimate Committee
(ii) Standing (Committee & IT)
(iii) Consultative (Petroleum)

सत्यमेव जयते

16A, Ferozshah Road
New Delhi-110001

Singh Kothi
Aurangabad (Bihar)

Telephone :
New Delhi : 011-23354155
Fax : 011-23354156
Aurangabad : 06186-226300

ii) Whether no spectrum was allotted by the DoT to the Telecom Operators between 2004 to 2007 and if allotted, why the impact of allotment of such spectrum was not included in the CAG Report or such impact was included in the earlier CAG Report?

3. **I feel that this potential loss to the exchequer would have been in the range of Rs.3,00,000 Crores if the impact of New Licenses issued and the Spectrum allotted in 2004 to 2007 was also included in this report. The reasons for downplaying the potential loss by excluding the period 2004 to 2007 cannot be incidental and it appears to me a calculated move by the CAG because a number of established operators and renowned entrepreneurs would have been exposed by this inclusion.**

4 It has come to my notice that Aircel / Dishnet owned by Dr.Pratap Reddy had received 7 new Telecom Licenses in 2004 and 14 new Telecom Licenses in 2006 at the price discovered in 2001. The company had only Telecom Licenses of Tamil Nadu / Chennai before 2004. It has also come to my notice that this company had received additional spectrum beyond its entitlement of 6.2 MHz absolutely free in respect of their telecom licenses held in Tamil Nadu and Chennai as per the details given below:

| Sr. No. | Date of Allotment of Excess Spectrum (beyond 6.2 MHz) | Amount of Spectrum Allotted in MHz | Service Area |
|---|---|---|---|
| 1. | 09.01.2004 | 1.6 (900 MHz) | Tamil Nadu |
| 2. | 03.12.2004 | 2.0 | Tamil Nadu |
| 3. | 20.01.2006 | 1.8 | Chennai |
| 4. | 15.11.2006 | 0.6 | Chennai |
| | Total | 6.00 | |

*Sushil Kumar Singh*
MEMBER OF PARLIAMENT
(LOK SABHA)

MEMBER :-
Estimate Committee
Standing (Communication & IT)
Consultative (Petroleum)

सत्यमेव जयते

16A, Ferozshah Road,
New Delhi-110001

Singh Kothi,
Aurangabad (Bihar)

Telephone :
New Delhi : 011-23354155
Fax : 011-23354156
Aurangabad : 06186-226300

5. It would be seen that not only the company owned by Dr.Pratap Reddy got 21 new Telecom Licenses in 2004 and 2006 at 2001 prices; the company also got 6 MHz of Spectrum beyond the amount mandated in the licenses and 1.6 MHz out of this in 900 MHz premium band and that too against the DoT guidelines that spectrum beyond 6.2 MHz should not be allotted in 900 MHz to anyone. In this case, Aircel got 7.8 MHz of Spectrum in this premium band. All this spectrum has been allotted to the company absolutely free and the licenses were awarded at a price of 2001. This allotment of excess spectrum has helped Aircel in saving CAPEX and OPEX worth Rs.2000 Crores. Surprisingly, the CAG has ignored such serious issues for the reasons unknown to me at least. Inclusion of these licenses and excess spectrum would have boosted the loss to the Government by another Rs.18,000 Crores.

6. **I will request you to kindly order investigation by CBI or any other appropriate authority:**

   a) **Why the CAG had omitted 21 licenses issued in 2004 and 2006 to Aircel / Dishnet in its report of 2010 ?**

   b) **Why the excess spectrum of 6 MHz was allotted to the Company in 2004 and 2006 absolutely free?**

   c) **Why 1.6 MHz of Excess Spectrum was allotted to the company in Tamil Nadu in 900 MHz band beyond the license conditions?**

With kind regards,

Yours,

(Sushil Kumar Singh)

3

*Sushil Kumar Singh*
Member of Parliament
(Lok Sabha)

Member :
(i) Estimate Committee
(ii) Standing (Committee & IT)
(iii) Consultative (Petroleum)

सत्यमेव जयते

16A, Ferozshah Road
New Delhi-110001

Singh Kothi
Aurangabad (Bihar)

Telephone :
New Delhi : 011-23354155
Fax : 011-23354156
Aurangabad : 06186-226300

**Copy for kind information:**

1. Shri Pranab Mukherjee , Hon'ble Minister of Finance,
2. Shri Kapil Sibal, Hon'ble Minister of Communication & Information Technology,
3. Shri Vinod Rai, Comptroller and Auditor General of India,
4. Shri P.J. Thomas, Central Vigilance Commissioner,
5. Dr. Murli Manohar Joshi, Chairman, Committee – Public Accounts (PAC)
6. All Members of PAC.
7. Ms. Vini Mahajan, Joint Secretary PMO

Ramesh Rathod
**MEMBER OF PARLIAMENT**
**(LOK SABHA)**

Member Standing Committee on Coal & Steel
Member Papers Laid on the Table

121 – South Avenue,
New Delhi – 110001
Mob : 901318028
Email: office.rameshrathod@gmail.com

Permanent Address: Sevadas Nagar Utnoor
Distt.: Adilabad, Andhra Pradesh
Tel. (08731) 274188, Mob: 9440435537
Fax : (08731) 274188

15th December, 2010

Dr. Manmohan Singh ji
Hon'ble Prime Minister of India
Govt. of India
South Block
New Delhi

Subject : **Excess Spectrum of up to 3.6 MHz has been given in 900 MHz band to incumbent operators –should be withdrawn and alternated spectrum should be provided in 1800 MHz band.**

**Initial allotment of 6.2 MHz spectrum was made to incumbent operators without any license guidelines. Why?**

**Spectrum up to 10 MHz has been given to incumbent operators free of cost and without any allocation guidelines. The excess spectrum should be charged as per the CAG method based on 3G auction, which comes to Rs 36993 Crores.**

**To institute an enquiry under retired Supreme Court Judge to examine the whole issue of allotment of spectrum since 1994 to unearth the ugly nexus between WPC officers and the telecom operators.**

Dear Dr Manmohan Singh Ji,

It is very painful that working of Democratic Institutions like Lok Sabha and Rajya Sabha have been granted to a halt now because of the so called scandal of 2G Spectrum. I am of the firm opinion that our policy makers in the DoT knew extremely well about the scarcity, limited availability of spectrum and the value of allotment of such spectrum to the operators right from the day the bids were invited for the first two cellular licenses in 1992. The custodians of spectrum have been manipulating the information with respect to the availability and allotment of spectrum in league and connivance with the telecom operators to suit their interests.

1

**Ramesh Rathod**
**MEMBER OF PARLIAMENT**
**(LOK SABHA)**

Member Standing Committee on Coal & Steel
Member Papers Laid on the Table

121 – South Avenue,
New Delhi – 110001
Mob : 901318028
Email: office.rameshrathod@gmail.com

Permanent Address: Sevadas Nagar Utnoor
Distt.: Adilabad, Andhra Pradesh
Tel. (08731) 274188, Mob: 9440435537
Fax : (08731) 274188

You may kindly recall that the allotment of spectrum to the cellular operators had been in the news very frequently at least during the last 3 to 4 years. The press articles covered wide range of distortions carried out by the DoT in the policies with respect to the allotment of spectrum during the last one decade.

It is surprising that CAG, CVC, CBI or any Government agency did not take any action on these reports which had been appearing in the media for a long time and it is a result of such apartheid shown by the Government towards such a valuable asset as spectrum that a scandal involving about Rs.2 Lacs Crores has been unearthed now by the CAG.

It has been brought to my notice that the DoT / WPC Officers responsible for the allotment of spectrum have always been keeping the availability of spectrum under close wrap and have been allotting the spectrum as per their whims and fancies and as per the dictates of the influential operators. Following issues of malpractices in the allotment of spectrum have been brought to my notice:

i) The WPC wing of the DoT had allotted 6.2 MHz as the startup spectrum to a certain set of operators who took part in the bidding of 4th Cellular License. This was a special favour shown by the WPC wing to these operators since 4.4 MHz was and had always been the startup spectrum till date barring some of the above indicated fourth cellular licensees. Some of the operators even got 6.2 MHz in 900 MHz band when it was clearly laid down in the license that all spectrum to 4th cellular licensees will be only in 1800 MHz band. This allotment of higher amount of spectrum as a startup helped the operators to save thousands of crores of CAPEX. The details of such operators are placed at **Annexure – 1.**

ii) The WPC wing of the DoT had allotted upto 8 MHz of spectrum in the premium 900 MHz band to a certain set of operators even though the policy guidelines prohibited allotment of more than 6.2 MHz in this band.

**Ramesh Rathod**
**MEMBER OF PARLIAMENT**
**(LOK SABHA)**

Member Standing Committee on Coal & Steel
Member Papers Laid on the Table

सत्यमेव जयते

121 – South Avenue,
New Delhi –110001
Mob : 901318028
Email: office.rameshrathod@gmail.com

Permanent Address: Sevadas Nagar Utnoor
Distt.: Adilabad, Andhra Pradesh
Tel. (08731) 274188, Mob: 9440435537
Fax : (08731) 274188

It is well known that 900 MHz band is at least two to three times more efficient than 1800 MHz band. By allotting upto 8 MHz in the 900 MHz band, the WPC wing of the DoT had helped the operators again to save thousands of crores of rupees of CAPEX. The details of such allotments are given in **Annexure – 2.**

iii) The WPC wing of the DoT allotted upto 10 MHz of spectrum to the operators without any guidelines and that too beyond the contracted amount of 6.2 MHz as laid down in the license conditions. I am informed that higher amount of allotment of spectrum has a much higher intrinsic value to the operators as they save disproportionately large amounts of CAPEX. This issue has been raised by CAG also in its report. The details of such allotments are given in **Annexure – 3.**

You would kindly notice that all the above favours shown to some of the selected operators definitely would not have been done by the DoT / WPC officers without any kickbacks and benefits coming to them. It is clear that the concerned officers in DoT / WPC have been in hand and glove with some of the telecom operators from the date of start of cellular services.

**6.Request :**

**Excess Spectrum of up to 3.6 MHz has been given in 900 MHz band to incumbent operatorshould be withdrawn and alternated spectrum should be provided in 1800 MHz band.**

**Investigations should be made regarding Initial allotment of 6.2 MHz spectrum,made to incumbent operators without any license guidelines.?**

**Spectrum up to 10 MHz has been given to incumbent operators free of cost and without any allocation guidelines. The spectrum should be charged as per the method based on 3G auction, which comes to Rs 36993 Crores.**

**Kindly institute an enquiry under retired Supreme Court Judge to examine the whole issue of allotment of spectrum since 1994 to unearth the ugly nexus between WPC officers and the telecom operators.**

Thanking you,

With warm regards,

( Ramesh Rathod )

CC : Shri Kapil Sibal, Hon'ble Minister Communication & IT.
Encl : **Annexure 1 to 3**

3

**Annexure - I**

| S. No. | Name of operator | City/Circle | Date/ Year | Spectrum Allocated |
|---|---|---|---|---|
| 1 | Bharti Cellular Limited | Gujarat | 01.04.2002 | 6.2+6.2 |
| 2 | Bharti Cellular Limited | Haryana | 01.04.2002 | 6.2+6.2 |
| 3 | Bharti Cellular Limited | Kerala | 11.03.2002 | 6.2+6.2 |
| 4 | Bharti Cellular Limited | MP | 01.04.2002 | 6.2+6.2 |
| 5 | Bharti Cellular Limited | Maharashtra | 01.04.2002 | 6.2+6.2 |
| 6 | Bharti Cellular Limited | Mumbai | 11.03.2002 | 6.2+6.2 |
| 7 | Bharti Cellular Limited | TN | 11.03.2002 | 6.2+6.2 |
| 8 | Bharti Cellular Limited | UP(W) | 03.04.2002 | 6.2+6.2 |
| 9 | Bharti Cellular Limited | UP(E) | 06.05.2004 | 6.2+6.2 (900 MHz) |
| 10 | Bharti Cellular Limited | Bihar | 06.05.2004 | 6.2+6.2 (900 MHz) |
| 11 | Bharti Cellular Limited | Orissa | 06.05.2004 | 6.2+6.2 (900 MHz) |

Annexure - 2

## Spectrum beyond 6.2 MHz ( 900 MHz band)

| Operator | Service Area | Spectrum in 900 MHz band |
|---|---|---|
| Bharti Airtel | Delhi | 8 MHz |
| " | AP | 7.8 MHz |
| " | Karnataka | 7.8 MHz |
| " | Punjab | 7.8 MHz |
| Vodafone | Kolkata | 7.8 MHz |
| " | Delhi | 8 MHz |
| " | Mumbai | 8 MHz |
| " | Gujarat | 7.8 MHz |
| BPL | Mumbai | 8 MHz |
| Aircel | Tamil Nadu | 7.8 MHz |
| Idea | Maharashtra | 7.8 MHz |
| Spice | Punjab | 7.8 MHz |

6

**Annexure - 3**

**Allotment of excess spectrum beyond the contracted value of 6.2 MHz.**

| Name | Amount of additional spectrum (MHz) | No. of Circles |
|---|---|---|
| Aircel | 3.6 | 1 |
| Bharti | 32.4 | 13 |
| BPL (Mumbai) | 3.8 | 1 |
| BSNL | 61.6 | 19 |
| IDEA | 12.6 | 6 |
| MTNL (Delhi & Mumbai) | 12.4 | 2 |
| Reliance | 1.8 | 1 |
| Spice (Punjab) | 1.6 | 1 |
| Vodafone | 19.6 | 7 |
| | 14.4 | |

**Khagen Das**
MEMBER OF PARLIAMENT
(LOK SABHA)

सत्यमेव जयते

**90, North Avenue,**
**New Delhi - 110 001**
**Tels. (011) 23094461,**
~~23094137~~

4[th] January 2011

Dr.Manmohan Singh,
Hon'ble Prime Minister
Government of India,
South Block
**New Delhi**

**Subject: Urgent need to review past failures in administering policy decisions by DOT.**

Dear Dr. Manmohan Singh ji,

Telecommunication services in the country have taken a big leap during a short span of 15 years since its privatisation. It is really heartening to note that telecom subscriber base reached 742 million at the end of October 2010, achieving a tele-density of 62% against the dismal figure of less than 1% in 1995. This has been really possible due to the progressive and liberal policies adopted by the successive Central Governments and the active role played by the private operators. It is a matter of great proud that India stands at second place after China in the ranking of total subscriber base in the World.

2. However, this remarkable growth in Telecom services has not been without a share of controversies. The Country has seen the biggest scam wherein the CAG has estimated a loss of Rs. 1,76,000 crores on account of issue of licences and excess spectrum held by the operators. The recent telecom scam which completely disrupted the functioning of Parliamentary democracy has really cast a dark shadow on the functioning of our politicians, bureaucrats & corporate houses.

3. The scandals in the Telecom Industry are not new. The first migration package given to the telecom operators in 1999 was a completely sell off to the private operators at that time. Even though the licenses for

1

**Khagen Das**
MEMBER OF PARLIAMENT
(LOK SABHA)

सत्यमेव जयते

**90, North Avenue,**
**New Delhi - 110 001**
**Tels. (011) 23094461,**
~~23094137~~

cellular services were awarded through auction and the operators had committed to pay annual license fees but all of them completely failed to pay the license fee to the Government. **The Government bailed out all these operators by migrating them to the revenue sharing arrangements instead of the license fees. The loss to the Government has been estimated to the extent of Rs. 50,000 crores. The CAG in its report of 2000 had commented adversely but no action was taken at that time.**

4. The mobile telephone operators have been the biggest beneficiaries of the concessions granted to them from 1999 till date. **It is true that these operators have brought the telecom services within the reach of the common man but if we see the various scams, it has been achieved at a very heavy cost to the Government and has brought a bad name to the nation.**

5. Some of the gross violations of license conditions of the telecom licenses committed from 1999 onwards are enumerated below:-

(i) Migration package of 1999 bailing out the first and second private telecom licensees.

(ii) Operators were granted additional spectrum of 1.8 MHz against the contracted value of 4.4 MHz without any guidelines.

(iii) Operators allotted spectrum upto 10 MHz without any policy guidelines.

(iv) Operators allotted 6.2 MHz of start up spectrum instead of 4.4 MHz mandated in the license.

(v) 4th Cellular operators allotted spectrum in 900 MHz premium band against the license conditions.

(vi) Operators allotted more than 6.2 MHz in 900 MHz band against the policy guidelines.

(vii) Concessions granted to NLD and ILD licencees without TRAI recommendations.

(viii) Issue of 51 new licences in 2004 to 2007 at the price discovered in 2001.

**Khagen Das**
MEMBER OF PARLIAMENT
(LOK SABHA)

सत्यमेव जयते

**90, North Avenue,**
**New Delhi - 110 001**
**Tels. (011) 23094461,**
**23094137**

6. **I am giving below a snapshot of irregularities committed during the tenure of each Minister of Communications & IT during 1999-2007.**

6.1 **Irregularities committed during the tenure of Sh. A.B. Vajapyee which are estimated at Rs. 50,000 crores.**

| Sr no | Irregularity | Operator | Circle | Period / Date | Secretary DOT | Wireless Advisor | DDG (VAS) | Chairman TRAI | Member (T)TRAI |
|---|---|---|---|---|---|---|---|---|---|
| 1 | Spectrum allotment beyond license up to 6.2 MHz without any guidelines | Bharti | Chennai | Aug-99 | Sh. Anil Kumar | Sh. R N Agarwal | Sh. J.R. Gupta | Justice S.S. Sodhi | Sh. R.R.N. Prasad |
| | -do- | -do- | Delhi | Aug-99 | -do- | -do- | -do- | -do- | -do- |
| | -do- | BPL | Mumbai | Aug-99 | -do- | -do- | -do- | -do- | -do- |
| 2 | Migration Package of 1999 | 1st and 2nd Cellular and Basic operators | All | Aug-99 | -do- | -do- | -do- | -do- | -do- |
| | • Validity of licenses increased from 10 years to 20 year | | | Aug-99 | -do- | -do- | -do- | -do- | -do- |
| | • Operators allowed revenue sharing instead of the fixed license fees. | | | Aug-99 | -do- | -do- | -do- | -do- | -do- |
| | • Effective date of license extended by 6 months. | | | Aug-99 | -do- | -do- | -do- | -do- | -do- |
| | • Metro operators allowed to increase the rental from Rs. 156 per month to Rs. 600 per month per subscriber. | | | Aug-99 | -do- | -do- | -do- | -do- | -do- |

**Khagen Das**
MEMBER OF PARLIAMENT
(LOK SABHA)

सत्यमेव जयते

**90, North Avenue,**
**New Delhi - 110 001**
**Tels. (011) 23094461,**
**23094137**

6.2 **Irregularities committed during the tenure of Sh. Ram Vilas Paswan**

| Sr no | Irregularity | Operator | Circle | Period / Date | Telecom Secretary | Wireless Advisor | Chairman, TRAI | Member (T)TRAI |
|---|---|---|---|---|---|---|---|---|
| 1 | Spectrum allotment up to 6.2 MHz without any guidelines | Aircel Digilink (Vodafone) | Chennai | Mar-00 | Sh. Anil Kumar | Sh. R N Agarwal | Justice S.S. Sodhi | Sh. R.R.N. Prasad |
| | -do- | Bharti | AP | Apr-00 | Sh. Shyamal Ghosh | -do- | -do- | -do- |
| | -do- | Bharti | Karnataka | Apr-00 | -do- | -do- | -do- | -do- |
| | -do- | Spice | Karnataka | Apr-00 | -do- | -do- | -do- | -do- |
| | -do- | Spice | Punjab | Apr-00 | -do- | -do- | -do- | -do- |
| | -do- | Aircel Digilink (Vodafone) | Haryana | Jan-01 | -do- | -do- | -do- | -do- |
| | -do- | -do- | Rajasthan | Jan-01 | -do- | -do- | -do- | -do- |
| | -do- | -do- | UP(East) | Jan-01 | -do- | -do- | -do- | -do- |

6.3 **Irregularities committed during the tenure of Sh. Pramod Mahajan**

| Sr no | Irregularity | Operator | Circle | Period / Date | Telecom Secretary | Wireless Advisor | Chairman, TRAI | Member (T)TRAI |
|---|---|---|---|---|---|---|---|---|
| 1 | Allotment of spectrum upto 10MHz without any fixed fee and without increase in spectrum usage charge | Bharti, Vodafone, Idea, BPL, Aircel | Various circles | 1.2.2002 | Sh. Shyamal Ghosh | Sh. P K Garg | Sh. M.S. Verma | Sh. R.R.N. Prasad |
| 2 | More than 6.2 MHz Spectrum allotted in 900 MHz | Bharti Airtel | Delhi | 17.7.2002 | Sh. Vinod Vaish | -do- | -do- | — |

**Khagen Das**
MEMBER OF PARLIAMENT
(LOK SABHA)

सत्यमेव जयते

**90, North Avenue,**
**New Delhi - 110 001**
**Tels. (011) 23094461,**
**23094137**

| | | | | | | | | |
|---|---|---|---|---|---|---|---|---|
| | premium band | | | | | | | |
| | -do- | Vodafone | Delhi | 17.7.2002 | -do- | -do- | -do- | --- |
| | -do- | Vodafone | Mumbai | 17.7.2002 | -do- | -do- | -do- | --- |

6.4 **Irregularities committed during the tenure of Sh. Arun Shourie**

| Sr no | Irregularity | Operator | Circle | Period / Date | Telecom Secretary | Wireless Advisor | DDG (VAS) | Chairman TRAI | Member (T)TRAI |
|---|---|---|---|---|---|---|---|---|---|
| 1 | More than 6.2 MHz Spectrum allotted in 900 MHz premium band | BPL | Mumbai | 13.3.2003 | Sh. Vinod Vaish | Sh. PK Garg | Sh. J.R. Gupta | Sh. Pradeep Baijal | Dr. D.P.S. Seth |
| | -do- | Bharti | Karnataka | 31.12.2003 | -do- | -do- | -do- | -do- | -do- |
| | -do- | Idea | Maharashtra | 31.12.2003 | -do- | -do- | -do- | -do- | -do- |
| | -do- | Vodafone | Gujarat | 31.12.2003 | -do | -do- | -do- | -do- | -do- |
| | -do- | Bharti | Punjab | 9.1.2004 | -do- | -do- | -do- | -do- | -do- |
| | -do- | Spice | Punjab | 9.1.2004 | -do- | -do- | -do- | -do- | -do- |
| | -do- | Aircel | Tamil Nadu | 9.1.2004 | -do- | -do- | -do- | -do- | -do- |
| | -do- | Bharti | AP | 9.2.2004 | Sh. Nripendra Misra | -do- | -do- | -do- | -do- |
| 2 | Spectrum allotted up to 10 MHz without any guidelines | Bharti | Delhi | Jul-03 | Sh. Vinod Vaish | -do- | -do- | -do- | -do- |

**Khagen Das**
MEMBER OF PARLIAMENT
(LOK SABHA)

सत्यमेव जयते

**90, North Avenue,**
**New Delhi - 110 001**
**Tels. (011) 23094461,**
**23094139**

| | | | | | | | | | |
|---|---|---|---|---|---|---|---|---|---|
| | -do- | Vodafone | Delhi | Oct-03 | -do- | -do- | -do- | -do- | -do- |
| | -do- | Vodafone | Mumbai | Oct-03 | -do- | -do- | -do- | -do- | -do- |
| | -do- | Bharti | Karnataka | Jan-04 | -do- | -do- | -do- | -do- | -do- |
| | -do- | Idea | Maharashtra | Apr-04 | Sh. Nripendra Misra | -do- | -do- | -do- | -do- |
| 3 | 27 UAS licenses issued on 2001 prices | Aircel | 7 circles | Apr-04 | -do- | -do- | -do- | -do- | -do- |
| | -do- | Bharti | 6 circles | Feb-04 | -do- | -do- | -do- | -do- | -do- |
| | -do- | Vodafone | 2 circles | Feb-04 | -do- | -do- | -do- | -do- | -do- |
| | -do- | Tata Tele | 12 circles | Jan-04 | -do- | -do- | -do- | -do- | -do- |

6.5 **Irregularities committed during the tenure of Sh. Dayanidhi Maran**

| Sr no | Irregularity | Operator | Circle | Period / Date | Telecom Secretary | Wireless Advisor | DDG (VAS/AS) | Chairman TRAI | Member (T)TRAI |
|---|---|---|---|---|---|---|---|---|---|
| 1 | Spectrum allotted up to 10 MHz without any guidelines | BPL | Mumbai | Sep-04 | Sh. Nripendra Misra | Sh. PK Garg | Sh. N Parmeshwaran | Sh. Pradeep Baijal | Dr. D.P.S. Seth |

**Khagen Das**
MEMBER OF PARLIAMENT
(LOK SABHA)

सत्यमेव जयते

**90, North Avenue,**
**New Delhi - 110 001**
**Tels. (011) 23094461,**
[illegible]

| | | | | | | | | | |
|---|---|---|---|---|---|---|---|---|---|
| | -do- | Aircel | Tamilna du | Dec-04 | -do- | -do- | -do- | -do- | -do- |
| | -do- | Vodafone | Gujarat | May-05 | Sh. Brijesh Kumar | -do- | -do- | -do- | -do- |
| | -do- | Bharti | Mumbai | Jan-06 | Sh. JS Sarma | -do- | -do- | -do- | -do- |
| 2 | Initial Spectrum allotted in 900 MHz premium band instead of 1800 MHz | Bharti | West Bengal | 12.08.20 04 | Sh. Nripendra Misra | -do- | -do- | -do- | -do- |
| | -do- | Bharti | U.P. (E) | 06.05.20 04 | -do- | -do- | -do- | -do- | -do- |
| | -do- | Bharti | Bihar | 06.05.20 04 | -do- | -do- | -do- | -do- | -do- |
| | -do- | Bharti | Orissa | 06.05.20 04 | -do- | -do- | -do- | -do- | -do- |
| | -do- | Hutch | West Bengal | 12.08.20 04 | -do- | -do- | -do- | -do- | -do- |
| | -do- | Hutch | U.P. (W) | 06.05.20 04 | -do- | -do- | -do- | -do- | -do- |
| | -do- | Vodafone | Kolkata | 30.6.200 4 | -do- | -do- | -do- | -do- | -do- |
| 3 | 24 Licenses issued on 2001 prices | Aircel | 14 circles | Dec-06 | Sh. D.S. Mathur | -do- | -do- | Sh. Nripendra Misra | Sh. A.K. Sahney |
| | -do- | Idea | 2 circle | Dec-06 | -do- | -do- | -do- | -do- | -do- |
| | -do- | Vodafone | 7 circles | Dec-06 | -do- | -do- | -do- | -do- | -do- |
| | -do- | Reliance | 1 circle | Sep-04 | Sh. Nripendra Misra | -do- | -do- | Sh. Pradeep Baijal | Dr. D.P.S. Seth |

**Khagen Das**
MEMBER OF PARLIAMENT
(LOK SABHA)

सत्यमेव जयते

**90, North Avenue,**
**New Delhi - 110 001**
**Tels. (011) 23094461,**
**23094137**

| | | | | |
|---|---|---|---|---|
| 4 | Concessions granted to NLD operators without TRAI Recommendations | • Entry fee reduced from Rs. 100 to Rs. 25 crores.<br>• Revenue share reduced from 15% to 6%.<br>• Roll out obligation diluted.<br>• Networth requirement reduced from Rs. 2500 crores to Rs. 2.5 crores. | -do- | -do- |
| 5 | Concessions granted to ILD operators without TRAI Recommendations | • Entry fee reduced from Rs. 25 crores to Rs. 2.5 crores.<br>• Revenue share reduced from 15% to 6%.<br>• Roll out obligations diluted.<br>• Networth requirement reduced from Rs. 25 crores to Rs. 2.5 crores.<br>• Performance Bank Guarantee waived off. | -do- | -do- |

7. It may be observed from above and the annexures that only a few selected incumbent operators have been benefitted right from 1999 onwards till date i.e. through migration package, allotment of spectrum in 900 MHz premium band, allotment of higher start up spectrum, allotment of spectrum above the mandated without any guidelines and the issue of new licenses in 2004-2007.

**Conclusion:-**

8. It may kindly be seen from above that if you take into account the above abnormalities, the present scandal relating to an estimated loss of Rs. 1,76,000 crores to the Government may be a shade poorer than the scandals committed during 1999 to 2007. **One thing is very clear that a select group of telecom operators viz Bharti, Vodafone, Idea and BPL have been the main beneficiaries as they have saved thousands of crores of Capex and Opex** also in thousands of crores of Rupees per annum by moving to revenue sharing regime instead of the annual license fees and getting spectrum free violating the license conditions. **The biggest loser is the Central Government which has been defrauded by a close liaison between the politicians, bureaucrats and the cellular operators.**

**Khagen Das**
MEMBER OF PARLIAMENT
(LOK SABHA)

सत्यमेव जयते

**90, North Avenue,**
**New Delhi - 110 001**
**Tels. (011) 23094461,**
**23094437**

**9. I will urge and request you to kindly:-**

**(a) Order Investigations by CBI and ED into all the above abnormalities.**

**(b) Summon the Secretaries and Wireless Advisors who were responsible for such manipulations and irregularities committed during 1999-2007 period so as to get to the root of the issues.**

**(c) Refer all these issues to one man committee.**

With best regards,

Yours sincerely,

Khagen 8/1/11

( Khagen Das )

Encl.: as above.

c.c.:

1. Sh. Murli Manohar Joshi, Chairman, PAC
2. Sh. Pranab Mukherjee, Finance Minister,
3. Sh. Kapil Sibal, Minister of Communications & IT
4. Dr. J. S. Sarma, Chairman, TRAI
5. Sh. P. J. Thomas, CVC
6. Sh. Vinod Rai, CAG
7. Sh. A. P. Singh, CBI Director
8. Sh. Arun Mathur, Director, Enforcement Directorate

सत्यमेव जयते

RAJEEV CHANDRASEKHAR
MEMBER OF PARLIAMENT
RAJYA SABHA

Member of Standing Committee on Information Technology
Member of Consultative Committee on Finance
Member of Parliamentary Forum on Youth
Co-Chairman, Vigilance & Monitoring Committee, Bangalore Urban District

11th January, 2011

Respected Prime Minister,

This is with regard to the press conference held by Mr. Kapil Sibal, Hon'ble Minister of Communications & IT, trashing the CAG and mounting humiliation on a constitutional body, as well as making a mockery of the CAG's detailed analysis by suggesting, through some bizarre arithmetic, that the actual loss caused due to the 2G spectrum scam is, in fact, zero.

His decision to publicly announce that the loss resulting from the 2G scam is in fact zero by issuing an official press release, is an unprecedented and dangerous move which has compromised the Government, the Supreme Court hearing that is currently in progress, the CBI investigation, and in fact, even the residual (according to Mr. Sibal) task of investigating the improprieties that have been committed.

Mr. Sibal has overstepped the line which defines the dignity of a Union Minister who is duty bound to cooperate with the ongoing investigation and the Supreme Court Order, or is completely misled by those who have committed the crime (both DoT officials and corporates in collusion) based on whose advise he chose to lead this misadventure. Specifically, he can easily be held responsible for various acts and omissions which are detrimental to the overall investigation process, as listed in the *Annexure.*

Mr. Sibal also needs to be reminded that the arguments that he made are a bland repetition of what has already been made in great detail in the affidavits that the Department of Telecom and Mr. A. Raja submitted in the Supreme Court – in spite of which an investigation has been ordered on the issue of losses by the Supreme Court. Clearly, these arguments have failed to persuade the Supreme Court, or else, the Supreme Court would not have expanded the scope of investigation to include losses which are included in the CAG Report.

Additionally, his criticism of the CAG Report is also completely unwarranted. As anyone in government knows or should know, the CAG would have given the DoT every opportunity to respond during the audit process between January-September 2010. The CAG Report itself openly lays out the process followed by it in its Chapter 2 'Audit Approach'. It makes clear that the information is based on DoT files and TRAI recommendations.

..2..

211 North Avenue, New Delhi-110001 India
Tel: + 91-11-23094044 Fax : + 91-11-23094042
E-mail : rajeev.c@nic.in
www.rajeev.in

सत्यमेव जयते

-2-

The Report takes into account replies by DoT and Ministry of Finance in response to the audit observations communicated to them in July 2010 and September 2010. Performance audit guidelines were followed by the CAG to perfection, including holding of entry and exit conferences in December 2009 and May 2010. DoT sought and was given additional meetings to discuss the report, and extension to provide responses. All the arguments forwarded by Mr. Sibal have been included and analyzed by the CAG at the end of which they have arrived at this Report. Mr. Sibal is neither stating anything new nor revealing anything that the department officials and lawyers have not already argue unsuccessfully, both in front of CAG and Supreme Court – both of whom were unimpressed with DoT's replies. The attack on the CAG is made even more tragic, given that you as Prime Minister just recently praised the CAG and the trend of independent constitutional bodies seemingly becoming extinct in our country.

I can assure you that Mr. Sibal's arithmetic of bringing the loss down to zero is thoroughly erroneous and a gross misrepresentation. It flies in the face of obvious evidence available of many Private companies profiteering from this spectrum allocation. Most of his other conclusions in the press release aimed at defending Mr. A. Raja's decision of giving away spectrum in 2008 at 2001 prices without an open, transparent auction, are deeply flawed, without logic, and misrepresent facts while cherry picking statements from government documents (policy and Five Year Plan), DoT notifications and TRAI recommendations.

Apart from insulting the intelligence of the many Indians concerned with corruption in our governance, his repeated statements that the 'Prime Minister did not ask for auctions' also has him implying that you had, as Prime Minister, chosen to ignore all the letters to you on the subject that were written by various well meaning persons in Parliament, Government and elsewhere, seeking a more transparent and fair form of allocating a scarce national asset. While that may be Mr. Sibal's views, I believe that you were genuinely concerned about seeking an alternative to this dubious method of giving spectrum – this is clear from your letter dated 02 November, 2008 addressed to Mr. A. Raja. Mr Sibal also needs to be informed that spectrum is a national asset – and the trusteeship of this asset by the Government is on behalf of the people of India, and cannot be a private dispute between Political parties.

I am perfectly willing to give him the benefit of the doubt that, he may have been ill advised by some bureaucrats or private companies who are currently fearing prosecution. Through this letter, I request you to kindly advise him to recall his press release and the presentation, but more specifically, the official statement relating to the fact that "the loss emanating from the 2G spectrum scam is zero." This statement has wide ranging implications on the judicial and investigative process. Additionally, he should seriously consider apologizing for his erroneous choice of words in describing the efforts of the

...3..

सत्यमेव जयते

-3-

diligent and fearless officials of CAG, presented through its Report covering the shortcomings since 2003. The most recent interview by him, has him justifying the losses, as the "consumers have benefited". As all of us are aware, most scams are almost always under the garb of benefitting the consumer!!

Mr. Sibal is badly misreading the mood of the people and the nation in the face of this scam. The correct thing for the government would be address the scam squarely and assist the various investigations to identify the crime and its perpetrators, punish them and recover the moneys/spectrum lost. The people of India expect the Government of India, and their representatives in Parliament and media to discharge their solemn duty and investigate this crime. Any amateurish efforts to sweep this under the carpet, such as the one being attempted by Mr. Sibal, will backfire and be severely rejected by the people of India.

I request that my letter be given careful consideration for the wider good of justice and to safeguard the current investigation whose completion is the only way to restore citizens' trust in the functioning of your government and to show due respect for the Supreme Court Order dated 16 December 2010.

I will keenly await Mr. Sibal's retraction.

Yours Sincerely,

**RAJEEV CHANDRASEKHAR**

**Dr Manmohan Singh**
Hon'ble Prime Minister
Government of India
New Delhi

Annexure

## Implications of Mr. Kapil Sibal's Press Statement

1. **Insult to Supreme Court Judgment bordering on contempt**

As a lawyer, Mr. Sibal should know that the Supreme Court, after hearing detailed defense by the lawyers of DoT and Mr. Raja, has not only allowed for the investigation to proceed, but in fact, expanded its terms, including a decision to supervise the CBI. Specifically, the Supreme Court has stated that it is "prima facie satisfied with the allegations contained in the writ petition and affidavits filed before this Court which are supported not only by documents produced by them, but also the report of the CVC and the findings recorded by CAG in its performance audit report need a thorough and impartial investigation." Further, it has given a specific direction to the CBI to "conduct thorough investigation into various issues highlighted in the report of the CVC and the report of CAG who have prima facie found serious irregularities .....and the huge losses to the public Exchequer running into several thousand crores."

Mr. Sibal's position second guesses the finding of the Court and its decision to direct an enquiry into the losses. As a Minister, he should be assisting the process of justice, rather than thwarting the investigation into the issue of losses due to the 2G scam.

2. **Misused position as Union Minister to influence / prejudice the CBI Investigation**

The CBI, as you are aware, has registered a specific FIR on 20 October 2009. Apart from being under directions to investigate losses from the 2G scam (not just procedural irregularities), the CBI FIR specifically mentions that "officials of DoT entered into criminal conspiracy with certain private persons / companies and misused their official position in grant of UASL causing wrongful loss to the government and corresponding wrongful gain to these private companies." Further, it mentions even back in 2009, an independent figure of an estimated loss of "more than Rs.22,000 crores" without including dual technology or spectrum beyond 6.2 MHz. Mr. Sibal has now thwarted this investigation process by informing the CBI and the nation that the loss is, in fact, zero – thus unduly influencing the Supreme Court monitored investigation by CBI.

3. **Makes it impossible for Government to recover lost revenues**

By making a public statement and issuing an official press release criticizing the CAG's report by concluding that "a large loss to the exchequer has no merit", he has made it virtually impossible for the Government to recover even a small portion of the said loss, regardless of whether he agrees with the loss of Rs.1.76

crores. His conclusion that the loss is, in fact, zero - aided by a press release and a presentation – will be a permanent defense for the beneficiaries of the scam in all forums, including courts, against any efforts by the Government to recover the losses. It is a self goal that has robbed the Exchequer of any opportunity to recover additional revenues.

4. Attempt to whitewash scams and giving safe passage to the beneficiaries

If according to Mr. Sibal, the loss is zero, and by consequence, there are no gains to private parties - then it would be virtually impossible to prosecute the beneficiaries of this scam. Any irregularity that does not lead to a loss to the Exchequer will go virtually unpunished. In one sweeping statement, Mr Sibal has compromised your government's position, that of CBI and the entire investigation process, since the beneficiaries will now argue that the Union Minister himself has given them a clean chit (since procedural irregularities can only accrue to DoT, and not the beneficiaries).

5. Undermined PAC and breach of Parliamentary privilege

As the Union Minister, whose department is required to respond to the PAC, he has bordered on breaching Parliamentary privilege and put his position out in public, before his department has fully responded to the queries of PAC – a process that has only just begun. It would have been up to the PAC to conclude, based on his department's responses, on whether or not the CAG report is accurate. While he has every right to defend the department (even if for political reasons), the defense should have been aimed at PAC under the protocol that needs to be followed in the Parliament, rather than jumping to an external press release – that too, without any provocation. Moreover, the argument that he is making should have been made by the Secretary at his deposition in front of PAC.

6. Publicly humiliated, compromised and undermined institution of CAG

Without going into the language that Mr. Sibal has used, his phraseology to describe the workings and analysis of CAG is to say the least "humiliating and demotivating". The Government's auditor as it is has an extremely difficult job to point misuse of power, leading to losses by senior Ministers. In this case, it had done an outstanding job of providing multiple options to calculate presumptive losses without favoring one over the other. It had detailed the irregularities in decision making and left it to the PAC to draw final conclusions. It is extremely unbecoming of Mr. Sibal to put the CAG under such pressure by humiliating its honest and diligent officers and demotivating and discouraging them from producing such honest and detailed reports which have served as an eye opener for the nation in the future. He owes the CAG an apology for his language.

7. **Insult to the intelligence of a Billion Indians**

While Mr. Sibal had the right to his opinion and could have debated on the actual level of loss rather than the 1.76 crore which caught the attention of the media and the nation – his attempt to suggest that it is "zero loss" is a pure simple insult to the intelligence and sensitivities of a nation that is seething with anger and frustration due to this episode. He should have demonstrated at least minimal sensitivity and some basic level of rigor while dealing with this sensitive issue of losses to the Exchequer.

Ramesh Rathod
MEMBER OF PARLIAMENT
(LOK SABHA)

Member Standing Committee on Coal & Steel
Member Papers Laid on the Table

सत्यमेव जयते

121 – South Avenue,
New Delhi –110001
Mob : 901318028
Email: office.rameshrathod@gmail.com

Permanent Address: Sevadas Nagar Utnoor
Distt.: Adilabad, Andhra Pradesh
Tel. (08731) 274188, Mob: 9440435537
Fax : (08731) 274188

**20th January, 2011**

**Dr. Manmohan Singh**
**Hon'ble Prime Minister**
**Government of India**
**South Block**
**NEW DELHI – 110 001.**

**Sub: Uninor is the Front Company of Tata Group**

**Tata Group funded the entire amount of Rs. 1700 crore paid by Unitech Group for acquiring UAS License**

**Deal was brokered by Niira Radia who had both Tata Group and Unitech Group as her clients**

**No action yet taken by any Regulator – neither against Tatas nor against Unitech**

**Respected Dr. Manmohan Singh Ji**

I wish to bring to your notice some startling facts, which not only have a potential threat on the safety and integrity of the nation but also are a classical example of open violation of the law of the land by Tata Group.

Given below is the modus operandi showing how Tata Group has craftily skirted around the policies and procedures and flouted laws to create Unitech as its Front Company to secure UAS License to fulfill its ambitions to foray in GSM telephony.

**Facts**

1. Tatas were desperately in need of GSM spectrum to diversify their existing CDMA based mobile services and had applied for offering GSM based services under dual technology. Since Tatas were not sure to get GSM spectrum under dual technology policy, in October 2007, they in a clandestine manner resorted to use Unitech Limited as Front to receive UAS License and spectrum as part of the process initiated by DoT.

2. Tata Group, through one of its group entity Tata Reality and Infrastructure Limited (Tata Realty advanced an amount of Rs 1,700 crore to Unitech Limited (Unitech) in the financial year i.e. 2007-08, under the guise of commercial advance.

   Tata Realty in its Annual Report for the FY 2007-08 has mentioned that it has entered into a Memorandum of Understanding (MOU) with "a party" for the proposed acquisition of land /

1

Ramesh Rathod
MEMBER OF PARLIAMENT
(LOK SABHA)

Member Standing Committee on Coal & Steel
Member Papers Laid on the Table

सत्यमेव जयते

121 – South Avenue,
New Delhi –110001
Mob : 901318028
Email: office.rameshrathod@gmail.com

Permanent Address: Sevadas Nagar Utnoor
Distt.: Adilabad, Andhra Pradesh
Tel. (08731) 274188, Mob: 9440435537
Fax : (08731) 274188

land owning companies. On the basis of MOU, it has advanced a sum of Rs. 1700 Crs as part consideration / advance towards the proposed acquisition of land / land owning companies. It is also mentioned that the terms of the deal were not finalized but then also a huge sum of Rs. 1700 Crs was given as an advance.

Please refer **Annexure 1 - Annual Report of Tata Realty** for the period from 2nd March, 2007 to 31st March, 2008 - Note No. 28 – Notes to Accounts, showing MOU entered with "a party" and advance given of Rs. 1,700 crore.

3. The above amount of Rs. 1700 crore availed by Unitech from Tata Realty was used in back-to-back funding to 8 subsidiaries of Unitech, which applied for and were awarded UAS License in early 2008. These funds were used by Unitech in funding these 8 subsidiaries not only as loan but also for acquiring their equity capital, as under:

| Licensee Company | Equity | Loan | Total |
|---|---|---|---|
| Unitech Wireless (Delhi) Private Limited | 10 | 163.59 | 173.59 |
| Unitech Wireless (Mumbai) Private Limited | 10 | 196.66 | 206.66 |
| Unitech Wireless (Kolkata) Private Limited | 10 | 70.89 | 80.89 |
| Unitech Wireless (Tamil Nadu) Private Limited | 10 | 225.89 | 235.89 |
| Unitech Wireless (East) Private Limited | 22 | 50.32 | 72.32 |
| Unitech Wireless (West) Private Limited | 25 | 297.59 | 322.59 |
| Unitech Wireless (North) Private Limited | 26 | 219.4 | 245.4 |
| Unitech Wireless (South) Private Limited | 25 | 332.51 | 357.51 |
| **Total** | **138** | **1556.85** | **1694.85** |

The chart given below clearly reflects the funding by Tata and their use by Unitech in acquiring UAS License through subsidiaries:

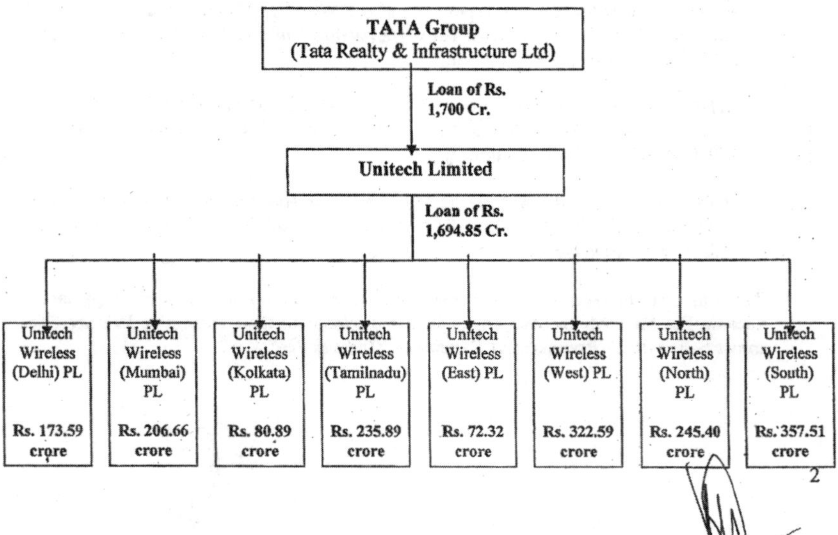


2

Ramesh Rathod
MEMBER OF PARLIAMENT
(LOK SABHA)

Member Standing Committee on Coal & Steel
Member Papers Laid on the Table

सत्यमेव जयते

121 – South Avenue,
New Delhi –110001
Mob : 901318028
Email: office.rameshrathod@gmail.com

Permanent Address: Sevadas Nagar Utnoor
Distt.: Adilabad, Andhra Pradesh
Tel. (08731) 274188, Mob: 9440435537
Fax : (08731) 274188

4. **The above back-to-back funding i.e. from Tata Realty - to - Unitech - to – Subsidiaries of Unitech applying for UASL is also very clear from the Annual Reports of the each of the above 8 subsidiaries, as per details given below:**

   a. **Refer Annexure 2 - Annual Report of Unitech Wireless (Delhi) Pvt. Ltd** for 2007-08 – Schedule 6 point No. 7 "Related Party Transactions" of showing unsecured loan of Rs. 163.59 crores from Unitech Limited;

   b. **Refer Annexure 3 - Annual Report of Unitech Wireless (Mumbai) Pvt. Ltd** for 2007-08 – Schedule 6 point No. 7 "Related Party Transactions" of showing unsecured loan of Rs. 196.66 crores from Unitech Limited;

   c. **Refer Annexure 4 - Annual Report of Unitech Wireless (Kolkata) Pvt. Ltd** for 2007-08 – Schedule 6 point No. 7 "Related Party Transactions" of showing unsecured loan of Rs. 70.89 crores from Unitech Limited;

   d. **Refer Annexure 5 - Annual Report of Unitech Wireless (Tamilnadu) Pvt. Ltd** for 2007-08 – Schedule 6 point No. 7 "Related Party Transactions" of showing unsecured loan of Rs. 225.89 crores from Unitech Limited;

   e. **Refer Annexure 6 - Annual Report of Unitech Wireless (East) Pvt. Ltd** for 2007-08 – Schedule 6 point No. 7 "Related Party Transactions" of showing unsecured loan of Rs. 50.32 crores from Unitech Limited;

   f. **Refer Annexure 7 - Annual Report of Unitech Wireless (West) Pvt. Ltd** for 2007-08 – Schedule 6 point No. 7 "Related Party Transactions" of showing unsecured loan of Rs. 297.59 crores from Unitech Limited;

   g. **Refer Annexure 8 - Annual Report of Unitech Wireless (North) Pvt. Ltd** for 2007-08 – Schedule 6 point No. 7 "Related Party Transactions" of showing unsecured loan of Rs. 219.40 crores from Unitech Limited;

   h. **Refer Annexure 9 - Annual Report of Unitech Wireless (South) Pvt. Ltd** for 2007-08 – Schedule 6 point No. 7 "Related Party Transactions" of showing unsecured loan of Rs. 332.51 crores from Unitech Limited;

**The said amount received by Licensee Companies from Unitech is used in payment of License Fee for UAS License, which is also disclosed in their respective Balance Sheets under Schedule 2 – Preoperative Expenses – "License Fee".**

3

Ramesh Rathod
MEMBER OF PARLIAMENT
(LOK SABHA)

Member Standing Committee on Coal & Steel
Member Papers Laid on the Table

सत्यमेव जयते

121 – South Avenue,
New Delhi – 110001
Mob : 901318028
Email: office.rameshrathod@gmail.com

Permanent Address: Sevadas Nagar Utnoor
Distt.: Adilabad, Andhra Pradesh
Tel. (08731) 274188, Mob: 9440435537
Fax : (08731) 274188

**Fraudulent Motives and Violations**

5. The above clearly shows that the motive of Tata Group was never to acquire the land / land owing companies as they have attempted to camouflage in the Annual Repot of Tata Realty. Their motive to fund Unitech was evidently to create a Front to grab UAS License bundled with GSM spectrum.

6. Tata Group had advanced this huge loan of Rs. 1700 crore to Unitech with a tacit understanding wherein Unitech would have acted as a plan for Tata Group to acquire GSM spectrum and offer GSM based services.

7. This has also been corroborated by the fact that infamous corporate lobbyists and undesirable person Niira Radia had brokered this deal of Rs. 1700 crore between Tatas and Unitech. Taped conversation between Niira Radia and Ratan Tata which is now in possession of the Supreme Court clearly reveal that both Tatas and Unitech are clients of Niira Radia. This is also a matter of investigation that these undesirable persons were actively working to get the UASL licence for Tata Group / Unitech by resorting to policy maneuvering and adopting corrupt practices.

8. It is thus proved beyond doubt that Tata Group in a clandestine manner advanced huge loan of Rs. 1700 crore to Unitech, flouting all rules, regulations and applicable laws. Unitech has diverted that money received from Tatas to pay for 2G GSM licence fee in early 2008.

9. It is also important to note that in 2008, once Tata Group received LOI for Dual Technology, their need to have a Unitech as a "Front" Company for GSM License was over and the funding provided by Tata Group to Unitech was reversed.

10. In October, 2008, Unitech sold 60% stake in its Licensee Companies for an aggregate amount of US 1.07 billion. With these funds and other funds availed from financial institutions, Unitech refunded the loan taken from Tatas. Tata Realty in its Balance Sheet of 2008-09 has mentioned that it has received a refund of Rs. 1,007.95 Crs and acquired land owning companies aggregating Rs. 601.84 Crs. A sum of Rs. 90.21 Crs was still pending repayment – refer **Annexure 10.**

11. Looking into the timing of such huge loan by Tata Group and the sequence of events leading to award of LOI for Dual Technology to Tatas and UAS License and spectrum to Unitech, the whole issue needs to be investigated thoroughly.

12. **Accordingly, in the national interest it is necessary that the above matter is investigated on top priority and immediate penal / corrective steps are taken by the relevant authorities as under:**

4

Ramesh Rathod
MEMBER OF PARLIAMENT
(LOK SABHA)

Member Standing Committee on Coal & Steel
Member Papers Laid on the Table.

सत्यमेव जयते

121 – South Avenue,
New Delhi –110001
Mob.: 901318028
Email: office.rameshrathod@gmail.com

Permanent Address: Sevadas Nagar Utnoor
Distt.: Adilabad, Andhra Pradesh
Tel. (08731) 274188, Mob: 9440435537
Fax : (08731) 274188

**a. CBI:**

- **To investigate the relationship/nexus of and financial transaction between Tata Group and Unitech and violation of laws committed by them;**

- **To investigate the end use of funds received by Unitech from Tata Group.**

**b. The Ministry of Communications and Information Technology, Department of Telecommunications (DOT) to take an immediate action to:**

- **Cancel the UASL License issued to Uninor, obtained by it fraudulently.**

- **Cancel the Dual technology License issued to Tata Group, for violation of applicable policy norms.**

- **Take back the spectrum allotted to Uninor and Tata Group.**

**c. The Ministry of Corporate Affairs and Registrar of Companies to conduct an inspection of the affairs of Tata Realty and Unitech under Section 209A of the Companies Act, 1956 for financial irregularities and violations of laws.**

**d. Income Tax Department (investigation wing) to investigate tax evasion in these transactions;**

**e. Reserve Bank of India, Enforcement Directorate and anti Money Laundering Authorities to investigate the trail of funds and violations of FEMA and Money Laundering laws.**

The above information is sourced from the publicly available data. I request you to direct Investigating authorities to obtain additional relevant data from the concerned sources.

Thanking you,

With warm Regards

( Ramesh Rathod )

5

सत्यमेव जयते

RAJEEV CHANDRASEKHAR
MEMBER OF PARLIAMENT
RAJYA SABHA

Member of Standing Committee on Information Technology
Member of Consultative Committee on Finance
Member of Parliamentary Forum on Youth
Co-Chairman, Vigilance & Monitoring Committee, Bangalore Urban District

10 February, 2011

Respected Prime Minister,

**Sub. : TRAI's 2G Report of 30.01.2011 confirms Spectrum Scam, losses and raises serious questions about administrative failure and wilful illegalities committed by MoCIT in 2008**

This is with further to my various letters to you on the issue of valuable 2G spectrum that has been given in 2008 without auctions at 2001 prices – thus causing a massive loss to the National Exchequer. Today's letter is with reference to the TRAI's latest Report on the 2010 Value of Spectrum in the 1800 MHz Band dated 30 January, 2011.

This Report obviously seems far more detailed in its calculations regarding the technical and economic values to be assigned for 2G spectrum vis-a-vis 3G auction prices. Even by this Report, it is clear that 2G spectrum up to 6.2 MHz is pegged at 53% of the 3G spectrum value and beyond 6.2 MHz, at 136%.

Consequent upon this detailed finding and based on the methodology used by the CAG, the loss to the Exchequer arising out of 6.2 MHz spectrum contracted (though only 4.4 MHz have been given till now) and spectrum held by operators beyond 6.2 MHz would still be pegged at upwards of Rs.1.2 lakh crores.

Further, the Report also conceals the fact that auctions must be held for spectrum that is returned from approx. 74 licenses that may be liable for cancellation, based on failure to meet license conditions.

211 North Avenue, New Delhi-110001 India
Tel: + 91-11-23094044 Fax : + 91-11-23094042
E-mail : rajeev.c@nic.in
www.rajeev.in

सत्यमेव जयते

While I welcome TRAI's view that 2G spectrum reverted back to the DoT in case of cancellation of licenses of defaulting companies can be placed for auction, it raises serious questions relating to the following:

1. What stopped the Government from resorting to auctions in 2008 – since similar level playing field considerations would have existed as they exist in 2011?

2. The accountability and rigour of TRAI's Recommendations which seems to have given conflicting views on auctions in 2008 and 2010, but supports auctions when new 2G spectrum becomes available.

3. Why was your letter of 02 November, 2007 to the then MoCIT, specifically seeking consideration of "spectrum auctions" or "revision of entry fee", ignored, since you had appropriately pointed towards recovering the "correct price of spectrum" – which is now been reaffirmed in no uncertain terms, by the TRAI's Report of 30 January, 2011?

All of these necessitate serious administrative review of the manner in which TRAI is functioning and MoCIT is handling direct correspondence from your office.

There is also a striking similarity between the announcements made by the Hon'ble MoCIT, Shri Kapil Sibal on 07 January, 2011 and TRAI's Report of 30 January, 2011, both on account of :

- Value of 2G spectrum vis-a-vis 3G auction price; and
- The decision to oppose auctions for 2G in general, but auction new spectrum which comes back to DoT as a result of license cancellations.

Unless this is purely coincidental, the TRAI Report would seem like a "command performance", even though it still reaffirms the massive loss caused to the Exchequer on account of the 2G spectrum scam.

Finally, with this report in hand and evidence of serious wrongdoing during 2008 (in spite of your letter dated 02 November, 2007 to the then MoCIT), may I please request you to have the Government accept its mistake and start the process of cleanup by cancelling licenses given illegally, and recovering the value of spectrum either through re-auctions of spectrum or benchmark pricing, where appropriate – consistent with your letter of 02 November, 2007. It will also be greatly helpful if the

2

सत्यमेव जयते

Hon'ble MoCIT can stop managing the optics of this huge loss and defending the indefensible acts of the then MoCIT.

While I have decided to oppose and expose any cover-up attempts, I am equally available to discuss constructively the best possible way forward to resolve the issues at hand, and move forward - but not without identifying and penalizing the perpetrators of the 2G spectrum scam, ensuring recovery of lost revenue and on the back of a policy decision to auction all scarce, national resources in an open, transparent manner.

Yours Sincerely,

RAJEEV CHANDRASEKHAR

**Dr. Manmohan Singh**
Hon'ble Prime Minister
Government of India
New Delhi

*Sushil Kumar Singh*

MEMBER OF PARLIAMENT
(LOK SABHA)

MEMBER :-
Estimate Committee
Standing (Communication & IT)
Consultative (Petroleum)

सत्यमेव जयते

16A, Ferozshah Road,
New Delhi-110001

Singh Kothi,
Aurangabad (Bihar)

Telephone :
New Delhi : 011-23354155
Fax : 011-23354156
Aurangabad : 06186-226300

11th February, 2011

Dr. Manmohan Singh
Hon'ble Prime Minister,
Government of India
South Block
**New Delhi-110001**

**Subject : TRAI recommendations on the charging of 1800 MHz spectrum need to be investigated by an independent agency like CBI.**

Dear Dr. Manmohan Singh ji,

This refers to the report in the Economic Times of 10th February, 2011 under the caption 'GSM Cos slam proposed TRAI fee of Rs.1700 Crores for extra spectrum'. The report is based on the TRAI recommendations on pricing of 1800 MHz spectrum for the purpose of charging the excess 2G spectrum held by the operators. It is observed from the media reports that the operators who have been holding excess spectrum would have to pay about Rs.17,513 Crores to the Government. Copy of the media report is attached Annexure – 01.

It may kindly be recalled that these TRAI recommendations are in continuation to its earlier recommendations of 11th May, 2010 on 'Spectrum Management and Licensing Framework', wherein one of the recommendations of the TRAI was to charge the excess spectrum held by the operator above the contracted amount of 6.2 MHz on the basis of 3G auction price.

Salient points of TRAI recommendations of 11th May, 2010 were as follows:

- Excess 2G spectrum in 1800 MHz band should be charged as per auction determined price of 3G spectrum in 2100 MHz.
- Excess 2G spectrum held in 900 MHz band should be charged at 1.5 times of the auction determined price of 3G spectrum in 2100 MHz since 900 MHz hand has better quality characteristics.
- Charges of excess spectrum should be enhanced by 30% in case the spectrum held in the service area is beyond 8 MHz since it provides trunking efficiency to the operators and saves them lot of Capex.
- The spectrum charges for this excess spectrum would be for the balance period of the license subject to a minimum period of 7 years.
- Based on these recommendations, the liability of various operators worked out as follows to a total of Rs.23270 Crores:

*Sushil Kumar Singh*

MEMBER OF PARLIAMENT
(LOK SABHA)

MEMBER :-
Estimate Committee
Standing (Communication & IT)
Consultative (Petroleum)

सत्यमेव जयते

16A, Ferozshah Road,
New Delhi-110001

Singh Kothi,
Aurangabad (Bihar)

Telephone :
New Delhi : 011-23354155
Fax : 011-23354156
Aurangabad : 06186-226300

| Sr. No. | Name of the operator | Amount payable for excess spectrum as per TRAI Recommendations dated 11th May, 2010 in Rs. Crores |
|---|---|---|
| 1 | Vodafone Essar | 4411.00 |
| 2 | Bharti Airtel | 5484.00 |
| 3 | Loop Telecom | 1500.00 |
| 4 | BSNL / MTNL | 9625.00 |
| 5 | Aircel | 478.00 |
| 6 | Idea Cellular | 1734.00 |
| 7 | Reliance Comm | 38.00 |
| | TOTAL | 23270.00 |

These recommendations of TRAI were vehemently opposed by the old GSM operators like Bharti Airtel, Vodafone, Loop and Idea who have been holding spectrum much beyond the license mandated 6.2 MHz which saved them thousands of crores of Capex and Opex at the cost of exchequer since all the spectrum was given to them without any fees.

Faced with the opposition from old GSM operators, within a week of issuing the recommendations on 11th May, 2010, the TRAI asked the DoT to hold on these recommendations on the plea that the TRAI would be sending another set of recommendations on the pricing of 2G spectrum shortly. <u>This short period has ended after 9 months of delay, giving the operators excess spectrum lease of another 9 months, which they have been holding for the last 8 to 10 years without any payment.</u>

The TRAI had now recommended a new set of prices for charging 1800 MHz spectrum which have been reduced to a very low level in some of the Metros and major Circles as compared to the other service areas for the reasons best known to the TRAI. A comparison of per MHz of 1800 MHz spectrum charges recommended in May, 2010 and recommended now is attached as Annexure II. It would be observed that in the new recommendations, 2G spectrum prices are 19% to 877% of the earlier recommended prices and the major beneficiaries are Delhi, Mumbai and Maharashtra where the prices have been reduced to a level of 19% to 38%. These are the areas where most of the excess spectrum is held. The states like West Bengal, Madhya Pradesh, U.P.(East), Bihar, Himachal Pradesh, Orissa, Assam and J&K etc have been hardest hit where the charges have been increased between 378% to 877%.

*Sushil Kumar Singh*

MEMBER OF PARLIAMENT
(LOK SABHA)

MEMBER :-
Estimate Committee
Standing (Communication & IT)
Consultative (Petroleum)

सत्यमेव जयते

16A, Ferozshah Road,
New Delhi-110001

Singh Kothi,
Aurangabad (Bihar)

Telephone :
New Delhi : 011-23354155
Fax : 011-23354156
Aurangabad : 06186-226300

Further, the TRAI has given another bonanza to these operators by recommending that the excess spectrum charges will be payable from 1.4.2010 onwards till the expiry of the license period knowing fully well that the licenses in these areas will be expiring in the next 4 to 5 years.

**It may kindly be appreciated that some of these operators have got the spectrum beyond the mandated value of 6.2 MHz as back as in 2002 but will pay for it only from 1.4.2010 onwards. The earlier recommendations required payment for excess spectrum held for at least 7 years.**

Based on the recent recommendations of TRAI, the operators holding excess spectrum will now have to pay the amounts as indicated in the table below. **It would be observed that Bharti Airtel would be gaining Rs.119 Crores, Vodafone Rs.2642 Crores and Loop Rs.1308 Crores respectively as compared to the earlier recommendations of May, 2010.**

| | | | |
|---|---|---|---|
| a) | Vodafone | : | Rs.2500 Crores |
| b) | Bharti Airtel | : | Rs.1200 Crores |
| c) | Loop | : | Rs.13000 Crores |

**In this process, the Government would be losing Rs.5700 Crores. As a Member of the Standing Committee on Communication & IT, I will suggest that the recent recommendations of TRAI should be scrapped and operators should be asked to pay for the excess spectrum held by them as per May, 2010 recommendations.**

It is an irony that the independent regulator had issued recommendations on charging of excess spectrum on 11th May, 2010 and has now completely revised these charges only after 9 months, for the reasons best known to the TRAI only. **It looks to me that such a downward revision is at the behest of operators like Bharti Airtel, Vodafone and Loop who have gained substantially.**

It may be of further interest that CAG in its report of 2010 on 'Issue of Licenses and Allocation of 2G Spectrum' had also adversely commented for not charging for the extra spectrum allotted to the various operators. **The CAG in its report under para 5.5 has indicated a loss of Rs.36,993 Crores on account of excess spectrum.**

Urgent need of the day :

**To order an investigation by an independent agency like CBI to look into the entire process undertaken by TRAI in arriving at the recent recommendations which will make the Government to lose another Rs.5756 Crores as compared to TRAI's earlier recommendations and Rs.19400 Crores, if the CAG's report is taken into account.**

With warm regards,

Yours sincerely,

( Sushil Kumar Singh )

Encl: Annexure 01 & 02

CC : 1. Finance Minister 2. Minister of Communication & IT
3. Comptroller & Auditor General of India 4. Director CBI

Annexure. 01

GSM cos slam proposed Trai fee of Rs 17kcr for extra spectrum
10 Feb, 2011, 0713 hrs IST, ET Bureau

NEW DELHI: India's top GSM operators have torn into telecom regulator Trai for suggesting that mobile phone companies be charged a one-time pan-India fee of 4,572 core for every unit of airwaves they hold beyond the contracted limit.

Calculations by ET revealed that the industry would have to shell out 17,513 crore if the government accepts the regulator's recommendations, with state-owned BSNL and MTNL bearing the brunt, as they will have to cough up about 50% of this amount (refer table).

Trai also said these changes should be implemented with effect from last April. The regulator also found support in telecom minister Kapil Sibal, who told media that the regulators recommendations seem acceptable in principle to the government.

The sector has been mired in a controversy regarding the pricing of 'excess' second generation spectrum, used for basic mobile services since 2008. Industry executives said that leading GSM operators are examining the possibility of approaching courts seeking relief.

These companies-notably Bharti Airtel, Vodafone Essar, Idea Cellular and BSNL-claim that mobile permits entitle them to as 15 units of airwaves in every region and, therefore, cannot be subject to a one-time fee for all spectrums beyond the 6.2 MHz limit as prescribed by the regulator.

Incumbent GSM telcos also accused the regulator of seeking to overcharge established players and destroy mobile phone firms, who have been battling falling profits and revenues for several quarters. These companies hold airwaves beyond the 'contracted' 6.2 MHz limit in several circles. In some regions their holdings are as high as 10 units of airwaves.

"The recommendations by Trai goes against the stated principle of the government to offer affordability, fairness and level playing field," Bharti Airtel, the country' leading mobile phone company by revenues and customers said. The Sunil-Mittal promoted company will have to shell out about 4,285 crore if the government were to accept the regulator's latest recommendations.

Vodafone Essar, which will have to pay 1,769 crore under Trai's latest pricing formula, termed the proposals as 'flawed, illogical and discriminatory' and said the regulator was acting against the interests of 'operators who were the first to invest deeply to build the sector'.

Using unusually harsh language, Vodafone Essar CEO Marten Pieters said Trai's recommendations do "rectify the completely illogical difference in the treatment of spectrum given to GSM operators and to dual technology operators (such as Reliance Communications and Tata Teleservices). Although dual technology players have 10-40% more spectrum than Vodafone, the new Trai recommendations suggest that they will pay insignificant amounts as one-time spectrum fees while the incumbent GSM operators will have to pay thousands of crores rupees as a one-time spectrum fee - Bharti 4000 cr, Vodafone 1,740 cr, RCom 70 cr and Tata nil!," Pieters added.

4

Bharti Airtel also appealed to telecom minister Kapil Sibal to reject the regulator's latest recommendations to 'ensure level playing field among all operators and ensure that all types of 2G spectrum pricing - 800 CDMA, 900 GSM, 1800 GSM - be given similar treatment'.

New operators, including dual technology companies who were given mobile permits in 2008, have been given only 4.4 MHz of startup spectrum. While Trai has not recommend pricing for additional airwaves be applied for airwaves beyond the 4.4 MHz mark for these companies, it, however, said that every unit of airwaves between 4.4 MHz and 6.2 MHz could be valued at 1,770 crore (pan-India).

Sibal had recently said that the telecom ministry will charge mobile operators for additional spectrum at market-determined prices beyond the 4.4 MHz mark, indicating that companies such as RCOM and Tata Teleservices will also have to pay up. Both RCOM and Tatas did not comment on Trai's proposals, while Uninor said the one time fee should only be applicable for airwaves beyond the 6.2 MHz limit.

Last year, Trai had recommended that the GSM telcos pay a one-time fee for 2G spectrum over 6.2 MHz at rates determined for 3G auctions. The regulator then said it was reviewing its recommendations after leading operators said that the proposals were discriminatory and could harm a sector already struggling to cope with an intense tariff war.

But, telecom companies said the new proposals would result in them paying a higher amount, when compared to last year. ET's calculations reveal the industry would have to pay about 16,095 crore under Trai's earlier methodology.

"For 2G spectrum pricing, Trai, while moving away from its earlier arbitrarily-linked 3G pricing levels, has now in many cases gone beyond 3G values. This goes against Kapil Sibal's and the government's acknowledged position that 3G is significantly more efficient than 2G, and services must remain affordable for the masses. There seem to be huge inconsistency in terms of the differences of prices in various circles. For instance, up to 6.2MHz the price vis-a-vis 3G prices range from a low of 16% to a high of 208% while beyond 6.2MHz, it ranges from a low of 24% to a high of 868%. This defies logic," Bharti Airtel added .

Following Trai's recommendations, shares of telecom companies were dumped by investors who fear that the sector, burdened by price wars and the imminent expenses for 3G services, are not as attractive as before. Bharti Airtel scrip ended 0.27% down at 332.35. Reliance Communications scrips touched new lows. Its stock tanked by more than 14.3% and MTNL's stock eroded by more than 7.4%. while Idea Cellular's stock also slipped by 3.07%, closing at 66.3.

Annexure.02

Per MHz price as per TRAI Recommendations

| S. No. | Circle | Per MHz price as per TRAI recommendations of 11th May, 2010 | Per MHz price as per TRAI recommendations as per 8th February, 2011 | TRAI recommendations of 8th Feb 2011 % of 11th May, 2010 |
|---|---|---|---|---|
| 1 | Delhi | 663.386 | 249.73 | 38% |
| 2 | Mumbai | 649.414 | 157.34 | 24% |
| 3 | Maharashtra | 251.564 | 47.6 | 19% |
| 4 | Gujarat | 215.212 | 374.47 | 174% |
| 5 | AP | 274.628 | 355.37 | 129% |
| 6 | Karnataka | 315.982 | 431.95 | 137% |
| 7 | Tamilnadu | 292.988 | 345.92 | 118% |
| 8 | Kolkata | 108.852 | 426.05 | 391% |
| 9 | Kerala | 62.496 | 232.16 | 371% |
| 10 | Punjab | 64.402 | 180.56 | 280% |
| 11 | Haryana | 44.516 | 107.90 | 242% |
| 12 | UP (E) | 72.914 | 318.76 | 437% |
| 13 | UP(W) | 102.808 | 252.55 | 246% |
| 14 | Rajasthan | 64.206 | 278.84 | 434% |
| 15 | MP | 51.672 | 254.45 | 492% |
| 16 | WB | 24.726 | 216.96 | 877% |
| 17 | HP | 7.446 | 28.12 | 378% |
| 18 | Bihar | 40.692 | 153.69 | 378% |
| 19 | Orissa | 19.396 | 73.26 | 378% |
| 20 | Assam | 8.296 | 31.33 | 378% |
| 21 | NE | 8.46 | 31.95 | 378% |
| 22 | J &K | 6.06 | 22.89 | 378% |
| | | 3350.116 | 4571.85 | |

**Naranbhai Kachhadiya**
MEMBER OF PARLIAMENT
(LOK SABHA)
• **Member:**

* **Parliamentary Standing Committee, On Ministry of Agriculture**

***Consultative Committee on Ministry of Steel**

सत्यमेव जयते

**107, South Avenue**
**New Delhi -110011**
**Telefax: 011 - 23795324**

**Date: 17 /02/2011**

Dr. Manmohan Singh
Hon'ble Prime Minister
Government of India,
South Block
**NEW DELHI – 110 001.**

**Subject :** **Investigate the allotment of spectrum and the issue of license from 1994 onwards in respect of Bharti Airtel Ltd.**

Dear Sir,

This is regarding the on going media reports on 2G spectrum scam, wherein the investigations by CBI are going on under the supervision of Hon'ble Supreme Court of India. On one hand, the opposition parties are insisting for probe by JPC and on the other hand, the Department of Telecom (DoT) had set up a one man committee under Justice Shivaraj V. Patil. I am aware that Justice Patil had submitted its report on 31st January, 2011 and the same is available on DoT Website for the last few days.

The Terms of Reference of this one man committee included the identification of short comings and lapses in the implementation of laid down procedures and identification of the public Officials responsible for such lapses and to further examine whether the procedures adopted were fair and transparent and were keeping in line with the principles of natural justice.

Review of Justice Patil's report indicates that the GSM operators like Bharti Airtel have benefited immensely in terms of allotment of spectrum illegally as the Department of Telecom played partition and did not follow proper procedures. Though the report contains the names of many operators who were beneficiaries of unfair and non-transparent procedures of DoT, I am giving below some of the crucial abnormalities noticed in the report in respect of Bharti Airtel.

i) In para xv of page 88, it has been noted that the 4th Cellular operator was given an option to seek allotment of additional 1.8 MHz + 1.8 MHz in the beginning itself subject to only payment of additional 1% of revenue as license fee. This was done without being considered by Telecom Commission and without the recommendations of TRAI. Based on this, Bharti Airtel got start-up spectrum of 6.2 MHz instead of license mandated 4.4 MHz in respect of 11 service areas of Gujarat, Haryana, Kerala, Madhya Pradesh, Maharashtra, Mumbai, Tamil Nadu, UP(East) UP(West) Bihar and Orissa service areas which helped them in saving capex worth thousands of crores.

**Naranbhai Kachhadiya**
MEMBER OF PARLIAMENT
(LOK SABHA)
• **Member:**

* **Parliamentary Standing Committee, On Ministry of Agriculture**

***Consultative Committee on Ministry of Steel**

**107, South Avenue**
**New Delhi -110011**
**Telefax: 011 - 23795324**

सत्यमेव जयते

Date: / /2011

ii) Vide para xvii of page 88, para xx of page 103 and para xix of page 134 of the report, the committee has noted that the allotment of additional spectrum beyond 8 MHz was approved on 18.8.2003 but the same was not notified to the existing operators or intending entrants and as such was opposed to the extent policy requirements of transparency and fairness. **The committee has further noted that in case of Bharti Airtel Ltd, an allotment of 2+2 MHz beyond 8 MHz was made on 15.7.2003 for Delhi Service area though no criteria for allotment of the same was in existence. The committed has noted that this was arbitrary and selective.**

The committee had further noted in its report on para xvii of page 102 that in respect of Chennai service area, two operators i.e. Aircel Ltd. and Bharti Airtel Pvt. Ltd. had sought allotment of additional spectrum. **While Aircel Ltd had the priority and spectrum available was 1.4 + 1.4 MHz only, the DoT gave a go by to the first come first serve criteria and allotted 0.6 MHz + 0.6 MHz each to these two operators. This favoured Bharti Airtel at the cost of Aircel.**

Further the committee had noted vide para iv of page 108 that at the time of decision taken in the year 2003 to consider the applications for grant of UASL on first come first serve basis, applications from two operators viz. Bharti Airtel and Tata Telecommunications were already pending. As such, first come first serve as the basis of grant of UASL <u>was unfair to other intending applications who could not anticipate such decision and consequently could not make applications to take advantage of first come first serve basis.</u>

From above it would be seen that Bharti Airtel had taken lot of undue advantages in the grant of spectrum and the issue of licenses in connivance with some of the DoT officials.

The violations noted above pertained only to the period 2001 to 2008 and the committee had not commented anything before 2001. For the period upto 2001, the CAG in its report of 2000 had noted very adversely that the concession granted by the Government during 1999 to Bharti Airtel, Essar (Vodafone), BPL (Loop) and Sky Tel (Aircel) had caused a loss of about Rs.50,000 Crores to the Government because of migration from fixed fee to revenue sharing, extension of licensing period from 10 years to 20 years without payment of any fees and increase in the per month rental from the mobile subscribers for Rs.156 to Rs.600 per subscriber.

The CAG had also noted in its report of 2010 that Bharti Airtel had 32.4 MHz of excess spectrum spread in 13 service circles without payment of additional fee. This excess allotment of spectrum has caused a loss of **Rs.5500** Crores to the exchequer.

It may be of interest to note that Bharti Airtel immediately after the grant of license for Delhi service area 1994 for almost free, got investment of Rs.200 crores in 1996 even though the license along with 4.4 MHz spectrum was completely free at that time. There had been a number of equity stake sales in Bharti Airtel upto a sum of about Rs.2500 Crores upto 2001 alone. Some these transactions are given below:

**Flat No. 107, South Avenue New Delhi-110 011, Tele+fax: 23795324**

**Naranbhai Kachhadiya**
MEMBER OF PARLIAMENT
(LOK SABHA)
• **Member:**

**107, South Avenue**
**New Delhi -110011**
**Telefax: 011 - 23795324**

सत्यमेव जयते

*** Parliamentary Standing Committee,**
**On Ministry of Agriculture**

***Consultative Committee on Ministry of Steel** Date: / /2011

| Year | Investor | Amount Invested In Rs. Corores | Equity Stake (purchased) |
|---|---|---|---|
| 2001 | Singapore Telecom | US$200 Million (Rs.900 Crores) | 12.96% |
| 2001 | Warburg Pincus | US$ 200 Million (Rs.900 Crores) | 12.96% |
| 2001 | Asian Infrastructure Funds Management | US$ 35 Million (Rs.158 Crores) | 2.27% |
| 2001 | International Finance Corporation | US $ 20 Million (Rs.90 Crores | 1.30% |
| 2001 | New York Life Insurance Fund | US$ 5 Million (Rs.23 Crores) | 0.32% |

It could be well established that all these stakes sales were mainly based on the spectrum holding by Bharti Airtel and that too unfairly and non-transparently in a number of cases as mentioned in the one man committee's report.

In the light of above, it is clear that Bharti Airtel lead by Shri Sunil Mittal had been indulging in unfair and illegal deals right from the beginning of its starting mobile operations in Delhi in 1995. This has been corroborated by the CAG report of 2000, CAG Report of 2010 and the findings of One Man Committee headed by Justice Shivaraj Patil. It is thus recommended that the case should be investigated thoroughly by CBI into the alleged linkage of the company with the officials in the Government right from 1994 onwards till date.

Since Bharti Airtel has been the beneficiary of allotment of spectrum breaking all rules and regulations; the spectrum allotted to the company in violation of rules should be withdrawn immediately and allotted to the needy companies. The Government should also charge the company for extra spectrum held by it so far.

Bharti Airtel Ltd. has been receiving bonanzas right from 1995 onwards and as such the nexus between Shri Sunil Mittal and the top officers of DoT during the period 1995-2010 should be investigated and guilty DoT officers punished suitably.

Thanking you,

With warm regards

( Naranbhai Kachhadiya )

Flat No. 107, South Avenue New Delhi-110 011, Tele+fax: 23795324

D.O. No...1572/MP/LS/VIP/11

**Maheshwar Hazari**
Member of Parliament
(Lok Sabha)
**Member :**
• Standing Committee, Petroleum & Natural Gas
• Consultative Committee, Power
**Chairman :**
• District Vigilance & Monitoring Committee
For Rural Development Programmes, Samastipur (Bihar)

सत्यमेव जयते

14-C, Ferozshah Road,
New Delhi-110001
Phone : 23327374
23327375

Ref. No. ................................

21 FEB 2011
Dated ........................

Dr. Manmohan Singh
Hon'ble Prime Minister
Govt. of India
South Block
**NEW DELHI – 110 001.**

Dear Sir,

My attention has been drawn to the report of one man committee under Justice Shivaraj V. Patil, Former Judge, Supreme Court of India, which has been submitted to the Government of India on 31.01.2011. It is shocking that the top brass in the DoT has not followed any rules and regulations in the issue of Telecom licenses and in the allotment of spectrum, which is a very valuable and scarce resource. The reading of this report indicates that the rules have been bent very often so that the big corporate houses could be advantaged irrespective of the fact that the Government loses money on this worth thousands of crores of rupees.

I find it shocking that a company held by Birla Group i.e Idea Cellular Ltd. had received lot of favours in the grant of licenses during 2001-2008 and grant of spectrum breaking the DoT guidelines and the license conditions. The CAG report of 2010 has also indicted the company for issuance of telecom licenses in 2008 at 2001 price and for holding of excess spectrum. All these has caused huge loss amounting to more than Rs.10,000 Crores to the Government of India. Some of the irregularities committed by the company are given in the attachment.

I am sure that if the company is indulging in malpractices in the field of telecommunication, certainly the company will also be indulging in similar activities in other fields. I would therefore suggest a full fledged inquiry into the dealings of the company spread over various businesses managed by Birla Group.

The telecom licenses allotted to the company in violation of rules and regulations should be cancelled and spectrum allotted to the company in violation of the license conditions should be withdrawn immediately. The DoT officials who had helped the company in acquiring these telecom licenses and in allotment of excess spectrum should be interrogated and action taken against each of them.

Thanking you,

With warm regards,

Maheshwar Hazari

( Maheshwar Hazari )

CC : 1. Director – CBI, 2. DIG – CBI, 3. Addl. SP - CBI

**Attachment**

**DETAILS OF ISSUES PERTAINING TO IDEA CELLULAR LIMITED**

| Subject | Issue in brief |
|---|---|
| 1. One man committee headed by Justice Shivaraj V. Patil. | Undue benefit in the grant of Telecom Licenses<br><br>**i. The committee has noted vide para 7.1 (vi) that Idea Cellular Limited had applied for grant of license on 4.8.2005 for Mumbai service area. LoI was issued only on 20.11.2006 and in the intervening period, time was extended to enable the applicant to acquire eligibility. Even though extension of time for rectification of deficiencies could maximum be 30 days but in this case it was granted more than one year.**<br><br>**ii. As per para 4.1 (viii) of the report it is noted that on the date of application, Tata Industries was holding 31.69% equity in applicants company. The DoT considered Idea Cellular Ltd. ineligible for the grant of UASL as this was in breach of restriction that an applicant must not have substantial equity in any other operator in the same service area. The company was allowed to retain its priority from date of application subsequent transfer of equity by Tata Industries Ltd.**<br><br>**iii. The committee has further noted that though Idea Cellular Ltd. did not have the eligibility on the date of application yet his subsequent acquisition of eligibility was taken into account for granting LoI by retaining the priority of the applicant from the date of original application.**<br><br>**iv. Vide para 2.41(xv) of the report, the committee has noted that in case of Idea Cellular Ltd, while LoI was issued on 10.1.2008 and the compliance was submitted on the same day, the demand draft for payment of entry fee was dated 8.1.2008. Though the decision was made public through press release on 10.1.2008, the submission of demand draft dated earlier to the notification of the decision indicates the possibilities of some of the applicants having known the changed procedure in advance. This is opposite to the** |

| | |
|---|---|
| | **principles of fairness.** |
| 2. Irregularities in the allotment of spectrum | **i) Idea Cellular Ltd. got spectrum upto 10 MHz in April, 2004 without any provision in the license agreement and without any guidelines of the DoT.**<br><br>**ii) Idea Cellular Ltd. received 6.2 MHz spectrum as start-up against 4.4 MHz as laid down in the license conditions in the service area of Delhi in October, 2002.**<br><br>**iii) Idea Cellular Ltd. received more than 6.2 MHz of spectrum in 900 MHz against the license conditions and policy guidelines. The company received 7.8 MHz in Maharashtra against the maximum stipulation of 6.2 MHz.** |
| 3. CAG Report of 2010 | **CAG in its report of 2010 had noted that Idea Cellular Ltd. had 12.6 MHz of excess spectrum spread over in 6 service areas. This has caused a loss of about Rs.2300 to the Government.** |
| **4. Miscellaneous** | **i) Idea received two UAS Licenses in 2006 and 9 UAS Licenses in 2008 at the prices discovered in 2001, thus, causing a loss to the Government to the extent of more than Rs.8000 Crores.**<br><br>**ii) Idea Cellular sold 15% of its stake to Telecom Malaysia at a price of about Rs.6,000 Crores in 2008 immediately after the receipt of licenses during this period. This premium should have accrued to the Government.** |

**Parimal Nathwani**
Member of Parliament
(Rajya Sabha)

**Member:**
Standing Committee on Personnel, Public Grievances, Law & Justice
Consultative Committee, Ministry of Commerce and Industry
**Permanent Special Invitee:**
Consultative Committee, Ministry of External Affairs

165, South Avenue,
New Delhi - 110 011
Ph.: 011-23794010
e-mail : parimal.nathwani@sansad.nic.in

B/107, Harmu Housing Colony, P. O. Doranc
P. S. Argora, Ranchi - 834 012
Ph. : 0651-2244144

CONFIDENTIAL

**February 23, 2011**

To,
**Dr. Manmohan Singh ji,**
**Hon'ble Prime Minister of India**
Government of India
New Delhi

Respected Sir,

I would like to mention that the decision to constitute the JPC has taken place for the 2G Spectrum. In this JPC, Member of Parliament, Rajya Sabha & Lok Sabha are going to be appointed from the political parties, but we would like to mention that one of the Member of our house, Sh. Rajeev Chandrasekhar is thoroughly knowledgeable person of the telecom sector and also at the same time he is not presently involved in this business sector. We are suggesting his name strongly. Although he is Independent but we would like to request to keep him in the JPC as his kind of knowledgeable and resourceful person will be helpful in JPC in larger interest for which this JPC has been constituted.

**We also suggest that any member directly or indirectly involved in the telecom sector or any other group company which has been called by CBI should not be a part of this JPC.**

I am sure you will consider this suggestion.

With regards

Yours sincerely
Parimal Nathwani

Yours sincerely
Bharatkumar Raut

*Sushil Kumar Singh*
MEMBER OF PARLIAMENT
(LOK SABHA)

MEMBER :-
Estimate Committee
Standing (Communication & IT)
Consultative (Petroleum)

सत्यमेव जयते

16A, Ferozshah Road,
New Delhi-110001

Singh Kothi,
Aurangabad (Bihar)

Telephone :
New Delhi : 011-23354155
Fax : 011-23354136
Aurangabad : 06186-2263..

**25.2.2011**

Dr. Manmohan Singh
Hon'ble Prime Minister
South Block
**NEW DELHI. – 110001.**

Dear Dr. Manmohan Singh ji,

A number of scams involving the allotment of spectrum either by the Department of Telecom or by Department of Space have been highlighted in the media during the last few months. CAG has also made serious observations with regard to the issue of 122 telecom licenses in 2008. The CAG had gone to the extent of estimating the loss to the government to the extent of Rs.1.76 Lakhs Crores because of issue of licenses and allotment of spectrum. I am aware that the issues are being investigated by the CBI under the supervision of Hon'ble Supreme Court of India and by one man committee constituted by shri Kapil Sibal, Minister of Communication and IT.

Since the scams involve lakhs of crores of public money, I am watching the progress of various investigations very keenly. It appears that the CBI has submitted the progress report to Hon'ble Supreme Court, the details of which are not made public. However, the one man committee constituted by Minister has submitted its recommendations on 31.1.2011.

I have gone through the report covering 143 pages, and am surprised to note that the rules, regulations and guidelines instituted by the DoT have been thrown to the winds. There have been violations everywhere, whether it is allotment of spectrum or issue of licenses.

It is distressing to note that a real estate company i.e. Unitech, which had no experience in telecom had been issued licenses in all the circles under various names and companies. It is a clear case that the DoT has not bothered to go into the details of the applications and award them licenses, even though they were not qualified.

The grant of licenses to the company cannot be without the involvement of the Minister and senior officer of the DoT. **The one man committee has observed that some of the applicants including Unitech collected LoI on 10 January, 2008 and submitted compliance on the same day along with the demand drafts which were dated earlier to 10.1.2008.**

The one man committee has observed as follows vide para 2.42 (xv) of page 120 of the report:

> *"In case Unitech Infrastructure Pvt. Ltd., Volga Properties Pvt. Ltd., Azka Projects Ltd., Azare Properties Ltd., Unitech Builders and Estates Pvt. Ltd., Adonis projects Pvt. Ltd. Hudson Properties Ltd., while the LoIs were issued on 10.1.2008 and compliance was submitted on the same day, the demand drafts for payment of entry fee was dated 24.12.2007.----- For the first time, the procedures for according priority to those applicants, who complied with the terms of LoI first, was mentioned in the letter of MOCIT to the Prime Minister dated 26.12.2007. The decision in the files of DoT to the said effect is taken only on 7.1.2008. The decision was made public through press release dated 10.1.2008."*

*Sushil Kumar Singh*

MEMBER OF PARLIAMENT
(LOK SABHA)

MEMBER :-
Estimate Committee
Standing (Communication & IT)
Consultative (Petroleum)

सत्यमेव जयते

16A, Ferozshah Road,
New Delhi-110001

Singh Kothi,
Aurangabad (Bihar)

Telephone :
New Delhi : 011-23354155
Fax : 011-23354156
Aurangabad : 06186-226300

The Committee has further noted that submission of demand draft dated earlier to the notification of the decision indicates the possibility of some of the applicants having known the changed procedures to be notified in advance and kept the demand draft ready for payment of entire fee.

Thus, the committee has clearly exposed a clear nexus between the Minister, Unitech and the Senior Officers of the DoT as Unitech was privy to the on-going policy decisions in the DoT. In normal course nobody would have dared to keep the demand draft valuing Rs.1658 crores ready on 24.12.2007 when the decision to issue the licenses was taken only on 10.1.2008, that is after 45 days of preparation of demand draft.

**This is a very serious and clear case of nexus involving Unitech, Minister and the DoT officers and should be investigated by CBI as to how demand drafts valuing Rs.1658 crores were got ready by Unitech on 24.1.2007 when the LoIs were issued only on 10.1.2008.**

I will be thankful if I am kept informed of the progress of these investigations and its outcome.

Thanking you,

Yours sincerely,

( Sushil Kumar Singh )

Copy to :
1. Sh. Kapil Sibal, Hon'ble Minister for Communication & IT
2. Shri A P Singh, Director, CBI
3. Sh. Vinod Rai, CAG.

सत्यमेव जयते

DR. ASHWANI KUMAR
Minister of State
Ministry of Planning, Parliamentary Affairs, Science & Technology, Earth Sciences
Government of India

April 30, 2011

Respected Dr. Sahib,

Please find enclosed herewith a copy of my statement issued to the Press yesterday on the PAC issue. Parts of the statement have been reported in the Press as per the enclosures.

With deepest regards,

Yours sincerely,

(ASHWANI KUMAR)

DR. MANMOHAN SINGH JI
HON'BLE PRIME MINISTER
7, RACE COURSE ROAD
NEW DELHI

Office : 132, Yojana Bhawan, Sansad Marg, New Delhi - 110001 Tel.: 011-23096561 / 62 / 63 Fax : 011-23096713
Resi. : 18, Ashoka Road, New Delhi - 110001 Telefax : 011-23354222

For Publication

A. The indecent haste with which Dr. Murli Manohar Joshi has sought to push for the adoption the draft report of the PAC despite strong and persistent reservations expressed by a majority of the members has done incalculable damage to established parliamentary conventions.

B. It is well established that parliamentary committees do not work on partisan basis. But by seeking to ignore the specific and expressed reservations of a majority of its members, Dr. Joshi has betrayed an inclination to subserve the political agenda of his party rather than to uphold the dignity of the institution of the PAC. The politicization of the work of PAC, writ large in an unabashed attempt to further the political agenda of the BJP is a matter of grave national concern. The conduct of Dr. Joshi strikes at the root of the healthy functioning of our parliamentary democracy.

- Parts of the draft report are legally vitiated because of the prima facie disconnect between evidence considered and brought before the full committee and the conclusions sought to be drawn therefrom.

- That parts of the draft report are ex facie patently partisan, outsourced and factually flawed is established amongst others by a statement therein that officials of the PMO, the Cabinet Secretary and the AG had been examined, whereas it is in public domain that they could not offer their testimony

- Those sought to be faulted were not examined and condemned unheard. This is a clear violation of the first principles of natural justice which renders the draft report a nullity in law.

- The established conventions of parliament mandate the adoption of the Report of PAC by consensus. Not only is there no consensus, but a majority of members have serious and valid reservations about the draft report.

- Such a document is no report at all in the eyes of law and is without any precedent whosoever. A document which cannot be said to be a Report as contemplated, can in law be neither presented to, nor acted upon by any constitutional functionary.

- It is incorrect to suggest that the next committee of the PAC is precluded from hearing the matter afresh or to review the deliberations of the previous PAC.

Ashwani Kumar
MOS (Parliamentary Affairs & Planning)

Dharampal Sabharwal
MEMBER OF PARLIAMENT
(RAJYA SABAH)

सत्यमेव जयते

Tel. : 23315733
Mobile : 9868181137
C-201, Swarna Jayanti Sadan,
Dr. B.D. Marg,
New Delhi - 110 001.

January 16, 2007

Dear Mr. Prime Minister,

**Sub: Mismanagement & Financial irregularities in DoT**

I would like to draw your attention to observations made by CAG on functioning of Department of Telecom (DoT). I am in receipt of CAG's Regulatory audit Report no 9 (2004 -2005) of Non Tax Receipts. Chapter 2 of this report deals with Revenue management in Department of Telecommunications. There are some *startling observations of mismanagement made by CAG in this* report. Some of important inconsistencies brought out in CAG report are:

**Inconsistency in allotment of Spectrum:**

1. Department of telecommunication (DoT) had allocated radio frequencies to ineligible operators resulting in substantial loss to the exchequer. There are many instances of this brought out in the CAG report.

   a. *The license conditions stipulated that initially a maximum of* 4.4+4.4MHz radio frequency (spectrum) be allotted to cellular operators in a service area based on fulfillment of minimum subscriber base criteria. Further, allocation was to be based on the usage pattern *and availability of additional radio frequency. However in the audit* scrutiny it was revealed that in violation of norms, DoT had made initial allotments of 6.2+6.2 MHz radio frequency to four cellular operators. The excess allocation was not justified in terms of *subscriber base of the operators.*
   b. DoT did not insist upon the clearance of outstanding amounts while allocating additional spectrum to six operators although they had dues of Rs.73.94 crore outstanding against them.
   c. There is a condition existing for withdrawal of spectrum following inefficient usage from basic service operators (CDMA operators) however there is no provision of withdrawal in case of GSM operators.

**Lack of coordination between different wings of DoT:**

a. Lack of internal coordination between Licensing Finance (LF) wing and Wireless Planning & coordination (WPF) resulted in short remittance of spectrum charges of Rs.17.72 crore.
b. Lack of internal coordination between LF wing and Accounting Wing: *No reconciliation of books were done between the years* 2001-02 to 2004-05, which resulted in a net difference of Rs.700.40 crore of revenue shown in these two sets of records.

-1-

website : http://parliamentofindia.nic.in
*Permanent Address : # 53-A, Bahadurpur, HOSHIARPUR-146001 (PUNJAB)*

Dharampal Sabharwal
MEMBER OF PARLIAMENT
(RAJYA SABHA)

Tel.: 23315733
Mobile: 9868181137
C-201, Swarna Jayanti Sadan,
Dr. B.D. Marg,
New Delhi - 110 001.

-2-

**Lax attitude of DoT in recovering outstanding payments:**

a. DoT failed to communicate the new financial conditions of the revenue-sharing regime to MTNL in time, which resulted in non-levy of interest of Rs. 43.51 crore on it for delays in payment of license fees.
b. DoT did not realize spectrum dues of Rs.241.60 crore from five Central Government organizations.

Spectrum has been a controversial issue & DoT mismanaging this is an issue is of grave concern. In past, on number of occasions, this subject has been discussed in Parliament, Parliamentary Standing Committees. In 2005 Standing Committee has given its observation in a report. On many occasion there has been allegation on DoT for favoring GSM technology and the same has been brought to light in CAG report also. DoT should follow technology neutral approach in all circumstances and should immediately take action to remove all anomalies including the one described in CAG report.

Financial irregularities in the various wings of DoT especially in WPC needs through investigation. The proposal of having a separate National Frequency Allocation Plan was a good proposal and can bring in some amount of synergy in working of WPC, LF and Accounting wings of DoT.

Looking forwards for an appropriate action in the matter.

With kind regards,

Yours sincerely,

D.P. Sabharwal

(DHARAM PAL SABHARWAL)

Shri Manmohan Singh,
Hon'ble Prime Minister,
Government of India,
New Delhi.

website : http://parliamentofindia.nic.in
Permanent Address : 6 53-A. Bahadurpur, HOSHIARPUR-146001 (PUNJAB)

*Rayapali Sambasiva Rao M.P.*
(Lok Sabha)

**CHAIRMAN**
Standing Committee on Water Resources

सत्यमेव जयते

Off : 129, Parliament House Annexe
New Delhi-110001
Phone : 23034356
Telefax : 23016836

Res. : C-I/20, Pandara Park,
New Delhi-110003
Tel. : 23388272 Fax : 23388252

27th October, 2007

Respected Prime Minister ji,

Kindly find enclosed a copy of the representation dated the 27th October, 2007 addressed to your honour by M/s ByCell Telecommunications India P. Ltd., New Delhi regarding issue of UAS Licenses for five circles in India. The said applications are pending for a long period in the Department of Telecommunications (DOT) even though the ByCell Telecommunications have completed all the formalities and found to be eligible for issue of licenses.

I shall be personally grateful if you could kindly have the matter looked into by the DOT for issue of licenses at the earliest.

With warm regards,

Yours sincerely,

(R. Sambasiva Rao)

Dr. Manmohan Singh ji,
Hon'ble Prime Minister
Government of India
South Block, New Delhi

4th Line, Lakshmipuram, GUNTUR-522007, Andhra Pradesh Tel. : 2221924, 2350500, Fax : 2356793, 2240500
HYDERABAD - Tel. : 23401234, 23402345

**ByCell Telecommunications India Pvt. Ltd.**

October 27, 2007

Respected Hon'ble Prime Minister of India

**Sub: Issue of UAS Licenses**

We are enclosing herewith a copy of our letter dated the 6th October, 2007 addressed to the Hon'ble Minister of Communication & Information Technology, Government of India, regarding issue of UAS Licenses applied for way back in January, 2006 in our favour.

Briefly the mater is that we had submitted applications for issue of UAS Licenses for five circles, namely Assam, Bihar, Orissa, West Bengal & North-East on 31st January 2006. The said applications were submitted after requisite approval from FIPB. Our applications were thoroughly examined by the Department of Telecommunications (DOT) in the early part of 2006 and we were asked to clarify on certain points. The points raised by DOT were replied to their full satisfaction. We would like to emphasis that at the time of our submission of applications, the policy of the DOT was to grant the licenses on first come first serve basis. Further, our applications were duly cleared in all respects in accordance with the criteria applicable on the date of our applications and we understand that spectrum is also available in all the five circles for which we had submitted the applications. Therefore, we feel that our applications are being with-held without any valid reasons.

In view of above, it is our humble request to your honour to kindly issue necessary directions to the Department of Telecommunications to issue us the licenses without any further delay.

With respectful regards and thanks,

Yours sincerely,
For ByCell Telecommunications India Pvt. Limited

Director

To:

The Hon'ble Prime Minister
Government of India
New Delhi

Regd. Office : C-367, LGF, Defence Colony, New Delhi - 110 024
Tel : +91 11 2433 6105, Fax : +91 11 2433 6083, e-mail :hq.delhi@bycell.com

**ByCell Telecommunications India Pvt. Ltd.**

October 6, 2007

Hon'ble Mr. A. Raja
Minister of Communication & Information Technology
Electronics Niketan
CGO Complex, Lodhi Road
NMew Delhi – 110 003

Mr. K. Sridhara
Member (Technical)
Department of Telecommunications
Sanchar Bhawan
20 Ashoka Road
New Delhi – 110 001

Mr. A.K. Srivastava
DDG (AS)
Department of Telecommunications
Sanchar Bhawan
20 Ashoka Road
New Delhi – 110 001

Mr. HJS Kachwaha
Joint Wireless Advisor
Department of Telecommunications
Sanchar Bhawan
20 Ashoka Road
New Delhi – 110 001

Mr. R. N. Padukone
Sr. DDG
Telecom Engg Centre
Khursheed Lal Bhawan
Janpath
New Delhi

**Re: ISSUE OF UASLICENSES**

Dear Sir,

We are an applicant for the UAS licence for different circles, in India. In this regard, we had submitted our initial applications for five circles, vis-à-vis Assam, Bihar, Orissa,

Regd. Office: C-582, LGF, Defence Colony, New Delhi-110 024
Tel: +91 11 2433 6105, Fax: +91 11 2433 6083, e-mail :hq.delhi@bycell.com

West Bengal and North-East way back on January 31, 2006. The said applications were submitted after having received due approval from the FIPB with respect to the following shareholder in our Company.

After submission of our applications, we were called upon to submit certain additional information and to respond to the queries raised by the DoT in the months of February/March 2006. All the information was provided and queries were answered to, to the satisfaction of the DoT by mid March 2006. Thereafter, no further queries were raised and we were given to understand that we were eligible for issue of licences, having satisfied the criteria of the DoT.

Thereafter, we have been waiting for the issue of the licences for the aforesaid five circles. The licenses have not been issued to us till today for reasons not known and/or intimated to us have not been issued to us till today. This is when our applications were duly cleared in all respects in accordance with the applicable criteria as on the date of our applications and to the best of our knowledge spectrum is available in the five circles for which we have made the application.

Subsequently, we have applied for UAS licences for seventeen (17) other circles in India to become a Pan India operator. However, over the last few days we have become concerned with various news articles appearing in the press suggested that certain new criteria are being considered for the issue of UASA licences.

We would like to mention here that ByCell applied for 5 UAS licences in January 2006 in accordance with the criteria applicable as on that date. Thereafter, the said applications were duly cleared by the DoT. Therefore, we fail to understand as to why a new criteria should be used to evaluate the applications filed and cleared after almost eighteen (18) months of the applications having been scrutinized and processed. We may mention that as on the date of our application for the 5 UAS licence, the criteria of the DoT was clearly 'first come, first serve' basis and we believe that the said criteria should not be disturbed for cases like ours which have already been clearly the scrutiny of the DoT. It is relevant to note here that even the discussions on the concept paper held by the TRAI were formulated in the year 2007 which is long after our applications had been filed (in

January 2006) and cleared by the DOT (mid-March 2006). TRAI also appreciated the fact that there was no requirement for change of policy and we have been and continue to be hopeful of getting the licences within a short time.

We hereby urge that the evaluation criteria be not changed at this late stage for cases like ours which already stands cleared by the DoT itself over 18 months back and such cases should be considered on a priority basis and we be awarded the five licenses for Assam, Bihar, Orissa, West Bengal and North East at the earliest possible, since spectrum is available in the said five circles.

Thanking you,

Yours sincerely,
For ByCell Telecommunications India P. Ltd.

(Ram Nath Babu)
Director

**AMAR SINGH**
MEMBER OF PARLIAMENT
(RAJYA SABHA)
NATIONAL GENERAL SECRETARY & SPOKESMAN
(SAMAJWADI PARTY)

27, LODHI ESTATE,
NEW DELHI-110003
TEL. : 32565397 / 32542188 / 2461682
FAX : 91-11-24636299
Email : amarsingh@bol.net.in

November 12, 2007

Respected Manmohan Singh ji,

I would like to draw your kind attention to some nefarious activities of the Cellular Operators Association of India (COAI) whose main aim is anti-consumer.

The COAI is holding the Department of Telecom, and in other words, the country to ransom by being a stumbling block for entry of new entrants in the sector.

Over the past 6 months some of the prominent members of the COAI have cartelized and increased the charges on consumers in a concerted manner. The increases have been as high as 30%, hurting the consumers.

Every time the Government brings about measures to improve spectrum efficiency to conserve the precious natural resource, the COAI has been opposing as they do not want to bring in efficiencies as it would entail them to invest more capital. In other words, COAI wants to thrive on Country's resources without any payment.

As per the licence agreements signed with the Government, these companies are entitled to get only 6.2 MHZ of spectrum. Curiously the companies in the forefront of litigation before the TDSAT on spectrum issues have amassed 10 MHZ spectrum each raising the question as to how and in what manner they obtained additional spectrum. This begs a CBI enquiry without any delay.

COAI and their principal sponsor have recently attacked the Government for allotting spectrum to the National Telecom companies, BSNL and MTNL forgetting that the National units have heavy social obligations to cater to.

The Department of Telecom should strongly defend their action in the TDSAT and expose the cartel, that is, COAI..

**Thanking you**

**With** regards,

**Yours** Sincerely
Amar Singh

**(Amar Singh)**

**Dr. Manmohan Singh**
**Hon'ble Prime Minister**
**Government of India**
**152 South Block**
**New Delhi-110001**

Permanent Address : E-593, GREATER KAILASH - II, NEW DELHI - 110048 Phone : 29226507 / 29225377
OFFICE : 8, SOUTH AVENUE, NEW DELHI - 110011 PHONE : 23792324 / 23794013 FAX : ...

S.M. LALJAN BASHA
MEMBER OF PARLIAMENT
(RAJYA SABHA)
CHAIRMAN
JOINT PARLIAMENTARY COMMITTEE
ON WAKF

सत्यमेव जयते

OFF. : 128, PARLIAMENT HOUSE ANNEXE,
NEW DELHI-110 001
TEL. : 23034898, 23015733

RES. : AB-15, MATHURA ROAD,
NEW DELHI-110 002
TEL. : 23782136
FAX : 23782116
E-MAIL : nbasha@sansad.nic.in

Sub: Hoarding of telecom spectrum by monopolies.

Dear Dr. Manmohan Singh ji Dec. 3, 207.

The entire country has learnt that telecom companies have hoarded spectrum, which is a national resource . Private Telecom Companies have cornered the entire Mobile sector . This is Crony Capitalism. Recently, you said that excess spectrum , held by telecom companies should be returned. I doubt whether TRAI or Telecom secretary can do it. Your office must take the initiative , as I doubt whether TRAI /Telecom Ministry can face the biggest /richest people in the world, who own the telecom sector.

In last 10 years, private telecom companies have earned huge amounts and the promoters are amongst world's richest people. Obviously, this means that they enjoy a monopoly & are fleecing the consumer.Only Mexico permits this situation and the world's richest man is a Mexican telecom operator. Mexico is not a good example for India.

I wonder whether the public controversy about spectrum hoarding is a mere "staged" fight . This controversy might be stage-managed. The controversy convinces everyone that there is rivalry. But in reality, we now hear of an "AMICABLE" settlement engineered by Ministry of Telecom. After a media fight, the Minister calls a meeting and everyone is happy.

The main effort of existing telecom companies is to ensure that no new entrants get into telecom. New entrants will reduce their super profits.

**Suggestions :**

a. Newcomers must be encouraged. Any newcomer should be able to start a telecom company and offer better rates .There should be no ban on entry . It should be an open sector .

ermanent Add. : "Bismillah Manzil", Mithila Nagar Colony, Road No.12, Banjara Hills, Hyderabad-500034 (A.P.)

2

b. Presently, the entire telecom sector of India is being manipulated and controlled by 2 or at most 3 people. Government should ensure that telecom prices are not so high-priced. TRAI is doing nothing,.

It is obvious that by hoarding Spectrum, the existing dominant players want to prevent future entries. They have plans for the next 25 years. If government wants to bring down service costs, then there should be free entry for new-comers.

Huge fortunes were made within 10 years. Such abnormal profits result only from monopoly situations. If government had ensured that there was competition, then such profits would not have been made.

The Indian consumer had paid more than is due. Please ensure that there is competition . The role of TRAI and its utility is now being publicly questioned.

With regards

Yours sincerely,

6.12.2007

**Dr. Manmohan Singh,**
Prime Minister ,
New Delhi.

**Laljan Basha S.M.**

# SHIV SENA PARLIAMENT PARTY

126 (II), PARLIAMENT HOUSE, NEW DELHI - 110 001
TEL. : 011-23014453; TELEFAX : 011-23034913

Ref. No. : *SS-1/GI/2007* Date : *5.12.2007*

Hon'ble Prime Minister,

**(Regarding; Spectrum allocation)**

Further to our letter dated 23rd November, certain new facts have come to our light and we would like to make some more suggestions for your consideration:

The DoT has appointed an expert committee consisting of Professors from IIT Chennai and Delhi to review the concerns of GSM as well as CDMA operators regarding spectrum allocation. The Government must ensure that independence of this committee is not compromised, nor the Committee pressurized by any lobby to adjust its findings / recommendations to suit any specific category of operators. Finally, the scientific and technically viable recommendations as made by Telecom Engineering Center (TEC) should be adopted by the Government for allocation of spectrum to all opretors.

It has also been brought to our notice that the TRAI has not recommended auction for 2G spectrum i.e. 800-900-1800 MHz and this view has also been accepted by DoT and GoI in order to create competition and a level playing field between all operators- new and old.

Accordingly, our view is the Government should go by existing policies, practices, and procedures and allocate spectrum and licenses on a non-discriminatory basis. The Government also must expeditiously issue instructions for the allocation of spectrum to all the applicants based on established guidelines to enhance number of players, increase competition and reduce tariffs in the interest of millions of consumers.

Further, in line with TRAI's recommendation, DoT must auction all available spectrums for both 3G and WIMAX, as and when available for allocation, through a transparent auction process which many well garner over Rs. 50,000 cr. in spectrum fees to the GoI.

We hope these suggesting will receive due consideration.

With regards,

Yours Sincerely,

**(MANOHAR JOSHI)**
**Leader: Rajya Sabha**

**(ANANT G. GEETE)**
**Leader: Lok Sabha**

**Dr. Manmohan Singh**
**Hon'ble Prime Minister,**
**Government of India**
**New Delhi.**

S.M. LALJAN BASHA
MEMBER OF PARLIAMENT
(RAJYA SABHA)
CHAIRMAN
JOINT PARLIAMENTARY COMMITTEE
ON WAKF

सत्यमेव जयते

OFF. : 128, PARLIAMENT HOUSE ANNEXE,
NEW DELHI-110 001
TEL. : 23034898, 23015732

RES. : AB-15, MATHURA ROAD,
NEW DELHI-110 002
TEL. : 23782136
FAX : 23782116
E-MAIL : gbasha@sansad.nic.in

Sub: Telecom policies :

Dear Dr. Manmohan Singh ji

Feb. 17, 2008.

I had written earlier on the need to increase competition in the telecom sector. Now, what has emerged is that 3 or 4 telecom players control entire telecom sector. If you look 6 years down the line, it is obvious that there will be 3 major players in the country and no more.

An oligarchic situation or " **crony capitalism**" to quote you, has emerged because existing players have managed to fix rules, so that new entrants cannot enter. The threshold for new telecom entrants has been raised so high that no new company can come and offer cheaper services .Only **Take-Overs** can happen.

Kindly consider the following ;

a. To keep open telecom sector for new entrants and new technology?
b. How to reduce the threshold for new entrants ?

c. How to have an **"anytime policy"** for new entrants and not some vague and un-fixed time in the future ? Such an **anytime open policy** will keep the existing dominating telecom players alert and cautious .

d. To examine role of **TRAI** . There is a feeling in the country that TRAI is loyal to private telecom companies. Now and then , some symbolic noise is made. Nothing serious or spontaneous, but orchestrated to the tune of telecom companies. Even a simple demand to reduce nuisance calls / SMS messages by marketing companies was not done . The scheme for tackling marketing calls was designed to fail and it has failed . This purposeful sabotage was done so that telecom companies will not lose revenue.

e. **Spectrum policy :**
The country wants to know why no auction was done and why highest revenues were not obtained. There is no transparency in this matter. I request you to review the entire episode of spectrum allotment and sale.

2

f. **Excess spectrum :**

The country is aware that excessive spectrum has been hoarded by telecom companies. A natural resource has been cornered by a few companies. Actually, majority of shares of such companies are closely held . Hence , excessive spectrum has gone to some individuals.

The country wants to know whether this is what a free economy means. That some private companies make super-profits , in the name of competition, when no competition exists .

g. **High price of phone calls :**

If you adjust price of Indian phone tariff with Purchasing Power Parity of Rupee, then our calls are very expensive. What telecom companies and TRAI are doing is to simply convert the present price of phone calls in India into dollar-terms and then say our calls are cheap.. When compared to incomes in India and Western countries, our calls are over-priced.

That is why telecom companies make profits of tens of thousands of crores every year.. They make super-profits at the expense of the public .It is estimated that our phone calls cost 7 times as much calls in the USA. **TRAI** has not done anything to bring down prices .TRAI is not regulating anything at all.

You frequently mention the virtues of competition and that a free economy is good for India . Then I request you to control and reduce the emerging monopolies which have already established themselves in the telecom sector, all in the name of free enterprise.

I hope you will initiate action before it is too late..
With regards

Yours sincerely,

16. 2. 2008

**Laljan Basha S.M.**

Dr. Manmohan Singh
Hon. Prime Minister,
Govt. of India
New Delhi.

Confidential

D.O. No. 30/8/SPS(S)/ND-08

**Dharampal Sabharwal**
MEMBER OF PARLIAMENT
(RAJYA SABHA)

Tel. : 23315733
Mobile : 9868181137
C-201, Swarna Jayanti Sadan,
Dr. B.D. Marg,
New Delhi - 110 001.

सत्यमेव जयते

November 06, 2008

Dear Dr. Manmohan Singh ji,

**Illegal & undue favour shown to Swan Telecom**

You may be aware that since last several months, the affairs of ADAG Group is in the news and in our Parliament. The main trust of all these are the "undue favours" being shown to this group. The recent case pertains to favours shown by the Department of Telecommunication to Swan Telecom Private Limited (Swan Telecom) which has been given license early this year is based on an invalid application.

Swan Telecom Private Limited was a company incorporated by Anil Ambani Group in July 2006 (Details in Annexure 1). This company filed application for UAS License on 2nd March 2007. Swan Telecom was further sold by Anil Ambani to Dynamix Balwan Group (A real estate company owned by Shahid Balwan) & its associates. It is understood that the sale was done for a hefty consideration as the company was ahead in the queue. Department of Telecom has publicly said that they want to strictly abide by the so called first come first serve basis which is reproduced below:

The application was invalid on the date of filing as per clause 8 of the Guidelines for Unified Access Services License issued by the Ministry of Communications and Information Technology, Development of Telecommunications, Government of India No. 10-21/2005-BS.I (Vol.II)/49 dated 14th December 2005 which is reproduced below:-

> "8. No. single company/legal person, either directly or through its associates, shall have substantial equity holding in more than one LICENSEE Company in the same service area for the Access Services namely; Basic, Cellular and Unified Access Service. 'Substantial equity' herein will mean 'an equity of 10% or more A Promoter company/Legal person cannot have stakes in more than once LICENSEE Company for the same service area. A certificate to this effect shall be provided by the applicant's company secretary alongwith application."

As per the above clause Anil Ambani group which also owns Reliance Communications has operation in the circles where application for Swan Telecom was filed. For the purpose only 9.99% holding was shown against Reliance Communications. Instead of rejecting the invalid application concerned officers of the Department processed this application and gave the license to Swan.

The favours shown to Swan did not stop here, some of the other favours shown to Swan Telecom are:

1. Two officers of DoT namely Mr.R.J.S.Kushwaha & Mr.D.Jha were transferred from WPC as they refused to unduly favour Swan Telecom. After transfer of these officers, spectrum was allotted to Swan Telecom for Delhi.

**Dharampal Sabharwal**

MEMBER OF PARLIAMENT
(RAJYA SABHA)

Tel. : 23315733
Mobile : 9868181137
C-201, Swarna Jayanti Sadan,
Dr. B.D. Marg,
New Delhi - 110 001.

2. BSNL which has never done any roaming agreement with any operator was forced to do a roaming agreement with Swan Telecom. The same favour was not extended to any other operator. I am told that the policy was made by BSNL only to suit Swan Telecom.

I would therefore request you to order a high level investigations to enquire into:

1. The application of Swan Telecom Limited on illegal application and license issued to them. The role of concerned DoT officers acting in collusion with Swan Telecom.
2. The transfer of WPC official and role of senior Department official in these transfers.
3. Role of BSNL official in entering in roaming agreement with Swan Telecom.

In view of above, I would request you that issues raised above and in the enclosed notes be addressed thoroughly and thoughtfully. If this is not done with the promptitude it deserves, I am afraid, it may give rise to another scam-like situation in this country.

With regards

Yours sincerely,

D.P. Sabharwal

(DHARAM PAL SABHARWAL)

Dr. Manmohan Singh,
Hon'ble Prime Minister,
Government of India,
New Delhi.

website : http://parliamentofindia.nic.in

## Annexure -1: Swan Telecom Private Limited

A. Swan Telecom Private Limited (the "Company") was incorporated on 13th July 2006 as Swan Capital Private Limited with registered office at 7th Floor, Raheja Point- 1, Jawaharlal Nehru Marg, Vakola Market, Santa Cruz (E), Mumbai – 400 055. The subscribers to the Memorandum of Association were:

| Person | No. of equity shares of Rs. 10 each |
|---|---|
| Himanshu Agarwal (employee of ADA Group) | 1 |
| Powersurfer Interactive (India) P Ltd. (A ADA Group Company) | 4,999 |
| Reliance Energy Management Services P Ltd. (an ADA Group Company) | 5,000 |
| Total | 10,000 |

On 22nd January 2007, the Company allotted equity shares of Rs. 10 each as given below:

| Person | No. of equity shares of Rs. 10 each |
|---|---|
| Tiger Trustees Private Limited (formerly Tiger Traders Private Limited) | 27,03,000 |
| Reliance Telecom Limited (a wholly owned subsidiary of Reliance Communications Limited) | 2,97,000 |
| Total | 30,00,000 |

On 2nd March 2007, the Company further allotted equity shares of Rs. 10 each as given below:

| Person | No. of equity shares of Rs. 10 each |
|---|---|
| Tiger Trustees Private Limited (formerly Tiger Traders Private Limited) | 9,55,06,000 |
| Reliance Telecom Limited (a wholly owned subsidiary of Reliance Communications Limited) | 1,04,94,000 |
| Total | 10,60,00,000 |

The Company made an application for Unified Access Service Licence (UASL) on 2nd March 2007 and the shareholders of the Company on that date were:

| Shareholder | No. of shares | Percent |
|---|---|---|
| Tiger Trustees Private Limited (formerly Tiger Traders Private Limited) | 9,82,19,000 | 90.10% |
| Reliance Telecom Ltd. (a wholly owned subsidiary of Reliance Communications Limited) | 1,07,91,000 | 9.90% |
| Total | 10,90,10,000 | 100.00% |

B. Tiger Trustees Private Limited was incorporated on 20th March 2006 as Tiger Traders Private Limited with registered office at Reliance Energy Centre, 3rd Floor, Santacruz East, Mumbai 400055. The shareholders of Tiger Trustees Private Limited as on 2nd March 2007 were:

| Shareholder | No. of shares | Percent |
|---|---|---|
| Swan Infonet Services Private Limited (formerly Parrot Consultants Private Limited | 5,000 | 50.00% |
| Swan Advisory Services Private Limited(formerly Zebra consultants Private Limited) | 5,000 | 50.00% |
| Total | 10,000 | 100.00% |

The directors of Tiger Trustees Private Limited on incorporation were:

| Name of the Director | Address |
|---|---|
| Mr. Ashish Karyekar (employee of ADA Group) | 704, Reliance Energy Quarters, Chembur, Receiving Station, Deonar, Mumbai 400088 |
| Mr. Paresh Rathod (employee of ADA Group) | 204, Reliance Energy Quarters, Chembur, Receiving Station, Deonar, Mumbai 400088 |

C. Swan Infonet Services Private Limited was incorporated on 17th March 2006 as Parrot consultants Private Limited with registered office at Reliance Energy Centre, 3rd Floor, Santacruz East, Mumbai 400055. The shareholders of Swan Infonet Services Private Limited as on 2nd March 2007 were:

| Shareholder | No. of shares | Percent |
|---|---|---|
| Tiger Trustees Private Limited (formerly Tiger Traders Private Limited) | 5,000 | 50.00% |
| Swan Advisory Services Private Limited (formerly Zebra Consultants Private Limited) | 5,000 | 50.00% |
| Total | 10,000 | 100.00% |

The directors of Swan Infonet Services Private Limited on incorporation were:

| Name of the Director | Address |
|---|---|
| Mr. Ashish Karyekar (employee of ADA Group) | 704, Reliance Energy Quarters, Chembur, Receiving Station, Deonar, Mumbai 400088 |
| Mr. Paresh Rathod (employee of ADA Group) | 204, Reliance Energy Quarters, Chembur, Receiving Station, Deonar, Mumbai 400088 |

D. Swan Advisory Services Private Limited was incorporated on 21st March 2006 as Zebra Consultants Private Limited with registered office at Reliance Energy

Centre, 3rd Floor, Santacruz East, Mumbai 400055. The shareholders of Swan Infonet Services Private Limited as on 2nd March 2007 were:

| Shareholder | No. of shares | Percent |
|---|---|---|
| Tiger Trustees Private Limited (formerly Tiger Traders Private Limited) | 5,000 | 50.00% |
| Swan Infonet Services Private Limited (formerly Parrot Consultants Private Limited ) | 5,000 | 50.00% |
| Total | 10,000 | 100.00% |

The directors of Swan Infonet Services Private Limited on incorporation were:

| Name of the Director | Address |
|---|---|
| Mr. Ashish Karyekar (employee of ADA Group) | 704, Reliance Energy Quarters, Chembur, Receiving Station, Deonar, Mumbai 400088 |
| Mr. Paresh Rathod (employee of ADA Group) | 204, Reliance Energy Quarters, Chembur, Receiving Station, Deonar, Mumbai 400088 |

**From the above, it is apparent that on 2nd March 2007,when the Company made application for Unified Access Services Licence, it was owned 100% by Reliance Communications Limited and its associates viz. Reliance Telecom Limited, Tiger Trustees Limited, Swan Infonet Services Private Limited, and Swan Advisory Services Private Limited. As pictorically presented below:**

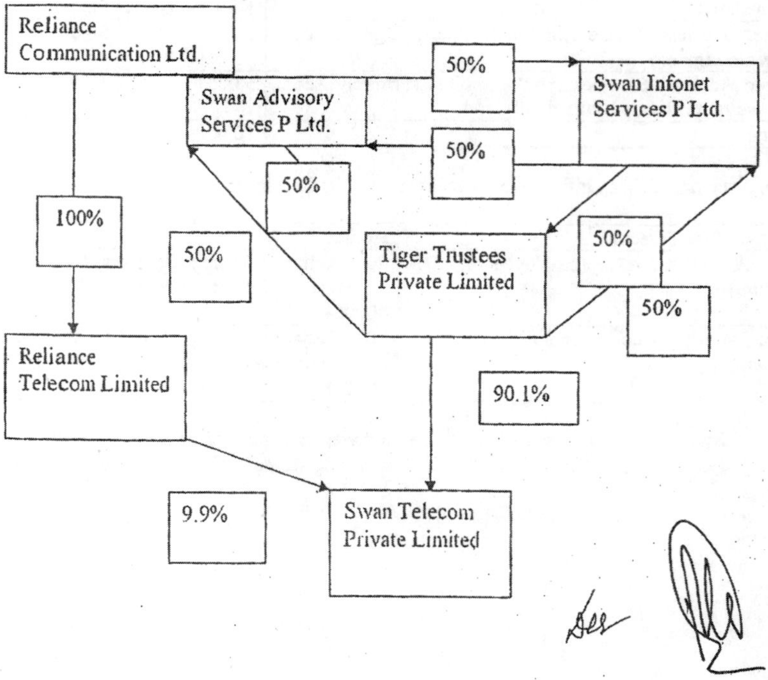

AMAR SINGH
MEMBER OF PARLIAMENT
(RAJYA SABHA)
NATIONAL GENERAL SECRETARY & SPOKESMAN
(SAMAJWADI PARTY)

27, LODHI ESTATE,
NEW DELHI-110003
TEL. : 32565397 / 32542188 / 2461682
FAX : 91-11-24636299
Email : amarsingh@bol.net.in

November 17, 2008

Respected Manmohan Singh ji

**Subject:** **Charging Annual Spectrum Charges for 2G spectrum, contrary to TRAI recommendation and at the behest of the private dominant operators which is also not pro level-playing field for new operators**

This is further to my letter dated 22nd August'08 regarding spectrum charges for the extra spectrum over 6.2 MHz allotted to the private cellular operators completely free of cost, as well as, the issue of annual spectrum charges for 2G spectrum.

I have now been given to understand that the Telecom Commission has reviewed the same and is increasing the spectrum usage charges by charging 1% across the board with a new slab at 8 MHz and beyond, where the increase is by 2%.

I would like to highlight that this decision is contrary to the TRAI recommendation in 2007, wherein it specifies that there should be no increase of spectrum usage charge up to 6.2 MHz in GSM and 5 MHz in CDMA. This was considering that the entry licensee fee of Rs.1650 crores for pan-India license includes the start-up spectrum as well as to ensure a level playing field for the new and existing operators. This also fulfilled the objectives of increasing the competition as well as acting as a pro-consumer measure.

**"Clause 2.83 – After examining various options for rationalizing the spectrum charges, the Authority, recommends adoption of revenue share spectrum charges as given in the table 8 below :**

| Spectrum | Current | Proposed |
|---|---|---|
| Upto 2x4.4 MHz | 2% | No change |
| Upto 2x6.2 MHz / 2x5 MHz | 3% | No change |
| Upto 2x8 MHz | 4% | No change |
| Upto 2x10 MHz | 4% | 5.00% |
| Upto 2x12.5 MHz | 5% | 6.00% |
| Upto2x15 MHz | 6% | 7.00% |
| Beyond 2x15 MHz | - | 8.00% |

A comparison of the current rates, TRAI's recommended rates and the Telecom Commission's proposed changes are given below:

AMAR SINGH
MEMBER OF PARLIAMENT
(RAJYA SABHA)
NATIONAL GENERAL SECRETARY & SPOKESMAN
(SAMAJWADI PARTY)

सत्यमेव जयते

27, LODHI ESTATE,
NEW DELHI-110003
TEL. : 32565397 / 32542188 / 2461682
FAX : 91-11-24636299
Email : amarsingh@bol.net.in

| GSM | Rates current | Rates trai | Rates proposed | Per MHz | Increase |
|---|---|---|---|---|---|
| 4.4 | 2% | 2% | 3% | 0.68% | 50% |
| 6.2 | 3% | 3% | 4% | 0.65% | 33% |
| 7.2 | 4% | 4% | 5% | 0.69% | 25% |
| 8 | 4% | 4% | 5% | 0.63% | 25% |
| 8.2 | 4% | 5% | 5% | 0.61% | 25% |
| 9.2 | 4% | 5% | 6% | 0.65% | 50% |
| 10 | 4% | 5% | 6% | 0.60% | 50% |
| 10.2 | 5% | 6% | 6% | 0.59% | 20% |
| 11.2 | 5% | 6% | 7% | 0.63% | 40% |
| 12.2 | 5% | 6% | 7% | 0.57% | 40% |
| 13.2 | 6% | 7% | 8% | 0.61% | 33% |
| 14.2 | 6% | 7% | 8% | 0.56% | 33% |
| 15.2 | not defined | 8% | 9% | 0.59% | |

| Spectrum | TRAI Recommendations | Telecom Commission DOT proposal | Comments |
|---|---|---|---|
| upto Contracted spectrum including 4.4 MHz start up spectrum and 6.2 MHz spectrum in GSM | No Change | 1% increase | DOT proposal contrary to TRAI recommendation<br><br>No change recommended by TRAI as licence fee paid by new operator includes the strartup Spectrum<br><br>Also to ensure level playing field between new operators and existing opertors<br><br>New operators will be hit the hardest |
| Beyond 6.2 Mhz of spectrum in GSM | One time fee beyond 10Mhz of Rs 16 crore per MHz, 8 crore per MHz and 3 crore per MHz for based on category of circle<br><br>1% increase beyond 8 MHz | 1% increase across board upto 8 Mhz and 2% beyond | Special category of 8MHz increase by 2% has little impact as most spectrum is held between 7 and 8 Mhz for the key operators and little Spectrum beyond 8 Mhz is held.<br><br>Charging One time fee recommended by TRAI has been derferred. |

It is clearly noticed from the above that:

a) It skews the level playing field, as the new entrants are hit the hardest, since they would need to pay increased charges. This is also contrary to the TRAI recommendation wherein it recommends no change in the spectrum charges up to 6.2 MHz for GSM and 5 MHz for CDMA.

b) The increase for new entrants with start-up spectrum is 50%, whereas, the increase for the existing operators with spectrum at 6.2 MHz is 33% and beyond 6.2 MHz to 8.2 MHz, the increase is 25%.

c) The per MHz charges (as % of AGR) reduces as MHz allocation increases. This does not support spectral efficiency.

d) The increase is higher at lower spectrum allocation and is lower at higher spectrum allocation of 7 - 8 MHz band where most private operators hold

AMAR SINGH
MEMBER OF PARLIAMENT
(RAJYA SABHA)
NATIONAL GENERAL SECRETARY & SPOKESMAN
(SAMAJWADI PARTY)

सत्यमेव जयते

27, LODHI ESTATE,
NEW DELHI-110003
TEL. : 32565397 / 32542188 / 246168
FAX : 91-11-24636299
Email : amarsingh@bol.net.in

spectrum. This also does not support the objective of promoting spectral efficiency.

e) Creating a special slab of 8 MHz and beyond where the charge increases by 2% instead of 1%, is clearly a grand design of increasing the charges where spectrum is not actually held by dominant private operators.

In my earlier letter, I had recommended an approach where there is no increase in spectrum charges up to contracted spectrum, which is also in line with the TRAI recommendation and meets the objective of a level playing field. I had also recommended the approach of charging for spectrum beyond 6.2 MHz by promoting the objective of spectral efficiency which has also been publicly stated by you. The letter dated 22nd April'08 is attached herewith for your ready reference.

**I would urge the Government to:**

- **Adopt the TRAI recommendation up to contracted spectrum and not charge 1% across the board, which is clearly at the behest of the existing dominant players and is against the interests of the new operators.**
- **Not to go ahead with the current proposal of 2G spectrum charge revision and refer the matter to the TRAI for review once again.**
- **Charge spectrum beyond contracted spectrum, which promotes spectral efficiency and do not allow creation of the new slab, which will not help the Government Exchequer and is clearly an attempt at lip-service increase on the behest of the dominant private operators.**

**Thanking you**

**With** regards,

**Yours** affectionately,

Amar Singh

**(Amar Singh)**

**Dr. Manmohan Singh**
**Hon'ble Prime Minister**
**Government of India**
**152 South Block**
**New Delhi-110011**

जयप्रकाश नारायण सिंह
JAIPRAKASH NARAYAN SINGH
Member of Parliament
Rajya Sabha
Member-Standing Committee on Coal & Steel

116, North Avenue
New Delhi-110001
Phone : 011-23093141
Mob. : 09868181381
Deoghar Ph. - 06432-225000
Mob.: 09431183181

**5th November, 2009**

Dr. Manmohan Singh
Hon'ble Prime Minister
South Block
<u>NEW DELHI.</u>

Dear Dr. Manmohan Singhji

The recent controversies in the telecom sector are real matter of concern to all citizens of the country, especially in view of the forthcoming 3G and BWA auction to be undertaken in the month of January 2010. Such controversies and alleged arbitrary practices will dampen the spirits of the operators, including the foreign operators who may be wishing to participate in the forthcoming auction and bring in the foreign direct investment.

The media reports are alarming that the spectrum allocation has been done in an inappropriate manner, causing lose to the national exchequer to the tune of about Rs. 1 Lakh Crore as stated by the Hon'ble Minister of Communication reported in the media today.

It is known that CBI is presently investigating the issue of license and spectrum allocation to some operators in January 2008 and the operators having made huge money by selling a part of their equity to the foreign operators.

However, it is painful that the actual lose to the exchequer to the tune of Rs. 1 Lakh Crore is being brushed aside and is not being investigated at all.

From the discussion with various quarters, I understand that the spectrum to the private operators has been issued from 1994-1995 onwards for the provision of cellular services. However, right from the beginning not even a single rupee has been charged. for the allocation of spectrum to the private operator which has been given as a state largesse. Not only the spectrum has been allocated beyond what has been contemplated in their licenses, this additional spectrum has also been allocated without any procedure or guidelines or systems being put in place. It is not surprising that the beneficiaries of this state largesse have acted in connivance with the powers within the DOT at all levels, be it official or political.

Contd......2/.....

किसान सेवा, देश सेवा

जयप्रकाश नारायण सिंह
JAIPRAKASH NARAYAN SINGH
Member of Parliament
Rajya Sabha
Member-Standing Committee on Coal & Steel

116, North Avenue
New Delhi-110001
Phone : 011-23093141
Mob. : 09868181381
Deoghar Ph. - 06432-225000
Mob.: 09431183181

:: 2 ::

The spectrum allocation has been done without even any study being made as to whether the spectrum allocation is being utilized efficiently or not. I also understand that the Hon'ble High Court of Delhi in one of the matters on the subject of spectrum allocation has adversely commented about the allocation of spectrum on the basis of some vague criteria and the operators serving much large number of subscribers within the given spectrum. This clearly shows that the operators earlier had much more spectrum than was required and they cornered the spectrum perhaps with a view to block the entry of new operators and gain at the cost of national exchequer.

It is surprising that today we are reading in the media about the value of spectrum being in thousands of crores whereas the same scarce spectrum has been given without any payment for additional spectrum. The only charge which the government made was for the usage of spectrum which varied from time to time based on the annual revenue. This usage charge cannot be equated with the initial cost of spectrum which has clearly led to loss to the national exchequer as has been reported in the media today.

The spectrum allocation issue needs to be investigated further and deeper right from the beginning as to how and when the spectrum was allocated and on what basis and why no charge was taken for the additional allocation of spectrum beyond what was mandated in the licence of the private operators.

With warm regards,

05.11.09

( Jaiprakash Narayan Singh )

CC :

a) Finance Minister
b) Minister for Communication & IT
c) CAG, New Delhi
d) Director, CBI
e) CVC, New Delhi.

ललित किशोर चतुर्वेदी
संसद सदस्य (राज्यसभा)
सदस्य : रेल्वे स्टेण्डिग कमेटी

सत्यमेव जयते

निवास
4 भ 21, जवाहर नगर, जयपुर–302004
दूरभाष : 0141-2652644
फैक्स : 0141-2655638
मोबा. : 94140 55699

क्रमांक : 603

PRIME MINISTER'S OFFICE
26 APR 2010
DAK SECTION

दिनांक 17/4/2010

प्रिय श्री मनमोहन सिंह जी

सप्रेम नमस्कार,

स्पैक्ट्रम 2 जी के आवण्टन में भ्रष्टाचार की बहुत चर्चा हुई है और इसी कम में सरकार की तरफ से स्पष्टीकरण के रूप में एक लघु पुस्तिका का प्रकाशन किया जाकर मंत्रीजी एवं विभाग पर लगे आरोपों को नकारा गया है। फिर भी कुछ ऐसी बातें है जो यह इंगित करती है कि कही दाल में काला है। इसलिए तारांकित प्रश्न के माध्यम से मैंने जानकारी चाही थी किन्तु प्रश्न बैलट में नही आने से समस्त शंकाएं अनुत्तरित रह गई । अब बजट सत्र का अन्तिम काल है अतः पत्र के माध्यम से अपने सारे प्रश्न नीचे प्रस्तुत कर रहा हूँ–

1 क्या यह सही है कि स्पैट्रम 2 जी के आवण्टन में भ्रष्टाचार की शिकायतों पर सी.बी.आई. ने दूरसंचार मंत्री के कार्यालय के साथ अन्य राज्यों में भी छापामारी की थी।
2 क्या सन् 2008 में सन् 2001 में स्पेक्ट्रम नीलामी दर पर आवंटन किया गया।
3 सन 2008 में सन् 2001 की नीलामी दर पर आवंटन का आधार और औचित्य क्या था।
4 क्या स्वान एवं यूनिटेक द्वारा अपनी हिस्सेदारी 6 गुणे दामों पर बेचना सिद्ध करता है कि सन् 2001 का आधार सही नही था।
5 इस आवंटन से सरकार को कितना घाटा हुआ ।
6 क्या सरकार इस उच्च स्तरीय भ्रष्टाचार की जांच करवाएगी।

मेरा आपसे निवेदन है कि सारे प्रकरण की जांच करवाकर स्थिति से अवगत कराने की कृपा करें ।

सद्भावी

(ललित किशोर चतुर्वेदी)

श्री मनमोहन सिंह जी
मा. प्रधानमंत्री, भारत सरकार,
नई दिल्ली ।

निवास नई दिल्ली :
सी–103, स्वर्ण जयन्ती सदन, डॉ. विश्वम्भर दास मार्ग, ताल कटोरा रोड़, नई दिल्ली–110001
दूरभाष : 011-23351199, फैक्स : 011-23316161, मोबा. : 98681 81084

**Cpt. Jainarayan Prasad Nishad**
Member of Parliament
(Lok Sabha)
Member :
• Standing Committee, Ministry of HRD
• Consultative Committee, Ministry of Steel

सत्यमेव जयते

5, Balwantrai Mehta L
Kasturba Gandhi R
New Delhi-110(
Phone : 011-23070
Fax : 011-23782
Mobile : 90131800

Ref. No. 887/MP/J.N.P/10 Dated 14.Nov.

Time 10...
15 NOV 2010
PARLIAMENTARY NOTICE OFFICE

Respected PM Sir,

I would like to draw attention to the recent sequence of events that have occurred with regard to the controversy surrounding the allocation of 2-G Spectrum and the ensuing debate with regard to this issue.

I must place on record my deep concern and anguish at the way the events have unfolded; it seems without doubt that there seems to be deep rooted design which is well scripted by certain vested interests.

Of grave concern is the fact that reports which by means of Parliamentary Privilege must first be placed in Parliament are appearing on Television News Channels, the same is broadcast in an absolutely irresponsible manner while doing so several serious accusations are made in an unparliamentarily and obscene language against the entire political class. This grave misinterpretation of facts and deviation from the established procedures are a dangerous trend which would have long term implications and consequential damage to both the concept of Public and Parliamentary debate.

Contd...

Cpt. Jainarayan Prasad Nishad
Member of Parliament
(Lok Sabha)
Member :
• Standing Committee, Ministry of HRD
• Consultative Committee, Ministry of Steel

सत्यमेव जयते

5, Balwantrai Mehta Lane,
Kasturba Gandhi Road,
New Delhi-110001
Phone : 011-23070995
Fax : 011-23782125
Mobile :: 9013180088

Ref. No.............................. Dated ..................................

-: 2 :-

Moreover, on close examination of the recent and earlier developments it becomes evident that there is a Cartel in the Telecom Sector which has become so powerful that they are able to access information from important Governmental Offices and Constitutional Offices like CAG. and consequently influence both the proceedings and process of decision making, needless to say this unhealthy development if found true needs to be checked and the malaise contained.

We have been advocating freedom of press during our long political sojourn, but unfortunately it seems that certain Cartels have become so powerful that in collusion with certain Media Houses are daring to influence and determine issues like removal of ministers, composition of coalitions, in terms of who will remain and who will go and consequently Government formation.

With regards,

Yours sincerely,

14/11/10

**( JAINARAIN PRASAD NISHAD )**

**Dr. Manmohan Singh,**
Hon'ble Prime Minister of India,
South Block,
New Delhi.

Sushil Kumar Singh
Member of Parliament
(Lok Sabha)

Member :
(i) Estimate Committee
(ii) Standing (Committee & IT)
(iii) Consultative (Petroleum)

सत्यमेव जयते

16A, Ferozshah Road
New Delhi-110001

Singh Kothi
Aurangabad (Bihar)

Telephone :
New Delhi : 011-23354155
Fax : 011-23354156
Aurangabad : 06186-226300

Date: 13-11-2010

Dr. Manmohan Singh
Hon'ble Prime Minister
South Block
New Delhi

Dear Dr. Manmohan Singhji,

It is understood that the DoT is proposing to allocate 2G spectrum to M/s Tata, Teleservices, M/s Datacom and M/s Unitech in Delhi service area. The allocation to these companies would be in contravention of the TRAI recommendations on Spectrum Management and Licensing Framework dated 11th May, 2010 wherein TRAI has recommended that top priority should be given to service providers who have received the initial start up spectrum and have met the eligibility conditions for grant of additional spectrum upto 6.2 MHz. The priority for assignment of spectrum to these operators in the end even after those who have been assigned committed spectrum but are waiting to get additional spectrum upto the maximum limit. The relevant TRAI recommendations are reproduced below for your kind reference:

*3.61 The Authority recommends that the inter-se priority between the different categories of operators shall be as follows:*

*Licensees who have received the initial start up spectrum and have met the eligibility conditions for grant of additional spectrum up to 6.2/5 MHz will be given the top priority. The inter-se priority for such operators, subject to meeting the eligibility norms, would be the date of application for additional spectrum.*

CONTD..2

*Sushil Kumar Singh*
Member of Parliament
(Lok Sabha)

Member :
(i) Estimate Committee
(ii) Standing (Committee & IT)
(iii) Consultative (Petroleum)

16A, Ferozshah Road
New Delhi-110001

Singh Kothi
Aurangabad (Bihar)

Telephone :
New Delhi : 011-23354155
Fax : 011-23354156
Aurangabad : 06186-226300

::2::

*b. Licensees who have been assigned the committed spectrum but are waiting to get additional spectrum- up to the maximum permissible limit will be next in priority. The inter-se priority between operators within this group, subject to meeting the eligibility norms, would also be the date of application for additional spectrum.*

*c. Next in priority will be those who are waiting for the start up spectrum. The inter-se priority between such operators would be the date of UAS licence.*

Thus it may be seen from the above that the proposal to allocate initial spectrum to Tata Teleservices, Datacom or Unitech is contrary to the TRAI recommendations. As per the TRAI Act in the event DoT decides to reject the TRAI recommendations it can do so only after it is has been referred back to the TRAI for its reconsideration.

I understand that the government has not taken any decision to reject the TRAI recommendations on priority for assignment of spectrum and referred recommendations back to the TRAI for reconsideration.

In view of the above I would request your personal intervention to examine new allocation of spectrum in Delhi service area and direct the DoT to follow the proper procedure in allocation of 2G spectrum in line with the sector regulator's recommendations.

With kind regards

Yours sincerely

(Sushil Kumar Singh)

Copy : Sri A. Raja, Minister for Communication & IT

ASHWANI KUMAR MP

Member, Public Accounts Committee of Parliament
Member, Standing Committee of Parliament on External Affairs

November 20, 2010

Respected Dr. Sahib,

I. The Opposition has repeatedly stalled the functioning of Parliament over their demand for constituting a JPC on the ground that the PAC cannot be a substitute for JPC because the latter has larger powers and a wider jurisdiction to investigate the 2G Spectrum issue.

The enclosed piece by Riccardo Pelizzo and Rick Stapenhurst extracted from Pelizzo, R; Stapenhurst, R; and Olson, D.2006 entitled "Parliamentary Oversight for Government Accountability" WBI Working Papers – World Bank PP. 23-35" would show that the jurisdiction of PAC is wide enough to summon and receive depositions from public officials on issues under investigation. There is no specific bar upon the PAC from seeking clarifications even from Ministers, if required. (See Chart in Annexure/B.) It has also being brought about in various studies including the one by PRS Legislative Intent that "about 75% recommendations of the PAC were accepted by the Government during the period of the 14th Lok Sabha".

From the enclosed Note 'A' which contains relevant extracts from information on Committee on Public Accounts on http://164.100.24.208/ls/committees/p17.htm?comm code=26 it is clear that "the functions of the Committee extend beyond the formality of expenditure to its wisdom, faithfulness and economy". The PAC may thus examine cases involving losses and financial irregularities including negligence resulting in loss or extravagance. The Committee is entitled to express disapproval or pass strictures in the above situations. It is now well established that the PAC is competent and indeed called upon to discuss "points of financial discipline and principle". Although the PAC is not concerned with questions of policy in the broad sense which must remain in the domain of the Executive, the Committee is not absolutely precluded from pointing to the wisdom or otherwise of the policy where extravagance, waste or loss of public funds resulted from is implementation. In this view of the matter I believe that the Opposition's claim for a JPC can and should be forcefully and publicly rebutted.

II. HEARING IN THE SUPREME COURT

(A) Government Lawyers arguing in the Suprme Court on Tuesday (23rd Nov) should focus, on showing on an overall basis that this was not a case of inaction by the PMO and that, even assuming that the Sanctioning Authority was under a duty to take a decision either way, the discretion could not have been fairly exercised without the results of an independent official investigation being available to the PMO.

18, Ashok Road, New Delhi-110 001 Telefax: 23354222
C-9, Friends Colony (East), New Delhi - 110 065 Tel : 26832102, Telefax : 26842758
E-mail : contactaklawchambers@gmail.com

सत्यमेव जयते

ASHWANI KUMAR MP
Member, Public Accounts Committee of Parliament
Member, Standing Committee of Parliament on External Affairs

(B) In my considered view, the submissions should be limited to the allegation of delay without getting into the argument on whether the representation for sanction of prosecution was properly presented or not. This point even if available in law could have been agitated under normal circumstances in subordinate courts, but <u>in the present circumstances and at this stage it may not be prudent to focus on a technicality,</u> in which case there is a risk of keeping the issue alive. The end objective should be to convince the court that upon the results of the investigations being available (which may not be to far away) a suitable view would be taken.

(C) Submissions to be advanced in the Supreme Court should not be canvassed in the media as a matter of policy.

With deepest regards

Yours sincerely,
Ashwani Kumar
(ASHWANI KUMAR)

DR. MANMOHAN SINGH JI
HON'BLE PRIME MINISTER
7, RACE COURSE ROAD
NEW DELHI

18, Ashok Road, New Delhi-110 001 Telefax: 23354222
C-9, Friends Colony (East), New Delhi - 110 065 Tel : 26832102, Telefax : 26842758
E-mail : contactaklawchambers@gmail.com

## I. Introduction

In a parliamentary democracy like ours, the Committee system assumes great importance. Administrative accountability to the legislature becomes the *sine qua non* of such a parliamentary system. The check that Parliament exercises over the executive stems from the basic principle that Parliamenet embodies the will of the people and it must, therefore, be able to supervise the manner in which public policy laid down by Parliament is carried out. However, the phenomenal proliferation of governmental activities has made the task of legislatures very complex and diversified. By its very nature, Parliament, as a body cannot have an effective control over the government and the whole gamut of its activities. Administrative accountability to the legislature through Committees has been the hallmark of our political system. The Committee on Public Accounts enjoys the place of pride in our Committee System.

## II. Genesis of the Committee

The Committee on Public Accounts was first set up in 1921 in the wake of the Montague-Chelmsford Reforms. The Finance Member of the Executive Council used to be the Chairman of the Committee. The Secretariat assistance to the Committee was rendered by the then Finance Department (now the Ministry of Finance). This position continued right up to 1949. During the days of the Interim Government, the then Finance Minister acted as the Chairman of the Committee, and later on, after the attainment of Independence in August, 1947, the Finance Minister became the Chairman. This naturally restricted the free expression of views and criticism of the Executive. The Committee on Public Accounts underwent a radical change with the coming into force of the Constitution of India on 26 January, 1950, when the Committee became a Parliamentary Committee functioning under the control of the Speaker with a non-official Chairman appointed by the Speaker from among the Members of Lok Sabha elected to the Committee. The Minister of Finance ceased to be a Member of the Committee *vide* Rule 309(i) of the Rules of Procedure and Conduct of Business in Lok Sabha.

## III. Constitution of the Committee

The Public Accounts Committee is now constituted every year under Rule 308 of the Rules of Procedure and Conduct of Business in Lok Sabha. The Public Accounts Committee consists of not more than 22 members comprising of 15 members elected by Lok Sabha every year from amongst its members according to the principle of proportional representation by means of single transferable vote and not more than 7 members of Rajya Sabha elected by that House in like manner. Prior to the year 1954-55, the Committee consisted of 15 members who were elected by Lok Sabha from amongst its Members. But with effect from the year 1954-55, 7 members from the Rajya Sabha are also being associated with the Committee. Till 1966-67, a senior member of the ruling party used to be appointed by the Speaker as Chairman of the Committee. In 1967, however, for the first time, a member from the Opposition in Lok Sabha, was appointed as the Chairman of the Committee by the Speaker. This practice continues till date. The term of office of members of the Committee does not exceed one year at a time. A Minister is not elected a member of the Committee, and if a member, after his election to the Committee is appointed a Minister, he ceases to be a member of the Committee from the date of such appointment. The Chairman of the Committee is appointed by the Speaker from amongst the members of the Committee from Lok Sabha.

**IV. Scope and Functions**

The functions of the Committee, as enshrined in Rule 308(1) of the Rules of Procedure and Conduct of Business in Lok Sabha, include examination of accounts showing the appropriation of sums granted by Parliament for the expenditure of the Government of India, the annual finance accounts of the Government and such other accounts laid before the House as the Committee may think fit. In scrutinising the Appropriation Accounts of the Government of India and the Report of the Comptroller & Auditor General of India thereon, the Committee has to satisfy :

(a) that the moneys shown in the accounts as having been disbursed were legally available for, and applicable to, the service or purpose to which they have been applied or charged;

(b) that the expenditure conforms to the authority which governs it;

(c) that every re-appropriation has been made in accordance with the provisions made in this behalf under rules framed by competent authority.

It shall also be the duty of the Committee –

(a) to examine the statement of accounts showing the `income and expenditure of state corporations, trading and manufacturing schemes, concerns and projects together with the balance sheets and statements of profit and loss accounts which the President may have required to be prepared or are prepared under the provisions of the statutory rules regulating the financing of a particular corporation, trading or manufacturing scheme or concern or project and the report of the Comptroller and Auditor General thereon.

(b) to examine the statement of accounts showing the income and expenditure of autonomous and semi autonomous bodies, the audit of which may be conducted by the Comptroller and Auditor General of India either under the directions of the President or by a statute of Parliament; and

(c) to consider the report of the Comptroller and Auditor General in cases where the President may have required him to conduct an audit of any receipts or to examine the accounts of stores and stocks.

If any money has been spent on any service during a financial year in excess of the amount granted by the House for that purpose the Committee shall examine with reference to the facts of each case the circumstances leading to such an excess and make such recommendation as it may deem fit.

**Nature and Scope of Examination.**

An important function of the Committee is to ascertain that money granted by Parliament has been spent by Government " within the scope of the demand." The implications of this phrase are that (i) money recorded as spent against the grant must not be more than the amount granted, (ii) the expenditure brought to account against a particular grant must be of such a nature as to warrant its record against the grant and against no other, and (iii) the grants should be spent on purposes which are set out in the detailed demand and they cannot be spent on "any new service not contemplated in the demand." The functions of the Committee extent "beyond the formality of expenditure to its wisdom, faithfulness and economy". The Committee thus examines cases involving losses, nugatory expenditure and financial irregularities. When any case of proved negligence resulting in loss or extravagance is brought to the notice of the Committee, it calls upon the Ministry/Department concerned to explain what action, disciplinary or otherwise, it had taken to prevent a recurrence. In such a case it can also record its opinion in the form of disapproval or pass strictures against the extravagance or lack of proper control by the Ministry or Department concerned. Another important function of the Committee is the discussion on points of financial discipline and principle. The detailed examination of questions involving principle and system is a leading and recognized function of the Committee. The Committee is not concerned with questions of policy in the broad sense. As a rule, it expresses no opinion on points of general policy, but it is within its jurisdiction to point out whether there has been extravagance or waste in carrying out that policy.

**Regularisation of Excesses over Grants**

If any money has been spent by the Government on a service in excess of the amount granted by the House for the purpose, the Committee examines with reference to the facts of each case, the circumstances leading to such an excess and makes such recommendations as it may deem fit. Such excesses are thereafter required to be brought up before the House by Government for regularization in the manner envisaged in Article 115 of the Constitution. To facilitate speedy regularization of such excess expenditure by Parliament, the Committee presents a consolidated report relating to all Ministries/Departments in advance of other reports.

**Savings**

The Committee looks upon savings arising from incorrect estimating or other defects or other defects of procedure no more leniently than it does upon excesses. It regards estimating on the safe side to be as faulty as estimating on the low side. In the words of the Committee "from one point of view, 'safe' estimating might be regarded as even more objectionable, as it might easily lead to extravagance, waste or worse".

**Significance and Importance of Committee's Work**

Lok Sabha, having voted large sums of the taxpayers' money does, in the interest of the taxpayers, expect in due course a detailed account of how the moneys have been spent. It must satisfy itself that the moneys so voted were directed to the intended purposes and were spent prudently and economically. The Comptroller and Auditor General examines the yearly accounts of the Government and after scrutiny certifies the accounts, subject to such reservations as he chooses to make, and submits his reports to the President who causes them to be laid before Parliament. It is difficult, if not impossible, for Lok Sabha to examine in detail the accounts, which are complex and technical. Further it cannot spare the time required for such examination. It is for these reasons that Lok Sabha has constituted the Committee on Public Accounts and entrusted it with the detailed examination of those accounts.

Another important function of the Committee is the discussion on points of financial discipline and principle. The detailed examination of questions involving principle and system is a leading and recognised function of the Committee.

**The PAC at work**

The Committee's work depends a great deal upon the results of audit and examination of the Accounts of the Union Government carried out by the Comptroller and Auditor General (C&AG). The audit by the C&AG is comprehensive and manifold. To cite an example, it involves among others, (a) Accountancy Audit, (b) Regularity Audit, (c) Appropriation Audit, (d) Propriety Audit or what is also known as Discretionary Audit and (e) Efficiency-cum-performance Audit. In recent years, the technique of efficiency-cum-performance has been attempted in the audit of developmental schemes. The Audit examines as how far the implementing agency is adequately discharging its financial responsibilities in regard to the various schemes undertaken by it and ascertains whether the schemes are being executed effectively and their operations conducted economically and whether they are producing the results expected of them. In fact, the Institution of Audit plays a crucial role in the functioning of the Committee on Public Accounts and the Comptroller and Auditor General is often termed as "friend, philosopher and guide" of the Committee.

At the beginning of its term every year, the Committee makes a selection of Audit Paragraphs included in the various reports of C&AG for in-depth examination. After holding deliberations and taking note of the time available at its disposal, the Committee selects the most important paragraphs from the Audit Reports for detailed examination and submits its reports to the House on them.

**Action Taken on Recommendations**

A report has value provided it is properly followed up. In the case of original report, the Government is required to intimate to the Committee the action taken or proposed to be taken by it on the recommendations contained in the Report normally within six months of the presentation. The Action Taken replies of the Government are considered by the Committee and after due classification of the replies, an Action

Taken Report is presented to the Parliament. The Government is further required to intimate to the Committee the action taken or proposed to be taken by it on the recommendations contained in Chapter I of the Action Taken Report and also to furnish final replies in respect of the earlier recommendations contained in the Original Report in respect of which either no replies had previously been received or only interim replies had been received. The action taken thus reported by the Government is laid on the Table of the House in the form of a Statement without any further comments by the Committee. This system not only ensures accountability of the Executive to Parliament but also enables Parliament and also the general public to appraise Government's final replies to the Committee's recommendations. This completes the examination of a subject by the Committee.

**Follow-up on Action taken by Government on Audit paragraphs not selected by the Committee**

Till 1981, there was no practice of ascertaining the action taken by the Ministries/Departments on the Audit paragraphs not selected by the Committee for detailed examination. However, with a view to ensuring enforcement of accountability of the executive in respect of all the issues dealt with in various Audit Reports, the Committee on Public Accounts decided in 1982 that the Audit Reports for the year 1980-81 be referred to the Ministries/Departments concerned for furnishing notes, duly vetted by Audit, showing remedial/corrective Action Taken on all the paragraphs contained therein. The system has further been streamlined to review the remedial/corrective action taken notes furnished by Government on the non-selected Audit Paragraphs.

At their sitting held on 8.8.2000, the Committee decided that the remedial/correction Action Taken Notes received from Government are sent to Office of C&AG for categorization like (a) Accepted (b) Partially accepted and (c) not accepted and then circulated these to the Members of the Committee. Based on the categorization, the Committee may select Audit Paragraphs for detailed examination.

**VI. List of Chairmen since its inception**

LIST OF CHAIRMEN OF THE PUBLIC ACCOUNTS COMMITTEE OF PARLIAMENT SINCE INCEPTION (1921 to 2006-07)

| SL.NO. | NAME | YEAR | PARTY |
|---|---|---|---|
| 1. | Mr. W. M. Hailey | 1921 | - |
| 2. | Sir Basil P Blackett | 1922 | - |
| 3. | Sir Basil P Blackett | 1923 | - |
| 4. | Sir Basil P Blackett | 1924 | - |
| 5. | Sir Basil P Blackett | 1925 | - |
| 6. | Sir Basil P Blackett | 1926 | - |
| 7. | Sir Basil P Blackett | 1927 | - |
| 8. | Sir Bhupendra Nath Mitra | 1928 | - |
| 9. | Sir George Schuster | 1929 | - |
| 10. | Sir George Schuster | 1930 | - |
| 11. | Sir George Schuster | 1931 | - |
| 12. | Sir Alan Parsons | 1932 | - |
| 13. | Mr. A. H. Lloyd | 1933 | - |
| 14. | Sir James Grigg | 1934 | - |
| 15. | Sir James Grigg | 1935 | - |
| 16. | Sir James Grigg | 1936 | - |
| 17. | Mr. J. C. Nixon | 1937 | - |
| 18. | Sir James Grigg | 1938 | - |
| 19. | Sir Jeremy Raisman | 1939 | - |
| 20. | Sir Jeremy Raisman | 1940 | - |
| 21. | Sir Jeremy Raisman | 1941 | - |
| 22. | Mr. C. E. Jones | 1942 | - |
| 23. | Sir Jeremy Raisman | 1943 | - |
| 24. | Sir Cyril Jones | 1944 | - |
| 25. | Sir Archibald Rowlands | 1945 | - |
| 26. | Sir Eric Coates<br>Dr. John Matthai<br>Mr. Liaquat Ali Khan | 1946 | - |
| 27. | Mr. Liaquat Ali Khan<br>Shri R. K. Shanmukham Chetty | 1947 | - |
| 28. | Shri R. K. Shanmukham Chetty<br>Dr. John Matthai | 1948 | - |
| 29. | Dr. John Matthai | 1949 | - |

| | | | |
|---|---|---|---|
| 30. | Shri B. Das | 1950-51 | INC |
| 31. | Shri B. Das | 1951-52 | INC |
| 32. | Shri B. Das | 1952-53 | INC |
| 33. | Shri B. Das | 1953-54 | INC |
| 34. | Shri B. Das | 1954-55 | INC |
| 35. | Shri V. B. Gandhi | 1955-56 | INC |
| 36. | Shri V. B. Gandhi | 1956-57 | INC |
| 37. | Shri T. N. Singh | 1957-58 | INC |
| 38. | Shri T. N. Singh<br>Prof. N.G. Ranga | 1958-59 | INC |
| 39. | Dr. P. Subbarayan<br>Shri Upendranath Barman | 1959-60 | INC<br>INC |
| 40. | Shri Upendranath Barman | 1960-61 | INC |
| 41. | Shri C. R. Pattabhi Raman | 1961-62 | INC |
| 42. | Shri Mahavir Tyagi | 1962-63 | INC |
| 43. | Shri Mahavir Tyagi<br>Shri R. K. Khadilkar | 1963-64 | INC |
| 44. | Shri R. R. Morarka | 1964-65 | INC |
| 45. | Shri R. R. Morarka | 1965-66 | INC |
| 46. | Shri R. R. Morarka | 1966-67 | INC |
| 47. | Shri M. R. Masani | 1967-68 | Swatantra |
| 48. | Shri M. R. Masani | 1968-69 | Swatantra |
| 49. | Shri Atal Bihari Vajpayee | 1969-70 | Jan Sangh |
| 50. | Shri Atal Bihari Vajpayee | 1970-71 | Jan Sangh |
| 51. | Shri Era Sezhiyan | 1971-72 | DMK |
| 52. | Shri Era Sezhiyan | 1972-73 | DMK |
| 53. | Shri Jyotirmoy Basu | 1973-74 | CPI(M) |
| 54. | Shri Jyotirmoy Basu | 1974-75 | CPI(M) |
| 55. | Shri H. N. Mukherjee | 1975-76 | CPI |
| 56. | Shri H. N. Mukherjee | 1976-77 | CPI |
| 57. | Shri C. M. Stephen | 1977-78 | Cong(I) |
| 58. | Shri P. V. Narasimha Rao | 1978-79 | Cong(I) |
| 59. | Shri T. A. Pai<br>Shri R Venkataraman | 1979-80<br>(upto 30.7.79) | Cong(I)<br>Cong(I) |

| | | | |
|---|---|---|---|
| | | 1979-80<br><br>(w.e.f. 2.8.79) | |
| 60. | Shri Chandrajit Yadav | 1980-81 | Lok Dal |
| 61. | Shri Satish Agarwal | 1981-82 | BJP |
| 62. | Shri Satish Agarwal | 1982-83 | BJP |
| 63. | Shri Sunil Maitra | 1983-84 | Cong(I) |
| 64. | Shri Sunil Maitra | 1984 | Cong(I) |
| 65. | Shri E. Ayyapu Reddy | 1985-86 | TDP |
| 66. | Shri E. Ayyapu Reddy | 1986-87 | TDP |
| 67. | Shri Amal Datta | 1987-88 | CPI(M) |
| 68. | Shri Amal Datta | 1988-89 | CPI(M) |
| 69. | Shri P. Kolandaivelu | 1989<br><br>(upto 27.11.89) | AIADMK |
| 70. | Shri Sontosh Mohan Dev | 1990-91 | Cong(I) |
| 71. | Shri Atal Bihari Vajpayee | 1991-92 | BJP |
| 72. | Shri Atal Bihari Vajpayee | 1992-93 | BJP |
| 73. | Shri Bhagwan Shankar Rawat | 1993-94 | BJP |
| 74. | Shri Bhagwan Shankar Rawat | 1994-95 | BJP |
| 75. | Shri Ram Naik | 1995-96 | BJP |
| 76. | Dr Murli Manohar Joshi | 1996-97 | BJP |
| 77. | Dr Murli Manohar Joshi | 1997-98 | BJP |
| 78. | Shri Manoranjan Bhakta | 1998-99 | INC |
| 79. | Shri Narayan Datt Tiwari | 1999-2000 | INC |
| 80. | Shri Narayan Datt Tiwari | 2000-2001 | INC |
| 81. | Shri Narayan Datt Tiwari<br><br><br><br>Shri N. Janardhana Reddy | 2001-2002<br><br>(upto 1.3.2002)<br><br>2001-2002<br><br>(w.e.f. 15.3. 2002<br><br>to 30.4.2002) | INC<br><br><br><br>INC |
| 82. | Sardar Buta Singh | 2002-2003 | INC |
| 83. | Sardar Buta Singh | 2003-2004<br><br>(upto 6.2.2004) | INC |

| | | | |
|---|---|---|---|
| 84. | Prof. Vijay Kumar Malhotra | (2004-2005) | BJP |
| 85. | Prof. Vijay Kumar Malhotra | (2005-2006) | BJP |
| 86 | Prof. Vijay Kumar Malhotra | (2006-2007) | BJP |
| 87. | Prof. Vijay Kumar Malhotra | (2007-2008) | BJP |

*Note: Till 1966-67 Chairmen, PAC were appointed from members of the ruling Party.*

**VII. Reports presented by the Committee since January 1950**

Since the Committee became a Parliamentary Committee under the control of the Speaker from January, 1950, it has presented 1337 Reports till 30th April, 2006. The details of the Reports presented Lok Sabha wise are as follows:

| **Lok Sabha** | **Tenure** | **Report Presented** |
|---|---|---|
| 1st Lok Sabha | 1952-57 | 025 |
| 2nd Lok Sabha | 1957-62 | 043 |
| 3rd Lok Sabha | 1962-67 | 072 |
| 4th Lok Sabha | 1967-70 | 125 |
| 5th Lok Sabha | 1971-77 | 239 |
| 6th Lok Sabha | 1977-79 | 149 |
| 7th Lok Sabha | 1980-84 | 231 |
| 8th Lok Sabha | 1984-89 | 187 |
| 9th Lok Sabha | 1989-91 | 022 |
| 10th Lok Sabha | 1991-96 | 119 |
| 11th Lok Sabha | 1996-97 | 024 |
| 12th Lok Sabha | 1998-99 | 011 |
| 13th Lok Sabha | 1999-2004 | 063 |
| 14th Lok Sabha | 2004- continuing | 047 (As on 30.04.2007) |

Khagen Das
MEMBER OF PARLIAMENT
(LOK SABHA)

90, North Avenue,
New Delhi - 110 001
Tels. (011) 23094461,
~~23094137~~

4th January 2011

Dr.Manmohan Singh,
Hon'ble Prime Minister
Government of India,
South Block
**New Delhi**

**Subject: Urgent need to review past failures in administering policy decisions by DOT.**

Dear Dr. Manmohan Singh ji,

Telecommunication services in the country have taken a big leap during a short span of 15 years since its privatisation. It is really heartening to note that telecom subscriber base reached 742 million at the end of October 2010, achieving a tele-density of 62% against the dismal figure of less than 1% in 1995. This has been really possible due to the progressive and liberal policies adopted by the successive Central Governments and the active role played by the private operators. It is a matter of great proud that India stands at second place after China in the ranking of total subscriber base in the World.

2. However, this remarkable growth in Telecom services has not-been without a share of controversies. The Country has seen the biggest scam wherein the CAG has estimated a loss of Rs. 1,76,000 crores on account of issue of licences and excess spectrum held by the operators. The recent telecom scam which completely disrupted the functioning of Parliamentary democracy has really cast a dark shadow on the functioning of our politicians, bureaucrats & corporate houses.

3. The scandals in the Telecom Industry are not new. The first migration package given to the telecom operators in 1999 was a completely sell off to the private operators at that time. Even though the licenses for

**Khagen Das**
MEMBER OF PARLIAMENT
(LOK SABHA)

सत्यमेव जयते

**90, North Avenue,**
**New Delhi - 110 001**
**Tels. (011) 23094461,**
~~23094137~~

cellular services were awarded through auction and the operators had committed to pay annual license fee: all of them completely failed to pay the license fee to the Government. **The Government bailed out all tl operators by migrating them to the revenue sharing arrangements instead of the license fees. The los the Government has been estimated to the extent of Rs. 50,000 crores. The CAG in its report of 2000 l commented adversely but no action was taken at that time.**

4. The mobile telephone operators have been the biggest beneficiaries of the concessions granted to th from 1999 till date. **It is true that these operators have brought the telecom services within the reach the common man but if we see the various scams, it has been achieved at a very heavy cost to t Government and has brought a bad name to the nation.**

5. Some of the gross violations of license conditions of the telecom licenses committed from 1999 onwarc are enumerated below:-

(i) Migration package of 1999 bailing out the first and second private telecom licensees.

(ii) Operators were granted additional spectrum of 1.8 MHz against the contracted value of 4.4 MH: without any guidelines.

(iii) Operators allotted spectrum upto 10 MHz without any policy guidelines.

(iv) Operators allotted 6.2 MHz of start up spectrum instead of 4.4 MHz mandated in the license.

(v) 4th Cellular operators allotted spectrum in 900 MHz premium band against the license conditions.

(vi) Operators allotted more than 6.2 MHz in 900 MHz band against the policy guidelines.

(vii) Concessions granted to NLD and ILD licencees without TRAI recommendations.

(viii) Issue of 51 new licences in 2004 to 2007 at the price discovered in 2001.

**Khagen Das**
MEMBER OF PARLIAMENT
(LOK SABHA)

सत्यमेव जयते

**90, North Avenue,**
**New Delhi - 110 001**
**Tels. (011) 23094461,**
**23094137**

6. **I am giving below a snapshot of irregularities committed during the tenure of each Minister of Communications & IT during 1999-2007.**

6.1 **Irregularities committed during the tenure of Sh. A.B. Vajapyee which are estimated at Rs. 50,000 crores.**

| Sr no | Irregularity | Operator | Circle | Period / Date | Secretary DOT | Wireless Advisor | DDG (VAS) | Chairman TRAI | Member (T)TRAI |
|---|---|---|---|---|---|---|---|---|---|
| 1 | Spectrum allotment beyond license up to 6.2 MHz without any guidelines | Bharti | Chennai | Aug-99 | Sh. Anil Kumar | Sh. R N Agarwal | Sh. J.R. Gupta | Justice S.S. Sodhi | Sh. R.R.N. Prasad |
| | -do- | -do- | Delhi | Aug-99 | -do- | -do- | -do- | -do- | -do- |
| | -do- | BPL | Mumbai | Aug-99 | -do- | -do- | -do- | -do- | -do- |
| 2 | Migration Package of 1999 | 1st and 2nd Cellular and Basic operators | All | Aug-99 | -do- | -do- | -do- | -do- | -do- |
| | • Validity of licenses increased from 10 years to 20 year | | | Aug-99 | -do- | -do- | -do- | -do- | -do- |
| | • Operators allowed revenue sharing instead of the fixed license fees. | | | Aug-99 | -do- | -do- | -do- | -do- | -do- |
| | • Effective date of license extended by 6 months. | | | Aug-99 | -do- | -do- | -do- | -do- | -do- |
| | • Metro operators allowed to increase the rental from Rs. 156 per month to Rs. 600 per month per subscriber. | | | Aug-99 | -do- | -do- | -do- | -do- | -do- |

**Khagen Das**
MEMBER OF PARLIAMENT
(LOK SABHA)

**90, North Avenue,
New Delhi - 110 001
Tels. (011) 23094461,
23094137**

6.2 **Irregularities committed during the tenure of Sh. Ram Vilas Paswan**

| Sr no | Irregularity | Operator | Circle | Period / Date | Telecom Secretary | Wireless Advisor | Chairman, TRAI | Member (T)TRAI |
|---|---|---|---|---|---|---|---|---|
| 1 | Spectrum allotment up to 6.2 MHz without any guidelines | Aircel Digilink (Vodafone) | Chennai | Mar-00 | Sh. Anil Kumar | Sh. R N Agarwal | Justice S.S. Sodhi | Sh. R.R.N. Prasad |
| | -do- | Bharti | AP | Apr-00 | Sh. Shyamal Ghosh | -do- | -do- | -do- |
| | -do- | Bharti | Karnataka | Apr-00 | -do- | -do- | -do- | -do- |
| | -do- | Spice | Karnataka | Apr-00 | -do- | -do- | -do- | -do- |
| | -do- | Spice | Punjab | Apr-00 | -do- | -do- | -do- | -do- |
| | -do- | Aircel Digilink (Vodafone) | Haryana | Jan-01 | -do- | -do | -do- | -do- |
| | -do- | -do- | Rajasthan | Jan-01 | -do- | -do- | -do- | -do- |
| | -do- | -do- | UP(East) | Jan-01 | -do- | -do- | -do- | -do- |

6.3 **Irregularities committed during the tenure of Sh. Pramod Mahajan**

| Sr no | Irregularity | Operator | Circle | Period / Date | Telecom Secretary | Wireless Advisor | Chairman, TRAI | Member (T)TRAI |
|---|---|---|---|---|---|---|---|---|
| 1 | Allotment of spectrum upto 10MHz without any fixed fee and without increase in spectrum usage charge | Bharti, Vodafone, Idea, BPL, Aircel | Various circles | 1.2.2002 | Sh. Shyamal Ghosh | Sh. P K Garg | Sh. M.S. Verma | Sh. R.R.N. Prasad |
| 2 | More than 6.2 MHz Spectrum allotted in 900 MHz | Bharti Airtel | Delhi | 17.7.2002 | Sh. Vinod Vaish | -do- | -do- | -:- |

**Khagen Das**
MEMBER OF PARLIAMENT
(LOK SABHA)

सत्यमेव जयते

**90, North Avenue,**
**New Delhi - 110 001**
**Tels. (011) 23094461,**
**23094137**

| | | | | | | | | |
|---|---|---|---|---|---|---|---|---|
| | premium band | | | | | | | |
| | -do- | Vodafone | Delhi | 17.7.2002 | -do- | -do- | -do- | --- |
| | -do- | Vodafone | Mumbai | 17.7.2002 | -do- | -do- | -do- | --- |

6.4 **Irregularities committed during the tenure of Sh. Arun Shourie**

| Sr no | Irregularity | Operator | Circle | Period / Date | Telecom Secretary | Wireless Advisor | DDG (VAS) | Chairman TRAI | Member (T)TRAI |
|---|---|---|---|---|---|---|---|---|---|
| 1 | More than 6.2 MHz Spectrum allotted in 900 MHz premium band | BPL | Mumbai | 13.3.2003 | Sh. Vinod Vaish | Sh. PK Garg | Sh. J.R. Gupta | Sh. Pradeep Baijal | Dr. D.P.S. Seth |
| | -do- | Bharti | Karnataka | 31.12.2003 | -do- | -do- | -do- | -do- | -do- |
| | -do- | Idea | Maharashtra | 31.12.2003 | -do- | -do- | -do- | -do- | -do- |
| | -do- | Vodafone | Gujarat | 31.12.2003 | -do | -do- | -do- | -do- | -do- |
| | -do- | Bharti | Punjab | 9.1.2004 | -do- | -do- | -do- | -do- | -do- |
| | -do- | Spice | Punjab | 9.1.2004 | -do- | -do- | -do- | -do- | -do- |
| | -do- | Aircel | Tamil Nadu | 9.1.2004 | -do- | -do- | -do- | -do- | -do- |
| | -do- | Bharti | AP | 9.2.2004 | Sh. Nripendra Misra | -do- | -do- | -do- | -do- |
| 2 | Spectrum allotted up to 10 MHz without any guidelines | Bharti | Delhi | Jul-03 | Sh. Vinod Vaish | -do- | -do- | -do- | -do- |

**Khagen Das**
MEMBER OF PARLIAMENT
(LOK SABHA)

सत्यमेव जयते

**90, North Avenue,**
**New Delhi - 110 001**
**Tels. (011) 23094461,**
**23094159**

| | | | | | | | | | |
|---|---|---|---|---|---|---|---|---|---|
| | -do- | Vodafone | Delhi | Oct-03 | -do- | -do- | -do- | -do- | -do- |
| | -do- | Vodafone | Mumbai | Oct-03 | -do- | -do- | -do- | -do- | -do- |
| | -do- | Bharti | Karnataka | Jan-04 | -do- | -do- | -do- | -do- | -do- |
| | -do- | Idea | Maharashtra | Apr-04 | Sh. Nripendr a Misra | -do- | -do- | -do- | -do- |
| 3 | 27 UAS licenses issued on 2001 prices | Aircel | 7 circles | Apr-04 | -do- | -do- | -do- | -do- | -do- |
| | -do- | Bharti | 6 circles | Feb-04 | -do- | -do- | -do- | -do- | -do- |
| | -do- | Vodafone | 2 circles | Feb-04 | -do- | -do- | -do- | -do- | -do- |
| | -do- | Tata Tele | 12 circles | Jan-04 | -do- | -do- | -do- | -do- | -do- |

6.5 **Irregularities committed during the tenure of Sh. Dayanidhi Maran**

| Sr no | Irregularity | Operator | Circle | Period / Date | Telecom Secretary | Wireless Advisor | DDG (VAS/A S) | Chairman TRAI | Member (T)TRAI |
|---|---|---|---|---|---|---|---|---|---|
| 1 | Spectrum allotted up to 10 MHz without any guidelines | BPL | Mumbai | Sep-04 | Sh. Nripendra Misra | Sh. PK Garg | Sh. N Parmesh waran | Sh. Pradeep Baijal | Dr. D.P.S. Seth |

**Khagen Das**
MEMBER OF PARLIAMENT
(LOK SABHA)

सत्यमेव जयते

**90, North Avenue,**
**New Delhi - 110 001**
**Tels. (011) 23094461,**
**23094137**

| | | | | | | | | | |
|---|---|---|---|---|---|---|---|---|---|
| | -do- | Aircel | Tamilnadu | Dec-04 | -do- | -do- | -do- | -do- | -do- |
| | -do- | Vodafone | Gujarat | May-05 | Sh. Brijesh Kumar | -do- | -do- | -do- | -do- |
| | -do- | Bharti | Mumbai | Jan-06 | Sh. JS Sarma | -do- | -do- | -do- | -do- |
| 2 | Initial Spectrum allotted in 900 MHz premium band instead of 1800 MHz | Bharti | West Bengal | 12.08.2004 | Sh. Nripendra Misra | -do- | -do- | -do- | -do- |
| | -do- | Bharti | U.P. (E) | 06.05.2004 | -do- | -do- | -do- | -do- | -do- |
| | -do- | Bharti | Bihar | 06.05.2004 | -do- | -do- | -do- | -do- | -do- |
| | -do- | Bharti | Orissa | 06.05.2004 | -do- | -do- | -do- | -do- | -do- |
| | -do- | Hutch | West Bengal | 12.08.2004 | -do- | -do- | -do- | -do- | -do- |
| | -do- | Hutch | U.P. (W) | 06.05.2004 | -do- | -do- | -do- | -do- | -do- |
| | -do- | Vodafone | Kolkata | 30.6.2004 | -do- | -do- | -do- | -do- | -do- |
| 3 | 24 Licenses Issued on 2001 prices | Aircel | 14 circles | Dec-06 | Sh. D.S. Mathur | -do- | -do- | Sh. Nripendra Misra | Sh. A.K. Sahney |
| | -do- | Idea | 2 circle | Dec-06 | -do- | -do- | -do- | -do- | -do- |
| | -do- | Vodafone | 7 circles | Dec-06 | -do- | -do- | -do- | -do- | -do- |
| | -do- | Reliance | 1 circle | Sep-04 | Sh. Nripendra Misra | -do- | -do- | Sh. Pradeep Baijal | Dr. D.P.S. Seth |

**Khagen Das**
MEMBER OF PARLIAMENT
(LOK SABHA)

सत्यमेव जयते

**90, North Avenue,**
**New Delhi - 110 001**
**Tels. (011) 23094461,**
**23094137**

| | | | | |
|---|---|---|---|---|
| 4 | Concessions granted to NLD operators without TRAI Recommendations | • Entry fee reduced from Rs. 100 to Rs. 25 crores.<br>• Revenue share reduced from 15% to 6%.<br>• Roll out obligation diluted.<br>• Networth requirement reduced from Rs. 2500 crores to Rs. 2.5 crores. | -do- | -do- |
| 5 | Concessions granted to ILD operators without TRAI Recommendations | • Entry fee reduced from Rs. 25 crores to Rs. 2.5 crores.<br>• Revenue share reduced from 15% to 6%.<br>• Roll out obligations diluted.<br>• Networth requirement reduced from Rs. 25 crores to Rs. 2.5 crores.<br>• Performance Bank Guarantee waived off. | -do- | -do- |

7. It may be observed from above and the annexures that only a few selected incumbent operators have been benefitted right from 1999 onwards till date i.e. through migration package, allotment of spectrum in 900 MHz premium band, allotment of higher start up spectrum, allotment of spectrum above the mandated without any guidelines and the issue of new licenses in 2004-2007.

**Conclusion:-**

8. It may kindly be seen from above that if you take into account the above abnormalities, the present scandal relating to an estimated loss of Rs. 1,76,000 crores to the Government may be a shade poorer than the scandals committed during 1999 to 2007. **One thing is very clear that a select group of telecom operators viz Bharti, Vodafone, Idea and BPL have been the main beneficiaries as they have saved thousands of crores of Capex and Opex** also in thousands of crores of Rupees per annum by moving to revenue sharing regime instead of the annual license fees and getting spectrum free violating the license conditions. **The biggest loser is the Central Government which has been defrauded by a close liaison between the politicians, bureaucrats and the cellular operators.**

**Khagen Das**
MEMBER OF PARLIAMENT
(LOK SABHA)

सत्यमेव जयते

**90, North Avenue,**
**New Delhi - 110 001**
**Tels. (011) 23094461,**
**23094137**

**9. I will urge and request you to kindly:-**

**(a) Order Investigations by CBI and ED into all the above abnormalities.**

**(b) Summon the Secretaries and Wireless Advisors who were responsible for such manipulations and irregularities committed during 1999-2007 period so as to get to the root of the issues.**

**(c) Refer all these issues to one man committee.**

With best regards,

Yours sincerely,

Khagen 8/1/11

( Khagen Das )

Encl.: as above.

c.c.:

1. Sh. Murli Manohar Joshi, Chairman, PAC
2. Sh. Pranab Mukherjee, Finance Minister,
3. Sh. Kapil Sibal, Minister of Communications & IT
4. Dr. J. S. Sarma, Chairman, TRAI
5. Sh. P. J. Thomas, CVC
6. Sh. Vinod Rai, CAG
7. Sh. A. P. Singh, CBI Director
8. Sh. Arun Mathur, Director, Enforcement Directorate

सत्यमेव जयते

**RAJEEV CHANDRASEKHAR**
**MEMBER OF PARLIAMENT**
**RAJYA SABHA**

**Member of Standing Committee on Information Technology**
**Member of Consultative Committee on Finance**
**Member of Parliamentary Forum on Youth**
**Co-Chairman, Vigilance & Monitoring Committee, Bangalore Urban District**

24 January, 2011

Respected Prime Minister,

This is further to my letter to you dated 11 January, 2011 regarding the Press Conference held by Shri Kapil Sibal, Hon'ble Minister of Communications & IT.

As I had mentioned in that letter, the Minister's Press Conference had far ranging implications, including that of undermining the investigation under progress. The Supreme Court has also since commented similarly.

I would not have considered challenging the claims of Mr. Sibal and Mr. Ahluwalia, except for the fact they chose to undermine the CAG, knowing fully well that the CAG cannot respond with a detailed Public defense and also making arguments that have already been made in the Supreme Court. The country deserves to know the truth and not get misled by smooth talking and articulate spin.

So, I have chosen to research and analyze Mr. Sibal's contentions and the subsequent statements by the Dy. Chairman of the Planning Commission. After detailed research and reading of over 1600 pages of various documents, I have prepared a presentation that analyzes Mr. Sibal's claims in his Press conference.

The conclusion, purely based on evidence, is clear for all to see. It lays bare the claims :

a) That the DoT has followed the TRAI Recommendations (a claim made to me in Parliament by the then Minister as well)
b) That the CAG report is based on assumptions – There are no assumptions used by the CAG. Only evidence.

I have shared this with the media, and in the interests of transparency, also with the Minister himself, Petitioners of the PILs in court, and political leaders in Parliament, including leaders of the Opposition.

I am enclosing herewith the detailed analysis and annexures for your action. As always, I am available for any further discussions or explanations that you might seek emerging out these documents.

Sincerely,

RAJEEV CHANDRASEKHAR

**Dr. Manmohan Singh**
Hon'ble Prime Minister
Government of India
New Delhi

211 North Avenue, New Delhi-110001 India
Tel: + 91-11-23094044 Fax : + 91-11-23094042
E-mail : rajeev.c@nic.in
www.rajeev.in

नृपेन्द्र मिश्र
*Nripendra Misra*
अध्यक्ष/Chairman
भारतीय दूरसंचार विनियामक प्राधिकरण
*Telecom Regulatory Authority of India*

D.O. No.: 103-1/2008-MN
January 14, 2008

Dear Shri Baluru

It has been learnt from the press release of DoT dated 10th January, 2008 and information posted on DoT's website that about 120 Letters Of Intent (LOI) for award of license to provide unified access service have been issued.

2. In above said press release, it is also mentioned that "TRAI on 28.08.2007 recommended that no cap be placed on the number of access service providers in any service area. The Government accepted this recommendation of TRAI...... Accordingly, DoT has decided to issue LOI to all the eligible applicants on the date of application who applied upto 25.9.2007".

3. The Authority in its recommendation dated 28th August, 2007 had confirmed the maintenance of status-quo in the existing policy of no limit on the number of access service providers, which has been the policy of Government since 1999. However, the Authority wants to reiterate that its recommendation on the entry of new service providers has always been linked to the availability of spectrum. This was conveyed to DoT vide letter No. 101-5/2003-MN dated 22nd February, 2003 and subsequently reiterated in its recommendation on "Unified Licensing Regime" of October 27, 2003, wherein TRAI opined that "Induction of additional mobile service providers in various service areas can be considered if there is adequate availability of spectrum for the existing service providers as well as for the new players, if permitted." As there was no subsequent reference to the Authority on the issue, therefore, it is presumed that the Government had agreed with the above recommendation.

4. I also wish to draw your kind attention to D.O. No. CP/TRAI/2007 dated October 15, 2007 regarding the legal provisions of processing the recommendations of TRAI. This letter was followed by another D.O. No. CP/TRAI/2007 dated October 19, 2007 wherein it was clarified that "It would be unfair and misleading if any decision and consequent action is initiated without identifying and implementing the linkages elsewhere in the Recommendation". It was reiterated that the Authority should be formally consulted if there is any deviation from the totality of the Recommendation.

..2..

5. Also, the Authority in its recommendation on "Review of license terms and conditions and capping of number of access providers" dated 28th August, 2007 has recommended that it is necessary, to ensure that allocations of spectrum are made in accordance with the laid down policy and the information on such allocations and pending requests for allocation of spectrum, the reasons for pendency, the duration of pending requests, etc., is available in public domain. Above all, the likely availability of spectrum in different bands in all the circles, the time period by which it will be available for allocation, the criteria to be adopted for setting up a 'Q system' needs to be made public". Similarly in its recommendation on "allocation and pricing of spectrum for 3G and broadband wireless access service" dated 27th September, 2006, the Authority has emphasized that there is a need to ensure availability of adequate spectrum, efficient utilization of the spectrum and making the processes of spectrum allocation completely transparent, and based on a road map and well researched plan.

6. It is sincerely hoped that the above suggestions/observations and compliance of legal provisions would receive highest consideration as they have a long term bearing on the telecom sector.

With regards,

Yours sincerely,

(Nripendra Misra)

Shri Siddhartha Behura,
Secretary,
Department of Telecommunications,
Sanchar Bhavan,
New Delhi - 110001

RAJEEV CHANDRASEKHAR
MEMBER OF PARLIAMENT
RAJYA SABHA

Member of Standing Committee on Information Technology
Member of Consultative Committee on Finance
Member of Parliamentary Forum on Youth
Co-Chairman, Vigilance & Monitoring Committee, Bangalore Urban District

10 February, 2011

Respected Prime Minister,

**Sub. :** **TRAI's 2G Report of 30.01.2011 confirms Spectrum Scam, losses and raises serious questions about administrative failure and wilful illegalities committed by MoCIT in 2008**

This is with further to my various letters to you on the issue of valuable 2G spectrum that has been given in 2008 without auctions at 2001 prices – thus causing a massive loss to the National Exchequer. Today's letter is with reference to the TRAI's latest Report on the 2010 Value of Spectrum in the 1800 MHz Band dated 30 January, 2011.

This Report obviously seems far more detailed in its calculations regarding the technical and economic values to be assigned for 2G spectrum vis-a-vis 3G auction prices. Even by this Report, it is clear that 2G spectrum up to 6.2 MHz is pegged at 53% of the 3G spectrum value and beyond 6.2 MHz, at 136%.

Consequent upon this detailed finding and based on the methodology used by the CAG, the loss to the Exchequer arising out of 6.2 MHz spectrum contracted (though only 4.4 MHz have been given till now) and spectrum held by operators beyond 6.2 MHz would still be pegged at upwards of Rs.1.2 lakh crores.

Further, the Report also conceals the fact that auctions must be held for spectrum that is returned from approx. 74 licenses that may be liable for cancellation, based on failure to meet license conditions.

211 North Avenue, New Delhi-110001 India
Tel: + 91-11-23094044 Fax : + 91-11-23094042
E-mail : rajeev.c@nic.in
www.rajeev.in

सत्यमेव जयते

While I welcome TRAI's view that 2G spectrum reverted back to the DoT in case of cancellation of licenses of defaulting companies can be placed for auction, it raises serious questions relating to the following:

1. What stopped the Government from resorting to auctions in 2008 – since similar level playing field considerations would have existed as they exist in 2011?

2. The accountability and rigour of TRAI's Recommendations which seems to have given conflicting views on auctions in 2008 and 2010, but supports auctions when new 2G spectrum becomes available.

3. Why was your letter of 02 November, 2007 to the then MoCIT, specifically seeking consideration of "spectrum auctions" or "revision of entry fee", ignored, since you had appropriately pointed towards recovering the "correct price of spectrum" – which is now been reaffirmed in no uncertain terms, by the TRAI's Report of 30 January, 2011?

All of these necessitate serious administrative review of the manner in which TRAI is functioning and MoCIT is handling direct correspondence from your office.

There is also a striking similarity between the announcements made by the Hon'ble MoCIT, Shri Kapil Sibal on 07 January, 2011 and TRAI's Report of 30 January, 2011, both on account of :

- Value of 2G spectrum vis-a-vis 3G auction price; and
- The decision to oppose auctions for 2G in general, but auction new spectrum which comes back to DoT as a result of license cancellations.

Unless this is purely coincidental, the TRAI Report would seem like a "command performance", even though it still reaffirms the massive loss caused to the Exchequer on account of the 2G spectrum scam.

Finally, with this report in hand and evidence of serious wrongdoing during 2008 (in spite of your letter dated 02 November, 2007 to the then MoCIT), may I please request you to have the Government accept its mistake and start the process of cleanup by cancelling licenses given illegally, and recovering the value of spectrum either through re-auctions of spectrum or benchmark pricing, where appropriate – consistent with your letter of 02 November, 2007. It will also be greatly helpful if the

2

सत्यमेव जयते

Hon'ble MoCIT can stop managing the optics of this huge loss and defending the indefensible acts of the then MoCIT.

While I have decided to oppose and expose any cover-up attempts, I am equally available to discuss constructively the best possible way forward to resolve the issues at hand, and move forward - but not without identifying and penalizing the perpetrators of the 2G spectrum scam, ensuring recovery of lost revenue and on the back of a policy decision to auction all scarce, national resources in an open, transparent manner.

Yours Sincerely,

RAJEEV CHANDRASEKHAR

**Dr. Manmohan Singh**
Hon'ble Prime Minister
Government of India
New Delhi

3

**RAJEEV CHANDRASEKHAR**
**MEMBER OF PARLIAMENT**

# 2G SPECTRUM SCAM

## MOCIT's CLAIMS VERSUS FACTS

**New Delhi. 21 January, 2011**

# Today's Presentation

1. Why are the facts important and why this Meeting

2. The MoCIT/Planning Commission "zero loss" theory

3. Challenges step-by-step their contentions on :

    i. Zero loss
    ii. CAG's calculations outrageously erroneous / flawed
    iii. TRAI said no auctions, therefore Raja followed recommendations
    iv. Public interest is more important than Exchequer revenue, and therefore, no auctions
    v. Tenth Five Year Plan supports the theory of no auction
    vi. Telecom is comparable to Highways, fertilizers and coal subsidy
    vii. Had Supreme Court taken on board the CAG Report
    viii. Implications of MOCIT's "No Loss" Statements

4. Summary / Conclusions

**All evaluation based on evidence**

# Why are the facts important and why this Meeting

1. Too many scams go unpunished.

2. The main reason is that these are sophisticated Economic Crimes. The investigating agencies and prosecutors are most of the time over matched in investigating these crimes. Overmatched by the system and the perpetrators.

3. The media also, in most cases, overwhelmed by spin and complex techno-economic issues. "Policy" used to obfuscate matters.

4. The people of India don't relate to these scams – because they are not aware that they are paying for it.

5. Moneys lost or skimmed or swindled are tax payer money or assets and the victims of each of these scams is the people.

6. Politicians tend to make all things political,, because it suits them – and the people then tune out!

3

## Sibal's View on First Come, First Served Policy

**Sibal, as a lawyer in the "Home Communications Limited versus Union of India" case, in the Delhi High Court, has argued:**

*"FCFS methodology, as envisaged will result in black marketing of time slots by unscrupulous licensees, which could be at the costs of the public revenue as well as sufferings of the viewers. Policy promotes trafficking in licensees..."*

**Sibal, as the MoCIT in 2011:**

*"Policies aimed at maximizing growth and competition, rather than revenue and minimizing tariffs."*

**Change of Mind?**

4

## Basic Premise of MoCIT's Presentation

1. MoCIT says TRAI is a statutory body and Government has followed its recommendations.

2. TRAI did not recommend auction since 2003, and therefore, the auction route was not followed. How could the Government disagree with TRAI?

3. CAG's loss calculation is utterly erroneous. Actual loss is zero

4. Revenue maximization is not Government policy. Government acted in public interest. Lower prices and teledensity is more important than Exchequer revenue, and therefore, no auctions.

5. Policy documents – NTP'99 and 10th Five Year Plan oppose the notion of revenue maximization, and therefore, justify no auctions.

6. Sectors such as highways (free land), coal and fertilizer get subsidy. So why should telecom be any different?

5

# What this Presentation Evaluates

1. Is the loss zero, or is CAG correct in its evaluations?

2. Has CAG Performance Audit process demonstrated rigor or is it based on assumptions?

3. Is the Government bound by TRAI recommendations? Did TRAI oppose auctions?
   Did the government follow TRAI recommendations as it claims?

4. Is public interest better served if Exchequer loses money by allocating scarce resources at historical prices? Or does auction serve overall public interest and public policy objectives better?

5. Does the Tenth Five Year Plan support MoCIT's contention?

6. Are Highways, Coal and fertilizers relevant examples? Or an attempt to confuse?

7. Has the Supreme Court taken on board the CAG Report including the issue of losses?

8. What are the implications of MoCIT's 'No Loss' statement?

9. Summary

6

# 1. Is the loss zero, or is CAG correct in its evaluations?

Loss According to CAG based on 3G Auction Prices :

| | |
|---|---|
| New Licenses (122) | Rs. 1,02,498 crores |
| Dual technology (35 licenses) | Rs.37,154 crores |
| Spectrum beyond contracted quantity of 6.2 MHz | Rs.36,993 crores |
| **Total loss** | **Rs.1,76,645 crores** |

**However, MoCIT claims that this loss is zero**

# 1 - MoCIT's Questionable Arithmetic

MoCIT says :

I. Government has not made up its mind on the charge for spectrum beyond 6.2 MHz, therefore, loss of Rs.36,993 crores needs to be excluded.

II. The remaining loss of Rs.1,39,652 crores is only Rs.99,000 crores since government has only given 4.4 MHz spectrum, while CAG has wrongly calculated loss based on 6.2 MHz.

III. Since the 3G auctions were held in 2010, but 2G licenses were given in 2008, the "time value" of loss of spectrum is not Rs.99,000 crores, but Rs.56,000 crores. (46% discount – without calculation).

IV. Since spectrum was given late and not in 2008, license term is 19, not 20 years, loss is down to Rs.53,000 crores.

V. Since 3G spectrum is three times more efficient than 2G, the loss is further down to Rs.17,755 crores.

VI. Since 4.4 MHz is free with UASL license anyway, the actual loss is zero.

**Consequently, loss is zero, and not Rs.1.76 crores**

# 1 - Response to MoCIT's Questionable Arithmetic

I. **Government has not made up its mind on the rate for spectrum beyond 6.2 MHz, therefore, loss of Rs.36,993 crores needs to be excluded.**

1. **TRAI recommendations, 11 May, 2010, Section 3.99, states :**

***"Accordingly, the Authority recommends that all the service providers having spectrum beyond the contracted quantum should pay excess spectrum charges at the "Current Price", pro-rated for the period of the remaining validity of their license subject to a minimum of seven years."***
***(Page 6)***

Loss calculated on that basis alone.

2. "Current Price" defined in Section 3.82 and Table 3.4 of TRAI Recommendations dated 11 May, 2010 as 3G auction price. *(Pages 3, 5)*
3. Is CAG wrong in calculating recoverable Government revenue from the last 8 years as loss to the Government at the current time?
4. Till the Government recovers revenue, any auditor will consider this as a loss
5. Let the Government recover the revenue and then this figure can be reduced from the losses.

**MoCIT's arithmetic is wrong. Contradicts TRAI**

9

# 1 - Response to MoCIT's Questionable Arithmetic

II. **The remaining loss of Rs.1,39,652 crores is only Rs.99,000 crores since government has only given 4.4 MHz spectrum, while CAG has calculated 6.2 MHz.**

a) This is a blatant misrepresentation and a classical move to confuse those who are unfamiliar with the details of TRAI Recommendations and licensing regime.

b) **TRAI Recommendations of 11 May, 2010 (Section 2.47) concludes : *"Authority is clearly of the view that contracted spectrum for all access licenses issued in or after 2001 is 6.2 MHz."* CAG's calculation is based on this.** *(Page 18)*

c) TRAI bases its recommendations on :

- DoT action since 2000
- DoT Tender Document – 4th Cellular Mobile – 2001
- UASL License agreements (legal contract) – 2003-04
- UASL Guidelines dated 14.12.2005, Section 37
- DoT affidavit in TDSAT dated 18.08.2008
- DoT affidavit in Delhi High Court dated 14.01.2008 ***(Pages 11-17)***

d) The license entitlement is for 6.2MHz. That 4.4 MHz has been given initially, does not mean that the entitlement is limited to 4.4 MHz. In most cases, it is given in phases – 4.4 MHz, then 1.8 MHz and so on.

**MoCIT's arithmetic is wrong. Contradicts TRAI, license, guidelines, DoT affidavits**

10

# 1 - Response to MoCIT's Questionable Arithmetic

**III. Since the 3G auctions were held in 2010, but 2G spectrum was given in 2008, the time value of loss of spectrum is not Rs.99,000 crores, but Rs.56,000 crores.**

a) **TRAI Recommendations dated 11 May, 2010 had concluded that the 3G price has determined in May 2010 (middle of 3G auctions) that the 3G price discovered in 2010 should be the "current price" to be charged for 2G spectrum beyond 6.2 MHz in 1800 band and 1.5 times 3G price in 900 MHz band. MoCIT has contradicted these recommendations.** *(Pages 5, 8)*

b) This recommendation applies to spectrum beyond 6.2 MHz given since 2003, not just 2008. CAG has calculated loss based on TRAI's recommendation – no assumption here. *(Page 3)*

c) Curiously, MoCIT is willing to discount Government revenue by 46% between 2010 and 2008, but doesn't see the loss from spectrum given in 2008 at 2001 prices.

a) Clearly, MoCIT thinks time value of money works between 2008 and 2010, but fails between 2001 and 2008. Again, cherry-picking .

**MoCIT's arithmetic is wrong. Contradicts TRAI , basic economics**

## 1 - Loss based on MoCIT's Logic of Time Value of Money

1. According to MoCIT, a 140% increase in subscriber base from 249 million in January 2008 to 601 million in June 2010 translates into a 76% increase in time value of spectrum. (from Rs.99,000 crores to Rs.139,652 crores).
2. Spectrum value (76%) increases at approx. half the increase in subscriber value (140%).
3. By this calculation, the subscriber base in 2001 increased from 4 million to 249 million or an increase of 62 times. By MoCIT's logic, the spectrum value should increase by half or 31 times, i.e., Rs.1,658 crores X 31 = Rs.52,235 crores.
4. This would be approx. 2½ times 3G price. By this calculation, the total loss would be Rs.4.4 lakh crores
5. MoCIT might wish to reconsider the rationale of his arithmetic, apart from the fact that he is contradicting TRAI.

12

# 1 - Response to MoCIT's Questionable Arithmetic

**IV. Since spectrum was given late and not in 2008, license term is 19, not 20 years, loss is down to Rs.53,000 crores**

(a) **UASL guidelines, Section 37, clearly states spectrum allocation "subject to availability".** ***(Page 21)***

(b) Operators knew exactly what they were getting into. No demand from operators for extending license period.

(c) Why is MoCIT discounting Exchequer losses in favour of private interest, when the private companies have not sought any relief?

(d) Why did Raja give licenses in 2008 when he didn't have spectrum till 2009? What was the hurry to rush? Why did he not listen to TRAI? CAG has said "undue haste" – is that wrong?

(e) Can DoT take advantage of its own wrong (delay) to mitigate its crime (loss)?

(f) MoCIT exposes DoT to litigation / claims for extension of license by operators, in an attempt to defend Raja.

**MoCIT's arithmetic is wrong. Appropriate protection under UASL guidelines being ignored in favor of private companies**

13

# 1 - Response to MoCIT's Questionable Arithmetic

**V. Since 3G spectrum is three times more efficient than 2G, the loss is further down to Rs.17,755 crores**

(a) **TRAI Recommendations of 11 May, 2010 – Section 3.82 had clearly stated that :**

***"Spectral efficiency of 3G and 2G are comparable",***

**and therefore, concluded that 3G price should be the "current price" for 2G spectrum in 2010.** ***(Pages 4-5)***

(b) Gross misrepresentation vis-à-vis TRAI Recommendations.

(c) CAG cannot assume technical conclusions. It has based its calculations on TRAI recommendations.

(d) MoCIT is cherry-picking - cites TRAI recommendations to defend no auction, but rejects TRAI technical calculations of 3G and 2G being equated.

(e) Reportedly, TRAI is under pressure to take a U-turn to support MoCIT's position.

**MoCIT's arithmetic is wrong. Contradicts TRAI (may take a U-turn!)**

14

# 1 - Response to MoCIT's Questionable Arithmetic

**VI. Since 4.4 MHz is free with UASL license anyway, the actual loss is zero.**

(a) TRAI recommendations dated 13.01.2005, Section 9 states:

*"In the existing policy, spectrum charges are two components : (i)* ***one time spectrum charge which is paid as a part of the one time entry fee by service providers".*** ***(Page 23-24)***

(b) TRAI recommendations of 11 May, 2010 on Unified License (**without spectrum**) prices UASL + NLD + ILD + Internet + IP-1 as a single license **only Rs.20 crores**. ***(Page 26)***

(c) MoCIT wants us to believe that UASL license minus spectrum is Rs.1658 crores. Flies in the face of the above recommendations.

(d) Entry fee was discovered through an auction in 2001 where license came bundled with 6.2 MHz. Operators valued the 6.2 MHz, and not a piece of paper. Without spectrum, there is no mobility. Fixed line license is free in UASL.

(e) Bid for entry fee is a bid for bundled spectrum. Without spectrum, UASL is worthless.

**MoCIT's arithmetic is wrong. Contradicts TRAI, 2005 and 2010**

15

## 2. CAG has based its Report on DoT files, TRAI Recommendations and License Agreements; No Assumptions

a) MoCIT has justified all decisions citing TRAI's statutory status and recommendations of no auction.

b) CAG's calculations have only taken TRAI recommendations, licensing regime, tender documents and DoT affidavits into consideration.

c) CAG has depended (for calculations) on the exact same source (TRAI) as MoCIT (for not holding auctions).

d) MoCIT's loss figure is contradicted at every stage by the TRAI (since 2005) in what he calls statutory recommendations and have been the basis of DoT's actions since 2003. CAG has made no assumptions.

**Again like his predecessors, MoCIT is cherry picking TRAI Recommendations**

16

## 2 - Has CAG Performance Audit process demonstrated rigor?

(a) CAG's Performance Audit process includes the following :

- CAG-DoT Entry Conference – 23 December, 2009
- Performance audit tenure – Jan-September 2010
- Period covered under audit – 2003-2010
- Basis of Audit – Files of DoT, DoT files with CBI, TRAI's statutory recommendations, MoF files / comments, public documents on website of Ministry of Corporate Affairs, replies of DoT and MoF.

(b) Did DoT have a chance to reply to audit observations? : Yes, in July 2010 and September 2010

(c) Did MoF have a chance to respond to audit observations ? : Yes

(d) Was extra time given to DoT? : Yes

(e) Was meeting held to discuss draft audit report? – Yes, on 04 October, 2010

(f) CAG leads Dy. CAG and Advisor Finance DoT – Exit Conference - 20 May, 2010

**CAG Report is not ex-parte; deals with every single reply of DoT / MoF – through multiple opportunities**

17

## 2 - Has CAG been unfair in calculating loss without taking into consideration increase in tax, revenue share?

a) Tax and revenue share would accrue regardless of auctions or First Come, First Served. Bidders also need to pay revenue share, spectrum charge etc. It is not one or the other.

b) For revenue share and tax, there should be rollout and subscribers

c) Recent 2G beneficiaries have not rolled out, so no increase in tax revenue or revenue share

d) Market share of new entrants after two years less than 5%, so no impact on tax / revenue share, competition or prices.

e) Incumbents and not new entrants serving unserved areas even today

f) No public policy objective met – nor have taxes or revenue incomes increased on account of new entrants.

**CAG is entirely correct in basing loss on TRAI Recommendations. No perceptible increase in revenue or tax**

18

## 3. Are TRAI recommendations binding on the DoT?

An impression that TRAI recommendations are binding is entirely false. TRAI Act allows DoT to reject, modify or accept recommendations subject to procedure laid down under TRAI Act, Section 11, Fifth Proviso ***(Page 29)***

> *"Provided also that if the Central Government having considered that recommendation of the Authority, comes to a prima facie conclusion that such recommendation cannot be accepted or needs modifications, it shall refer the recommendation back to the Authority for its reconsideration, and the Authority may, within fifteen days from the date of receipt of such reference, forward to the Central Government its recommendation after considering the reference made by that Government. After receipt of further recommendation if any, the Central Government shall take a final decision."*

**DoT is fully empowered to reject or modify TRAI's recommendations – and it routinely does. It has to follow the statutory process of re-reference before modification.**

19

## 3 - Did the TRAI oppose auctions since 2003 as the MoCIT claims?

a) TRAI recommendations dated 27 October, 2003, Section 7.39

*"The induction of additional mobile service providers (became UASL in 2003) in various service areas can be considered if there is adequate availability of spectrum. As the existing players have to improve the efficiency of utilisation of spectrum and if Government ensures availability of additional spectrum then in the existing Licensing Regime, they may introduce additional players* ***through a multi-stage bidding process as was followed for 4th cellular operator*** *"* **(Page 31)**

b) Mobile licensing regime was converted into UASL regime in November 2003.

c) UASL is exactly similar to 4th mobile with fixed line thrown in free.

**MoCIT is wrong. TRAI did recommend auctions since 2003**

20

## 3 - Did the TRAI oppose auctions in August 2007as the MoCIT claims?

a) TRAI differentiated between spectrum auction and entry fee auction on 28 August, 2007 – basis of the current 2G scam, TRAI recommended in Section 2.73

*"The entry fee as it exists today is, in fact, a result of the price discovered through a markets based mechanism applicable for the grant of license to the 4th cellular operator. In today's dynamism and unprecedented growth of telecom sector, the entry fee determined then is also not the realistic price for obtaining a license. Perhaps, it **needs to be reassessed through a market mechanism**."* ***(Page 33)***

b) DoT quotes Section 2.78, 2.79 (no auction) ***(Pages 36-37)***

c) Why did the DoT not follow 2.73 regarding auction of entry fee?

d) Why did it not seek clarification from TRAI in case of conflicting Sections, i.e., Section 2.73 versus Section 2.78 / 2.79?

e) It has statutory powers to do so under Section 11 of the TRAI Act.

f) TRAI wrote three letters on 15 October, 2007, 19 October, 2007 and 14 January, 2008 asking DoT to consult it before issuing LoIs. Why were these letters ignored?

21

## 3 - MoCIT says TRAI Recommendations of 28 August, 2007 have been followed

What do the recommendations cover?

1. Issue of Entry Fee
2. Issue of spectrum auction
3. Issue of Cap on the Number of Service Providers
4. Issue of M&A
5. Issue of Rollout Obligations
6. Others

This is a single interlinked set of recommendations in response to DoT Reference of April 2007.

22

# 3 - Did the government follow TRAI Recommendations as it claims?

1. TRAI's Recommendations of August 28, 2007 recommended :

a) Section 6.1 : No cap – violated (122 out of 575 applications, by advancing cutoff date to 25.09.2007 from 01.10.2007) as per Delhi High Court Judgment – July 2009 ***(Pages 39, 42, 44)***

**This ensured that genuine bidders were kept out. Market created.**

b) Section 5.27 : No M&A till rollout obligations are met – violated by DoT. Acquisitions allowed, mergers linked to three years, and not rollout obligations. Allowed Unitech / Swan to sell within 8 months ***(Pages 47, 48, 51, 53)***

**This ensured that buyers could only buy from private companies. Sale ensured.**

c) Section 5.41, 5.2 : Rollout obligations unchanged, Linked to "effective date of license" – violated by DoT. Changed to "effective date of spectrum allocation". Therefore, no rollout and eventually, Show Cause Notices. ***(Pages 57/58 read with 55/56, 60)***

**This ensured that sale could be made at a windfall without any investment in infrastructure / rollout.**

**DoT has violated TRAI Act with impunity and violated recommendations / cherry picked at will. Has ignored TRAI letters**

23

# 3 - TRAI wrote three letters to DoT – Two before LoIs, one after LoI

a) TRAI cautioned DoT that its recommendations of 28 August, 2007 have to be read in its entirety. It warned against cherry-picking.

b) DoT / TRAI is hiding these letters (RTI reply).

c) TRAI warned DoT on 19 October, 2007 (three months before 122 LoIs were given at 2001 prices) :

*"It would be unfair and misleading if any decision and consequent action is initiated without identifying and implementing the linkages elsewhere in the Recommendation."* ***(Page 63)***

d) TRAI warned DoT on 14 January, 2008 (two months before licenses were given) :

*"It was reiterated that the Authority should be formally consulted if there is any deviation from the totality of the Recommendation."* ***(Page 63)***

e) RTI applications filed with TRAI have yielded no response. Attempt to hide? ***(Page 68)***

**Why were these letters ignored if MoCIT claims that TRAI Recommendations have been followed?**

24

# 4. Is public interest better served if Exchequer takes the loss by giving scarce resources at a loss?

**Public Interest more important than Exchequer revenue**

(a) Sacrificing auctions and causing loss to Exchequer does not mean consumer will not pay market price.

(b) Public auctions (2001,3G) were replaced by private auctions (Unitech and Swan). Consumer still pays a price which includes the asset's market price.

(c) By this logic, diesel, petrol, power, water should all be free. Taxes should be slashed.

(d) Giving scarce national resources at historical prices when companies are willing to pay market price is a bizarre logic.

25

## 4 - If Consumer interest is more important than Exchequer revenue, petrol should cost Rs.35.18 and not Rs.59 per litre

| Basic Price | Rs 28.93 |
|---|---|
| Dealer commission | Rs 1.05 |
| Transportation Charge | Rs 6.00 |
| Government Levies and Taxes | |
| Excise duty | Rs 14.35 |
| Education Tax | Rs 0.[illegible] |
| VAT | Rs 5.5 |
| Crude Oil Custom duty | Rs 1.1 |
| Petrol Custom Duty | Rs 1.54 |
| Total price | Rs 58.90 |

**Clearly, MoCIT / Planning Commission's logic is not acceptable to the Cabinet**

26

## 4 - Is public interest better served if Exchequer takes the loss by giving scarce resources at a loss?...Contd

**Auctions for revenue versus auctions for transparency / selecting winners / meeting policy objectives**

(a) Auctions goes beyond protecting Exchequer revenue

Only fair way to select winners when demand exceeds supply. Ex: 575 applications for 122 slots

(b) Market price forces operators to roll out asap. 3G 2010 (rolled out) versus 2G 2008 (Show Cause for rollout violation).

(c) Tariff based on 20-year license and subscriber acquisition, not merely recovery of auction price– Tata's pricing of 3G voice lower than 2G voice.

(d) Auction design can help prevent high bids and price regulation can protect consumer interest – TRAI Act, Section 11(2).

**From every aspect, well-designed auctions score higher** 27

## 5 - Tenth Five Year Plan - Comparing Demand Supply Equation 2001 vs 2008

| | 2001 | 2008 |
|---|---|---|
| Subscriber Base | 4 million | 249 million |
| No. of applications | 10-12 (at any one time) | 575 (with 01 October cutoff) |
| No. of Licenses Available (based on spectrum) | 210 (51 – 2003-07 + 157 – 2008 onwards) | 157 (122 + 35 Dual Tech) |
| Demand for spectrum from existing operators | None | 150 existing operators in queue |
| Relative Scarcity | Minimal | Acute |

**Going by Tenth Five Year Plan, demand supply recommendation or transparent need to select 122 out of 575 applicants – auctions was the only way forward**

## 5 - Does Tenth Five Year Plan support MoCIT Planning Commission's argument?...Contd.

**MoCIT states from the Tenth Five Year Plan:**

*"Spectrum policy needs to be promotional in nature : with revenue considerations playing a secondary role."*

**What the Tenth Plan, Box 8.5.7, Guiding Principles – Spectrum Policy, actually states :**

*"Spectrum policy needs to be promotional in nature : with revenue considerations playing a secondary role.*

*"Pricing and allocation should ensure that available spectrum is utilized optimally."*

*"Spectrum pricing needs to be based on relative demand and supply over space and time in a dynamic manner. Opportunity cost to reflect the relative scarcity of the resource in a given situation."*

***(Page 72)***

**MoCIT is quoting the Tenth Five Year Plan selectively. Tenth Five Year Plan is about dynamic pricing of spectrum based on demand / supply and stresses on efficient utilization (Prime Minister's letter of 02 November, 2007). Plan has no opposition to auction of entry fee**

29

## 5. Does Tenth Five Year Plan support MoCIT Planning Commission's argument?

a) MoCIT cites Tenth Five Year Plan of the NDA, but fails to cite the Eleventh Five Year Plan (2007) of the UPA – wonder why?

b) MoCIT states from the Tenth Five Year Plan:

*"Government's broad policy of taxes and regulation for telecom sector has to be a promotional one. Mopping up of resources or revenue generation by Government should not be a determinant of the ;policy governing the sector."*

c) What the Tenth Plan, Section 8.5.38 actually states :

*""Government's broad policy of taxes and regulation for telecom sector has to be a promotional one. Mopping up of resources or revenue generation by Government should not be a determinant of the ;policy governing the sector.* ***The incidence of license fees in the form revenue share and spectrum charges has to be guided by this principle. Keeping in line with the policy adopted by most of the progressive administrations in the world, the license fee need to be aligned to the cost of regulation and administration of Universal Service Obligations (USO)." (Page 70)***

**MoCIT is quoting the Tenth Five Year Plan selectively. The Tenth Plan is about lowering revenue share/spectrum charge, and not about auction of entry fee.** 30

## 6. Are Highways, Coal and fertilizer relevant?

**MoCIT in his Press Release quotes free land given for Highways, subsidized coal prices and fertilizers:**

(a) It is preposterous to compare highway with telecom. Highway has no takers while spectrum had 575 applicants waiting to bid in queue.

(b) Highway involves negative subsidy while telecom has generated Rs.70,000 crores as revenue in taxes and revenue share Rs.1,00,000 on sale of 3G and BWA.

(c) Coal and fertilizer subsidy is the equivalent of rural fixed line tariffs (70 paise) – served by the USO regime. India had lower fixed line tariffs for 60 years in rural India, just as coal and fertilizer.

(d) USO is the mechanism for subsidizing telephony, not largess to corporates by way of spectrum in 2008 at 2001 prices.

(e) Attempt to confuse Consumer targeted subsidy with largess to private companies ignoring the fact that consumer will bear the brunt of assets' market price.

(f) Unitech and Swan replace public auction with private auction. Consumer will bear market price of asset

**These comparisons are an insult to the intelligence of the people of India**

31

# 7. Has the Supreme Court taken on board the CAG Report including the issue of losses?

a) PIL in Supreme Court filed before CAG Report was released

b) CAG Report released in November, 2010

c) DoT affidavit in SC presented same arguments as MoCIT (on CAG calculation and TRAI Recommendations), in its affidavit – 11 November, 2010. Opposes SC supervision of CBI *(Page 73-83)*

d) A. Raja's affidavit in SC also argues the same points as MoCIT (on CAG calculation and TRAI Recommendations). *(Pages 84-89)*

e) Supreme Court Judgment of 16 December, 2010:

- Decides to supervise CBI
- **Expands scope to include CAG and period from 2001- 2007**
- **Specifically issues raised in CAG Report including "losses running into thousands of crores to the Exchequer".**

*(Pages 91, 92)*

**Supreme Court has considered MoCIT's defence of Mr. Raja's actions. Remains unimpressed – expanded investigation to CAG**

32

# 8. Implications of MoCIT's 'No Loss' statement

1. Pressure TRAI to take a U-turn on its 3G / 2G spectrum parity recommendations of 11 May 2010. (Section 3.82 /Table 3.4)

2. Makes it impossible for Government to recover lost revenues

3. Opens DoT to litigation and claims if license is 19 years, and not 20

4. Insult to Supreme Court Judgment bordering on contempt

5. Misused position as Union Minister to influence / prejudice the CBI Investigation which has specifically filed a FIR quoting "wrongful loss" and a figure of "more than Rs.22,000 crores." ***(Pages 97. 98)***

6. Attempt to whitewash scams and giving safe passage to the beneficiaries

7. Undermined PAC and breach of Parliamentary privilege

8. Publicly humiliated, compromised and undermined institution of CAG

**If there is no crime (loss), then there are no criminals (DoT officials / private companies)**

33

# 9. Summary

a) Corruption isn't a moral issue. Its an economic and governance issue.

b) The scams and swindles are no longer simple. They involve sophisticated capture of Public Policy, Regulatory policy and Contracts.

c) To stop this trend, media needs to build capacity and get behind this. This needs to be understood by the people as crimes against the taxpayer and citizens.

d) Only then will the institutions of democracy like Parliament really get pressured into addressing this.

e) No scams ever seem to be properly investigated and concluded.

f) Our desire must be to simply ensure that proper investigation into these scams isn't prevented by smooth talking ministers and their meekly complying bureaucrats and statutory bodies that are also meekly politically pliable.

g) The tendency of smooth talking ministers and politicians to talk and spin their way out of this can only be challenged by media.

h) We owe it to the people of India to ensure that these scams are not brushed under the carpet.

*In the interest of a transparent discussion, this Presentation is being sent to the Hon'ble Prime Minister, MoCIT, Chairman – PAC, Leader of the Opposition in Lok Sabha, Leader of the Opposition in Rajya Sabha, Vice Chairman - Planning Commission and Petitioners of the PIL in Hon'ble Supreme Court.*

34

Government of India
Ministry of Communications & I.T.
Department of Telecommunications
Wireless Planning & Co-ordination Wing
6th Floor, Sanchar Bhavan, 20, Ashoka Road, New Delhi-01.

No.L-14047/101/2005-NTG(Pt.II) Dated: 01 -11-2011

To,

Shri Vivek Garg , Advocate
Advocates International,
18/1, GF, Shakti Nagar,
New Delhi-110007

Subject: - Information required under the Right to Information Act 2005.

Sir,

I am to refer to your application no. RTI/PMO-Delhi/2011/489 dated 29-09-2011 transferred by Deputy Secretary & CPIO of PMO Office (received on 17/10/2011) seeking information under RTI Act, 2005 for the points 4,5,8,9 & 10.

2. The copies of correspondences i.r.o. S.No. 4, 5, 9 & 10 of the enclosed list(Annex-I) with the application are enclosed herewith. For point no. 8, your application has been transferred to Shri Piyush Srivastava, Director (PF-II), Department of Economic Affairs, New Delhi.

4. Appeal, if any, against the above decision of the CPIO may be preferred, within thirty days of the receipt of this letter to Shri T.K.Varda Krishnan, J.W.A. & Appelate Authority, Department of Telecommunications, Room No. 603, Sanchar Bhavan, 20 Ashoka Road, New Delhi.

Encl: A/A

Yours faithfully

(M.K.Rao)
Deputy Wireless Advisor& CPIO
To the Govt. of India

To,

1. Shri Piyush Srivastava, Director(PF-II), Room No. 168-C, North Block, New Delhi for providing the information i.r.o. point no. 8 of the enclosed list directly to the applicant. (RTI application attached)

Copy to:

1. Smt. Sanjukta Ray, Deputy Secretary & CPIO, PMO, South Block, New Delhi-110101 for information.

DO No.3/11/2003-Infra
भारत सरकार
वित्त मंत्रालय
आर्थिक कार्य विभाग
नार्थ ब्लाक,
नई दिल्ली–110 001 भारत
Government of India
Ministry of Finance
Department of Economic Affairs
North Block,
New Delhi - 110001 India
Tel (011) 2309 2611 Fax (011) 2309 4075
e-mail : ashokjha@nic.in

सत्यमेव जयते

वित्त सचिव
**Finance Secretary**

March 28, 2007.

Dear Shri Mathur,

Please refer to Cabinet Secretariat O.M.No.93/1/1/2006-Cab. dated 23.2.2006., 10.11.2006 and 7.12.2006 regarding Constitution of GoM on vacation of spectrum and raising resources for the purpose. Also refer to DEA OM of even number dated 18.5.2006 requesting that technology neutrality in spectrum allocation and spectrum pricing should be included within the terms of reference of the GoM.

2. The Terms of Reference (ToR) of the GoM do not include issues relating to technology neutral spectrum allocation and spectrum pricing which are of immense importance for further growth of telecom in the country. The methodology to be followed for allocation of spectrum and its pricing would logically follow the vacation of spectrum which is one of the issues included in the ToRs. A sound policy on spectrum allocation and pricing will not only result in optimum utilization of spectrum but would also have revenue implication.

3. As the GoM is being serviced by the Department of Telecom, I request you to ensure that these issues are included in the ToR for the GoM. I also request you to initiate action for scheduling the meeting of the GoM at an early date.

With kind regards,

Yours sincerely,

(Ashok Jha)

Shri D.S. Mathur,
Secretary,
Department of Telecom,
Sanchar Bhawan,
New Delhi.

S.No.23(I)

Tel. : +91-11-2371 9898
Fax : +91-11-2371 1514
e-mail : dsmathur@nic.in

**D. S. Mathur**
सचिव Secretary

भारत सरकार
संचार एवं सूचना प्रौद्योगिकी मंत्रालय
दूरसंचार विभाग
संचार भवन, नई दिल्ली-110 001
**Government of India**
**Ministry of Communications & Information Technology**
**Department of Telecommunications**
**Sanchar Bhawan, New Delhi-110 001**

DO No. L-14047/1/2006-NTG
April 2, 2007

Dear Shri Jha,

Kindly refer to your DO letter No 3/11/2003-Infra dated 28[th] March 2007 concerning the TOR for GOM on vacation of spectrum and raising resources for the purpose.

2. In this context, I may mention that DOT had proposed a draft TOR for the GOM in January 2006, which focused on the issues relating to vacation of spectrum in a time-bound manner for the growth of telecom sector, making available funds for relocation of existing systems and use of digital technology.

3. The TOR issued by Cabinet Secretariat in February 2006 included certain other issues, including spectrum pricing, which are within the normal work carried out by this Ministry. The Hon'ble MOC&IT had written to the Hon'ble PM accordingly in February 2006, requesting that the Terms of Reference may kindly be modified as suggested in our original proposal. The revised TOR were issued by Cabinet Secretariat in December 2006. I hope this clarifies the matter.

With regards,

Yours sincerely,

***(D.S.Mathur)***

Shri Ashok Jha
Finance Secretary
Ministry of Finance
North Block
New Delhi

**DO No.3/11/20**

सत्यमेव जयते

डॉ. डी. सुब्बाराव
**DR. D. SUBBARAO**

सचिव
आर्थिक कार्य विभाग
वित्त मंत्रालय
भारत सरकार
**SECRETARY**
**DEPARTMENT OF ECONOMIC AFFAIRS**
**MINISTRY OF FINANCE**
**GOVERNMENT OF INDIA**
नई दिल्ली/New Delhi
Tel.: 23092611, 23092555 Fax: 23094075

June 6, 2007

**Shri D.S. Mathur**
**Secretary**
**Department of Telecom**
**Sanchar Bhawan**
**New Delhi**

Dear Shri Mathur,

1. I am writing further to our earlier DO dated 28.3.2007 on the subject of Terms of Reference (ToRs) of the GoM on vacation of Sprectrum. We had pointed out therein that the ToRs of the GoM circulated vide Cabinet Secretariat OM No.93/1/1/2006-Cab. dated 7.12.2006 do not include issues relating to technology neutral spectrum allocation and spectrum pricing.

2. When I called you last week, you had told me that Department of Telecom has agreed to include 'Technology Neutrality' in the ToRs. However, you had expressed your disinclination to include 'Spectrum Pricing' in the ToRs.

3. This matter has been discussed at the level of the Finance Minister. It is our view that for optimum utilization of spectrum, a sound policy on spectrum pricing is necessary. The methodology to be followed for spectrum pricing would logically follow the vacation of spectrum which is the main task of the GoM.

4. I, therefore, request you to reconsider the matter and include spectrum pricing in the ToRs for the GoM. I shall be grateful for your reply at the earliest.

Best regards,

Yours sincerely,

**(D. SUBBARAO)**

1930/C/R2/07
8/6/07

***Secret***

Tel. : +91-11-2371 9898
Fax : +91-11-2371 1514
e-mail : dsmathur@nic.in

सत्यमेव जयते

**D. S. Mathur**
सचिव Secretary

भारत सरकार
संचार एवं सूचना प्रौद्योगिकी मंत्रालय
दूरसंचार विभाग
संचार भवन, नई दिल्ली-110 001
Government of India
Ministry of Communications & Information Technology
Department of Telecommunications
Sanchar Bhawan, New Delhi-110 001

DO No. L-14047/01/2006-NTG
June 15, 2007

Dear Dr. Subbarao,

Kindly refer to your DO letter No 3/11/2003-Inf dated June 6, 2007 regarding TOR for the Group of Ministers (GoM) on vacation of spectrum and raising resources for the same.

2. You may kindly recall that I had told you in the discussion referred to by you that we have always been technology neutral and this is therefore not an issue to be brought before the GOM.

3. As regards the issue of pricing of the spectrum, the then Minister of Communications & IT had written to the Hon'ble Prime Minister on January 11, 2006 that one major bottle-neck in the sustained growth of telecom sector is the availability of and not allocation of spectrum. The GOM should therefore focus its attention on the vacation of spectrum by the Defence and other agencies. The Minister had again written to the Hon'ble Prime Minister on Febrauary 28, 2006 that some of the Terms of Reference (TOR) impinge upon the work that is normally being carried out by this Ministry.

4. The revised draft of TOR was submitted by the Minister to the Hon'ble Prime Minister on November 16, 2006 and the final ToR was issued by the Cabinet Secretariat on December 7, 2006.

5. The spectrum pricing and charges for the use of the spectrum is a dynamic issue. It depends, inter-alia, on the region of use, the type of telecom service, the band of the spectrum used, etc. Hence, pricing of spectrum cannot be fixed for a long time to come at any stage. It is to be reviewed and considered from time to time in the context of the changing technology and international best practices in consultation with TRAI. As you are aware, TRAI is a statutory body.

6. The Telecom Regulatory Authority of India (TRAI) under its statutory provisions, provides recommendations on, among other matters, 'Efficient Management of available spectrum'. Appropriate pricing of spectrum is one of the important tools to ensure optimum & efficient use of the scarce resource. The Government has been consulting TRAI on several spectrum issues for different wireless based services / systems including new technologies. It may be mentioned that TRAI has recently given its recommendations on spectrum allotment & pricing of 3G services.

Contd....02/-

: 02 :

7. This matter was discussed in a meeting with Minister of Communications & IT and it was felt that the ToR may now remain as they were issued in December last year.

With regards,

Yours sincerely,

(D.S.Mathur)

Dr. D. Subbarao
Secretary
Department of Economic Affairs
Ministry of Finance, North Block
New Delhi

**By Regd. Post**

No.20-262(I)/2010-AS-I
Department of Telecommunications
(Access Services-I Section)
1203, Sanchar Bhawan, New Delhi.

February 25, 2011

To,

Shri Vivek Garg, Advocate
R/o 18/1, GF, Shakti Nagar,
Delhi – 110007.

**Subject: Application dated 12.01.2011 seeking information under RTI Act, 2005.**

With reference to your above mentioned application under RTI Act, 2005, the point-wise information are as under:

| Point No. | Information |
|---|---|
| 3, 5, 7 and 8 | UAS licences are granted as per Guidelines dated 14.12.2005 which does not prescribes the requirement of experience in telecom. 122 UAS licences were issued in year 2008. Company-wise list is enclosed at **Annexure-I.** Rs.9014.2405 crore was received as entry fee from these companies for the above said licences. The rate of entry fee paid by each company for the respective service area mentioned in annexure-I, is enclosed at **Annexure-II.** List of Address of the 17 companies, which were issued 122 UAS licences in 22 service areas in year 2008, is enclosed at **Annexure-III.** |
| 4 | 70 CMTS/UAS licences have been amended for uses of 3G spectrum for providing access services under the existing CMTS/UAS licences. Letters of amendments are available on the website of DoT viz. www.dot.gov.in. In case of any problem in getting a copy of aforementioned letters from the said website, you are requested to send an IPO/ DD of Rs.180/- (*@Rs.2/- per page for total of 90 pages document*) to enable us to send a copy of the same please. |
| 12 | Information sought does not relate to this public authority i.e. Department of Telecom. |
| 14, 39 | A copy each of the two letters dated 02.011.2007 & letter dated 26.12.2007 written by the then Hon'ble Minister of Communications & IT to Hon'ble Prime Minister in the relation of 2G spectrum allocation are enclose as **Annexure-IV to VI.** |
| 15, 17 to 23 | No such information is available in writing. |
| 16, 26, 39 | For seeking this information, PMO may be approached. |
| 25 | The related files are under the custody of CBI. As the matter is presently being investigated by CBI, this office is unable to provide the information sought as these are exempted under section 8(1)(e) & (h) of RTI Act as the same may impede the process of investigation. |

| | |
|---|---|
| **27** | The concerned public authority/ office may be approached for the requisite information. |
| **28** | Matter is under examination/ investigation by various agencies, such as Public Accounts Committee, CBI, etc. |
| **30** | Unified Access Services (UAS) licences are granted as per UAS guideline dated 14.12.2005 and copy of the said UASL guideline is available on the website 'www.dot.gov.in' of this Department. In case, a hard copy of the same is required, an amount of Rs.56/-{@Rs.2/- per page for total of 28 pages of the document} may be sent please. |
| **32, 34** | The terms & conditions of UAS Licence including the conditions of cancellation are available on the website 'www.dot.gov.in'. In case, a hard copy of the same is required, an amount of Rs.182/-(@Rs.@2/- per page for total of 91 pages of the document) may be sent please. |
| **36** | As per the provisions contained in the UAS licences agreement, the UAS licence is amended from time to time. Copies of which are available on the aforementioned website of DoT. |
| **24, 38** | The information sought seems to elicit the view of the CPIO in the matter which is not covered under the 'Right to Inforamtion Act' as per Section 2(j) of the Act. |
| **40** | The information sought pertain to office of C&AG. However, the report of C&AG on "Issue of Licences and Allocation of 2G Spectrum by the Department of Telecommunications" is available on the website of C&AG. |

The rest of the information sought pertaining to this public authority (DoT) are being transferred to various CPIOs as mentioned below for taking necessary action on the relevant points of the RTI Application.

Appeal, if any, against the above decision of the CPIO may be preferred, within thirty days of the receipt of this letter to 'Shri A.K. Mittal, DDG(AS) & Appellate Authority, Department of Telecommunications, Room No.1004, Sanchar Bhawan, 20, Ashoka Road, New Delhi'.

(R.K. Gupta)
Director (AS-I) & CPIO

**Copy to:**

1. Shri Jayant Kumar, Director (A), Room No.461, 4th Floor, Telecommunication Engineering Centre, Gate No.5, Khurshid Lal Bhawan, Janpath, New Delhi -01. TEC- for taking necessary action in r/o of Points **1 & 2** of the application.
2. Shri Rajiv Kumar, Director(AS-III), Room No.907, Sanchar Bhawan, New Delhi – for taking necessary action in r/o of Point **11** of the application.
3. Shri S.K. Singhal, Director(AS-IV) – Room No.1202, Sanchar Bhawan, New Delhi – for taking necessary action in r/o of Points **9, 10, 11 & 13** of the application.
4. Shri Rajiv Prakash, Director (WR)/Director (Finance) & CPIO- for taking necessary action in r/o of Points **6, 7 & 29** of the application.
5. Shri M.K. Rao, DWA & CPIO, WPC wing, 6th Floor, Sanchar Bhawan, New Delhi –in respect of information related to 3G as sought vide Points **14** to **23, 25** to **28, 31, 33, 35, 37** to **40** of the application.

ANNEXURE-I

## Company wise List of 122 UAS licences granted in 2008

| S. No. | Name of Licensee Company | Service Area | Effective Date of Licence |
|---|---|---|---|
| 1 | Etisalat DB Telecom Pvt. Ltd. | Andhra Pradesh | 25-Jan-2008 |
| 2 | Etisalat DB Telecom Pvt. Ltd. | Delhi | 25-Jan-2008 |
| 3 | Etisalat DB Telecom Pvt. Ltd. | Gujarat | 25-Jan-2008 |
| 4 | Etisalat DB Telecom Pvt. Ltd. | Haryana | 25-Jan-2008 |
| 5 | Etisalat DB Telecom Pvt. Ltd. | Karnataka | 25-Jan-2008 |
| 6 | Etisalat DB Telecom Pvt. Ltd. | Kerala | 25-Jan-2008 |
| 7 | Etisalat DB Telecom Pvt. Ltd. | Maharashtra | 25-Jan-2008 |
| 8 | Etisalat DB Telecom Pvt. Ltd. | Mumbai | 25-Jan-2008 |
| 9 | Etisalat DB Telecom Pvt. Ltd. | Punjab | 25-Jan-2008 |
| 10 | Etisalat DB Telecom Pvt. Ltd. | Rajasthan | 25-Jan-2008 |
| 11 | Etisalat DB Telecom Pvt. Ltd. | Tamilnadu (including Chennai Service Area) | 25-Jan-2008 |
| 12 | Etisalat DB Telecom Pvt. Ltd. | Uttar Pradesh (East) | 25-Jan-2008 |
| 13 | Etisalat DB Telecom Pvt. Ltd. | Uttar Pradesh (West) | 25-Jan-2008 |
| 14 | Idea Cellular Ltd. | Assam | 25-Jan-2008 |
| 15 | Idea Cellular Ltd. | Jammu & Kashmir | 25-Jan-2008 |
| 16 | Idea Cellular Ltd. | Karnataka | 25-Jan-2008 |
| 17 | Idea Cellular Ltd. | Kolkata | 25-Jan-2008 |
| 18 | Idea Cellular Ltd. | North East | 25-Jan-2008 |
| 19 | Idea Cellular Ltd. | Orissa | 25-Jan-2008 |
| 20 | Idea Cellular Ltd. | Punjab | 25-Jan-2008 |
| 21 | Idea Cellular Ltd. | Tamilnadu (including Chennai Service Area) | 25-Jan-2008 |
| 22 | Idea Cellular Ltd. | West Bengal | 25-Jan-2008 |
| 23 | Loop Telecom Ltd. | Andhra Pradesh | 25-Jan-2008 |
| 24 | Loop Telecom Ltd. | Assam | 25-Jan-2008 |
| 25 | Loop Telecom Ltd. | Bihar | 25-Jan-2008 |
| 26 | Loop Telecom Ltd. | Delhi | 25-Jan-2008 |
| 27 | Loop Telecom Ltd. | Gujarat | 25-Jan-2008 |
| 28 | Loop Telecom Ltd. | Haryana | 25-Jan-2008 |
| 29 | Loop Telecom Ltd. | Himachal Pradesh | 25-Jan-2008 |
| 30 | Loop Telecom Ltd. | Jammu & Kashmir | 25-Jan-2008 |
| 31 | Loop Telecom Ltd. | Karnataka | 25-Jan-2008 |
| 32 | Loop Telecom Ltd. | Kerala | 25-Jan-2008 |
| 33 | Loop Telecom Ltd. | Kolkata | 25-Jan-2008 |
| 34 | Loop Telecom Ltd. | Madhya Pradesh | 25-Jan-2008 |
| 35 | Loop Telecom Ltd. | Maharashtra | 25-Jan-2008 |
| 36 | Loop Telecom Ltd. | North East | 25-Jan-2008 |
| 37 | Loop Telecom Ltd. | Orissa | 25-Jan-2008 |
| 38 | Loop Telecom Ltd. | Punjab | 25-Jan-2008 |
| 39 | Loop Telecom Ltd. | Rajasthan | 25-Jan-2008 |
| 40 | Loop Telecom Ltd. | Tamilnadu (including Chennai Service Area) | 25-Jan-2008 |
| 41 | Loop Telecom Ltd. | Uttar Pradesh (East) | 25-Jan-2008 |
| 42 | Loop Telecom Ltd. | Uttar Pradesh (West) | 25-Jan-2008 |
| 43 | Loop Telecom Ltd. | West Bengal | 25-Jan-2008 |
| 44 | S Tel Pvt. Ltd. | Assam | 25-Jan-2008 |
| 45 | S Tel Pvt. Ltd. | Bihar | 25-Jan-2008 |
| 46 | S Tel Pvt. Ltd. | Himachal Pradesh | 25-Jan-2008 |
| 47 | S Tel Pvt. Ltd. | Jammu & Kashmir | 25-Jan-2008 |
| 48 | S Tel Pvt. Ltd. | North East | 25-Jan-2008 |
| 49 | S Tel Pvt. Ltd. | Orissa | 25-Jan-2008 |
| 50 | Sistema Shyam TeleServices Ltd. | Andhra Pradesh | 25-Jan-2008 |
| 51 | Sistema Shyam TeleServices Ltd. | Assam | 25-Jan-2008 |
| 52 | Sistema Shyam TeleServices Ltd. | Bihar | 25-Jan-2008 |

| S. No. | Name of Licensee Company | Service Area | Effective Date of Licence |
|---|---|---|---|
| 53 | Sistema Shyam TeleServices Ltd. | Delhi | 25-Jan-2008 |
| 54 | Sistema Shyam TeleServices Ltd. | Gujarat | 25-Jan-2008 |
| 55 | Sistema Shyam TeleServices Ltd. | Haryana | 25-Jan-2008 |
| 56 | Sistema Shyam TeleServices Ltd. | Himachal Pradesh | 25-Jan-2008 |
| 57 | Sistema Shyam TeleServices Ltd. | Jammu & Kashmir | 25-Jan-2008 |
| 58 | Sistema Shyam TeleServices Ltd. | Karnataka | 25-Jan-2008 |
| 59 | Sistema Shyam TeleServices Ltd. | Kerala | 25-Jan-2008 |
| 60 | Sistema Shyam TeleServices Ltd. | Kolkata | 25-Jan-2008 |
| 61 | Sistema Shyam TeleServices Ltd. | Madhya Pradesh | 25-Jan-2008 |
| 62 | Sistema Shyam TeleServices Ltd. | Maharashtra | 25-Jan-2008 |
| 63 | Sistema Shyam TeleServices Ltd. | Mumbai | 25-Jan-2008 |
| 64 | Sistema Shyam TeleServices Ltd. | North East | 25-Jan-2008 |
| 65 | Sistema Shyam TeleServices Ltd. | Orissa | 25-Jan-2008 |
| 66 | Sistema Shyam TeleServices Ltd. | Punjab | 25-Jan-2008 |
| 67 | Sistema Shyam TeleServices Ltd. | Tamilnadu (including Chennai Service Area) | 25-Jan-2008 |
| 68 | Sistema Shyam TeleServices Ltd. | Uttar Pradesh (East) | 25-Jan-2008 |
| 69 | Sistema Shyam TeleServices Ltd. | Uttar Pradesh (West) | 25-Jan-2008 |
| 70 | Sistema Shyam TeleServices Ltd. | West Bengal | 25-Jan-2008 |
| 71 | Spice Communications Ltd. | Andhra Pradesh | 25-Jan-2008 |
| 72 | Spice Communications Ltd. | Delhi | 25-Jan-2008 |
| 73 | Spice Communications Ltd. | Haryana | 25-Jan-2008 |
| 74 | Spice Communications Ltd. | Maharashtra | 25-Jan-2008 |
| 75 | Tata Teleservices Ltd. | Assam | 25-Jan-2008 |
| 76 | Tata Teleservices Ltd. | Jammu & Kashmir | 25-Jan-2008 |
| 77 | Tata Teleservices Ltd. | North East | 25-Jan-2008 |
| 78 | Unitech Wireless (Delhi) Pvt.Ltd. | Delhi | 25-Jan-2008 |
| 79 | Unitech Wireless (East) Pvt. Ltd. | Assam | 25-Jan-2008 |
| 80 | Unitech Wireless (East) Pvt. Ltd. | Bihar | 25-Jan-2008 |
| 81 | Unitech Wireless (East) Pvt. Ltd. | North East | 25-Jan-2008 |
| 82 | Unitech Wireless (East) Pvt. Ltd. | Orissa | 25-Jan-2008 |
| 83 | Unitech Wireless (East) Pvt. Ltd. | Uttar Pradesh (East) | 25-Jan-2008 |
| 84 | Unitech Wireless (East) Pvt. Ltd. | West Bengal | 25-Jan-2008 |
| 85 | Unitech Wireless (Kolkata) Pvt. Ltd. | Kolkata | 25-Jan-2008 |
| 86 | Unitech Wireless (Mumbai) Pvt. Ltd. | Mumbai | 25-Jan-2008 |
| 87 | Unitech Wireless (North) Pvt. Ltd. | Haryana | 25-Jan-2008 |
| 88 | Unitech Wireless (North) Pvt. Ltd. | Himachal Pradesh | 25-Jan-2008 |
| 89 | Unitech Wireless (North) Pvt. Ltd. | Jammu & Kashmir | 25-Jan-2008 |
| 90 | Unitech Wireless (North) Pvt. Ltd. | Punjab | 25-Jan-2008 |
| 91 | Unitech Wireless (North) Pvt. Ltd. | Rajasthan | 25-Jan-2008 |
| 92 | Unitech Wireless (North) Pvt. Ltd. | Uttar Pradesh (West) | 25-Jan-2008 |
| 93 | Unitech Wireless (South) Pvt. Ltd. | Andhra Pradesh | 25-Jan-2008 |
| 94 | Unitech Wireless (South) Pvt. Ltd. | Karnataka | 25-Jan-2008 |
| 95 | Unitech Wireless (South) Pvt. Ltd. | Kerala | 25-Jan-2008 |
| 96 | Unitech Wireless (Tamil Nadu) Pvt. Ltd. | Tamilnadu (including Chennai Service Area) | 25-Jan-2008 |
| 97 | Unitech Wireless (West) Pvt. Ltd. | Gujarat | 25-Jan-2008 |
| 98 | Unitech Wireless (West) Pvt. Ltd. | Madhya Pradesh | 25-Jan-2008 |
| 99 | Unitech Wireless (West) Pvt. Ltd. | Maharashtra | 25-Jan-2008 |
| 100 | Videocon Telecommunications Ltd. | Andhra Pradesh | 25-Jan-2008 |
| 101 | Videocon Telecommunications Ltd. | Assam | 25-Jan-2008 |
| 102 | Videocon Telecommunications Ltd. | Bihar | 25-Jan-2008 |
| 103 | Videocon Telecommunications Ltd. | Delhi | 25-Jan-2008 |
| 104 | Videocon Telecommunications Ltd. | Gujarat | 25-Jan-2008 |
| 105 | Videocon Telecommunications Ltd. | Haryana | 25-Jan-2008 |

Page 2 of 3

| S. No. | Name of Licensee Company | Service Area | Effective Date of Licence |
|---|---|---|---|
| 106 | Videocon Telecommunications Ltd. | Himachal Pradesh | 25-Jan-2008 |
| 107 | Videocon Telecommunications Ltd. | Jammu & Kashmir | 25-Jan-2008 |
| 108 | Videocon Telecommunications Ltd. | Karnataka | 25-Jan-2008 |
| 109 | Videocon Telecommunications Ltd. | Kerala | 25-Jan-2008 |
| 110 | Videocon Telecommunications Ltd. | Kolkata | 25-Jan-2008 |
| 111 | Videocon Telecommunications Ltd. | Madhya Pradesh | 25-Jan-2008 |
| 112 | Videocon Telecommunications Ltd. | Maharashtra | 25-Jan-2008 |
| 113 | Videocon Telecommunications Ltd. | Mumbai | 25-Jan-2008 |
| 114 | Videocon Telecommunications Ltd. | North East | 25-Jan-2008 |
| 115 | Videocon Telecommunications Ltd. | Orissa | 25-Jan-2008 |
| 116 | Videocon Telecommunications Ltd. | Rajasthan | 25-Jan-2008 |
| 117 | Videocon Telecommunications Ltd. | Tamilnadu (including Chennai Service Area) | 25-Jan-2008 |
| 118 | Videocon Telecommunications Ltd. | Uttar Pradesh (East) | 25-Jan-2008 |
| 119 | Videocon Telecommunications Ltd. | Uttar Pradesh (West) | 25-Jan-2008 |
| 120 | Videocon Telecommunications Ltd. | West Bengal | 25-Jan-2008 |
| 121 | Allianz Infratech (P) Ltd. | Bihar | 31-Jul-2008 |
| 122 | Allianz Infratech (P) Ltd. | Madhya Pradesh | 31-Jul-2008 |

सत्यमेव जयते

ஆ. இராசா
ए. राजा
A. RAJA

मंत्री
संचार एवं सूचना प्रौद्योगिकी
भारत सरकार,
इलेक्ट्रॉनिक्स निकेतन, 6, सी.जी.ओ. कॉम्प्लेक्स,
नई दिल्ली-110 003

MINISTER
COMMUNICATIONS & INFORMATION TECHNOLOGY,
GOVERNMENT OF INDIA,
ELECTRONICS NIKETAN, 6, C.G.O. COMPLEX,
NEW DELHI-110 003

D.O. No.L-14047/01/2006-NTG

Respected Sir, Vanakkam.

As you are aware, a Group of Ministers (GoM) on vacation of spectrum and raising resources for the purpose, under the chairmanship of Thiru. Pranab Mukherjee, Minister of External Affairs, has been constituted.

Today, India has almost 220 million telephone subscribers with a teledensity around 20%, making it the third largest network in the world. The Government recognizes that wireless is the fastest and most cost effective way of connecting rural India, with more than 90% of additions in telephone connections coming in the wireless/mobile segment. The demand on spectrum is growing exponentially with increase in subscriber base. We have the ambitious target of reaching 500 million subscribers by 2010. We need adequate availability of spectrum to fuel this envisaged growth.

Spectrum inadequacy will not only hamper the growth but also adversely affect the quality of service. The spectrum congestion is already hampering telecom operators in their bid to expand network and consumer base.

In this context, an assessment of the actual usage of spectrum by different organizations has been made by Wireless Planning and Coordination (WPC) Wing of my Ministry, which is the national spectrum management agency. They are reconciling this spectrum usage with these organizations. This process is expected to take some more time.

Contd...P/2..

-:: 02 ::-

Further, as a result of detailed discussions between the Ministry of Defence and my Ministry, a Project was conceived to provide alternative communication network, based on Optical Fibre Cable (OFC) capacity for some of the wireless communication links (between fixed locations) of the Defence services. With the implementation of the first phase of this Project for Indian Air Force, it is estimated that upto about 40-42 MHz of spectrum can be released from Defence links for mobile telephony services. The first phase is expected to be completed by August, 2007. Part of this spectrum released from Defence (Air Force), will enable allotment of additional spectrum for the growth of mobile telephony services by the existing operators.

Also, regarding spectrum for Broadband Wireless Access (BWA), discussions are in progress with the Department of Space, as part of the concerned spectrum is shared by terrestrial and satellite based services. Trials for Electro-Magnetic Interference (EMI) and Electro-Magnetic Compatibility (EMC) between terrestrial and satellite based application are also in progress.

I feel that the GoM would be able to deliberate on the issue relating to vacation of spectrum by various organizations in a more meaningful manner after the reconciliation of spectrum usage with them has been completed to a large extent. Hence, I propose to request the Chairman of the GoM, Thiru. Pranab Mukherjee, Minister of External Affairs to kindly defer the meeting of the GoM till that time.

I hope that you would kindly concur with this proposal.

With regards,

Yours sincerely,

(A. RAJA)

Dr. Manmohan Singh
Hon'ble Prime Minister of India,
South Block,
New Delhi - 110 011

- GOM was set up in 2006 to recommend measures for vacation of spectrum by existing users for growth of mobile telephony and broadband sectors.

- Mobile telephony (GSM) works on 900 MHZ (890-915 and 935-960 MHz) and 1800 MHz bands (1710-1785 and 1805-1880 MHz) worldwide. These bands cannot be changed due to availability of equipments and their usage globally.

- In case we go for some different band, India may not get economical handsets and also make international roaming difficult. Therefore, it is proposed to expand GSM in these bands only.

- The present ongoing Optical Fibre Cable (OFC) Network Project for Ministry of Defence will help in release of about 20 MHz (out of total 42.5 MHz with Air Force) spectrum in 1800 MHz band, which could be used for expansion of 2G mobile services.

- The remaining 20-22 MHz will be released by Air Force in 2100 MHz band which will be used for 3G services.

- Of the remaining about 40 MHz in 1800 MHz band, Ministry of Defence is using less that 30 MHz spread across the country.

- An exercise is being made by the WPC Wing of the Ministry to ascertain exact usage by the Ministry of Defence.

- The meeting of GOM will be useful once exact usage is recognized with the Ministry of Defence.

- Therefore, it is proposed to hold first GOM meeting after this information is finalised, which may take about three months.

அ. இராசா
ए. राजा
**A. RAJA**

सत्यमेव जयते

मंत्री
संचार एवं सूचना प्रौद्योगिकी
भारत सरकार,
इलैक्ट्रॉनिक्स निकेतन, 6, सी.जी.ओ. कॉम्प्लेक्स,
नई दिल्ली-110003

MINISTER
COMMUNICATIONS & INFORMATION TECHNOLOGY
GOVERNMENT OF INDIA,
ELECTRONICS NIKETAN, 6, C.G.O. COMPLEX,
NEW DELHI-110 003

D.O.No.L-14047/01/2006-NTG

09 AUG 2007

Respected Sir,

This is further to my letter of 20th June, 2007 regarding the Group of Ministers (GoM) on vacation of spectrum and raising resources for the purpose, under your esteemed Chairmanship.

One of the salient issues indicated by me then was the on-going reconciliation by WPC Wing of my Minister with Defence Services, of their spectrum usage in 1700-2000 MHz band (overlapping GSM 1800 MHz band and 1920-1980 MHz sub-band for 3G IMT-2000). The WPC Wing has exchanged many letters with Joint Communications & Electronic Staff (JCES), Ministry of Defence which coordinates the spectrum requirements of Defence Services; and the WPC Wing has also held discussion with them. However, every time JCES have brought up new issues.

One of the issues raised by JCES last time was regarding use of frequency band 1735-1775 MHz, upto 100 Kms along the border, based on WPC Wing general letter of agreement in 1997, which also requested them to provide details of proposed actual usage within 3 years (i.e. by 2000). However, they had not indicated any firm usage plan and hence the general letter of agreement of 1997 is no more valid. This has been conveyed to JCES, MOD by WPC Wing.

Another issue is regarding spectrum usage (and consequential vacation) by Air Force and Army. As indicated in my earlier letter, an alternative communication network based on Optical Fibre Cable capacity is being created through BSNL and MTNL. With the completion of the part relating to Air Force, it should be possible for Air Force to close the concerned wireless links, which should release a substantial portion of the spectrum requirement in GSM 1800 MHz band and 1920-1980 MHz sub-band for 3G IMT-2000. However, recently the MOD has written that even the Air Force would be able to vacate spectrum, only when complete alternate network (for Army, Air Force and Navy) is in place. It is worth mentioning

: 2 :

that frequencies for the concerned defence wireless network were authorised in phases and hence as a pragmatic approach, it should be possible to release the same in phases as the alternative network is build up.

As you are aware, there is urgency for vacation of spectrum by Defence so as to finalise and announce guidelines for introduction of 3G technology in the country as well as for additional spectrum for existing 2G services.

I discussed this issue with Thiru Pranab Mukherjee, Hon'ble Minister of External Affairs and Chairman, GoM on Vacation of Spectrum and he has desired that a meeting could be convened under his Chairmanship where Thiru A.K. Antony, Hon'ble Defence Minister and myself are present with concerned officers to sort out the issue before convening meeting of GOM.

With regards,

Yours sincerely,

(A.Raja)

**Dr. Manmohan Singh,**
Hon'ble Prime Minister of India,
South Block,
**New Delhi - 110 011.**

सत्यमेव जयते

प्रधान मंत्री

Prime Minister

New Delhi
August 15, 2007

Dear Shri Raja,

I have received your D.O. letters No. I-14047/01/2006-NTG dated nil and 9.8.2007 regarding the Group of Ministers constituted to go into issues concerning vacation of spectrum and raising resources for the purpose. The Group of Ministers was formed in February 2006 and is yet to meet. As you are well aware, there has been much public debate emphasizing the need of making spectrum available to mobile telephone service operators for the existing 2G services in the country as well as the proposed commencement of 3G services, so that the continued growth of the telecom sector is ensured. Therefore, it is essential that the Group of Ministers meets at the earliest and resolves spectrum vacation related issues.

Against this background, I would urge you to have a meeting of the Group of Ministers convened before 25th August 2007 and to ensure that all matters are resolved within a month of the first meeting.

I am also writing separately to the Minister of External Affairs in this regard.

Yours sincerely,

Manmohan Singh
(Manmohan Singh)

Shri A. Raja
Minister of Communications and Information Technology,
New Delhi

ஆ. இராசா
ए. राजा
**A. RAJA**

मंत्री
संचार एवं सूचना प्रौद्योगिकी
भारत सरकार,
इलैक्ट्रॉनिक्स निकेतन, 6, सी.जी.ओ. कॉम्प्लेक्स,
नई दिल्ली-110 003

**MINISTER**
**COMMUNICATIONS & INFORMATION TECHNOLOGY,**
**GOVERNMENT OF INDIA,**
**ELECTRONICS NIKETAN, 6, C.G.O. COMPLEX,**
**NEW DELHI-110 003**

D.O.No.L-14047/01/2006-NTG

16 AUG 2007

Respected Sir, Pradhan Mantri ji,

I have received your D.O. letter dated August 15. 2007 regarding the meeting of Group of Ministers concerning vacation of spectrum and raising resources for the purpose.

Telecom sector in our country is growing at an unprecedented pace. The addition of new subscribers to the subscriber base in the last month was 7.3 million. Since most of the growth is taking place in the mobile sector, the pressure on spectrum is also growing substantially.

I had requested Shri Pranab Mukherjee for an informal meeting with Shri A.K. Antony, Defence Minister so that certain involved issues regarding the vacation of spectrum could be addressed and consensus could be reached in finding solutions to them. My meeting with Shri Mukherjee and Shri Antony is going to take place on August 20, 2007. We can have a formal meeting of the Group of Ministers after this meeting, as you suggested.

With regards,

Yours sincerely,

(A.Raja)

**Dr. Manmohan Singh,**
Hon'ble Prime Minister of India,
South Block,
**New Delhi - 110 011.**

ஆ. இராசா
ए. राजा
A. RAJA

सत्यमेव जयते

मंत्री
संचार एवं सूचना प्रौद्योगिकी
भारत सरकार,
इलेक्ट्रॉनिक्स निकेतन, 6, सी.जी.ओ. कॉम्प्लेक्स,
नई दिल्ली-110 003

MINISTER
COMMUNICATIONS & INFORMATION TECHNOLOGY,
GOVERNMENT OF INDIA,
ELECTRONICS NIKETAN, 6, C.G.O. COMPLEX,
NEW DELHI-110 003

D.O. No.20-100/2007-AS.I
Dated 2nd November 2007.

Respected Sir,

After the announcement of TRAI Recommendations on Review of Licence Terms and Conditions for (Telecom) Access Service Providers on 28th August, 2007, an unprecedented number of applications were being received by the Department due to Recommendation of TRAI recommending " No Cap" on number of Licences in a Service Area.

2. As unprecedented number of applications were being received, a cut-off date of 1st October, 2007 was announced by the Department on 24th September, 2007 and a Press Release was given. In all 575 applications for 22 Service Areas were received.

3. The Department wanted to examine the possibility of any other procedure in addition to the current procedure of allotment of Licences to process the huge number of applications. A few alternative procedures as debated in the Department and also opined by few legal experts were suggested by the Department of Telecom to Ministry of Law & Justice to examine its legal tenability to avoid future legal complications, if any. Ministry of Law and Justice, instead of examining the legal tenability of these alternative procedures, suggested referring the matter to empowered Group of Ministers. Since, generally new major policy decisions of a Department or inter-departmental issues are referred to GOM, and, needless to say that the present issue relates to procedures, the suggestion of Law Ministry is totally out of context.

4. Now, the Department has decided to continue with the existing policy (first-cum-first-served) for processing of applications received up to 25th September 2007, i. e. the date when the news-item on announcement of cut-off date appeared in the newspapers. The procedure for processing the remaining applications will be decided at a later date, if any spectrum is left available after processing the applications received up to 25th September 2007.

4. As the Department is not deviating from the existing procedure, I hope this will satisfy the Industry.

5. You will appreciate that I am writing this letter to apprise you about the latest developments in the Department.

I take this occasion to extend my warm Diwali Greetings.

With regards,

Yours sincerely,

(A. RAJA)

Dr. Manmohan Singh,
Prime Minister of India,
New Delhi.

ஆ. இராசா
ए. राजा
A. RAJA

सत्यमेव जयते

मंत्री
संचार एवं सूचना प्रौद्योगिकी
भारत सरकार,
इलैक्ट्रॉनिक्स निकेतन, 6, सी.जी.ओ. कॉम्प्लेक्स,
नई दिल्ली-110 003

**MINISTER**
**COMMUNICATIONS & INFORMATION TECHNOLOGY,**
**GOVERNMENT OF INDIA,**
**ELECTRONICS NIKETAN, 6, C.G.O. COMPLEX,**
**NEW DELHI-110 003**

D.O. No. 20-100/2007-AS.I
**2nd November, 2007.**

Respected Sir, Vanakkam.

Kindly refer to your letter dated 2.11.2007 regarding various issues related to Telecom sector. In this regard I have already written to you a letter earlier today (copy enclosed) clarifying the position on processing of large number of applications received for fresh licences. Before giving clarifications to the averments contained in the Annexure to your letter, I would like to inform you that there was, and is, no single deviation or departure in the rules and procedures contemplated, in all the decisions taken by my Ministry and as such full transparency is being maintained by my Ministry and I further assure you the same in future also.

Clarifications with respect to other issues are as follows:

1. **<u>Enhancement of subscriber linked spectrum allocation criteria</u>**

TRAI had recommended in August 2007, enhancement in subscriber linked criteria for allotment of additional spectrum to existing operators in order to increase spectrum efficiency which is scarce. Independent to this, Telecom Engineering Centre (TEC), which is the competent body to look into such matter, was asked to examine the spectrum efficiency issues scientifically. TEC submitted its recommendations on 26.10.2007, which was in principle accepted by me. It has been placed on the website of the Ministry and therefore, anybody much less COAI is at liberty to challenge the report of TEC with scientific basis. **However, the fact still remains that no such attempts have been honestly made by them.**

.....2/-

-2-

2. **<u>Permission to CDMA service providers to also provide services on the GSM standard and be eligible for spectrum in the GSM service band</u>**

This matter was referred to TRAI for its comments on use of dual technology. TRAI, after due deliberations on the issue, recommended use of dual technology, enabling existing Universal Access Service licensees (USAL) to provide services under both (GSM and CDMA) technologies. It was examined in the Ministry and was agreed to as they will be able to rollout the network fast which will ultimately benefit the customers because of increase in teledensity and also resulting lower tariff. **These operators will get spectrum only after the allotment of spectrum to the existing operators according to their eligibility and also licence holders awaiting for initial spectrum.**

3. **<u>Processing of a large number of applications received for fresh licenses against the backdrop of inadequate spectrum to cater to overall demand</u>**

The issue of auction of spectrum was considered by the TRAI and the Telecom Commission and was not recommended as the existing licence holders who are already having spectrum upto 10 MHz per Circle **have got it without any spectrum charge**. It will be unfair, discriminatory, arbitrary and capricious to auction the spectrum to new applicants as it will not give them level playing field.

I would like to bring it to your notice that DoT has earmarked totally 100 MHz in 900 MHz and 1800 MHz bands for 2G mobile services. Out of this, so for a maximum of about 35 to 40 MHz per Circle has been allotted to different operators and being used by them. The remaining 60 to 65 MHz, including spectrum likely to be vacated by Defence Services, is still available for 2G services.

Therefore, there is enough scope for allotment of spectrum to few new operators even after meeting the requirements of existing operators and licensees. An increase in number of operators will certainly bring real competition which will lead to better services

......3/-

-3-

and increased teledensity at lower tariff. **Waiting for spectrum for long after getting licence is not unknown to the Industry and even at present Aircel, Vodafone, Idea and Dishnet are waiting for initial spectrum in some Circles since December 2006.**

I would like to bring to your kind notice that M/s Aircel and M/s Spice Telecom, who were party to the petition to the TDSAT challenging DoT orders on acceptance of TRAI recommendations, have disassociated with the petition after having clarifications from me. These operators have openly admitted that the COAI had misled them, media and the public in general.

Since assuming charge, on more than three occasions I have reviewed all the long pending TRAI recommendations **announced during the tenures of my predecessors** including Number Portability, 3G, Wimax etc. and directed my officers to process them in a transparent manner. As a result we are almost reaching to shape the modalities to auction 3G and Wimax as contemplated by TRAI. I am told that divergence of views on implementation of Number Portability have been expressed by various stakeholders and I am trying to resolve it. The final decision on all these recommendations will be taken soon.

To conclude, I would like to assure you that all my decisions and endeavours are honestly aimed at development of the telecom sector, increasing the teledensity and lowering the tariff for the benefit of the public in general and customers in particular.

With regards,

Yours sincerely,

**(A.RAJA)**

**Dr. Manmohan Singh**
Hon'ble Prime Minister of India
7, Race Course Road
New Delhi.

आ. इराजा
ए. राजा
A. RAJA

सत्यमेव जयते

मंत्री
संचार एवं सूचना प्रौद्योगिकी
भारत सरकार,
इलैक्ट्रॉनिक्स निकेतन, 6, सी.जी.ओ. कॉम्प्लेक्स,
नई दिल्ली-110 003
MINISTER
COMMUNICATIONS & INFORMATION TECHNOLOGY,
GOVERNMENT OF INDIA,
ELECTRONICS NIKETAN, 6, C.G.O. COMPLEX,
NEW DELHI-110 003

**D.O. No. 260/M(C&IT)/VIP/2007**

26th December, 2007.

Respected Sir, Vanakkam.

Kindly refer to my letters dated 2.11.2007, and subsequent personal discussions with you on various issues related to Telecom sector. As discussed with you I also had several discussions with the External Affairs Minister, who is also heading GOM on vacation of spectrum on these issues. The major issues viz., (i) Subscriber based criteria for additional spectrum to existing operators; (ii) issue of dual technology; and (iii) issue of new licences were discussed with External Affairs Minister at length. Since the cases filed by Cellular Operators Association of India (COAI) on these issues before Telecom Disputes Settlement & Appellate Tribunal (TDSAT) and Delhi High Court are being represented by Solicitor General of India, he was also called for the discussions to explain the legal position.

I must recall that there are three reports available with the DoT with regard to subscriber based criteria for additional spectrum to existing operators viz., Telecom Regulatory Authority of India (TRAI), Telecom Engineering Centre (TEC) and the Report of the Committee which was constituted under the chairmanship of Additional Secretary, DoT with two Professors from IIT, Kanpur and IIT, Chennai who have done their specialisation in Radio Frequency. For one or the other flimsy reason, COAI neither accepted any one of the report nor co-operated with the DOT to arrive at an amicable solution. Similarly, on use of Dual Technology also, they want to challenge the policy decision taken by the Government on the basis of TRAI recommendations.

Since TDSAT refused to grant stay they moved the Delhi High Court for stay on subscriber based criteria, dual technology and in addition to these, the issue of new licences. This clearly shows that the attitude of COAI is to maintain their monopoly in the sector by avoiding healthy competition and level playing field. The only malicious intention of COAI, it appears, is that they want to procrastinate the issues through frivolous and vexacious Court proceedings endlessly.

.......2/-

-2-

As I have already promised to you, my efforts in this sector are intended to give lower tariff to the consumer and to bring higher tele-density in the country, more specifically in rural areas. It is needless to say that the tariff in India is not as cheap as claimed in terms of purchasing power parity and standard of living of the people of the country since there is no tariff fixation.

In these circumstances, the discussions with the External Affairs Minister and Solicitor General of India have further enlightened me to take a pre-emptive and pro-active decision on these issues as per the guidelines and rules framed there under to avoid any further confusions and delay. The issue wise details and my decisions are given in the enclosed annexure.

This is for your kind information.

With regards,

Yours sincerely,

(A.RAJA)

**Dr. Manmohan Singh**
Hon'ble Prime Minister of India
New Delhi.

Encl: Annexure

**Annexure**

1. **Subscriber Linked Spectrum Allocation Criterion for CMTS/UAS Licensees**

DOT provides Radio spectrum for providing mobile services to Wireless Operating Licence holders for roll out of GSM / CDMA services. An initial spectrum of 4.4 MHz for GSM and 2.5 MHz for CDMA based technology is provided to operators. Additional spectrum is provided to operators based on the number of subscribers, availability of spectrum, optimal use of spectrum, competition and other interest of public. To ensure optimal utilization of spectrum, TRAI while giving recommendation on other issues as requested by the DOT, also recommended that **"there is a need to tighten the subscriber criteria for all the service areas so as to make it more efficient from the usage and pricing point of view. In order to frame new spectrum allocation criteria, a multi-disciplinary committee may be constituted. However, it is necessary to enhance the present subscriber norms as an ad-hoc measure so that the task of spectrum allocation is not stalled"**. This recommendation was accepted by the department on 17-10-2007.

However, COAI and existing GSM operators challenged recommendations of TRAI saying it lacks scientific basis. In the meantime, TEC which was simultaneously working on the subscriber based criteria for allocation of additional spectrum submitted its report to the Ministry which was accepted in-principal. Incidentally, TEC norms, which were based on scientific basis, came out to be stricter than TRAI norms. COAI challenged these reports in the TDSAT. To avoid any controversy and to find an amicable solution, as suggested by TRAI a Committee headed by Additional Secretary, DOT, including Representatives of COAI and AUSPI and two Professors from IIT Kanpur and IIT Chennai was setup. However, on 7-12-2007, COAI disassociated itself from the proceedings of the Committee. The committee has submitted its report and has suggested that another Committee as suggested by TRAI may be set up to look into broader issues of allotment of additional spectrum and till then recommended to go with TRAI's interim report for allotment of additional spectrum. This recommendation of the Committee is accepted.

**In view of above, DOT is proceeding ahead to implement the recommendation of TRAI on subscriber based criteria as an interim measure and allot additional spectrum to eligible existing operators as per TRAI norm, followed by those who got licence in Dec 2006, dual technology and to new applicants as and when licences are given. An affidavit to this effect will be filled in both TDSAT and Delhi High Court.**

2. **Use of Dual Spectrum (Alternate technology) by UAS Licensees**

DOT sought the recommendations of TRAI on Use of Dual Technology / Alternate Technology under USA License and other issues on 13-4-2007( prior to taking over by the present Minister). The recommendations of TRAI were received by DOT on 29-08-2007 which suggested that **"A licensee using one technology may be permitted on request, usage of alternative technology and thus allocation of dual spectrum. However, such a licensee must pay the same amount of fee which has been paid by existing licensees using the alternative technology or which would be paid by a new licensee going to use that technology"**. This recommendation was accepted by the department on 17-10-2007.

This policy makes existing UAS Licence holders (Reliance, TATA, Airtel, Vodafone, etc.) eligible for allotment of spectrum for alternate technology. COAI challenged Dual technology policy in the TDSAT. TDSAT has adjourned the case to 09-01-2008. Failing obtaining stay from TDSAT, COAI moved to Delhi high court on 20-12-2007. The matter was heard on 24-12-2007 and is posted for 3-1-2008 without granting any stay.

**In view of above, DOT is proceeding ahead for allotting initial spectrum under dual technology policy to eligible applicants subject to the court order, if any. Application of TATA Telecommunication will also be processed as per the policy and guidelines. An affidavit to this effect will be filled in both TDSAT and Delhi High Court.**

3. **Issue of New Licences**

Although UASL guidelines issued in December 2005 clearly indicates that **"Licences shall be issued without any restriction on the number of entrants for provision of Unified Acess Services in a service Area"**, DOT sought recommendation of TRAI on number of UAS licences to be issued in a Service Area on 13-4-2007( prior to taking over by the present Minister). The recommendations of TRAI were received by DOT on 29-08-2007 which suggested that **"No Cap be placed on the number of access service providers in any Service Area"**. This recommendation was accepted by the department on 17-10-2007 in order to encourage more competition in the Telecom Sector and decided to grant new UAS Licences. This is first time that December 2005 UASL guidelines are being implemented in letter and spirit in view of TRAI recommendation.

DOT has been implementing a policy of First-cum-First Served for grant of UAS licences. The same policy is proposed to be implemented in granting licence to existing applicants. However, it may be noted that grant of UAS licence and allotment of Radio Frequency is a three stage process.

1. **Issue of Letter of Intent (LOI):** DOT follows a policy of First-cum-First Served for granting LOI to the applicants for UAS licence, which means, an application received first will be processed first and if found eligible will be granted LOI.

2. **Issue of Licence:** The First-cum-First Served policy is also applicable for grant of licence on compliance of LOI conditions. Therefore, any applicant who complies with the conditions of LOI first will be granted UAS licence first. This issue never arose in the past as at one point of time only one application was processed and LOI was granted and enough time was given to him for compliance of conditions of LOI. However, since the Government has adopted a policy of **"No Cap"** on number of UAS Licence, a large number of LOI's are proposed to be issued simultaneously. In these circumstances, an applicant who fulfils the conditions of LOI first will be granted licence first, although several applicants will be issued LOI simultaneously. **The same has been concurred by the Solicitor General of India during the discussions.**

3. **Grant of Wireless Licence:** The First-cum-First Served policy is also applicable for grant of Wireless Licence to the UAS Licencee. Wireless Licence is an independent licence to UAS licence for allotment of Radio Frequency and authorising launching of GSM / CDMA based mobile services. There is a misconception that UAS licence authorises a person to launch mobile services automatically. UAS licence is a licence for providing both wire and wireless services. Therefore, any UAS licence holder wishes to offer mobile service has to obtain a separate Wireless Licence from DOT. It is clearly indicated in Clauses 43.1 and 43.2 of the UAS Licence agreement of the DOT.

**Since the file for issue of LOI to all eligible applicants was approved by me on 2-11-2007, it is proposed to implement the decision without further delay and without any departure from existing guidelines.**

सत्यमेव जयते

प्रधान मंत्री

Prime Minister

New Delhi
3 January, 2008

Dear Shri Raja,

I have received your letter of 26 December, 2007 regarding recent developments in the telecom sector.

With warm regards,

Yours sincerely,

(Manmohan Singh)

Shri A. Raja
Minister of Communications &
Information Technology
New Delhi

सत्यमेव जयते

ஆ. இராசா
ए. राजा
A. RAJA

मंत्री
संचार एवं सूचना प्रौद्योगिकी
भारत सरकार,
इलैक्ट्रॉनिक्स निकेतन, 6, सी.जी.ओ. कॉम्प्लेक्स,
नई दिल्ली-110 003
MINISTER
COMMUNICATIONS & INFORMATION TECHNOLOGY,
GOVERNMENT OF INDIA,
ELECTRONICS NIKETAN, 6, C.G.O. COMPLEX,
NEW DELHI-110 003

**D.O. No. 450/M (C&IT)/VIP/2008**

Dated the November 7, 2008

Respected Sir, Vanakkam.

Kindly recall my meeting with you on 4.11.2008 along with Hon'ble Finance Minister in connection with 3G spectrum auction and one time spectrum charges for 2G.

During the discussion, you have advised me to meet the Press to explain the policy and rules being adopted in granting new licenses and spectrum allotment in accordance with the TRAI recommendations.

Accordingly, I addressed the issues in the Press Conference today (7.11.2008) and explained the related issues including dilution of shares, as explained by the Finance Minister, of M/s. SWAN and M/s. UNITECH who are the new licensees.

A copy of the brief press note issued in the press conference is also enclosed for your kind perusal.

Yours sincerely,

(A.RAJA)

**Dr. Manmohan Singh**
Hon'ble Prime Minister of India
7, Race Course Road
New Delhi

**Department of Telecommunications**

**PRESS RELEASE**

**Dated: 07.11.2008**

There have been several reports in the media and other quarters regarding valuation of new licences and alleged loss to the exchequer.

It is clarified that there has been no deviation in the policy approved by the Cabinet on 31st October 2003 for issuance of new licenses. The above decision is based on NTP 1999 and supported by TRAI recommendations from time to time.

NTP-99 is the bedrock regarding issuance of licence and allocation of spectrum. NTP 99 in para 3.1.1 says,

> ***"The entry of more operators in a service area shall be based on the recommendations of the TRAI who will review this as required and no later than every two years.***
>
> ***CMSP operators would be required to pay a one time entry fee. The basis for determining the entry fee and the basis for selection of additional operators would be recommended by the TRAI. Apart from the one time entry fee, CMSP operators would also be required to pay licence fee based on a revenue share. It is proposed that the appropriate level of entry fee and percentage of revenue share arrangement for different service areas would be recommended by TRAI in a time-bound manner, keeping in view the objectives of the New Telecom Policy".***

In addition, the guidelines for Basic Service Licence dated 25.1.2001 in para 26 enunciates the policy of allocation of spectrum on first-come-first-served basis.

TRAI in 2003 recommended that ***"...entry fee of the fourth Cellular Operator would be the entry fee in the new Unified Access Licensing Region..."*** This amount is Rs.1658 crores for a PAN India license.

In consonance with NTP 99 & TRAI recommendations, the guidelines issued for UAS Licences in 2005 interalia contains in para 19 that ***"The LICENSEE shall pay spectrum charges in addition to the Licence Fees on revenue share basis...".***

Further Para 37 of Guidelines of UASL 2005 also stipulates the allocation of spectrum to licencees as follows :-

*"For wireless operations in SUBSCRIBER access network, the frequencies shall be assigned by WPC Wing of the Department of Telecom from the frequency bands earmarked in the applicable National Frequency Allocation Plan and in coordination with various users. Initially a cumulative maximum of upto 4.4 MHz + 4.4 MHz shall be allocated in the case of TDMA based system @ 200 KHz per carrier or 30 KHz per carrier or a maximum of 2.5 MHz + 2.5 MHz shall be allocated in the case of CDMA based system @ 1.25 MHz per carrier, on case by case basis subject to availability".*

Subsequently, TRAI has again in August 2007 recommended the following...

***"It is therefore recommended that in future all spectrum <u>excluding</u> in 800, 900 and 1800 bands should be auctioned so as to ensure efficient utilisation of this scarce resource. In the 2G bands (800 MHz/900 MHZ/1800 MHz), the allocation through auction may not be possible as the service providers were allocated spectrum at different times of their license and the amount of spectrum with them varies from 2x4.4 MHz to 2x 10 MHz for GSM technology and 2 x 2.5 MHz to 2 x 5 MHZ in CDMA technology. Therefore, to decide the cut off after which the spectrum is auctioned will be difficult and might raise the issue of level playing field" (para 2.79).***

Further, TRAI also recommended in August, 2007 that ***"No cap be placed on the number of access service providers in any service area" (para 2.37).***

In addition TRAI also recommended that ***"Keeping in view the objective of growth, affordability, penetration of wireless services in semi-urban and rural areas, the Authority is not in favour of changing the spectrum fee regime for a new entrant. Opportunity for equal competition has always been one of the prime principles of the Authority in suggesting a regulatory framework in telecom services. Any differential treatment to a new entrant vis-à-vis incumbents in the wireless sector will go against the principle of level playing field" (para 2.78).***

These established policy regarding issuance of license, allocation of spectrum and charges thereon have been followed by the successive governments till date.

Regarding sale of shares by SWAN and UNITECH, it is clarified that the foreign companies have entered into agreement to subscribe to the new equity shares of the Company. No share of the founding promoters of the companies have been sold. Hence, the question of windfall gain or for that matter any gain for the promoters does not arise. In the case of SWAN, Rs. 3500 crores aprox. is proposed to be inducted into the company. Similarly, in the case of UNITECH, Rs.6000 crores aprox. shall be inducted by the foreign partners in the company. This is as per FDI Policy of the Government and these transactions are going to result in infusion of above FDI into the country.

These funds in the company will be utilised for the establishment of network including infrastructure. It is clarified that it is necessary for such licensees to seek technical, managerial and financial support from suitable collaborators in order to successfully comply with license conditions which involves telecommunication operations. The valuations being quoted are "post-money" – it reflects the value of the funds applied to the business and not the value of the licence or spectrum.

**This matter has been discussed and clarified with the Finance Minister. In addition, MoC&IT has on 5.11.2008, directed that Telecom Commission may deliberate on the issue of prohibiting sale of equity by promoters.**

Since the introduction of revenue share regime in 1999, the Government has received more than Rs. 50,000 crores on account of only licence fee. In addition to above Government has received aprox. Rs. 9000 crores on account of spectrum charges and aprox. Rs.19500 crores (Rs. 12500 crores aprox. in 2007-08 alone) on account of entry fee. In 2007-08 alone Government received aprox. Rs. 12,000 crores from licence fee and spectrum charges. This annual fee has been increasing year after year as subscriber base has been increasing. Hence, loss of revenue for not resorting to auction is only a myth and is compensated by deferred revenue every year.

Regarding 3G, in line with TRAI recommendations, Government has already issued guidelines for 3G and BWA services. These have been shared with the Press on 1st August 2008. Since then the Government have received suggestions from various sources including media and the Government have issued certain modifications in full consultation and agreement with the Ministry of Finance. The auctioneer has already been appointed and the auctioning of 3G and BWA spectrum will be completed by January 2009.

********

Page 3/3

प्रधान मंत्री

Prime Minister

New Delhi
17 November, 2008

Dear Shri Raja,

I have received your letter of 7 November, 2008 regarding the press conference held by you on issues related to spectrum allocation.

With warm regards,

Yours sincerely,

(Manmohan Singh)

Shri A. Raja
Minister of Communications and
Information Technology
New Delhi

सत्यमेव जयते

அ. இராசா
ए. राजा
A. RAJA

मंत्री
संचार एवं सूचना प्रौद्योगिकी
भारत सरकार,
इलैक्ट्रॉनिक्स निकेतन, 6, सी.जी.ओ. कॉम्प्लेक्स,
नई दिल्ली-110 003

MINISTER
COMMUNICATIONS & INFORMATION TECHNOLOGY,
GOVERNMENT OF INDIA,
ELECTRONICS NIKETAN, 6, C.G.O. COMPLEX,
NEW DELHI-110 003

D.O. No. 20-100/2007-AS-I(Pt.)

April 1, 2009

Respected Sir, Vanakkam.

You may kindly recall the remarkable decisions that have been taken in this Ministry under your able guidance & leadership on following issues.

1. Permitting dual technology i.e. from CDMA to GSM and vice-versa,
2. Allocation of Spectrum on subscriber based criteria
3. Issuance of new Unified Access Services (UAS) Licenses.

Needless to say that a lot of controversy has been raked up by the vested interests through media and other forums despite legitimate and progressive decision making process arrived at by this Ministry on the basis of the TRAI recommendations and established procedure in the light of NTP-99.

All these decisions of the Government were challenged by the Cellular Operators Association of India (COAI) before the Hon'ble Telecom Dispute Settlement Appellate Tribunal (TDSAT) on the grounds of arbitrariness, haste and malafide. After hearing the case of all the parties to the proceedings, the Hon'ble TDSAT disposed of the petition filed by the COAI challenging the Government decision and categorically observed that the decisions of the Government do not warrant any judicial intervention as these were neither arbitrary nor malafide.

A gist of the judgment of the Hon'ble TDSAT is enclosed for information.

Yours sincerely,

(A.RAJA)

Encl: as above

**Dr. Manmohan Singh,**
Hon'ble Prime Minister of India,
South Block
New Delhi.

2-APR-2009 13:35 FROM: TO:00442073732828 P.4

**ANNEX-I**

**GIST OF JUDGMENT OF TDSAT IN PETITION NO. 286/2007 REGARDING DUAL TECHNOLOGY, SPECTRUM PERMISSION ETC.**

I. The Petitioners do not have any vested right to receive GSM spectrum beyond 6.2 MHz.

II. A reading of the NTP-99 document and the licence conditions reveals that the concept of dual technology is not a new concept and that this is contained in the above documents.

III. In taking the decision reflected in the letter dated 18.10.2007 or the Press Release dated 19.10.2007, no impropriety was committed by DOT.

IV. No ground to level mala fide intention on the part of DOT.

V. The contention of petitioners that the impugned decision of DOT dated 19.10.2007 has disturbed the level playing field was rejected.

VI. There is nothing irregular in grant of 4.4 MHz as start up spectrum to the Respondents (under dual technology).

VII. The contention of the petitioners that those with dual technology and dual spectrum should be charged the spectrum usage charges on the basis of the combined spectrum was rejected.

VIII. The contention that the DOT has disregarded the Recommendations of TRAI in respect of contingent roll-out obligation was rejected.

IX. The contention that the subscriber linked criteria was designed to adversely affect the interests of the existing GSM operators does not merit consideration.

X. DOT was right in adopting the criteria recommended by TRAI as an interim measure in the light of the Recommendations of TRAI, TEC and the DOT Spectrum Review Committee.

*********

सत्यमेव जयते

प्रधान मंत्री

Prime Minister

New Delhi
15 April, 2009

Dear Shri Raja,

I have received your letter of 1 April, 2009 enclosing a gist of the judgment of TDSAT on a petition challenging certain decisions of the Government of India.

With warm regards,

Yours sincerely,

(Manmohan Singh)

Shri A. Raja
Minister of Communications
and Information Technology
New Delhi

ஆ. இராசா
ए. राजा
**A. RAJA**

डी.ओ.सं. 71 सं.एवं सू.प्रौ.मंत्री/2010
D.O. No. 71 MOC & IT/2010
मंत्री
संचार एवं सूचना प्रौद्योगिकी
भारत सरकार,
इलैक्ट्रॉनिक्स निकेतन, 6, सी.जी.ओ. कॉम्प्लेक्स,
नई दिल्ली-110 003
MINISTER
COMMUNICATIONS & INFORMATION TECHNOLOGY,
GOVERNMENT OF INDIA,
ELECTRONICS NIKETAN, 6, C.G.O. COMPLEX,
NEW DELHI-110 003

21 APR 2010

Respected Sir,

Vanakkam.

I am herewith presenting for the kind attention of the Hon'ble Prime Minister the following facts regarding.W.P.(C) No. 2442/2010 filed by Dr. Subramaniam Swamy before the Delhi High Court.

2. The allegations made by him are all taken out of the news published in the magazine called "Pioneer", which is the party magazine of Bharathiya Janata Party. Dr. Subramaniam Swamy has chosen to call the articles published in the said magazine as "investigative reports". The term investigative reports attributed to the said magazine, particularly in respect of the news item in question can only be described as a misnomer. The various news items in question are absolutely motivated and malafide exhibiting a deliberate attempt to malign me. This malicious exercise had been started by this magazine against me since the year 2008. Dr. Subramaniam Swamy had deliberately chosen to place reliance on these reports because his intention in filing the above said Writ Petition before the Delhi High Court is not in any way different from the motive or intention behind the said reports published in the said magazine. Long before he filed the above said case before the Delhi High Court, Dr. Subramaniam Swamy, had been giving interviews particularly in a T.V. channel called "Jaya TV" operating from Chennai that he would be filing the case in the Delhi High Court.

3. It is brought to the kind attention of the Hon'ble PM that excepting the following two allegations viz., Allegation No. 9(g) and under the caption "persons involved" in the same paragraph under sub-para (e) all other allegations are subject matters of a suit filed by me for defamation against a bi-weekly called "Junior Vikatan" before the Madras High Court in C.S. No. 366/2009, in which as a counter to the application filed by me

...2/-

: 2 :

for the grant of injunction in O.A. No. 420/2009, the Printer and Publisher of the said bi-weekly magazine have raised all these allegations not only in the reports published by them in the said magazine, but also in their counter affidavit to my application for injunction culled out from the said Newspaper "Pioneer". It was on the basis of the pleadings between the parties in the said application for injunction pending disposal of the said suit that a Division Bench of the Madras High Court by order dated 1.10.2009 in the OSA No. 230 & 231/2009 was pleased to grant an order of interim injunction pending disposal of the aforesaid suit subject to certain conditions (**Copy enclosed - Flag 'A'**). The averments contained in my affidavits / counter affidavits and related papers thereto will reveal the strong denial of those allegations which are now being perpetrated by Mr. Subramaniam Swamy in the present petition (**Copy enclosed - Flag 'B'**). As a matter of fact, the magazine 'Junior Vikatan' neither preferred appeal as against the order of the High Court nor filed any new credentials or documents to substantiate the allegation. The suit is still pending and as such subjudice. The said judgment of the Division Bench of the Madras High Court has been reported in (2009) 5 L.W. 117.

4. It is also relevant to point out that this magazine "Pioneer" had published false news information regarding the subjects discussed between the Hon'ble Home Minister of India and the Hon'ble Chief Minister of Tamilnadu and when a lawyer's notice was sent on behalf of the Hon'ble Chief Minister of Tamilnadu, the said magazine has expressed unqualified regrets and had the same published in their newspaper. This is brought to the notice for the purpose of showing the news worthiness of this newspaper "Pioneer".

5. Weighing the credibility of the newspaper 'Pioneer' in terms of quality of worthiness and quantity of circulation, I did not institute any such legal proceedings as I did in the case of 'Junior Vikatan' and therefore this optional and intentional omission cannot be permitted as a shelter for Mr. Swamy whose public credibility is known to all.

6. Further, I have come across on verification of documents that the companies viz., Green House Promoters (P) Ltd., and Equaas Estates (P) Ltd., have also separately filed Criminal Complaints C.C. No. 9602/2009 and 9603/2009 respectively against the bi-weekly magazine "Junior Vikatan" and the said complaints have been taken on file and the same are pending before the XVII Metropolitan Magistrate, Saidapet, Chennai-15 (**Copy enclosed - Flag 'C' & 'D'**). The accused in the said complaints "Junior Vikatan" have taken notice and also appeared in person.

...3/-

: 3 :

7. Similarly, regarding Para 9(g), the allegation that "Earlier while serving as Minister for Environment & Forests Respondent No. 2 had appointed his nephew Dr. R. Sridhar as Deputy Director in the Ministry of Environment and Forest by flouting the Norms of Appointment". The real facts pertaining to the aforesaid allegation is that the said Dr. R. Sridhar applied for the post of Deputy Director pursuant to the Notification of inviting applications. He became successful on his own merits. I was in no way connected with the said appointment and at the time of his appointment I was also not the Minister of Environment and Forest as alleged.

8. As regards the other allegation under the caption "persons involved" sub para (e) viz., "Mr. A. Kaliaperumal (Brother of Respondent No. 2) arrested by the CBI in January 2010 on an FIR filed following the directions of the Chief Vigilance Commissioner on this matter", the said allegation is false and when this is false, one can estimate the veracity of the said publication, the so called Pioneer magazine, a party magazine of BJP and their motive in making such false publication. There was no proceedings taken against him by the CBI and therefore the question of his arrest, filing of FIR etc., are totally false.

9. With regard to another allegation in para 12 on page 20 which refers the order of Hon'ble Supreme court in S'Tel Vs Union of India, the petitioner Mr. Swami cannot rely upon it for his case as this case was filed to assail the cut off date chosen by the government to issue license, admitting the policy and procedure for issuance of license and allotment of Spectrum. It is pertinent to note that affidavit filed by M/s S'Tel itself admits that the order is not arbitrary after verification of Spectrum availability.

10. In any event it was never pleaded by S'Tel that the government suffers exchequer loss or undue favour to any company enabling them for unlawful enrichment. However to avoid legal repercussion on administrative domain of the government, the matter has been referred to the Law Ministry for further clarification. Thus the Order of the Supreme Court does not offer any sustenance or strength to the petitioner for either criminal interpretation of scam or exchequer loss.

11. It is clear that there are some 'vested interests' including the above named Petitioner in filing the case against me before the Delhi High Court and they are bent upon bringing down my image as well as the image of the Government of India on such false news and premises.

...4/-

: 4 :

12. Since the matter is coming before the High Court of Delhi on 18.5.2010 for hearing, I am placing on record the aforesaid facts for necessary further course of action with relevant copies of documents referred.

With regards,

Yours sincerely,

**( A. RAJA )**

**Dr. Manmohan Singh,**
Hon'ble Prime Minister of India,
South Block,
New Delhi.

प्रधान मंत्री

**Prime Minister**

New Delhi
26 April, 2010

Dear Shri Raja,

I have received your letter of 21 April, 2010 regarding W.P. (C) No.2442/2010 filed by Dr. Subramaniam Swamy before the Delhi High Court.

With warm regards,

Yours sincerely,

(Manmohan Singh)

Shri A. Raja
Minister of Communications and
Information Technology
New Delhi

आ. இராசா
ए. राजा
A. RAJA

सत्यमेव जयते

मंत्री
संचार एवं सूचना प्रौद्योगिकी
भारत सरकार
इलैक्ट्रॉनिक्स निकेतन, 6, सी.जी.ओ. कॉम्पलेक्स
नई दिल्ली-110 003

MINISTER
COMMUNICATIONS & INFORMATION TECHNOLOGY
GOVERNMENT OF INDIA
ELCETRONICS NIKETAN, 6, C.G.O. COMPLEX
NEW DELHI - 110 003

D.O. No. 20-281/2010-AS-I(Vol.II)
Dated : 02.07.2010

Respected Sir, Vanakkam.

The recommendations of the TRAI on Spectrum Management and licensing framework have been received in this department on 11.05.2010. Industry associations and service providers have been holding diverse views in this matter. A number of industry representatives have been meeting me over this issue. I have already proposed to hold an interaction with all Service Providers on 07.07.2010. Once the Industries' views are consolidated, we will constitute a Committee to hold detailed interactions in the Department to examine the recommendations of TRAI in the best interest of the country and the service providers.

The report of the Committee will be considered by the Telecom Commission. The Telecom Commission will recommend the final decision to be taken by the Government on those issues which are within the scope of the Telecom Commission.

The other contentious issues as well as major policy changes proposed such as revising the structure of UASL and delinking of spectrum etc., as suggested by TRAI, will have to be taken at the level of E-GoM or Cabinet, since those decisions were taken earlier by the Cabinet under the aegis of NTP '99. Any change in the letter and spirit of NTP '99 on licence and spectrum issues, no doubt, have to be subjected to the scrutiny of the Cabinet and Parliament.

Therefore, as per the above procedure, reference to the E-GoM will be appropriate for final decision on major contentious issues after the due deliberations in Telecom Commission. I will also keep your goodself informed about further developments in this regard.

With kind regards,

Yours sincerely,

(A. RAJA)

Dr. Manmohan Singh
Hon'ble Prime Minister of India
South Block
New Delhi.

प्रधान मंत्री

Prime Minister

New Delhi
7 July, 2010

Dear Shri Raja,

I have received your letter of 2 July, 2010 regarding the recommendations of the Telecom Regulatory Authority of India on spectrum management and licensing framework.

With warm regards,

Yours sincerely,

(Manmohan Singh)

Shri A. Raja
Minister of Communications &
Information Technology
New Delhi

प्रारंभिक जाँच पंजीकरण प्रतिवेदन

Preliminary Enquiry Registration Report

वि.पु.स्था.सी.-I

S.P.E.C.-I

बुक न 653
Book No.

क्रम सं. 5
Serial No.

1. जिला : District — थानाः PS: — वर्ष : Year — प्रा.जाँ.प्र.क्र. PE NO. — दिनांक : Date 4.1.2011

CBI ACB New Delhi 2011 PE-DAI-2011-A-0001

2. (क) प्रतीत अपराध :
(a) Suspected Offence Misconduct

(ख) दिन : Day — दिनांक Date — समय Time

(ग) थाने पर सूचना प्राप्त होने का Information received at PS — दिनांक Date

कायमी अपराध : Entry No. 08 — दिनाँक Date 4.1.2011 — समय Time 3:00 P.M.

3. सूचना का प्रकार : Type of Information — लिखित/मौखिक Written/Oral Direction of Hon'ble Supreme Court in order dt.16.12.1 in SLP(Civil) 24873/2010

4. घटना का स्थान : Place of Occurrence — (क) थाने से दिशा व दूरी : (a) Direction & Distance from PS

Deptt. of Tellecommunication

बीट नं./Beat No.

(ख) पता :
(b) Address Sanchar Bhawan, 20, Ashok Road, New Delhi & other places.

(ग) घटनास्थल अन्य थाना क्षेत्राधिकार में है तो थाना -
(c) In case, outside the limit of this Police Station, then

पुलिस थाना का नाम Name of PS — जिला District

1-90/CBI/ND/2002

2

5. अभियोगी/सूचनाकर्ता :
Complainant/Informant **As per direction of Hon'ble Supreme Court of India vide order dated 16.12.2010 in SLP(Civil) No. 24873/2010**

(क) नाम
(a) Name

(ख) पिता/पति का नाम
(b) Father's/Husband's Name

(ग) जन्म तिथि
(c) Date of Birth

(घ) राष्ट्रीयता :
(d)Nationality

(ङ) पासपोर्ट नं. ..........जारी दिनांक ........जारी होने का स्थान ...
(e) Passport No Date of Issue Place of Issue

(च) व्यवसाय
(f) Profession

(छ) पता -
(g) Address

6. ज्ञात//संदेही/अज्ञात/आरोपी का पूर्ण विवरण :
Details of known/suspected/unknown suspect with full particulars
(यदि आवश्यक हो तो अलग से पन्ना संलग्न करें)
(Attached separate sheet, if necessary)
(1) **Unknown officials of Department of Telecommunication & others.**
(2)
(3)

7. प्रथम सूचना विवरण :- (यदि आवश्यक हो तो अलग से पन्ना संलग्न करें)
First Information contents (Attach separate sheet, if required)
**As per separate sheet enclosed.**

2-90/CBI/ND/02.

Centre for Public Interest Litigation and others had filed a Writ Petition no. 3522/2010 before Hon'ble High Court of Delhi praying for a court monitored investigation by the Central Bureau of Investigation (CBI) or a Special Investigating Team into what has been termed as 2G Spectrum Scam for unearthing the role of Shri A. Raja, the then Minister for Communications & Information Technology (MOC&IT), senior officers of Department of Telecommunications, middlemen, businessmen and others. The said Writ Petition was, however, dismissed by the Hon'ble High Court of Delhi vide an order dated 25.05.2010. Aggrieved by this decision of the Delhi High Court, the petitioners moved Hon'ble Supreme Court of India by filing a Special Leave Petition (C) No. 24873 of 2010.

Vide an order dated 16.12.2010 the Hon'ble Supreme Court of India has granted leave and passed a detailed order directing inter-alia as following :-

> "The CBI shall, if it has already not registered first information report in the context of the alleged irregularities committed in the grant of licences from 2001 to 2006-2007, now register a case and conduct thorough investigation with particular emphasis on the loss caused to the public exchequer and corresponding gain to the licensees/service providers and also on the issue of allowing use of dual/alternate technology by some service providers even before the decision was made public vide press release dated 19.10.2007."

As regards 'the issue of allowing use of dual/alternate technology by some service providers even before the decision was made public vide press release dated 19.10.2010', the said issue is related to the allocation of licenses/spectrum in 2007-08 and is being investigated into the FIR No. RC DAI 2009 A 0045 (2G Spectrum Case) itself. In order to enquire into the irregularities committed in the grant of licenses & spectrum for Cellular Mobile Telephone Services / Basic (Telephone) Services / Unified Access Service by the Department of Telecommunications from 2001 to 2006-07, with particular emphasis on the loss caused to the public exchequer and corresponding gain to the licensees/service providers, a Preliminary Enquiry is hereby registered and endorsed to Sh. Vivek Priyadarshi, ASP, CBI, ACB, New Delhi for enquiry.